PLANNING CULTURES IN EUROPE

Urban and Regional Planning and Development Series

Series Editors: Professor Peter Roberts and Professor Graham Haughton

Based on over a decade of publishing the highest quality research, the Urban and Regional Planning and Development Series has developed a strong profile. It is internationally recognised for its high quality research monographs. The emphasis is on presenting original research findings which are informed by theoretical sophistication and methodological rigour. It is avowedly global in its outlook, with contributions welcomed from around the world. The series is open to contributions from a wide variety of disciplines, including planning, geography, sociology, political science, public administration and economics.

Other titles in the Series

De-coding New Regionalism
Shifting Socio-political Contexts in Central Europe and Latin America
Edited by James W. Scott
ISBN 978 0 7546 7098 8

Reshaping Planning with Culture
Greg Young
ISBN 978 0 7546 7077 3

Overcoming Fragmentation in Southeast Europe
Spatial Development Trends and Integration Potential
Edited by Panayiotis Getimis and Grigoris Kafkalas
ISBN 978 0 7546 4796 6

Partnership, Collaborative Planning and Urban Regeneration
John McCarthy
ISBN 978 0 7546 1375 6

Collective Action and Urban Policy Alleviation
Community Organizations and the Struggle for Shelter in Manila
Gavin Shatkin
ISBN 978 0 7546 4786 7

Government Discourse and Housing
Jago Dodson
ISBN 978 0 7546 4207 7

Planning Cultures in Europe
Decoding Cultural Phenomena in Urban and Regional Planning

Edited by
JOERG KNIELING
HafenCity University, Germany

and

FRANK OTHENGRAFEN
HafenCity University, Germany

ASHGATE

© Joerg Knieling and Frank Othengrafen 2009

All rights reserved. No part of this publication may be reproduced, stored in a retrieval system, or transmitted in any form or by any means, electronic, mechanical, photocopying, recording or otherwise without the prior permission of the publisher.

Joerg Knieling and Frank Othengrafen have asserted their right under the Copyright, Designs and Patents Act, 1988, to be identified as the editors of this work.

Published by
Ashgate Publishing Limited
Wey Court East
Union Road
Farnham
Surrey GU9 7PT
England

Ashgate Publishing Company
Suite 420
101 Cherry Street
Burlington, VT 05401-4405
USA

www.ashgate.com

British Library Cataloguing in Publication Data
Planning cultures in Europe : decoding cultural phenomena
 in urban and regional planning. -- (Urban and regional
 planning and development)
 1. City planning--European Union countries--Cross-cultural
 studies. 2. Regional planning--European Union countries--
 Cross-cultural studies.
 I. Series II. Knieling, Joerg. III. Othengrafen, Frank.
 711.4'094-dc22

Library of Congress Cataloging-in-Publication Data
Planning cultures in Europe : decoding cultural phenomena in urban and regional planning / by Joerg Knieling and Frank Othengrafen.
  p. cm. -- (Urban and regional planning and development series)
  Includes bibliographical references and index.
  ISBN 978-0-7546-7565-5 (hardcover) 1. Regional planning--European
Union countries--Cross-cultural studies. 2. City planning--European Union countries--
Cross-cultural studies. 3. Central planning--European Union countries--Cross-cultural
studies. 4. European Union countries--Economic policy. I. Knieling, Joerg. II.
Othengrafen, Frank.
 HT395.E8P566 2009
 307.1'216094--dc22

2009011775

ISBN 978-0-7546-7565-5

Printed and bound in Great Britain by
TJ International Ltd, Padstow, Cornwall

Contents

List of Figures, Maps and Tables	*ix*
List of Contributors	*xiii*
Acknowledgements	*xxi*
Preface	*xxiii*
Joerg Knieling and Frank Othengrafen	

PART 1: PLANNING CULTURE – THEORETICAL APPROACHES

1 Theoretical Reflections on Common European (Planning-) Cultures 3
   Hans Gullestrup

2 Planning Cultures en Route to a Better Comprehension of 'Planning Processes'? 23
   Dietrich Fürst

3 En Route to a Theoretical Model for Comparative Research on Planning Cultures 39
   Joerg Knieling and Frank Othengrafen

PART 2: PLANNING CULTURES IN NORTHWESTERN EUROPE

4 How German Is It? An Essay in Epistemological Eclecticism 65
   Friedhelm Fischer

5 Planning Culture in Austria – The Case of Vienna, the Unlike City 95
   Jens S. Dangschat and Alexander Hamedinger

6 Visualising Spatial Policy in Europe 113
   Stefanie Dühr

PART 3: PLANNING CULTURES IN EASTERN EUROPE – BETWEEN BREAKUP AND TRADITION

7 Remarks on the Features of Lithuanian Planning Culture 139
   Eugenijus Kęstutis Staniūnas

8	Planning Rationalities among Practitioners in St Petersburg, Russia – Soviet Traditions and Western Influences *Veli-Pekka Tynkkynen*	151
9	The House of Many Different Ages *Violeta Puşcaşu*	169

PART 4: PLANNING CULTURES IN SOUTHERN EUROPE

10	Planning Cultures in Italy – Reformism, Laissez-Faire and Contemporary Trends *Luciano Vettoretto*	189
11	Planning Culture and the Interference of Major Events: The Recent Experience of Athens *Konstantinos Serraos, Evangelos Asprogerakas and Byron Ioannou*	205
12	Coping with the Era of Change – Planning and Decision-Making under Globalisation in Turkey: The Case of the French Street Urban Transformation Project, Istanbul *Susanne Prehl and Gül Tuçaltan*	221

PART 5: INTERDEPENDENCIES BETWEEN EUROPEAN SPATIAL POLICIES AND PLANNING CULTURES

13	The Impact of Europeanisation on Planning Cultures *Bas Waterhout, João Morais Mourato and Kai Böhme*	239
14	A Missing Link in the Cultural Evolution of the European Union: Confronting EU Ideology with INTERREG III Practice Concerning Cultural Diversity *Roel During, Rosalie van Dam, André van der Zande*	255
15	Territorial Cohesion, European Social Model and Transnational Cooperation *Simin Davoudi*	269

PART 6: CONCLUSIONS

16	Planning Cultures between Models of Society and Planning Systems *Dominic Stead and Vincent Nadin*	283

17	Planning Cultures in Europe between Convergence and Divergence: Findings, Explanations and Perspectives *Joerg Knieling and Frank Othengrafen*	301
Index		*323*

List of Figures, Maps and Tables

Figures

1.1	The horizontal culture dimension	6
1.2	Culture as a complex entity consisting of culture segments and culture layers: the semi-static model	8
1.3	General dynamics culture model	11
3.1	The embeddedness of planning culture	44
3.2	The different levels of the mental programme	50
3.3	The levels of culture	51
3.4	The 'culturised planning model': the exposure of culture and its impact on spatial planning and development practices	57
4.1	Typically German?	67
4.2	Front cover of *How German Is It?*	68
4.3	Against sauerkraut and marching musik. Poster for a demonstration against right-wing tendencies	73
4.4	Invitation for conference on the reconstruction of lost buildings and spaces 2008	74
4.5	Figures of thought, theory formation and communication	76
4.6	Walter Christaller's central place diagram	79
4.7	August Loesch's trade centres' model	80
4.8	Walter Christaller's Central Place Diagram applied to re-plan conquered Poland	81
4.9	Total design for the mass production of traditional towns	82
4.10	Slogans of the conservative party of the post-war years: 'Against depersonalisation' in the working class districts and 'Individual home ownership as a bulwark against bolshevism'	85
4.11	Ludwig Hilberseimer: investigations into the modern city (1927)	87
4.12	The 'Weissenhof Siedlung' estate after completion. Stuttgart 1927	88
4.13	Attack and counter-attack: cartoons lampooning the 'Weissenhof Siedlung' estate as an Arab village	88
4.14	… and exposing its critics as over-fed bourgeois fossils of the pre-war era – 'Nichts fürs Gemüt'	89
5.1	Organisation of the 'Grätzlmanagement Volkert- und Alliiertenviertel 2004'	107
6.1	Cross-national comparison of the level of abstraction in Dutch, German and English strategic spatial plans	124

9.1	The house of many different ages – a metaphor for Romanian planning	184
11.1	Ellinikon Olympic Canoe/Kayak Slalom Centre	217
11.2	Faliro Bay Complex	217
12.1	French Street in 2006, newly renovated buildings house restaurants and bars, coloured awnings and restaurant seating characterise the street's appearance	231
13.1	Processes and influences underlying the Europeanisation of planning	243
16.1	Summary of Esping-Andersen's three worlds of welfare	285

Maps

3.1	The four major trends and traditions of spatial planning in Europe	46
3.2	The five legal and administrative planning families	47
5.1	Spatial concentrations of non-Austrians, Vienna 2008	99
5.2	Vienna's different Planning Regions	108
6.1a	Streekplan Noord-Holland Zuid – Streekplankaart (extract)	120
6.1b	Streekplan Noord-Holland Zuid – Streekplankaart – key	121
6.2	Landesentwicklungsprogramm III Rheinland-Pfalz (extract)	122
6.3	East of England Regional Key Diagram	123
6.4	North East and Europe	130
11.1	The Athens 2004 Olympic Venues	214
11.2	The spatial correlation of Olympic/post-Olympic poles with the areas of the basic poles of central activities, building density, population density and concentration of places of labour	216

Tables

6.1	Cross-national comparison of policy aims in text and graphical expression in regional-level statutory spatial planning documents in the Netherlands, Germany and England	126
9.1	Institutional competence coverage (selection)	175
9.2	Legislative synopsis	179
11.1	Key institutions of spatial planning	207
11.2	The general structure of the Greek planning system	208
11.3	Division of power in EU countries	210
13.1	Towards a typology of the Europeanisation of planning	247

16.1	Welfare state typologies	286
16.2	Planning system typologies	288
16.3	Traditions and criteria from the EU *Compendium of Spatial Planning Systems and Policies*	290

List of Contributors

Evangelos Asprogerakas, National Technical University of Athens, Greece
Evangelos Asprogerakas is an engineer in Surveying with a Masters degree from the National Technical University of Athens (NTUA, 1997). He holds a PhD in Urban and Regional Planning from the same university (2003) and he also holds an MSc in 'Development and Planning: Economics of Urbanisation and Management of the City Economy' from the University College of London (UCL, 1999). He is currently working as a Special Scientist in Regional Development at the Greek Ministry of Interior and as a Tutor at the Hellenic Open University. Previously, he taught Regional Planning at the University of Thessaly, Department of Planning and Regional Development. Since 2000 he has been an NTUA Researcher working on programmes concerning Urban and Regional Planning and Development, dealing especially with metropolitan planning, medium sized cities and the urban network, the spatial effects of innovation and information technologies and the development of tourism.

Kai Böhme, Spatial Foresight GmbH
Kai Böhme (1972) is Director of Spatial Foresight GmbH in Luxembourg. He specialises in European regional and territorial research and policies, international comparative studies in the fields of regional development policies, spatial planning, and in the territorial impacts of sector policies. In parallel to his consultancy and policy advice activities he holds visiting research fellowships at the Department of Town and Regional Planning at the University of Sheffield (UK) and the Centre for Spatial Development and Planning at the Blekinge Institute of Technology (Sweden). He has work experience from the ESPON Secretariat in Luxembourg, Nordregio in Sweden and the Secretariat for Future Studies (SFZ) in Germany. His educational background includes a PhD in Management Science from the University of Nijmegen (Netherlands) and a Masters in Spatial Planning from the University of Dortmund (Germany).

Jens S. Dangschat, Vienna University of Technology, Section Sociology (ISRA)
Since 1998 Jens S. Dangschat has been Professor for Urban and Regional Sociology and Demography, Department of Architecture and Spatial Planning, at the Vienna University of Technology. Between 1992–1998 he was Professor for Sociological Theory and Urban Sociology at the University of Hamburg. Jens S. Dangschat has published more than 200 books and articles on different topics of urban sociology such as segregation, gentrification and urban sprawl and on social inequalities, planning theory, theory of space, sustainability, and regulation theory. He is a member of the Executive Board

of the European Urban Research Association (EURA) and a member of the Steering Committee of the RC43 Housing and Built Environment of the International Sociological Association (ISA) and Chairman of the 'Urban Research' Section of the Austrian Association of Sociology (ÖGS).

Simin Davoudi, Newcastle University
Simin Davoudi is Professor of Environmental Policy and Planning and Co-Director of the Institute for Research on Environment and Sustainability (IRES) at Newcastle University. Before this, she was Director of the Centre for Urban Development and Environmental Management at Leeds Metropolitan University (2000–2006). She has held the Wibaut Visiting Professorship at the Amsterdam Institute for Metropolitan and International Development Studies, University of Amsterdam (2007) and Presidency of the Association of European Schools of Planning (AESOP: 2004–2006). She is currently a member of the advisory groups for ESPON UK Contact Point, the Irish Social Science Platform, Swedish School of Planning at BTH, the UK government's Housing and Planning Expert Panel and the North East of England Academic Panel. Her research interests include UK spatial planning, European territorial development, governance and institutional relationships, social dimensions of sustainability and strategic waste management. She is published widely. Her latest books include: *Conceptions of Space and Place in Strategic Spatial Planning* (Routledge, 2009) and *Planning for Climate Change* (Earthscan, 2009)

Stefanie Dühr, Radboud University Nijmegen
Stefanie Dühr is Reader in the Department of Spatial Planning at Radboud University Nijmegen, the Netherlands. Previously she worked in the European Commission, DG Regio, as UK Contact Point for the INTERREG IIIB North-west Europe programme, and as senior researcher at the University of the West of England. She holds a PhD in spatial planning from the University of the West of England, Bristol, and a geography degree from the University of Trier, Germany. Her main research interests are comparative planning systems and European territorial cooperation. Stefanie is currently involved in the ex-post evaluation of INTERREG III for the European Commission, and has previously coordinated the drafting of the new transnational territorial cooperation programme ('INTERREG IVB') for North West Europe. She is the author of *The Visual Language of Spatial Planning* (Routledge, 2007), and editor of the policy debates section of the journal *Regional Studies*.

Roel During, Wageningen University and Research Centre, The Netherlands
Roel During is Senior Researcher of spatial planning and cultural heritage at Alterra, Green World Research, Wageningen University, The Netherlands. Additionally, he is Assistant Professor at the Belvedere Chair of Wageningen University and Research Centre. He has many years' experience in national and international projects concerning the analysis and development of methods

and strategies regarding spatial planning and policy processes. Furthermore, he has been responsible for the coordination of research programme transition processes as well as of institutions and policy processes regarding the policy-advisory programme 'Quality of Environment' and the policy-advisory commission 'Trends and Land Use'. Recently, as lead partner, he has been involved in the INTERACT project CULTPLAN, which is analysing cultural influences in and their impacts (how to recognise, cope with or manage cultural differences) on international planning processes as INTERREG.

Friedhelm Fischer, HafenCity University Hamburg, Germany

Friedhelm Fischer is Visiting Professor for Culture and History of the Metropolis at the HafenCity University Hamburg (HCU) and Assistant Professor for Urban Regeneration at the University of Kassel. He studied Urban Planning at the universities of Aachen, Berkeley and Canberra and thereafter held research and teaching positions in each of these. He also completed a degree in English and American literature. From 1984 on he worked as a researcher and a 'scientific assistant' at the Institute for Urban, Regional and Environmental Planning of the Technical University Hamburg. Since 1993 he has held a position as Assistant Professor at the University of Kassel and since 2006 as a Professor at the HCU. His research focuses on comparative studies regarding urban planning, urban regeneration, conservation and planning history. His books and articles deal with case studies and approaches to planning and urban development in Germany, Britain and Australia.

Dietrich Fürst, University of Hannover, Germany

Dietrich Fürst studied economics and between 1981 and 2003 was the head of the Institute of Spatial Planning and Research at the University of Hannover (Germany). He is an expert in to regional planning and modes of regional development, especially in the fields of regional governance, regional management and with regard to the coordination and cooperation in development processes. He has wide experience in the administrative system of local authorities in Germany up to regional EU policies, regional cooperation and networks in regional structures. He published a wide range of scientific books and articles regarding these objects.

Hans Gullestrup, University of Aalborg, Denmark

Hans Gullestrup is Professor for Social and Economic Planning at the Centre for International Studies, Department of Business Studies, at the University of Aalborg. His research interests focus on theoretical research in intercultural understanding, general culture theory and analytical models for empirical cultural studies as well as on cross-cultural management and communication. He is a member of several scientific and social federations and boards. His is the author of, among other works, *Cultural Analysis – Towards Cross-Cultural Understanding* (2006).

Alexander Hamedinger, Vienna University of Technology, Department of Spatial Development, Infrastructure and Environmental Planning, Centre of Sociology (ISRA)
Alexander Hamedinger is Assistant Professor at the Centre of Sociology since 1998. He is an economist and sociologist; his research and teaching interests are mainly in the topics of urban/regional governance, urban/regional planning, planning and spatial theories, and urban sociology. In his research projects he is concentrating on the 'Europeanisation of cities', 'city-regional governance' and 'strategic planning'. His recent publications include the collaborative work *Strategieorientierte Planung im kooperativen Staat* (2008) and 'The Impact of EU Area-Based Programmes on Local Governance: Towards a "Europeanisation"?', in *Urban Studies* (2008).

Byron Ioannou, National Technical University of Athens, Greece
Byron Ioannou studied Architecture and Planning at the National Technical University of Athens, obtaining a Diploma of Engineer (1999), Master's (2002) and Doctoral degrees (2005). His PhD thesis concerned insular town networking and the spatial impacts of tourist development. Since 2000 he has been a researcher at the Laboratory of Urban Research at NTUA. During the period 2003–2006 he was a visiting lecturer at the Democritus University of Thrace and since 2005 has taught environmental and urban planning at the Hellenic Open University. He also works as a private planning consultant. His publications and his research work focus on planning dynamics, currently investigating the influence of development trends on the city image.

Joerg Knieling, HafenCity University Hamburg
Joerg Knieling is Vice-President for Research Affairs at the HafenCity University Hamburg (HCU) and holds the Chair for Urban Planning and Regional Development. He acquired a diploma and his PhD in urban and regional planning and a master in political sciences and sociology from the University of Hanover. From 1992 until 2001 he was managing director of a private planning and research agency, then a member of the Office of the Senate of the Free and Hanseatic City of Hamburg. In 2003 he was appointed Professor for Spatial Planning at Dresden Technical University. In 2004 he moved on to Technical University Hamburg-Harburg, since 2006 he has been a member of the HCU. His main research subjects are strategies of regional and metropolitan development, territorial governance, and planning theory.

João Morais Mourato, The Bartlett School of Planning – UCL, London, UK
João Morais Mourato (1975) trained as an architect (TU Lisbon) and currently follows the RTPI-accredited PhD Town Planning at the Bartlett School of Planning in London. He has worked as a Research Consultant for the Directorate General for Spatial Planning and Urban Development of the Portuguese Republic. His doctoral research interests are specifically focused

on the influence European spatial planning policies have had in shaping the Portuguese National Spatial Planning Policy Programme and on the consequent institutional culture shift.

Vincent Nadin, Delft University of Technology
Vincent Nadin is Professor of Spatial Planning and Strategy in the Department of Urbanism, Faculty of Architecture, Delft University of Technology. He is Visiting Professor at the Institute of Environmental Planning, Leibniz University, Hannover, and was previously Professor of Town Planning at the University of the West of England. Vincent jointly led the preparation of the EU *Compendium of Spatial Planning Systems and Policies* (1997) and the technical work on the *Spatial Vision for North West Europe* (2000). He has led a number of other major international research projects including sustainability and spatial planning; subsidiarity and proportionality in EU planning and a comparison of environmental planning systems. Vincent is joint author of *Town and Country Planning in the UK* and editor-in-chief of the Taylor and Francis international peer reviewed journal *Planning Practice and Research*.

Frank Othengrafen, HafenCity University Hamburg
Frank Othengrafen graduated as an Urban and Regional Planner from the University of Dortmund. Since 2004 he has worked as a researcher at the Chair for Urban Planning and Regional Development at HafenCity University Hamburg (HCU). His main research topics are European spatial planning and development, territorial governance, European planning cultures and planning theory. He has extensive experience of international comparative research, including projects dealing with planning strategies in metropolitan regions, territorial cohesion and territorial governance.

Susanne Prehl, Bauhaus-University Weimar, Germany
Susanne Prehl graduated from the Masters Programme in European Urban Studies at the Bauhaus-University Weimar in 2007. In her Masters thesis she analysed the constellations of actors and the distinction of lifestyles in Istanbul's public space at the case study of the French street. Before that, she studied Landscape Architecture at Anhalt University of Applied Sciences, Germany, from where she graduated in 2003. Her main research interest focuses on comparative studies dealing with public spaces and related processes of transition.

Violeta Puşcaşu, University 'Dunarea de Jos' Galati, Romania
Violeta Puşcaşu is Professor for Territorial Planning at the University Dunărea de Jos Galaţi. Before that, she was a researcher and lecturer (economic geography and urban and land planning) at the same university. She holds a PhD in Geography from the University of Bucharest. Her research interests

focus on urban and land planning, economical geography, and regional development, on which she has published several articles and books. She also has on-going visiting professorships in the Université du Havre, France and the Haute Ecole Leon Eli Troclet in Liege, Belgium.

Konstantinos Serraos, National Technical University of Athens, Greece
Konstantinos Serraos studied Architecture at the National Technical University of Athens (NTUA). He was awarded his Masters Degree in Urban Planning from the University of Munich (1990) and a PhD on Urban Planning from the Technical University of Vienna. He is currently Assistant Professor at the NTUA – School of Architecture, Department of Urban and Regional Planning. He also teaches Environmental Urban Planning at the Hellenic Open University, as well as at the Centre of Continuous Learning of the NTUA. In addition, until 2004, he taught Urban Planning at the University of Thessaly – Department of Urban and Regional Planning. He has undertaken extensive research concerning spatial problems, land use and threats from natural disasters. He has published many articles and books examining the management processes of Urban Development.

Eugenijus Kęstutis Staniūnas, Vilnius Gediminas Technical University, Lithuania
Eugenijus Staniunas is Associate Professor at the Department of Urban Design, Faculty of Architecture, at the Technical University in Vilnius. He has longstanding experience in the planning systems and planning practices as well as in the transitions of these traditions in the Baltic States. Recently, he participated in the INTERREG III B project 'COMMIN-Promoting Spatial Development by Creating Common Mindscapes', which consisted mainly of a comparative approach to describing and analysing the spatial planning systems in all Baltic Sea Region States.

Dominic Stead, Delft University of Technology, The Netherlands
Dominic Stead is Senior Researcher at Delft University of Technology. He has a PhD in Planning Studies from UCL, London, a Masters Degree in Town and Country Planning from University of the West of England, Bristol, and a Masters Degree in Environmental Management from Imperial College, London. His research primarily focuses on the processes of spatial planning and transport policy-making and the impacts of these policies. He has wide experience of pan-European research projects and has recently been involved in a projects funded by ESPON (European Spatial Planning Observation Network), European Framework Programmes, INTERACT, INTERREG and the United Nations Economic Commission for Europe. He has published widely in academic books and international journals.

Gül Tuçaltan, Middle East Technical University, Ankara, Turkey
Gül Tuçaltan attained her Bachelor's degree in City and Regional Planning in 2006 and her Master's degree in Urban Policy Planning and Local Governments in 2008 from the Middle East Technical University in Ankara, Turkey. She is currently working as Research Assistant at the Department of City and Regional Planning and is continuing her research studies at the Department of Urban Policy Planning and Local Governments at the same university. Her research interests focus on urban policy planning, urban and societal (dis)integration and urban political sociology.

Veli-Pekka Tynkkynen, University of Helsinki and Academy of Finland
Veli-Pekka Tynkkynen is a Post-doctoral Research Fellow at the Department of Geography, University of Helsinki. Between 1999 and 2006 he was Assistant Professor in the same department. Between 2006 and 2008 he also worked at Nordregio, Stockholm as a Senior Research Fellow concentrating, concentrating on Nordic spatial development issues. He holds a PhD in planning geography from the University of Helsinki. His research interests are urban and regional planning, sustainable development and governmentality in Northern Europe, including northwestern Russia. He has published various articles, publications and books on urban and regional planning, environmental policy and the geography of northwestern Russia.

Rosalie van Dam, Wageningen University and Research Centre, The Netherlands
Rosalie van Dam holds an MSc in Public Administration and currently works as policy analyst at Alterra, Green World Research, a research institute attached to Wageningen University, The Netherlands. She is active in the field of environmental and spatial planning research and is involved in national and international projects concerning the analysis and development of methods and strategies regarding spatial planning and policy processes, power structures between involved actors, stakeholder involvement, and social, spatial and administrative trends and their consequences as well as administrative and social cultures in the context of a complex and changing society. She was recently involved in the INTERACT project CULTPLAN, which is analysing cultural influences in and their impacts (how to recognise, cope with or manage cultural differences) on international planning processes as INTERREG.

André van der Zande, Wageningen University and Research Centre, The Netherlands
Andre van der Zande is Secretary General at the Dutch Ministry of Agriculture, Nature and Food Quality. In 2005 he was also appointed as Professor for Spatial Planning and Cultural Heritage at Wageningen University and Research Centre in the Netherlands. There he holds the Belvedere Chair and

is chair of the group on land-use planning. His research interests focus on cultural heritage and spatial planning, ecology, and landscape ecology.

Luciano Vettoretto
Luciano Vettoretto is full professor of Urban and Regional Planning, Director of the Department of Planning and of the Graduate Program in Urban and Regional Planning Sciences at the IUAV University of Venice. He is a member of the Editorial Board of *Archivio di Studi Urbani e Regionali*, and author of numerous essays, on topics such as planning theories and European spatial planning and policies. His recent studies have examined the outcomes of some European programmes on local societies and policy-making, and the meanings of some new regulative instruments in planning processes and local development policies.

Bas Waterhout, Delft University of Technology, The Netherlands
Bas Waterhout (1974) is a Research Fellow and Lecturer at OTB Research Institute for Housing, Urban and Mobility Studies at Delft University of Technology. His research focuses on strategic spatial planning and governance at EU and lower levels. Together with Andreas Faludi he co-authored the acclaimed book *The Making of the ESDP*. Bas Waterhout has carried out several commissioned projects for the Dutch National Spatial Planning Agency and was involved in INTERREG and ESPON projects. He trained as a spatial planner at the University of Amsterdam and holds a PhD from Delft University of Technology on the institutionalisation of European spatial planning.

Acknowledgements

The preparation of this book was inspired by the research agenda of the Institute for Urban, Regional and Environmental Planning of the HafenCity University Hamburg on planning theory and planning culture. Our interest in the field of comparative planning studies had increased in particular through the research project 'CULTPLAN – Planning as Culture in Europe: Learning from Differences in Planning Related to the Cultural Context', but also through collaborative research with the National Technical University of Athens and Helsinki University of Technology as well as a research fellowship at the Institut d'Études Avancées in Paris.

The CULTPLAN project included partners from five different European countries and was funded by the European Union. CULTPLAN analysed cultural influences and their manifestations in INTERREG projects and the way cultural similarities and differences had been recognised and handled as potentials or restraints. The objective was to conclude recommendations for dealing with cultural differences in international planning and cooperation processes. By analysing the cultural influences of INTERREG projects, all project partners of the international project consortium themselves had to take into account the cultural traits of their partners. This contributed fundamentally to our own awareness of cultural differences and strengthened our interest in the field of comparative planning studies. For the stimulating and successful cooperation during the CULTPLAN project we thank our partners and their teams from Alterra, Wageningen University (Roel During), ANEM, Development Company of Magnesia (Aristarhos-Aristeidis Nizamis), Consvipo, Consortium for the Development of Polesine (Davide Bonagurio), EUROREG, Warsaw University (Grzegorz Gorzelak), TRANSCOOP, Agency for Transnational Training and Development (Sakis Karamoschos), and from the University of Venice, Department of Urban Planning (Luciano Vettoretto). Many thanks are also due to Athanasios Papaioannou who was part of our research team at the HafenCity University Hamburg.

Within the duration of CULTPLAN we had the pleasure of organising the International Symposium 'Planning Cultures in Europe – Exploring Cultural Differences as Resources and Restrictions for Interregional Cooperation' in 2007 in Hamburg. The aim of the Symposium was to analyse cultural influences on planning processes and practices and, against the background of territorial cohesion and cooperation, to contribute to a better understanding of planning cultures throughout Europe. The Symposium included a Call for Papers, which addressed both experienced scientists and practitioners in the field of European Planning Cultures. The jury, including Dietrich Fürst and Luciano Vettoretto as external evaluators, reviewed all submitted papers and we are very grateful for their support. This book mainly consists of papers related to the presentations given at the Symposium. We thank all authors for their persistency and their willingness to contribute to this volume. Furthermore, we thank Dietrich Fürst and Luciano Vettoretto who joined the book project, adding important further features for decoding cultural phenomena in urban and regional planning practices in their contributions.

During the preparation of the book we incorporated further experiences from additional research initiatives, in particular from two research exchanges funded by the German Academic Exchange Service. The two years research with Athens ('The City as Arena. Events as Motor for Metropolitan Development') and Helsinki ('Innovative Planning Strategies in Metropolitan Regions') both included the analysis of planning cultures in urban and regional planning. Furthermore, the project 'Paris Métropoles en miroir – L'Ile de France comme region métropolitaine' offered the chance to analyse the current visioning process of the metropolitan region of Paris, including a deeper understanding of the French planning culture. We would like to thank our partners and their teams in Helsinki (Peter Ache), Athens (Konstantinos Serraos) and Paris (Jean-Louis Cohen, Cristiana Mazzoni, Hartmut Frank, Mario Gandelsonas and Yannis Tsiomis for the pilotage and coordination of the research programme as well as Jean-Luc Lory as secretary general of the Institut d'Études Avancées).

This book is hard to imagine without the assistance of Jakob F. Schmid. We would particularly like to thank him for both his excellent support in organising the International Symposium and for his continuous commitment in assembling the manuscript, his design of the book cover and his general technical support. Many thanks also to Christine Ahlert, Robert Nehls and Marco Schwartz for their support during the International Symposium and their assistance during manuscript preparation.

Furthermore, we would like to thank Val Rose, Carolyn Court, Sarah Horsley and Pauline Beavers at Ashgate Publishing for their patience and continuous support in preparing the book for publication.

Finally, we thank Nadine Appelhans and Pat FitzGerald, who – at various stages at the preparation process – worked so sedulously to transcribe the translation of this book in a prose style that retains the subtlety of the original without thereby sacrificing either clarity or readability.

We hope that the book will be stimulating for both scientists and practitioners in urban and regional planning who work and think 'international'. We would be glad if it contributes to a better understanding of European diversity, and thus assists the efforts of integrating Europe to a vibrant, lively and tolerant area of cross-border and inter-regional cooperation.

Joerg Knieling and Frank Othengrafen
Hamburg
July 2009

Preface
Spatial Planning and Culture – Symbiosis for a Better Understanding of Cultural Differences in Planning Systems, Traditions and Practices

Joerg Knieling and Frank Othengrafen

Territorial development, including not only urban and regional planning but also concepts of territorial cohesion and cooperation, has become of increasing importance throughout the world, but especially Europe: economic globalisation and the challenges posed by the European integration process have led to a 'spatial turn' and a more coherent approach to territorial development such as the European Spatial Development Perspective (CEC 1999) and the Territorial Agenda of the European Union (EU 2007). In these documents the role of space as 'territorial capital' (space as an important and distinguishable local production factor) and as dimension for 'spatial justice' (space as an integrating and balancing factor) is emphasised (Faludi 2005; Davoudi 2005; Soja 2008). The repositioning of space and territory is intensified by a 'new' interpretation of the category 'space': It is no longer a neutral category as it was between the 1960s and the 1980s that is viewed as a 'container' for economic and social processes, but it is rather the result of social relations among people living in a certain area or region (territory as social constructed space) where culture and cultural influences play a crucial role.

In other terms, urban and regional planning and development are strongly rooted in and restricted to the cultural contexts or traits of a society. To view planning as a technical or apolitical activity seems to be unrealistic and is furthermore seen to be incapable of achieving planning's goals:

> Instead, planners and planning systems need to be responsive to difference, to be genuinely participatory and to strive to create deliberative contexts that, as far as possible, minimise inequalities of power and knowledge. Methods of studying planning therefore also emphasize the importance of listening to planners' view of their worlds; tracing the forms of communication they use among themselves and with their publics; and understanding their ethical dilemmas. (Huxley 2000, 369)

Thus, urban and regional planning and development are to be understood and practiced differently depending on their institutional settings and cultural roots that vary significantly across countries and regions (Friedmann 2005, 29; CEC 1997). Each national or regional context is characterised by particularities of history, by attitudes, beliefs and values, political and legal traditions, different socio-economic patterns and concepts of justice, interpretations of planning tasks and responsibilities, and different structures of governance – in other terms: by its specific cultural characteristics.

In the context of the European integration process, and with regard to the European Union's objectives of a balanced, polycentric, sustainable and competitive development of its territory (EU 2007), this requires knowledge of the specific 'planning cultures' of countries or regions to promote a professional discourse of knowledge and opinions on these issues. The term 'planning culture' in this sense particularly refers to the different planning systems and traditions, institutional arrangements of spatial development and the broader cultural context of spatial planning and development. It consists of more than planning instruments and procedures; it is the aggregate of the social, environmental, and historical grounding of urban and regional planning (Young 2008, 35) describing the specific 'cultural contexts' in which planning is embedded and operates.

The 'Cultural Turn' and its Impact on Urban and Regional Development

One reason for the greater awareness of cultural contexts for urban and regional planning can be found in the 'cultural turn' in the 1990s which marked a watershed in recognising the significance of culture (and also space) compared to the discussions in the 1970s and 1980s when culture specific contexts and settings among nations and regions were neglected.[1] But with the cultural turn, economic globalisation and other challenges such as migration and integration policies, environmental policies or climate change led to a greater awareness and recognition of both cultural and territorial contexts. Friedmann (2005), for example, argues that despite the unifying and culturally homogenising powers of global interconnections and global policies, various culturally affected ways and strategies remain to react towards the global challenges for nations or regions. As a consequence, the cultural turn emphasises the value of

---

1 In the 1980s especially the worldwide trend, 'with Reagan and Thatcher in the lead, seemed to support the theory of neoclassical economists that people all over the world are the same in their pursuit of self-interests and are best served by entrepreneurial states' (Sanyal 2005, xx). Specific cultural contexts and settings among nations and regions were not recognised although the ways in which these neoliberal approaches were implemented in national policies varied widely, due to the different cultural contexts of nations, regions or places.

cultural diversity. From the point of view of urban and regional development, it becomes obvious that this diversity also has a spatial component, bringing together the 'cultural turn' and the 'spatial turn', the latter having been a subject in economical sciences since the 1990s (Krugman 2002). This explains that each area or region has its own culture, its own institutional context, its own traditions, values and attitudes which provide solutions different from those of other places (Dear 2000, 2). Together with postmodern ideas and concepts, this underlines the heterogeneity of social groups, the pluralism of values and the significance of difference. Culture is no longer necessarily seen as a general or universal concept, but it is also recognised as pluralistic, fragmentary, ambivalent, dynamic and reflective.

Together, the 'cultural turn' and the 'spatial turn' can be seen as basis for an increasing awareness for the concepts of space and territory in times of globalisation, with its cultural contexts and social consequences. The awareness of culture and cultural aspects has already been reflected in global governance policies, such as the UN Convention on the Protection and Promotion of the Diversity of Cultural Expressions, the UN Universal Declaration on Cultural Diversity or the UN Convention for the Safeguarding of the Intangible Cultural Heritage. These programmes and declarations have in common that they aim at enhancing the role of culture in national (planning) policies, recognising the knowledge of cultural, ethnic, linguistic and religious diversity and strengthening intercultural dialogue and skills.

Besides, 'development thinking in the last decade has experienced a cultural turn' (Radcliffe 2006, 2). The failure of certain projects, in particular huge infrastructure projects, during the 1970s and 1980s has led to a change of policies in the 1990s, for example, those of the World Bank. Since then the World Bank has incorporated 'strong rationales for planning perspectives and opportunities that are based on culture' (Young 2008, 2). In other terms, the focus of the World Bank's development policy has tried to integrate local and regional traditions, practices and habits (intellectual, emotional, moral and spiritual routines) more intensively.

Cultural Variety as Principle: The Role of Culture for the European Integration

For Europe, with its 27 member states and many further partners, the awareness of culture and cultural contexts is of high importance. Europe's cultural heterogeneity and diversity on one hand is a burden and a challenge for a common policy, on the other hand it is seen as an 'indispensable feature to achieve the EU's strategic objectives of prosperity, solidarity and security' (CEC 2007, 3).

The basis for the action of the EU in the field of culture lies in the EU Treaty (EU 2008). Article 167 (the 'culture chapter') states that:

> The Union shall contribute to the flowering of the cultures of the Member States, while respecting their national and regional diversity and at the same time bringing the common heritage to the fore.
>
> Action by the Union shall be aimed at encouraging cooperation between member States and, if necessary, supporting and supplementing their action ....
>
> The Union and the Member States shall foster cooperation with third countries and the competent international organisations in the sphere of culture, in particular the Council of Europe.
>
> The Union shall take cultural aspects into account in its action under the provisions of the Treaties, in particular in order to respect and to promote the diversity of its cultures ....

This article, which was introduced into the Treaties in 1992 for the first time, recognises the EU's cultural diversity as one of its greatest assets. In this context, the EU interprets culture, amongst other things, in an anthropological way:

> Culture lies at the heart of human development and civilisation. Culture is what makes people hope and dream, by stimulating our senses and offering new ways of looking at reality. It is what brings people together, by stirring dialogue and arousing passions, in a way that unites rather than divides. Culture should be regarded as a set of distinctive spiritual and material traits that characterize a society and social group. (CEC 2007, 2)

This also finds its expression in the European Year of Intercultural Dialogue 2008 but even more in the European Commission's *Communication on a European Agenda for Culture in a Globalising World* (CEC 2007), which was approved in 2007. The European agenda for culture proposes the first-ever comprehensive European strategy for culture, aiming amongst other things at the recognition of cultural diversity and the promotion of intercultural dialogue.

The role of culture can also be found in programmes of international collaboration in the field of spatial planning and development, which have been practiced since the 1990s in cross-border and transnational contexts (e.g. INTERREG, URBAN, URBACT etc.). These EU programmes and initiatives have the aim of helping Europe's regions in forming partnerships on joint projects. They have been designed to strengthen economic and social cohesion throughout the EU by fostering a balanced development of the continent through cross-border, transnational and interregional cooperation.

All these different programmes and initiatives highlight the role of culture in the European integration process. This again, shows the necessity of analysing the 'cultural contexts' of the programmes in which spatial planning and development are embedded and operate, to organise these programmes, as well as the European integration process, successfully.

Purpose of this Publication

Despite the increased cooperation in the field of urban and regional development across the European Union and various European planning processes and documents as the European Spatial Development Perspective (CEC 1999) or the Territorial Agenda (EU 2007), it is obvious that the term 'planning', with reference to urban and regional planning and development, is understood and practiced differently in the European countries. Depending on the particular perception and practice of urban and regional planning, the French term 'aménagement du territoire', the German *Raumordnung* or *Raumplanung*, the Dutch *Ruimtelijke Ordening* and the Spanish *urbanismo* do not necessarily share the same understanding of planning or pursue compatible objectives, models, strategies and instruments, due to different cultural contexts (CEC 1997, 23; Friedmann 2005, 31).

Urban and regional planning are influenced by culture through manifestations in history or by contemporary developments and via tangible and intangible ways. As a result planning systems and traditions, development processes in cities and regions, planning concepts and decision-making are always influenced by cultural contexts and the cultural background of the people involved in planning processes. Different perceptions and meanings of space, as well as different understandings of planning, planning systems and processes, affect the Europe-wide collaboration of actors. Even within a national context, cultural differences between regions can be found, but in cross-border or transnational activities especially there can be great contrasts in terms of the planning traditions and decision-making of collaborating countries and regions. To identify the cultural influences on spatial development and to use the European cultural diversity for the development of the European territory, contemporary comparative studies on urban and regional planning and development inevitably have to recognise the impact of culture. It is no longer acceptable to deal with spatial planning and development as a nationally isolated issue because the global interconnections and the EU integration policies have to be considered.

This publication recognises the need to study the relations between cultural variety and planning practice on a regional scale in Europe. The objective is to analyse the relations between different perceptions and meanings of space, specific planning traditions and philosophies, and cultural rules, norms, traditions, and values on the one side, and the practice of regional planning and development on the other side. All contributions in this volume aim at contributing to the European integration process by gaining a better understanding of the role of culture for spatial planning. According to Breulliard and Fraser (2007, xiv):

> the emphasis of the work however is not to describe what is happening in each country's professional practice but to compare practice and to examine in more depth the nature of the similarities and differences which arise, with a view to achieving a better understanding of the rationale ... behind each.

The objective of this volume is to develop a theoretical basis and conceptual framework for a systematic analysis and comparison of different planning cultures (planning models and practices related to an institutional and social context) on the basis of a consistent system of criteria. This may contribute to achieving a better understanding of the relationship between the cultural context (including the specific socio-economic patterns and related cultural norms, values, traditions, and attitudes) and spatial planning as an operative instrument of territorial policy. By combining cultural studies, social sciences and planning theory it is also intended to enrich the discussion about the use and the application of theories in planning research. To achieve these aims, the contributions of this volume consider the following main research questions:

- Analysis of planning practices: are there significant variations in urban and regional planning and development practices? Do such variations arise from differences in planning cultures, meaning the (historical) 'collective ethos and dominant attitudes of planning regarding the appropriate role of the state, market forces, and civil society in influencing social [and spatial] outcomes' (Sanyal 2005: xxi)? Which social practices in a society influence the dominant planning culture?
- Analysis of culture: how can culture be defined or what is the role of culture in planning and development processes? How are planning cultures formed? What are the core cultural traits which distinguish planning models and practices in different countries or regions? In which way do they differ from each other? Which influences do different sets of political, administrative and legal traditions, socio-economic patterns and structures of governance have? Are 'notions of social efficiency, social justice, and moral responsibility redefined to suit the needs of the changing global economy' (Sanyal 2005, xxii)?
- Analysis of theoretical (planning) approaches: how can these empirically classified cultural traits be ascertained theoretically? Which criteria are useful to describe and identify planning cultures? What could a consistent system of criteria look like and how can 'planning culture' be operationalised for comparative studies? Can elements of

cultural theories and social sciences be transferred to the field of spatial planning and development?
- Analysis of convergence or divergence of planning cultures: how does the continuous process of European integration with its social, political and technological changes affect planning models and practices in European member states and how do they structure institutional responses? What are the affects on planning models and practices?

Outline of the Book

Cultural diversity is the main characteristic but also a challenge for a multiple community such as the European Union. By analysing and understanding this cultural variety, and in particular the impacts of culture on urban and regional development, this volume tries to contribute towards a better understanding of Europe and the European integration process. All contributions aim at identifying cultural influences on spatial development and, through a conceptual framework and a systematic comparison, to enable professionals and scientists as well as practitioners to value and to make use of the European cultural diversity in the field of urban and regional planning for the common development of the European territory.

Planning Culture – Theoretical Approaches

The first part of the volume sets the frame for all the following contributions by presenting and connecting cultural theories and planning theories to develop a concept of an analytical model that explains the influences of culture on planning procedures and practices in a comparative perspective.

Hans Gullestrup, in his contribution 'Theoretical Reflections on Common European (Planning-) Cultures', presents a theoretical and anthropological approach for a better understanding of the concept of culture. To analyse the complexity of culture, Gullestrup distinguishes a horizontal and vertical dimension of culture. The horizontal dimension of culture consists of immediately visible cultural traits and is completed by the vertical dimension, i.e. the analysis of the fundamental legitimating cultural traits which will create a deeper insight into the culture observed. In conclusion, Gullestrup presents common European values as well as remarks and recommendations regarding the transferability of the analytical model for analysing planning practices and cultures.

In his contribution 'Planning Cultures En Route to a Better Comprehension of Planning Processes?', Dietrich Fürst approaches planning culture as a scientific concept. Referring to theoretical concepts of political, public administration and organisational sciences, he presents research results with regard to spatial planning systems but, at the same time, underlines a lack of comparative studies about influence of culture on planning practices. He stresses that attitudes, beliefs and values of individuals and groups as well as their interactions within societies are becoming more important for the comparative analysis of planning practices. He concludes that the discussion on cultural differences in planning could improve planning practices if it was translated into learning devices helping to understand and deal with cultural diversity.

According to the contributions of Hans Gullestrup and Dietrich Fürst, the following chapter, 'En Route to a Theoretical Model for Comparative Research on Planning Cultures', by Joerg Knieling and Frank Othengrafen, presents a theoretical model to encourage a scientific and systematic comparison of planning cultures on the basis of a consistent system of criteria. The outlined 'culturised planning model' is able to consider and decode cultural phenomena of planning not only on the visible 'surface' (horizontal) but also on a 'hidden' (vertical) level. By introducing the dimensions of (1) 'planning artefacts', (2) 'planning environment' and (3) 'societal environment' the model allows the systematic and comprehensive analysis and comparison of planning cultures. In this context, the 'culturised planning model' includes possible interrelations between cultural and (postmodern) planning theories to explain the influences of culture on planning procedures and practices. The model and its (analytical) cultural dimensions describe a culture-based planning paradigm which provides the framework for the analysis and description of the various planning cultures in the following contributions.

Planning Cultures in Northwestern Europe

Following the theoretical derivations the next contributions describe attributes of planning cultures and practices of Northwestern European member states. Friedhelm Fischer starts by describing the German planning culture in his contribution 'How German Is It? Planning Cultures and Different Types of Government – An Essay in Epistemological Eclecticism'. He identifies some of the important cultural origins of the German planning traditions and cultures by means of analysing the Prussian virtues (e.g. punctuality, modesty and diligence, rule of law, obedience to authority, reliability and the focus on (scientific) theories as basis for decision-making) and their consequences for the contemporary German planning system and culture. He also explains the relation of the tradition of a belated political modernisation and radicalisation to the tradition of an issue-related or result-oriented culture of decision-making.

In their contribution 'Planning Culture in Austria – The Case of Vienna, the Unlike City', Jens Dangschat and Alexander Hamedinger underline the 'shift from government to governance' in Vienna. In this context, they particularly focus on the spatial impacts of the clientelist relationship between local government and citizens, the high concentration of decision-making processes in the administration and within the extended structure of the ruling Social Democratic Workers Party, the Austrian form of cooperatism (*Sozialpartnerschaft*), and on the provision of services of general interest to the public.

In most traditions of spatial planning, planning policy documents involve a symbolic representation of the territory in the form of icons, diagrams and maps. In her contribution 'Visualising Spatial Policy in Europe' Stefanie Dühr shows that the visualisation of spatial policy is deeply rooted in a planning culture: a cross-national comparative analysis of the cartographic and symbolic representations of spatial policy in Germany, Great Britain and the Netherlands illustrates significant differences in the understanding of planning in different European countries affecting the content and design of 'policy maps'. The contribution concludes by discussing practical implications for visualising spatial policy in future cooperation processes of transnational spatial planning.

Planning Cultures in Eastern Europe

Due to the collapse of the Soviet Union and the former Eastern Bloc the analysis of planning culture in countries which used to belong to one of these 'groups' seems to be very promising to examine possible shifts in planning practice that have taken place recently. In his contribution 'Remarks on the Features of Lithuanian Planning Culture' Eugenijus Staniunas, amongst others, deals with the inconsistency and different perceptions of planning culture. By showing important facts and features of the planning cultures in Lithuania – e.g. the non-existence of an education for and profession of planners, numerous changes in spatial planning law, the lasting influence of former attitudes of the Soviet Union and the continuing problem of illegal construction – the chapter outlines the logical inter-relations between ideologies and planning practices and illustrates tendencies of the contemporary planning culture of the Baltic States.

Veli-Pekka Tynkkynen examines 'Planning Rationalities among Practitioners in St Petersburg, Russia – Soviet Traditions and Western Influences', analysing how the planning discourse in Russia has changed since the collapse of the Soviet Union. He concludes that, although planning seems to 'borrow' from the Soviet paradigm the idea of overarching instrumental rationality, including affording a superior position to planning professionals and neglecting aspects of democracy and sustainability, the present planning discourse in St Petersburg also underlines that urban planning and development is performed and led by powerful developer corporations in an extremely incremental manner. It is illustrated in this context that in Russia both planning and planning studies resemble Soviet times and that the gap between theorising and 'Realpolitik' remains wide.

Violeta Puşcaşu's objective in her contribution 'The House of Many Different Ages' is to build an argument for the diversity of the components in Romanian planning in an expository manner. Therefore, she introduces the image of 'the house of many different ages', a model of describing the Romanian planning culture by means of its cultural and historic traditions. She emphasises the administrative institutions and territorial levels of administration in which former and new levels and structures coexist, the normative level which displays a simple and discontinuous legislative synopsis, the opposable political context with direction and rhythm shifts, the external influences of proximity (former USSR versus EU, the Balkans versus the West) and the weak local planning culture and theory, where the consistent and hermetic Western theory reaches with difficulty.

Planning Cultures in Southern Europe

After various national and regional planning cultures and practices of Northwestern and Eastern Europe have been analysed, Part 4 presents some prominent features from Southern Europe. By showing features of the planning cultures in Italy Luciano Vettoretto outlines some interrelations between ideologies and planning practices. In his contribution 'Planning Cultures in Italy – Reformism, Laissez-Faire and Contemporary Trends' he describes recent changes in Italian planning culture, especially the impact of the European Union's key principles on the technical and administrative culture of local authorities that have overcome the sectoral and hierarchical orientation of public policies and spatial planning. Furthermore, he underlines the importance of the traditions and principles of 'reformism', 'patronage' (clientelism), and 'familism' for the understanding of planning practices in Italy.

The contribution 'Planning Culture and the Interference of Major Events, The Recent Experience of Athens' by Konstantinos Serraos, Byron Ioannou and Evangelos Asprogerakas gives a brief revision of the fundamental cultural features and spatial standards of Athens metropolitan area and the Olympic Games in Athens in 2004. Against the background of the administrative structure, institutional framework and planning instruments, the interference of the planning of the Olympic Games in Athens in 2004 as well as the post-Olympic use of these venues are presented and analysed. The authors evaluate the yields, potential detrimental effects and unexploited opportunities of the Olympic Games for Athens' metropolitan area and its inhabitants on the basis of regional and urban planning practices.

The aim of Susanne Prehl and Gul Tuçaltan's contribution 'Coping with the Era of Change – Planning and Decision-making under Globalisation in Turkey: The Case of French Street Urban Transformation Project, Istanbul' is to examine the effect of globalisation and neoliberal policies, and the related interdependent variables of economy, technology, society, politics, administration and space, on planning and decision-making processes in Turkey. By means of selected urban development and regeneration processes in the city of Istanbul, the authors show how Turkish planners and decision-makers cope with the influences of globalisation and with changes of related ethical and cultural values.

Interdependencies between European Spatial Policies and Planning Culture

Planning cultures are not only affected by endogenous (national or regional) practices, rules and developments but also by exogenous frameworks or developments. Spatial planning in Europe, for example, is undergoing an incremental process of Europeanisation. In their contribution 'The Impact of Europeanisation on Planning Cultures', Bas Waterhout, Joao Mourato and Kai Böhme argue that Europeanisation consists of processes of construction, diffusion, and institutionalisation of formal and informal rules and norms, procedures, policy paradigms, styles, 'ways of doing things' and shared beliefs which are first defined and consolidated in the EU policy process and then incorporated into national and regional contexts under the influence of their cultural contexts. They explore the question of whether the Europeanisation of spatial planning as such also leads to changing planning cultures in Europe. They go on to consider where these changes in planning systems may lead – to convergence or even to a European planning culture.

Roel During, Rosalie van Dam and André van der Zande focus on the present EU ideology and policy that recognise cultural variety as an important characteristic of Europe. In their contribution 'A Missing Link in the Cultural Evolution of the European Union: Confronting EU Ideology with INTERREG III Practice Concerning Cultural Diversity' they show that the desired synergy between maintaining cultural diversity and simultaneously achieving economic and political development in practice is to some extent a 'fairytale'. By analysing and evaluating EU policy and ideology on the one side and (culturally manifested) INTERREG practices on the other side, the chapter provides answers to the question of whether the EU really is respecting and supporting the cultural diversity of its constituting regions and if the regions recognise the grounding cultural aspects of their planning practice.

Simin Davoudi's contribution 'Territorial Cohesion, European Social Model and Transnational Cooperation' aims at providing a deeper understanding of the concept of territorial cohesion by tracing its roots in the two influential but different planning cultures and traditions of France and Germany and by positioning it in the wider debate on the European social model. She suggests that the concept can be interpreted as the spatial manifestation of the European model but that, at the same time, the application of territorial cohesion as a spatial concept is likely to be fragmented and diverse, due to the diversity of the national planning systems and their underlying social philosophies and cultural values.

Conclusions

The goal of this volume is to give a systematic and comprehensive introduction to the enduring phenomenon of culture and its impact on contemporary spatial planning and development practices. Against this background Dominic Stead and Vincent Nadin argue in their concluding contribution 'Planning Cultures between Models of Society and Planning Systems' that the characteristics of spatial planning systems and practices are embedded in wider models of society. They review the parallel dynamics of models of society and typologies of planning systems and identify the level of correspondence between them. Drawing on evidence from various European countries presented in the chapters of this volume they show that many planning systems are undergoing similar types of changes although the underlying cultural context, the model of society and the nature of the planning system are quite different. The extent to which these changes in planning systems lead to convergence is also considered.

In the final chapter, 'Planning Cultures in Europe between Convergence and Divergence: Findings, Explanations and Perspectives', Joerg Knieling and Frank Othengrafen summarise the different approaches to and elements of planning culture on the basis of the culturised planning model (see earlier contribution of Knieling and Othengrafen). On basis of the (theoretical) distinction between 'planning artefacts', 'planning environment' and 'societal environment' they summarise whether and to what extent cultural phenomena are considered and decoded in planning practices.

Bibliography

Breulliard, M. and C. Fraser (2007) 'Preface', in P. Booth, M. Breuillard, C. Fraser and D. Paris (eds) *Spatial Planning Systems of Britain and France, A Comparative Analysis*, Routledge, London, xiii–xv.

Commission of the European Communities – CEC (1997) *The EU Compendium of Spatial Planning Systems and Policies*, Regional Development Studies, Office for Official Publications of the European Communities, Luxembourg.

Commission of the European Communities – CEC (1999) *The European Spatial Development Perspective, Towards Balanced and Sustainable Development of the Territory of the European Union*, Office for Official Publications of the European Communities, Luxembourg.

Commission of the European Communities – CEC (2007) *Communication from the Commission to the European Parliament, the Council, the European European Economic and Social Committee and the Committee of the Regions on a European Agenda for Culture in a Globalizing World*, COM(2007) 242 final, Brussels.

Davoudi, S. (2005) 'Understanding Territorial Cohesion', *Planning Practice and Research* 20(4), 433–41.

EU Informal Ministerial Meeting on Urban Development and Territorial Cohesion (2007) *Territorial Agenda of the European Union: Towards a more Competitive and Sustainable Europe of Diverse Regions*, Leipzig 24–25 May.

EU (2008) *Consolidated Version of the Treaty on the Functioning of the European Union*, Office Journal of the European Union, 9 May, Brussels.

Faludi, A. (2005) 'Territorial Cohesion: An Unidentified Political Objective, Introduction to the Special Issue', *Town Planning Review* 76(1), 1–14.

Friedmann, J. (2005) 'Planning Cultures in Transition', in B. Sanyal (ed.) *Comparative Planning Culture*, Routledge, London, 29–44.

Huxley, M. (2000) 'The Limits to Communicative Planning', *Journal of Planning Education and Research* 19(4), 369–77.

Krugman, P. (2002) *Development, Geography and Economic Theory*, 6th edn, MIT Press, Cambridge, MA.

Radcliffe, S.A. (2006) *Culture and Development in a Globalizing World: Geographies, Actors, and Paradigms*, Routledge, London.

Sanyal, B. (2005) 'Preface', in Sanyal, B. (ed.) *Comparative Planning Culture*, Routledge, London, xix–xxiv.

Soja, E. (2008) 'Vom "Zeitgeist" zum "Raumgeist", New Twists on the Spatial Turn', in J. Döring and T. Thielmann (eds) *Spatial Turn, Das Raumparadigma in den Kultur- und Sozialwissenschaften*, transcript-Verlag, Bielefeld.

Young, G. (2008) *Reshaping Planning with Culture*, Ashgate, Aldershot.

PART 1
Planning Culture – Theoretical Approaches

Chapter 1
Theoretical Reflections on Common European (Planning-) Cultures

Hans Gullestrup

Introduction: A Way of Understanding Culture and the Cultural Foundation of Societies

This chapter attempts to show how a theoretical inter-cultural model of understanding can be useful for the description and understanding of how research, planning and social measures of development are strongly rooted in, and restricted to, the dominant world conception of cultures. In a globalised world this is the case in any given field at any given time.

On the basis of a brief account of the concept of culture and of my general understanding of this concept, I will reflect on some common features of European cultures of importance for European spatial planning. Let me stress that these are reflections based on the perceptions and experiences of a Danish development researcher with a business economics background. That is, I will observe European cultures in the way they can be perceived with a cultural background such as mine, or in the way they can be perceived with my own cultural preparedness. It is my clear understanding that 'reality' will always be perceived and understood through one's own culture, i.e. through one's own cultural glasses. 'Reality' – or a substantial part thereof – is thus constructed on the basis of one's own cultural background and experience. I will primarily reflect on the impact these dominant cultural features exert on how we in Europe perceive, acknowledge and define relevant issues in society. I will also reflect on how these recognised culturally related issues are of importance for the knowledge and insight that we ordinarily demand and obtain, in contrast to the knowledge we fail to recognise and therefore do not demand or try to obtain through research and developmental initiatives, related to our way of urban and regional planning in the European countries.

A Proposal for the Understanding of Culture

The concept of culture is unclear and difficult to define within humanistic and social science research. Nevertheless, or perhaps for this very reason, it is a concept that many researchers from many different schools have worked with, and one in which many researchers are still deeply involved. If one is to attempt to explain why this is so, the reason must be that culture is something that is relevant to all of us. It is something that we all have, and something which we want to preserve and yet at the same time try to change, consciously or unconsciously. Culture provides security and gives us a feeling of belonging, as well as a feeling of distance from others. But, for better or worse, culture is also a strong guide for our way of being and our way of perceiving 'reality' as the base for our acting.

If we are to understand much of what is happening in the world today, we have to take into account the concept of culture. If we are to understand the situation in the Middle East, and what is happening and has happened in former Yugoslavia, in Palestine and Israel, or if we are to try to understand the debate about the Muhammad cartoons in the Danish daily paper *Jyllands-Posten*, and the whole debate in Europe about refugees and immigrants, then we have to deal with the concept of culture. And if we want to understand why we are doing as we do – or why we are doing something differently, such as the way in which we teach our children or plan our society in Europe – we have to understand our cultures and the differences between them. In recent years, the concept of culture has also become part of a tool for understanding organisational development and international cooperation in different types of organisations, such as multinational companies, the European Union, the United Nations etc. (see also contribution of Knieling and Othengrafen in this volume).

But what, then, does the concept of culture mean? Well, to me culture is the world conception and the values, moral norms and actual behaviour – as well as material and immaterial results thereof – which people (in a given context and over a given period of time) take over from a past generation, which they – possibly in a modified form – seek to pass on to the next generation; and which make them different in various ways from people belonging to other cultures.

Thus, culture is manufactured and acquired by definition, and therefore in a way it is a contrast to what is 'not manufactured' – to nature. However, the distinction between 'nature' and 'culture' is not as simple and clear as it may appear initially. Firstly, the mere distinction between culture and nature is itself culturally determined. Secondly, the boundary between what is and what is not manufactured is becoming increasingly blurred because of technological advances. For instance, if we are able to create new plant and animal species by means of gene splicing, then are these new plants or animals part of nature, or are they examples of material products of culture?

The boundary between what is nature and what is culture is thus in no way unequivocal, in the same way that it is not independent of culture. In spite of this, I will, however, maintain a distinction between what is manufactured and what is not at an abstract level – between culture and nature – in order to focus more on the concept of culture.

To me the concept of culture can be understood by means of three different dimensions on an abstract and meaningful level: the horizontal culture dimension; the vertical culture dimension; and a culture dimension of time. Below, I will briefly outline these three dimensions and the relationships between them with the strongest focus on the horizontal and the vertical dimension. In empirical studies that look at specific sectors of the society, such as the planning, education or production sectors, the focus will be on various elements of the three cultural dimensions, depending on the aim of the study and the sector in question.

The Horizontal Culture Dimension and its Different Segments of Cultural Dimensions

A distinctive feature of all living creatures is that their survival as individuals and species depends on the relationship between their biological needs (for food, protection against the climate, reproduction and socialisation into new generations, etc.) and the opportunities that surrounding nature offers them. Where more than one person is present in nature, humankind will always seek to fulfil their basic needs in social co-action through one form or another. Not necessarily by means of social cooperation, because an actual example of co-action may very well be characterised by suppression and exploitation, but in some way it takes the form of co-action. The actual ways of fulfilling the basic needs and of organising co-action can, and will, vary greatly in time and space, from one group of people to another, or from one culture to another, even within similar natural conditions.

At the same time, we can observe a multitude of different ways of co-existing and co-acting to fulfil fundamental needs in cultural contexts. We can note certain patterns, or certain common features in these ways, which make up the essential parts or central segments of culture in human co-action. In connection with my studies of different cultures I have found it purposeful to work with eight such segments of culture; in an etics culture analysis, in the words of Marvin Harris (1999, 224). These segments can be found in any chosen culture, but each of them (and their relation to one another) can manifest itself in quite different forms. The difference between them can only be analysed and understood by means of an actual, empirical culture analysis or by means of an emics culture analysis.

Together the eight segments of culture make up what I call the horizontal culture dimension. Horizontal because the eight segments of culture are manifested on the same level of the culture, so to speak. That is on the 'perceivable' level. Which kind of observations are most interesting and important for empirical studies and understanding depends on the actual purpose of each study; for example, the purpose of understanding European planning cultures. The eight segments, each of which describes different

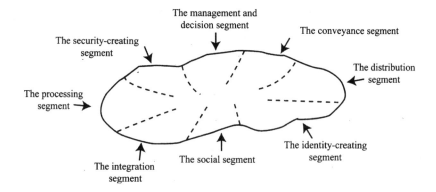

Figure 1.1   The horizontal culture dimension

Source: Gullestrup 2006, 75.

aspects of human co-action, can briefly be characterised in the following way and as in Figure 1.1:

1. the processing segment – or technology (for example, the use of statistical data, interviews or visual data, etc.);
2. the distribution segment – or economic institutions (for example, through (planning) legislation, advice of public teaching, etc.);
3. the social segment – or social institutions (for example, official state monopoly, community based or organisational planning institutions or individual planning);
4. the management and decision segment – or the political institutions. (for example, state or private decisions, community or cooperative decisions, etc.);
5. the conveyance segment – or language and communication (for example, professional languages, cases, pictures, etc.);
6. the integration segment – or reproduction, socialisation and learning (for example, part of school syllabus, TV announcing, legislating, etc.);
7. the identity-creating segment – or ideology (for example, the prestige of spatial planning and the planners, etc.); and
8. the security-creating segment – or religious institutions (for example, the legislation and/or political or religious support of spatial planning etc.).

The Vertical Culture Dimension and its Different Layers

In the encounter with a foreign culture certain perceptions will invariably be more noticeable than others. They thereby create a 'first-hand perception' of the observed culture. Actual behaviour, dress code and available products of different kinds will usually provide the foundation for this first-hand image. Soon after, the culture actor will also be able to perceive the underlying and difficult-to-perceive social structures, moral norms etc. A little later the social values will begin to materialise before the 'observer'. These materialisations will contribute to a more nuanced perception of the immediately perceived culture image.

Consequently, not all observations are equally important for culture understanding, in as far as some – the more immediately perceivable and 'observable' culture features – may only be an expression, or symptom, of a deep culture characteristic, such as attitudes and values. Therefore it is useful to speak of a hierarchy of observations – of the vertical culture dimension. My argument here is that a deeper insight into the immediately perceivable cultural layers can only be understood and grasped through the symbolising culture layers above. Thus understanding the manifest culture layers is significant on their own merit, but they might also carry a symbolising significance for penetrating the deeper symbolised culture layers. In other words, the core culture can only be understood via the symbolising culture layers.

I have thus found it useful to work with six different culture layers. The three upper layers belong to the perceivable or manifest culture layers with their own significance, as well as a symbolising significance for the understanding of the three lower layers. The latter belong to the hidden layers of the culture, but also the more fundamental core culture.

   a. Manifest culture layers – or the symbolising culture layers.
      i. The immediately perceivable process layer and its resultant outcome (for example, the dress formality of the planners, their language, etc.).
      ii. The difficult-to-perceive structural layer (for example, how the planning institutions are organised, other people's respect for planning and the planners, people's acceptance of plans, etc.).
      iii. The formalised layers of norms and rules (for example, the contents of planning, consideration for handicapped and 'people far away' etc. and the formal influences of the population, etc.).
   b. Core culture layers – or the symbolised culture layers.
      iv. The non-perceivable existence – or 'that which is without being there' (for example, the understanding of the 'strength' of different planning concepts and language, etc., the meaning 'of being there' at public meetings, etc.).

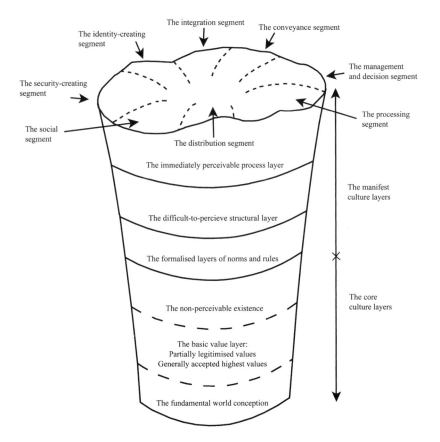

Figure 1.2 Culture as a complex entity consisting of culture segments and culture layers: the semi-static model

Source: Gullestrup, 2006, 101.

    v. The basic value layer (for example, respect for democracy, the various 'value- foundations' for decisions such as 'money-based economic reality perspective', 'growth philosophy' or consideration of nature and/or the future, etc.).
    vi. The fundamental world conception (for example, the priority of material income to religious consideration of various kinds, the superiority of the own society to others, etc.).

The horizontal and vertical dimensions of culture thus make up a kind of 'skeleton' for the individual cultures and by adding 'flesh and bone' to the skeleton through a culture analysis, a so-called 'emics analysis', the culture actor can receive a kind of instant picture, or a semi-static culture description of the observed culture (see Figure 1.2).

The Culture Dimension of Time

However, no culture is static, thus the term 'semi-static cultural description'. Just think about the influence of the automobile at the beginning of last century and how it changed the whole planning potential in Europe, and how, in turn, that changed the possibilities for developing train transportation as a consequence. And how can we expect climate change to alter our possibilities and limitations for future planning in Europe? On the contrary, any culture is exposed to a perpetual pressure to undergo changes, both from external and internal factors – what I refer to as change-initiating factors. These factors are called 'initiating' because by means of changes in many different ways, they 'push' changes in the observed culture. These pushes may not necessarily lead to changes, though. Whether there really will be a change in the observed culture and in which direction such a change will move is determined by quite different sets of change factors, namely the so-called change-determining factors.

Among the culture-external change-initiating factors we can find both conditions in nature, as well as situations in and from other cultures. Nature's constant change in itself means that human co-action, or human culture, which precisely makes a group of people's existence under certain natural conditions possible, is exposed to a perpetual pressure of change. Any culture therefore has a kind of two-way relationship with nature. On the one hand, the culture makes up the total complex of culture segments and culture layers which a group of people have developed over time with the purpose of fulfilling their own and their descendants' fundamental needs under the given social and natural conditions. On the other hand, this culture, in all respects, changes these exact social and natural conditions. The very same social and natural environment which makes up an essential part of the conditions of existence for the culture.

However, in most cases culture-external factors which come from other cultures, are of greatest significance. This can be noted from the fact that major elements of a given culture have usually been taken over from other cultures, whereupon they have been made part of the existing culture (see for example the contributions of Staniunas, Puşcaşu, Vettoretto and Serraos et al. in this volume). In such cases elements which have been assessed and adapted to the observed culture, consciously or unconsciously, but which nevertheless are foreign elements, have been taken from other cultures through external change-initiating factors. These changes happen particularly because of modern communication technology. The resulting changes for the individual cultures may be good or bad. In particular, the creation of the EU, as well as the still growing cooperation across the European borders have created a lot of change-initiating factors within the 'European planning industry' in current time.

The culture-internal change-initiating factors are factors that have arisen 'within' the observed culture in the shape of new creations, research, political changes in attitude and other types of creative action (see for example the contributions of Fischer, Puşcaşu, Vettoretto as well as Dangschat and Hamedinger in this volume).

Whether a given impact of change actually leads to changes in culture will, as mentioned, be determined by the change-determining factors, the relations between these and the initiating factors of change. In this connection I operate with four factors: 1) the degree of integration, which is an expression of the similarity and uniformity between the different values of a culture; and 2) degree of homogeneity, which is an expression of the breadth and width of the aggregated knowledge and insight into the observed culture; 3) the culture-internal power relations; and 4) the interplay between the change-initiating factors and the relevant values of the observed culture.

The degree of integration thus primarily has an effect on the strength with which the observed culture rejects or accepts a given impact of change. A highly integrated culture will react very strongly towards a change-initiating factor, either positively or negatively, depending on the interplay between the content of the integrated values and the value-related content of the change-initiating factors. Whereas a disintegrated culture will react more weakly and unpredictably. In a strongly disintegrated culture the culture-internal power relations will thus gain much influence on the actual course of change, in as far as the contents of the accepted values of the powerful persons will exert a decisive influence.

The degree of homogeneity will be of immense importance for the outcome of the reactions of the observed culture. Thus, a very homogeneous culture will solely 'relate to' culture changes that are as good as 'tailor made' to a very homogenous knowledge and insight into the culture. A more heterogeneous culture, however, by means of a broader understanding, will relate to far more diverse culture impacts. Thereby the contents and shape of the change-initiating factors receive far bigger importance in homogenous cultures than in more heterogeneous cultures. In such a way the differences of the various European (planning) cultures influence the different responses to common European planning (see the following contributions in this volume).

Culture as a Dynamic Totality and the Three Dimensions of Culture

By applying the three dimensions of culture to a dynamic understanding of culture of a given culture (see Figure 1.3) we get a semi-static picture of the cultural 'reality' of which the individuals are part and in which they, at the same time, contribute to making changes. This might be seen in the planning culture of each of the European countries. At the same time we are given a picture of the reality, which, for better or worse, partly determines the actions of the very same people. Thereby culture becomes a central element in the understanding of the way in which a given person or group of people perceive and interpret their surroundings, in as far as they perceive 'reality' through their own culture. As a result, they 'see' 'reality' through their own cultural glasses – or through their own cultural preparedness, which I prefer to call glasses, whereby the perceived reality in itself becomes culturally rooted – and thereby becomes a kind of social construction.

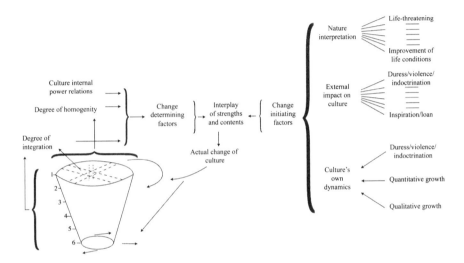

Figure 1.3   General dynamics culture model

Source: Gullestrup 2006, 153.

The single elements of the manifest culture in the different segments of culture thereby help to define society's 'undecided' issues, and thus the issues which researchers and politicians 'choose' to deal with, and to which practical solutions are sought. They are also the ones who have 'a voice in' which solutions are demanded and ultimately accepted. It is, however, on the basis of the deep core culture that the overall formulation and management of the perceived and conscious problems are made, in as far as the actually perceived problems in society are clearly rooted and justified in the fundamental world conception and values of the individual cultures.

In Europe in the early Middle Ages all topical problems in society took their point of departure from the then prevalent world conception. This was that the Earth was flat and the centre of the universe and every living creature was created by God in the form and shape it had at the time. Any scholarly or political issues had to be based on this world conception. It was not until a growing acceptance of the inability of the existing fundamental world conception to explain such issues had gained ground that a basis to present issues and embark on research and initiatives of development based on another world conception and culture values was created. A case in point is the groundbreaking research conducted by people such as Newton and Darwin. This in turn paved the way for new questions towards 'the new world conception' which led to more changes. But – and this is crucial to remember – this ongoing process of development, in which we continue to find ourselves, did not change the fact that the prevalent world conception at any given time, and the existent values at any given time, were, are and remain the guide for the issues that will be recognised and perceived and will be political and research issues in a given culture. The same holds true for the European cultures of today.

Therefore there is every reason to take interest in common features, if any, in the European cultures and areas of these cultures such of the European planning culture. And, not least, to assess whether in this plurality of cultures it is possible to ascertain any common characteristics and world conceptions which are of crucial importance for the content of the European social debate and the way in which problems in society are identified and sought to be solved.

In the following I will briefly mention how some common characteristics exert influence on three central phases in the debate in society. I want to illustrate this impact by a brief discussion of Denmark's attitude to some topical issues in society.

The three central phases in the social debate can be described this way:

1. The way in which we acknowledge social and planning issues in Europe: that is, the way in which we acknowledge and formulate the issues which will become the conscious product of our observations and experiences a) in the individual European cultures, b) in the relationships between the single European cultures and other culture inside and outside Europe, and c) in the relationship between the single European cultures and the surrounding nature.
2. The determination of the contents of the knowledge and insight we demand, and which we consciously seek to achieve through research and developmental work: this content is partly influenced directly by cultural characteristics and common features, partly influenced more indirectly as a result of the acknowledged and formulated issues.
3. The unconsciousness of the contents of the knowledge and insight that are not demanded, and which we accordingly do not seek to achieve through research or developmental work: that is, the knowledge we do not seek because we fail to acknowledge the issue, but which we could have acknowledged through conscious research and developmental work, which in turn could have contributed to developing alternative

solutions to the perceived problems in Europe and the countries outside Europe.

It is essential to keep in mind that the model of cultural understanding that I have presented above is abstract and theoretical in the way that it operates with a (clearly) delineated culture, which more or less unequivocally can be set apart from other cultures. In practice, in the real world, such a distinction is, however, very unclear, as the individual cultures will merge with each other and move in different directions. It is therefore meaningful to introduce a dimension of category where the individual forms part of different categories of culture in different contexts and at different times. Examples of such categories include national cultures (for example, Danish, Swedish, German, Indian, etc.) and cultures of education (for example, craftsmen, academics, health workers, unskilled workers, etc.) The individual will thus not only be influenced by his or her national culture, but also by other culture categories such as professional cultures like the planning cultures that he or she is part of – either technical or more economical – with, however, varying degrees of consciousness and force, depending on the situation and point of time.

The other dimension is the 'dimension of hierarchy', on the basis of which individuals will perceive themselves – and others will perceive the individual – as part of the different levels within the different categories of culture they are part of. Within the national category of culture a person may in some situations perceive him- or herself – and be perceived by others – as part of the Danish culture. In other situations, it may be that they are seen as being part of a wider culture within the national category of culture, for example, as part of Scandinavian culture or Northern European culture in contrast to Southern European culture, or perhaps merely as part of European culture. In contrast to this, the individual can also be seen as part of a culture on a lower level of the hierarchy than Danish culture. They may, for instance, be seen as part of the culture around Copenhagen, of the peninsula of Jutland, or as part of the culture of the area of 'Vensyssel' in the Northern part of Jutland. The culture category and level of the hierarchy of the category in question that will be essential for the intercultural understanding altogether depend on the context and point in time that the intercultural understanding is sought. In this chapter it would be the national category and the European level of the hierarchy which would be relevant.

I will build on this understanding to present, in brief, some common European features which I find to have tremendous influence on the three mentioned phases above, as well as on planning cultures in general, and which must be presumed to carry similar significance in the other European countries, as well as in the different 'branches' (specific sector of the society) represented in Europe.

Characteristics of European Cultural Values and European World Conceptions

The European way of life and the ways in which the single European countries have planned and structured their societies offer a diversity which immediately renders it difficult to point out common features in the European core cultures. Yet there seems to be a number of areas in which the European cultures, partly alongside their 'derived cultures' in Australia, New Zealand, USA and Canada, mutually deviate from a number of other cultures. Even though there is a diversity of cultures in Europe, this diversity also presents a number of characteristics, which makes it meaningful to speak of cultural common features in Europe. High up in the hierarchy, we can thus speak of a 'European culture'; further down in the hierarchy we can speak of a 'Southern European culture', an 'Eastern European culture' and a 'Northern European culture'.

Naturally, it is difficult to determine what these common features are, not only because of the mentioned diversity of cultures but also because of the contents of such common features – or rather the contents of the observed and recognised cultural common features. As has already been mentioned, such observations rely strongly on the eyes of the observer and on the perspective through which the culture actor observes them. It goes without saying that this does not mean that the European cultures in fact change in reality depending on the eyes that observe them, but it means that the culture actor's own culture, i.e. his or her own cultural preparedness, will be of decisive importance for which European culture elements he or she is aware of, and in which direction he or she relates the acknowledged common features of the social debate.

Some culture actors will thus focus on the Christian faith and put this down as a common feature of the European cultures, with a Protestant variety in the north and northwest and a Roman-Catholic variety in the south and southwest, as well as an Orthodox variety in the east and southeast of Europe. Other observers will focus on the relationship between the citizens and the state, and thus underline the democratic element of culture, such as in the planning cultures where the decisions might be made by the political elected politicians in the government, by the local elected politicians or individually by private companies or individuals.

In the following I have chosen to present a perspective relevant to the planning culture, which is technical, economical, rational and business-oriented, and to use this perspective for my reflections on common European features. The main focus therefore is on the initial question of which European cultural common features can one reasonably observe on the basis of the above-mentioned cultural preparedness.

A Money-based Economic Reality Perspective

The results that can be expected from an actual decision or action in a money-based economic society are given a utility value. Its size depends on the individual's assessment of what the observed result or utility can be used for (a coat, for instance, can be used both as protection against the climate and to signal a social belonging). They also depend on the different ways the utility can be used (for example, does the individual already have other coats, or do they only have this one? Is there any doubt about their status, or is it certain, with or without the coat?).

Beside the utility value, it also has a barter value which expresses the value which can be achieved in exchange of the observed utility (is it, for example, possible to get 10 shirts in exchange for the coat, or is it only worth five?). This barter value – usually expressed in the value of money – has gained a crucial importance in assessing single decisions and actions in European culture. Expectations of huge barter values measured in money-economic revenue or in money-economic savings will usually be more important in the planning processes than the expectations of a less rewarding money-economic result if another action is chosen, although the latter action will involve fewer resources in terms of raw materials and time, less pollution and perhaps even less human malaise. That is, Europeans prefer an action that, based on a greater money-economic rationality, leads to the same expected utility value rather than an action with less money-economic rationality, and thereby less barter value, but which would result in a greater real economic rationality achieved through less raw material and time consumption, as well as less pollution. That is, rationality measured in terms of consumption of materials and time, pollution and possible human happiness.

The implication of the money-economic mindset combined with the applied principles of calculation seen in the light of the massive investments in production facilities and public works have thus meant that many alternative decisions with far-reaching real economic consequences for the utility value are basically determined on the basis of their short-term money-economic barter value!

Mini Socially Oriented Stakeholder Considerations Bordering on Individual Considerations

The culture's generally accepted fundamental values exert tremendous influence on which social entities the individual feels most attached to and therefore is most loyal towards. At one extreme, the social entity valued most highly by the individual can consist of just one single person. Often this person is the individual him- or herself, but it can also be another person, such as a charismatic leader. At the other extreme, a person may feel attached to, and be fundamentally loyal towards, the collective entity of humanity or towards each single human being on earth. In such case, the individual will be attached to a larger social entity, such as a nation, a universal political or religious ideology or something similar. Between these two extremes there are other cultures where the individual is mostly oriented towards medium-sized social entities, such as the family, the tribe, a village or local community.

The mini social oriented consideration bordering on an individual stakeholder consideration is, however, in certain situations met with a sort of contrast, because in other contexts strong national feelings approaching nationalism can be observed. This nationalism does not necessarily follow formal state borders; rather, it often transgresses these, and in different contexts it may have a significant influence on everyday life, which – for one – can be seen in the former Yugoslavia. It is, however, my opinion that nationalism ousts the mini social oriented group loyalty outlined in the above only in special and extreme situations.

That this is the case can clearly be seen from the way in which Europeans perceive, both consciously and unconsciously, some types of economic crime against the totality: society or international cooperating organisations such as the EU or other similar organisations. Tax avoidance bordering on tax fraud, fraud in connection with subsidies and similar creative economic transactions receive far more lenient punishment than similar, or far less serious economic crimes, towards individuals, such as shoplifting or plain burglary.

This mini social orientation bordering on an individual orientation together with the other common European features is a strong contributing factor in the failure to recognise many issues relevant for large social entities or the whole of humanity. Even when such recognition is found – for instance in connection with aid to support 'less-developed' country exports – it is after all often downplayed in such a way that it only governs the political agenda to a lesser degree. This is visible, for instance, when Europe wants to protect its own companies against imports of goods from the same third world countries to which they have just donated production and export aid through development assistance.

The Unknown, Anonymous Human Being as an Instrumental Object

In connection with many decisions and acts in European culture man – or rather the unknown, anonymous human being – is seen as an object or instrument that does not in itself have an independent intrinsic value as a living individual. The unknown, anonymous human being is merely perceived as an object whose *raison d'être* is solely based on its importance as an instrument in relation to something else, for instance, in relation to one or more of the common features mentioned above. This 'objectification' is most clearly seen in national wars and civil wars, in which the anonymous individual is largely perceived as a necessary instrument for the battling parties whose fate the decision makers rarely accord much significance. On the other hand, the consideration of the individual, unknown, anonymous human being is given some importance in cases where his or her fate can be seen as having a certain utility value in relation to one or more of the dominating values in the actual situation. An example can be that the propaganda machine can present the fate of an otherwise anonymous individual as a suffering victim of acts of terrorism by the counter party. But even in such a case, the unknown, anonymous person is actually merely perceived as an object.

This trend of objectification is not only seen in extreme situations, however; it is also seen in everyday life where the consideration for the single individual very often takes second place to other values than his or her own as a living human being. Examples of this are situations in which money-economic profitability is accorded so much importance that even almost 'certain' statistical knowledge that certain incidents of death at workplaces and in traffic will occur by such and such a number within a certain period of time will not lead to decisions that are likely to save the lives of many anonymous people. But the most obvious example of people's instrumental status is their role in the production process and as consumer, where they are equated with an instrument or regarded just as a user.

The situation is changed if the unknown, anonymous individual is made 'personal' by being given a name and a face. When this happens, for example, by means of media publicity, political accounts, etc., most considerations are put aside to 'save' this, by now, personalised individual.

This tendency of objectifying anonymous people in European culture, linked with the individually-oriented attitudes, has the effect that the majority of humanity, including 'other Europeans', in the mindset of the Europeans is largely perceived as individuals – or objects – without any intrinsic value. They are perceived as 'things' which by and large can be equated to instruments in the ordinary production process or as consumer entities of the finished products of this production process.

Nature as an Objectified Object

In the same way that anonymous people are 'instrumentalised', nature is also perceived as an object or merely as a 'thing' by most Europeans. Nature is both seen as an (almost) inexhaustible resource of all kinds of raw materials and as an (almost) endless garbage site for all kinds of waste. Thus, in itself nature amounts to nothing, and even the living parts of nature – the animals and plants – are not accorded any value or *raison d'être* in their own right. Living nature is merely perceived as an object and thing whose only *raison d'être* is to be useful for humanity and, in the European culture, especially useful for Europeans.

In recent decades more and more Europeans have become increasingly environmentally conscious. This is positive, seen in the light of many considerations. But this change is hardly a basic change in the perception of nature itself, for instance towards attributing a value to living nature or a *raison d'être* in itself. Rather, it is a realisation that more and more people acknowledge that if we do not 'treat nature decently' humanity itself will ultimately pay the price.

The considerable attention which was directed towards the great whales some years back is thus difficult to see as an example of a radical change in the perception of nature as anything more than an object, in as far as this attention is not directed towards other and smaller species that are equally in danger of becoming extinct, such as the wolf and warthog. Perhaps the reason is that these animals have not become 'humanised' to the same degree as the whales. We speak of the songs of whales and the play of dolphins, but not of the songs or play of wolves; they merely howl and roam about.

Therefore, the heightened consciousness of nature hardly changes the situation that today living nature is only perceived as an object or 'thing' by Europeans, which humanity can exploit as they please and as best serves the individual human being's consideration. Only future generations will show whether heightened environmental consciousness will change this situation in a long-term perspective.

Partial Perception of Reality and Orientation towards Action

The last common feature of European culture I find relevant to stress in this chapter is the tendency to let many activities be guided by a limited – or partial – perception of the surrounding world. Thus many activities have been pursued based solely on the wish to optimise an actual activity without being aware of possible negative side effects in other areas. For example, the gain of many redeployments and restructurings within the public and private sectors based on the money-economic considerations may turn out to be less than the costs that are added to other 'sectors', such as the public sector within the social and health sector and the individual economic and human costs of those laid off. Overall, many situations can be registered where a skilful rationalisation has been made of partial elements of the totality, but at the same time the totality has become far less efficient than it was before the rationalisation. Just think of the many automatic answering machines and their offers to 'press for extensions to receive service'. These are no doubt extremely cost-effective for the organisation in question but at the same time highly time-consuming for those who make the calls, and therefore they add to the costs for the individuals.

Partial optimisation is a culture feature which has produced many excellent results within European technology and science. But the research, development and administration are, and have been, concentrated on optimisation of single elements of the whole of society. Unfortunately, this development has also produced many side effects in the shape of manufactured environmental destructions and human collapse in the form of stress and marginalisation of minority groups who have been made superfluous.

Summary

Summing up these characteristics, it can be stated that even though the individual European countries naturally have many different themes in their political debates, there are a number of recurrent themes in most of these countries. It goes without saying that the relevant weight of these will vary, and in one European country one theme may dominate the debate whereas it will hardly be debated in other countries. On the basis of my general outline of the European political debate and my own technical economic rationality perspective, however, I will venture to state that the following political themes carry a certain weight in all the European countries:

- technological development and the effects of technology;
- the growing inequality among different groups of populations;
- the problems of refugees and immigration;
- the European Union – EU;
- relations with third world countries;
- relations between employees and the public and private sector;
- the way the planning activities are organised and implemented;

Because of lack of space, however, these subjects will have to be investigated more carefully at another time.

Concluding Remarks

On the basis of a theoretical model of culture understanding, in this chapter I have reflected on some common European features and their significance for social debate and the planning situation in Europe. In doing so I do not mean to postulate that all of the common features mentioned are uniquely European and are not found anywhere else in the world. What I rather have attempted to demonstrate is that, by taking a point of departure in a more precisely defined culture perception, and on the basis of a closely defined perspective, one can focus on certain common characteristics of European culture. These common features, that through their contents possess strong guiding characteristics on how we in Europe are made aware of and acknowledge the social issues which are 'selected' for the political agendas and which are 'selected' as subjects for research, development initiatives and planning activities of different kinds, enable us to gain more insight into the nature of the issue. Furthermore, I wanted to demonstrate that culture embeddings also impose some limitations on the possible solutions to which insight is sought. Therefore the result is that, in many instances, alternative solutions do not even enter the political agenda and therefore do not become part of knowledge-demanding activities of research and development work, either.

The strengths of the presented analytical model are – as far as I can see – that it creates a way of thinking according to which the cultural actor can see him- or herself as a member of an intercultural world in which there are no clear, objective pictures of the various cultures. And it might therefore create a kind of humility and acceptance that 'reality', as we think we can see it, is not only a function of 'the others' but just as much a function of our own cultural foundation. It might therefore create a kind of better understanding for people belonging to other cultures and thus possibilities for better cooperation between people belonging to different cultures. The weaknesses are that there will be no exact pictures of how an individual's own culture has to be evaluated, in the same way that there will be no exact and objective evaluation of other cultures. Other weaknesses are that, according to this model, we will get no exact pictures of other cultures such as some researchers think themselves able to make. We have to create our own understanding of our own and other cultures by relating our knowledge from others; through observations; our data and our experiences in relations to the cultural model's three dimensions as well as to the relevant segments, layers and factors needed in the actual contents and for the actual purpose (see also contribution of Knieling and Othengrafen in this volume).

It is most important to be aware of cultural differences. The aim of planning, for example, a public transport system within a city raises various questions: How do we plan for better transportation or a better city? How can we define and measure what is 'better'? Is that in the short or in the long run? For whom is that to be measured? Based on which criteria? In this context the analytical model presented here might assist planners trying to describe the differences and to understand the reasons why there are different (cultural related) approaches. It would be dangerous to 'look away from the differences', just going on with planning based on one's own understanding of planning as well as on one's own power to carry through the way of understanding planning, and the way of making qualitative planning. In this way we might create better intercultural understanding and better possibilities for future intercultural cooperation.

Acknowledgement

This chapter draws on an earlier and more detailed discussion presented in Gullestrup 2003 and 2006.

Bibliography

Gullestrup, H. (2003) *Kulturanalyse – en vej til tværkulturel forståelse*, Akademisk Forlag, København.

Gullestrup, H. (2006) *Cultural Analysis, Towards Cross-Cultural Understanding*, Aalborg University Press, Aalborg.

Harris, M. (1999) *Theories of Culture in Postmodern Times*, Sage Publication, London.

Chapter 2
Planning Cultures en Route to a Better Comprehension of 'Planning Processes'?

Dietrich Fürst

Introduction

Planning culture is not a scientific term; it is rather ill defined, addresses a diffuse research area and is not bound to a specific body of theories. More often than not, planning culture is used as a mere integrating term covering an ensemble of variables which can be observed in practical planning. In publications, in the Anglo-Saxon ones in particular, 'planning culture' is applied synonymously with the term 'planning styles', often very widely defined as 'a general model of professional practice behaviour' (Hemmens 1988, 85). Therefore no difference will be made between 'planning style' and 'planning culture' in the following.

It is not quite clear when the term 'planning culture' first emerged. According to John Friedmann it was Klaus Selle et al. (Keller et al. 1993) who introduced the term by hermeneutically approaching the changes of planning in four different European countries[1] (Friedmann 2005b, 30). However, the term can also be found in earlier works. According to Andreas Faludi (2005, 286) this is the case already with Bolan (1973, cited in Faludi 2005). However it may be, the term still remains on the level of a mere research perspective today. Even the term 'culture' is used very differently — in 1993 there were already more than 160 different definitions to be found in literature (Faure 1993, cited in Jann 2000, 328).

Nonetheless, a pre-scientific consensus exists among experts that differences in cultural formation have a strong impact on interactions. It is well known from practical experience, in particular from INTERREG cooperations, that cultural differences may hamper processes of interaction. This is due to conflicting mutual expectations, to different cultures of participation, to different ways of addressing and resolving conflicts or that 'cultures of distrust' raise the transaction-costs of cooperation considerably. But on the other hand it is not very easy to separate cultural influences from other influences (e.g., institutional differences, language problems) — which is all the more difficult since institutional and language barriers can also be culturally determined (see

---

[1] France, Germany, Italy and Switzerland.

also contribution of Knieling and Othengrafen in this volume). In addition, planning cultures are 'learning systems' – the longer actors collaborate in planning activities the more they develop to share.

The scientific debate on 'planning culture' is therefore a risky activity. In the following, planning culture will be put into relation to similar discourses in other disciplines, followed by a short overview of international comparative studies on planning systems and their relations to planning culture. This overview indicates that an international comparison of planning cultures will meet particular difficulties, although publications establish that we experience a convergence of planning systems with well-put arguments, due to a convergence of framing conditions but modified by strong path-dependencies. On the other hand, the discussion of planning cultures shows close links to the 'governance discussion'. In the concluding section we will address the question of how to deal with cultural differences in practice.

Planning Culture in the Context of Culturally Determined Patterns of Collective Actions

Planning culture may be seen within the context of the 'cultural turn' observed in many disciplines concerned with human behaviour (see also the preface of this volume). The basic idea is that behaviour is not just rational but culturally determined, which holds true in particular for modes of interaction. The knowledge that social processes are embedded in regional traditions, norms, values, attitudes and mind sets is rampant in the social sciences and triggered different research perspectives. In the political sciences we talk of 'political culture' (Berg-Schlosser 2005) or culturally imbued 'policy styles' (Richardson et al. 1982), in public administration there is much talk of 'administrative cultures' (Jann 2000), in the organisational sciences a similar discussion refers to 'corporate culture' (Sackmann 2006) and in the managerial sciences we find the term 'planning styles' which indicates different planning procedures resulting from different traditions, routines, specific constellations of actors within an organisation. Even in the theory of science there is the notion of culturally tainted 'styles' (Galtung 1983, see also contribution of Fischer in this volume). All these different approaches have in common that processes should not be discussed and interpreted detached from their respective contexts and that we have to take into account the *longue durée* of cultural determinations.

The concept of 'planning culture' is closest to the approaches adopted in the political sciences, public administration and organisation sciences which refer to attitudes, mind sets and values shared and reinforced by participants of the same collective actor but also conserved by the supporting institutions (see also contribution of Knieling and Othengrafen in this volume). For instance, the term 'political culture' refers to 'different perceptions, mentalities, typical mind sets and behaviour patterns ascribed to groups or whole societies. It comprises all politically relevant individual traits, the attitudes and values latently imbued in predispositions for political actions and also in their symbolic appearances and the concrete political behaviour' (Berg-Schlosser 2005, 743). Jann (2000, 329) declares more concisely: 'Political culture refers to patterns and orientations, a mind set towards social and political facts ... In a more simplified version: Political culture is what can be registered by opinion polls.'

Culturally-bound communalities between actors may facilitate processes of interaction, while differences tend to aggravate them. Common cultural features support trust building, reduce risks and complexities of interactions and facilitate consensus building.

A study of some of the major contributions to planning culture shows that the research questions and the definition of what the authors consider 'planning culture' to be differ greatly, as explained below.

For the Area of Urban Planning

Keller et al. (2006, 279f.) are interested in how planning culture relates to values, role models and interpretation of tasks which planners hold vis-à-vis planning procedures and instruments. Walter (1995) is interested in how planning culture may be influenced by planning contents induced by changes of the roles planners play within a society. Others connect planning culture with participation and how affected interests are dealt with in the planning processes (Sandner 1998; Wentz 1992). The German Federal Agency for Construction and Regional Research (BBR) considers 'planning culture' as the production of the built-up environment and everyday dealing with it (BBR 2002). The German Association of Urban, Regional and Governmental Planners (SRL) defines planning culture as a normative concept: the behavioural norms to which planners of the SRL should subscribe.[2]

In the United States the term is less used (Friedmann 2005a) and if employed it usually refers to the whole practice of planning (Cullingworth 1993, 7f.). The term 'planning styles' is in use more frequently instead, in particular after the study of Carl Abbott ('The Oregon Planning Style') became widely known and local/regional initiatives came up to foster 'smart growth' (Hovey 2003, who draws attention to the structural power of language).

On the Level of Regional Planning/Spatial Planning

When talking of 'planning cultures' Faludi (2005, 285) points to ethical and paradigmatic predispositions of planning vis-à-vis interventions of the state and the integration of private actors. According to him planning culture is 'the collective ethos and dominant attitude of planners regarding the appropriate

---

2 Information on www.srl.de/srl/selbst/index.php.

role of the state, market forces, and civil society influencing social outcomes'. Friedmann (2005a, 183) considers 'planning culture' 'as the ways both formal and informal, that spatial planning is conceived, institutionalized, and enacted' and in another contexts he says 'local, regional and national differences in planning institutions and practices – I shall call them cultures' (Friedmann 2005b, 30). Others, like Kühn and Moss (2001) discuss planning culture primarily under aspects of governance and planning systems.

All the authors argue in common that planning culture refers to mental predispositions which the majority of those involved share. That means planning culture has much to do with mutual expectations which guide the actors' behaviour in planning processes, or put differently: planning culture refers to values, attitudes, mind sets and routines shared by those taking part in planning; it influences the perceived planning tasks, the behaviour in groups or communities and the pursuit of particular interests therein.

The problem is how to operationalise that concept. Following Gullestrup (2006) the research group CULTPLAN (see also contribution of During et al. in this volume; see also CULTPLAN 2007) used a very complex approach which distinguishes different societal functions of actors' behaviour (horizontal differentiation) on one hand, and considers culture as an overlay of different societal institutions affecting attitudes and values on the other (vertical differentiation). Gullestrup's system is multidimensionally juxtaposing societal and individual characteristics on the horizontal level and mixing behaviour-forming elements with other cultural traits in the vertical dimension. Although intellectually highly appealing, it may be difficult to translate the concept into practical empirical research.

The interdependencies between actors forcing them to coordinate their activities are mainly determined by five groups of variables (Scharpf 2000):

a. Variables of interaction:
   1. individual action orientation comprising attitudes, beliefs, values, interests and capabilities (competences);
   2. the interaction orientation of actors essentially based on norms and attitudes (competitive vs cooperative, person-oriented vs task-oriented,[3] consensus-oriented vs outcome-oriented[4]);
   3. the constellation of actors indicating the power-relations between actors and the room for manoeuvre of persons acting within organisations;

---

3 Thus the French culture of interaction is supposed to be more person-oriented while the German is more task-oriented, which leads to disturbances of intercultural interchanges.

4 The Dutch culture of interaction is supposed to be more consensus-oriented than the German, which is seen as more outcome-oriented.

b. Variables of external influences:
   4. the institutional framework referring to legal, organisational, administrative and language rules and routines. Language barriers, differences in the legal framework (e.g., Common Law in Great Britain vs Roman Law on the continent, e.g., Booth 2005), different levels of impact of legal regulations on societal interactions (e.g., legalistic culture in Germany), differences in the administrative structures (e.g., degree of decentralisation) and in administrative behaviour (top-down interventionist vs horizontal negotiations) could impede cross-cultural interactions. Institutions could mitigate the impact by engendering faith in interactions and in the rules of living together;
   5. the situation which is mainly determined by the problem-field and the factors shaping it which also comprise a general change of sentiments and paradigms.

For planning cultures, however, only the variables which are consistent long-term and are situation-independent are of relevance, which gives importance to groups (1) to (4). But even those may change (Keller et al. 2006). Hence, based on a long-term international discourse on 'changes in planning cultures' Keller et al. (2006) not only observe changes of behaviour patterns (towards 'communicative planning' and towards more intensive use of informal instruments) but also changes in the institutional approach: more destandardisation, more project based planning within the framework of the 'renaissance of the grand plans', reorientation towards 'planning without growth', enforcing private place-making within the trend towards deregulation and rescaling the state (Brenner 2004).

'Planning Culture' – the Neglected Dimension in International Comparative Studies on Planning Systems

It is remarkable that the rampant international approaches to identify differences between the planning systems within the EU context (Böhme 2002; CEC 1997; Healey et al. 1997; Hildenbrand 1996; Marcou 2004; Nadin et al. 2001; Newman and Thornley 1996; Roberts et al. 2000; Salet and Faludi 2000; Williams 1996) hardly addressed the issue of 'planning culture'. That may partly be excused by the fact that the studies were conducted for special purposes which vindicated their neglect of the cultural dimension: e.g., one of the reasons for doing the studies was the discussion on the European Spatial Development Perspectives at EU level (ESDP), making member states susceptible to the necessity that cross-border coordination of plans and the EU spatial programming would require a certain unification of planning systems. Secondly, on the regional level in most of the member states spatial planning had expanded towards strategic development planning thus being integrated into the regional endeavours to improve the region's competitive edge. Thirdly, in many member states we observe new patterns of governance supported or even induced by spatial planning. Fourthly, on the international level a renaissance of the discussion on spatial planning is restarting – primarily related to metropolitan areas in global competition but intensified by challenges for 'sustainable regional development'.

In addition, comparative studies were closely related to the institutional side (organisation, plans, formal procedures) – while the planning processes (problem solving, patterns of planning behaviour, weighing competing demands, etc.) hardly received much attention. But implicitly those studies drew attention to differences in planning cultures. For, where stark differences could be detected, equifunctional mechanisms or structures were frequently at work to cushion the practical impact of the differences. Such equifunctional mechanisms affect

- the relationship between planning functions of land-use regulation on one hand and regional developing strategies on the other: frequently, the regulatory functions only come to the fore in conjunction with projects, e.g., via a series of negotiating and supervising procedures;
- the relationship between national and subnational planning: due to a vertical division of labour the scope of planning may range very widely on different levels but in sum it may not differ much between member states;
- the coordinating mechanism: while some states prefer negotiations, others may rely more strongly on governmental regulations or persuasive strategies;
- the relationship between public and private planning: While the European planning tradition is primarily shaped by public planners we find a very lively, privately initiated concept of spatial planning in the USA (Schönig 2007; Yaro 2007).

However, institutional structures tell little about how they fare in praxis. This depends on how the actors make use of them or how beneficial they consider informal negotiating procedures or disregard institutional procedures or even use illegal actions. The way how actors' behaviour is shaped by institutions is determined by socio-cultural factors to a certain degree. Hence, there is no getting away from the fact that comparative institutional studies should also make reference to 'planning cultures'.

International and Inter-regional Comparisons of Planning Cultures

A methodologically demanding international comparative study on planning cultures is still missing, despite the efforts made by the research group CULTPLAN (CULTPLAN 2007). Although there are many studies dealing with interactions and communications within planning processes on the national or sub-national level, it is very difficult to interpret them on an international comparative scale. Some of the reasons are that:

- they were carried out at different times, i.e. the institutional and other context conditions vary greatly;
- the context conditions to be taken into account are too heterogenous;
- they were established according to criteria corresponding to the respective research question which, however, do not match the requirements of international comparative studies: the variables chosen, the weighing of the variables, the methods used and the interpretation attached to the results do not fit together;
- the notions of 'planning culture' adopted in those studies strongly differ;
- by choosing adequate case studies, some of the problems could certainly be solved ('the prudent comparativist does not choose his countries (i.e.: case study) by choice: he is guided by pertinent criteria' (Dogan and Pelassy 1981, 38, cited in Nohlen 2005a, 510). But even then the result will remain sub-optimal in comparison to a genuine comparative study if the research questions attached to the different case studies differ too much. Rather, comparing case studies is very demanding (Lauria and Wagner 2006) and the more so when different countries are involved. For the field of international comparative studies is 'densely populated by non-comparativists, by scholars, who have no interest, no notion, no training in comparing' (Sartori 1991, 243);[5]
- The predominant methods adopted for international comparative studies referring to cultural aspects are:
  - expert discourses (Keller et al. 2006, 1996; Sanyal 2005);[6]

---

5 Some of the main problems of international comparative studies on the basis of qualitative indicators (like attitudes, values, paradigms) are linked to the need that proxies must be used instead of directly measurable indicators and that identical questions may be perceived differently in different cultural contexts and hence be answered differently (van Deth 2003)

6 Donald Keller, Michael Koch and Klaus Selle (1996) report on expert discourses on changes of spatial planning in Germany, France, Italy and Switzerland; Bishwapriya Sanyal (2005) published the results of an international series of lectures at MIT in the summer of 2002 on planning cultures of urban planning in advanced developing countries and industrialised countries.

- participating observations and expert experiences (Friedmann 2005a, 2005b);
- and in particular case studies (CULTPLAN).

Hitherto not used were comparisons on the basis of 'cultural indicators' (e.g., content analysis of different resources) or 'semiological interpretations' (evaluation of rituals, symbols and narratives) (Berg-Schlosser 2005, 746). However, they may be very important for understanding actions within political-administrative systems not least because 'images' and 'cultural semantics' became the 'key words of our time' (Jay 1998). A good example of a creative use of content analysis and semiological interpretations is the international comparative study of governance patterns of different political-administrative systems guided by Rod A.W. Rhodes (Bevir and Rhodes 2003).

Do Planning Systems Converge in the EU Context?

Are we observing a withering away of socio-cultural differences in planning behaviour subsequent to EU integration (Eatwell 1997; see also contributions of Davoudi and Waterhout et al. in this volume)? In the publications, we are frequently confronted with the opinion that institutional structures of planning systems would converge due to EU interventions. That seems to fit in oddly with the observable differences in the planning cultures of the member states.

The conjectures on convergence are mainly based on four influences:

1. First, a Europe-wide discussion on rescaling the state in the wake of globalisation, neoliberal paradigms and an intensified competition between locations with subsequent strengthening of the regional level exists and can be observed in all member states (Keller et al. 1996; NSL 2002; Friedmann 2005a). That refers to processes of regionalisation (critical: MacLeod 2001), to new modes of regional governance (Newman 2000; Martin 1999; Keating 2000), to mobilising support of the so-called 'third sector' (Priller and Zimmer 2006; Backhaus-Maul 2006) or to the general turn to 'strategic planning' (Healey et al. 1997). Regional planners must take the concept of 'sustainable development' seriously and think and act on four levels: spatial, economical, ecological and socio-cultural.
2. A second push towards convergence comes from the EU. With the management approaches in structure funds and planning approaches in environment and nature protection (water framework directive, habitats directive, SEA directive) the EU pushes the member states to give more weight to planning endeavours in order to prevent risks and to mobilise

collective self-help patterns (Howe and White 2002; Tewdwr-Jones and Williams 2001; Sturm and Pehle 2005). Empirical evidence from Mediterranean member states seems to indicate a 'process of cultural innovation in southern European planning traditions' (Giannakourou 2005, 321).
3. A third impulse results from planning itself. Due to the restructuring of national governments (decentralisation, deregulation, privatisation) planners and the planning systems come under pressure to prove their societal relevance in order not to be derided as impedimental planners. On a European scale, beliefs seem to gain currency that spatial planning will become more relevant for society by managing the increasing interdependencies of regional actors. That is in line with a new understanding of the role of governments emphasising societal self-help and down-scaling the paternalistic welfare state. In many countries new planning institutions have come into existence 'in the form of development corporations, rather than planning agencies, because what inspired the moment was entrepreneurship and development, not regulations and planning' (Sanyal 2005, 9).
4. In addition, the internationalisation of planning education and the international exchange within the planning sciences play a strong role.[7] Thus, mind sets and value systems tend to be harmonised but also the methodological approaches of spatial planning converge with immediate impact on the planning praxis via the education system.

These four influences are strengthened by facilitating policies reacting to the increasing societal need for coordination and leadership. Although spatial planning faces a growing number of competing institutions in sector policies (regional structure policies, integrated rural development strategies) planning still has very strong potentials to be competitive via its spatial organising capacity.

Nonetheless, conjectures on planning systems to converge seem to be based on thin grounds, for in practice the process to adopt changes is rather slow and restrained by high transaction costs: systems tend to change primarily if the pressure to change is very strong or if ignoring the need to change will be met by severe sanctions. 'In general, transaction costs are the higher, the stronger formalized and institutionalized the processes are. Administrative procedures therefore are much more change-resistant than planning processes: EU directives are subsumed under existing routines and regulations rather than that they were able to transform them' (Sommermann 2002, 143).

More often than not, planning systems could only be changed if the institutional frame-work was altered at the same time (Sommermann 2002 for

---

7 The Association of European Schools of Planning, which recognised the need for international cooperation and interchange very early, has an important role.

a similar area: administrative procedures in comparison to administrative law). In addition, changes of the planning system must be supported by planners. But that is hardly to be expected if the changes will lead to the planners' loss of steering power. Therefore Sanyal (2005, 15) maintains that 'these planning cultures seem to have evolved with social, political, and economic influences, both internal and external, creating hybrid cultures whose complexity can only be understood through deep historical analysis'.

The Contribution of the Discussion on Planning Culture to the Governance Discourse

Governance arrangements are a mixture of different coordinating mechanisms: normative interventions (with reference to standards and norms of action like solidarity, altruism, traditions or paradigmatic mind-sets), bargaining (via the market or incentive systems) and coercive modes of steering (e.g., via majority rules, hierarchical intervention, 'conditional programmes'[8]). Different modes of regional governance reflect different 'governance cultures' or 'governance styles'.

The discussion on regional governance refers to similar phenomena as in planning culture: New constellations of actors and their influences must be addressed, new issues and solutions have to be dealt with, the modes of interaction change in favour of negotiations and contracts, the different modes of interaction (governance) must be integrated into the existing institutional framework, etc. Hence, planning culture could be linked to the discourse on regional governance (Healey 2006; Albrechts et al. 2003). In fact, the new modes of regional governance work very similarly to planning cultures:

- they primarily address mental structures (values, mind sets, attitudes) and action orientation and interaction orientation in particular;
- they are bound to the cultural variables which shape interactions within a certain society reflected in political cultures, institutional systems and in the behaviour patterns of public actors;
- they are directed towards processes of coordination and interaction in the public domain and their organisation (degree of decentralisation, tradition and importance of the voluntary sector, the ways how conflicts are resolved and critique is dealt with, etc.).

---

8 'Conditional programmes' are rules of action which only allow the addressee a limited 'if-then-decision': if the criteria of the regulation hold then certain decisions must be taken according to the given rules.

Conclusions

Although receiving more and more attention, cultural diversity as impediment to interactions is no surprise in a globalised world. However, while research on that subject may lead to ever more knowledge, the question of how to deal with cultural differences in the day-to-day work will be more important (see also Knieling and Othengrafen's introductory contribution to this volume). In the case of spatial planning that refers to the interactions between planning culture, regional planning and regional governance. Regional planning could become a mediator between different logics of action and different cultures to address issues. For one, planning is ever more intertwined with improving regional competitiveness ('strategic planning'). Second, the rampant success of new public management in the public administration will require regional planners to intensify their division of labour with other sector policies. And, finally, regional planning could play a big role in pursuing concepts of sustainable development which are closely linked to different actors and policies. Planning is a learning device which induces the actors involved to modify their mind sets, to clarify their interests and to accept and appreciate the diverging interests of other stakeholders. It is a process of give-and-take which requires an attentive sensitivity to the sentiments of others. What often is lacks in planning processes is what the Chinese multinational company Lenovo advises its employees to do: 'In all situations: assume good intentions; be intentional about understanding others and being understood; respect cultural differences.'

Hence, the discussion on cultural differences in planning could improve planning practices if it would be translated into learning devices helping to understand and play with cultural diversity. Multinational companies, military units deployed abroad and international aid organisations have been long aware of the problems and have found practical solutions to them. Planners could learn from those experiences.

Bibliography

Abbott, C. (1994) 'The Oregon planning style', in: C. Abbott, D. Howe and S. Adler (eds) *Planning the Oregon way. A Twenty-Year Evaluation*, Oregon State University Press, Corvallis.

Albrechts, L., P. Healey and K. Kunzmann (2003) 'Strategic Spatial Planning and Regional Governance in Europe', *Journal of the American Planning Association* 69(2), 113–29.

Backhaus-Maul, H. (2006) 'Gesellschaftliche Verantwortung von Unternehmen', *Aus Politik und Zeitgeschichte* 12, 32–38.

BBR (Bundesamt für Bauwesen und Raumordnung) (ed.) (2002) 'Baukultur – Planungskultur', *Informationen zur Raumentwicklung*, 11/12.

Berg-Schlosser, D. (2005) 'Politische Kultur/Kulturforschung', in: D. Nohlen and R.-O. Schultze (eds) *Lexikon der Politikwissenschaft*, vol. 2, 3. edition, Beck, München, 743–48.

Bevir, M. and R.A.W. Rhodes (2003) 'Searching for Civil Society: Changing Patterns of Governance in Britain', in: *Public Administration* 81, 41–62.

Bevir, M., R.A.W. Rhodes and P. Weller (2003) 'Traditions of Governance: Interpreting the Changing Role of the Public Sector', *Public Administration* 81, 1–17.

Böhme, K (2002) *Nordic Echoes of European Spatial Planning: Discursive Integration in Practice*, Nordregio, Nordregio Report Nr. 8, Stockholm.

Booth, Ph. (2005) 'The Nature of Difference: Traditions of Law and Government and Their Effects on Planning in Britain and Franc', in: B. Sanyal (ed.) *Comparative Planning Cultures*, Routledge, New York, 259–84.

Brenner, N. (2004) *New State Spaces: Urban Governance and the Rescaling of Statehood*, Oxford University Press, Oxford.

Commission of the European Communities (CEC) (1997) *The EU Compendium of Spatial Planning Systems and Policies, Regional Development Studies*, Office for Official Publications of the European Communities, Luxembourg.

Cullingworth, J.B. (1993) *The Political Culture of Planning: American Land Use Planning in Comparative Perspective*, Routledge, New York.

CULTPLAN (2007) *Cultural Differences in European Cooperation. Learning from INTERREG Practice*, final report of the INTERACT project CULTPLAN (ed. R. During and R. van Dam), Alterra, Wageningen UR, Wageningen.

Eatwell, R. (ed.) (1997) *European Political Cultures. Conflict or Convergence?*, Routledge, New York.

Faludi, A. (2005) 'The Netherlands: A Culture with a Soft Spot for Planning', in B. Sanyal (ed.) *Comparative Planning Cultures*, Routledge, New York, 285–308.

Friedmann, J. (2005a) 'Globalization and the Emerging Culture of Planning', *Progress in Planning* 64, 183–234.

Friedmann, J. (2005b) 'Planning Cultures in Transition', in: B. Sanyal (ed.) *Comparative Planning Cultures*, Routledge, New York, 29–44.

Fürst, D. (2001) 'Regional Governance – ein neues Paradigma der Regionalwissenschaften?', *Raumforschung und Raumordnung* 59, 370–80.

Fürst, D. (2003) 'Steuerung auf regionaler Ebene vs regional governance', *Informationen zur Raumentwicklung* 8/9, 441–50.

Fürst, D. (2005) 'Entwicklung und Stand des Steuerungsverständnisses in der Raumplanung', *DISP* 163, 16–27.

Galtung, J. (1983) 'Struktur, Kultur und intellektueller Stil. Ein vergleichender Essay über sachsonische, teutonische, gallische und nipponische Wissenschaft', *Leviathan* 11, 304–38.

Giannakourou, G. (2005) 'Transforming Spatial Planning Policy in Mediterranean Countries: Europeanisation and Domestic Change', *European Planning Studies* 13(2), 319–31.

Gullestrup, H. (2006) *Cultural Analysis. Towards Cross-Cultural Understanding*, Aalborg University Press, Aalborg.

Healey, P. (2006) 'Relational Complexity and the Imaginative Power of Strategic Spatial Planning', *European Planning Studies* 14(4), 525–45.

Healey, P. et al. (1997) *Making Strategic Spatial Plans: Innovation in Europe*, UCL-Press, London.

Hemmens, G.C. (1988) 'Thirty Years of Planning Education', *Journal of Planning Education and Research* 7, 85–91.

Hildenbrand, A. (1996) *Política de Ordenación del Territorio en Europa*, University of Seville, Seville.

Hofstede, G. (2001) *Culture's Consequences: Comparing Values, Behaviors, Institutions, and Organisations across Nations*, 2nd edn, Sage, Thousand Oaks, CA.

Hofstede, G. and G.J. Hofstede (2005) *Cultures and Organisations. Software of the Mind*, McGraw-Hill, New York.

Hovey, B. (2003) 'Making the Portland Way of Planning: The Structural Power of Language', *Journal of Planning History* 2(2), 140–74.

Howe, J. and I. White (2002) 'The Potential Implications of the European Union Water Framework Directive on Domestic Planning Systems: A UK Case Study', *European Planning Studies* 10, 1027–38.

Jann, W. (2000) 'Verwaltungskulturen im internationalen Vergleich. Ein Überblick über den Stand der empirischen Forschung', *Die Verwaltung* 33, 325–50.

Jay, M. (1998) *Cultural Semantics: Keywords of our Time*, Athlone Press, London.

Keating, M. (2000) *The New Regionalism of Western Europe*, Edward Elgar, London.

Keller, D.A., M. Koch and K. Selle (eds) (1993) *Planungskulturen in Europa. Erkundungen in Deutschland, Frankreich, Italien und in der Schweiz*, Verlag für Wissenschaftliche Publikationen, Darmstadt.

Keller, D.A., M. Koch and K. Selle (1996) "Either/Or' and 'And': First Impressions of a Journey into the Planning Cultures of Four Countries', *Planning Perspectives* 11(1), 41–54.

Keller, D.A., M. Koch and K. Selle (2006) 'Verständigungsversuche zum Wandel der Planungskulturen. Ein Langzeit-Projekt', in: K.Selle (ed.) *Zur räumlichen Entwicklung beitragen. Konzepte, Theorien, Impulse*, Reihe '*Planung neu denken*', Vol. 1, Rohn-Verlag, Dortmund, 279–91.

Knodt, M. (1998a) *Tiefenwirkung europäischer Politik: Eigensinn oder Anpassung regionalen Regierens?*, Nomos, Baden-Baden.

Knodt, M. (1998b) 'Die Prägekraft regionaler Politikstile', in: B.Kohler-Koch et al., (eds), *Interaktive Politik in Europa: Regionen im Netzwerk der Integration*, Leske + Budrich, Opladen, 97–152.

Kühn, M. and T. Moss (eds) (2001) *Planungskultur und Nachhaltigkeit*, 3rd edn, Verlag für Wissenschaft und Forschung, Berlin.

Lauria, M. and J.A. Wagner (2006) 'What Can we Learn from Empirical Studies of Planning Theory? A Comparative Case Analysis of Extant Literature', *Journal of Planning Education and Research* 25(4), 364–81.

MacLeod, G. (2001) 'New Regionalism Reconsidered: Globalization and the Remaking of Political Economic Space', *International Journal of Urban and Regional Research* 25, 804–29.

Marcou, G. (2004) 'La planification à l'echelle des grands territories. Etude comparative (Allgemagne, Expagne, Italie, Pay-Bas, Royaume-Uni)', unpublished paper, Paris.

Martin, R. (1999) 'The New "Geographical Turn" in Economics: Some Critical Reflections', *Cambridge Journal of Economics* 23, 65–91.

Nadin, V., C. Brown and S. Dühr (2001) *Sustainability, Development and Spatial Planning in Europe*, Routledge, London/New York.

Netzwerk Stadt und Landschaft (NSL) – ETH Zürich (1993) *DISP* 115, Special Issue on 'Planungskulturen in Europa', Zürich.

Netzwerk Stadt und Landschaft (NSL) – ETH Zürich (2002) *DISP* 148, Issue on 'Zukunft der Raumplanung', Zürich.

Newman, P. (2000) 'Changing Patterns of Regional Governance in the EU', *Urban Studies* 37, 895–908.

Newman, P. and A. Thornley (1996) *Urban Planning in Europe. International Competition, National Systems, and Planning Projects*, Routledge, New York.

Nohlen, D. (2005) 'Vergleichende Regierungslehre/ Vergleichende Politische Systemlehre', in: D. Nohlen and R.-O. Schultze (eds), *Lexikon der Politikwissenschaft*, vol. 2, Beck, München, 1099–95.

Priller, E. and A. Zimmer (eds) (2001) *Der Dritte Sektor international. Mehr Markt – weniger Staat?*, sigma, Berlin.

Priller, E. and A. Zimmer (2006) 'Dritter Sektor: Arbeit als Engagement', *Aus Politik und Zeitgeschichte* 12, 17–24.

Reichel, P. (ed.) (1982) *Politische Kultur in Westeuropa. Bürgerschaft und Staat in der Europäischen Gemeinschaft*, Campus, Frankfurt/New York.

Richardson, J.J., G. Gustaffson and G. Jordan (1982) 'The Concept of Policy Style', in: J.J. Richardson (ed.) *Policy Styles In Western Europe*, Allen & Unwin, London, 1–16.

Roberts, P., D. Shaw and J.A. Walsh (eds) (2000) *Regional Planning and Development in Europe*, Ashgate Press, London.

Sackmann, S. (2006) *Success Factor: Corporate Culture. Developing a Corporate Culture for High Performance and Long-term Competitiveness*, Bertelsmann, Gütersloh.

Salet, W. and A. Faludi (eds) (2000) *The Revival Of Strategic Planning*, Royal Netherlands Academy of Arts and Sciences, Amsterdam.

Sandner, R (1998) 'Stadtteilforen in Berlin. Ein Beispiel zur neuen Planungskultur?', *DISP* 134, 20–23.

Sanyal, B. (2005) 'Hybrid Planning Cultures: The Search for the Global Cultural Commons', in: Sanyal, B. (ed.) *Comparative Planning Cultures*, Routledge, New York, 3–28.

Sartori, G. (1991) 'Comparing and Mis-Comparing', *Journal of Theoretical Politics* 3, 243–57.

Scharpf, F.W. (2000) *Interaktionsformen. Akteurzentrierter Institutionalismus in der Politikforschung*, Leske + Budrich, Opladen.

Schönig, B. (2007) 'Regionalplanung als Eliteprojekt. Ambivalenzen der Regionalplanung durch zivilgesellschaftliche Akteure in den Stadtregionen New York und Chicago', in: U.Altrock, H.Hoffmann and B.Schönig (eds) *Hoffnungsträger Zivilgesellschaft? Governance, Nonprofits und Stadtentwicklung in den Metropolregionen der USA*, Reihe Planungsrundschau H.15, Berlin,137–54.

Selle, K. (1999) 'Neue Planungskultur – Raumplanung auf dem Weg zum kooperativen Handeln?', in: K.M. Schmals (ed.) *Was ist Raumplanung?*, Dortmunder Beiträge zur Raumplanung, Vol. 89, Dortmund, 210–26.

Sommermann, K.-P. (2002) 'Konvergenz im Verwaltungsverfahrens- und Verwaltungsprozessrecht europäischer Staaten', *Die öffentliche Verwaltung* 55, 133–43.

Sturm, R. and H. Pehle (2005) *Das neue deutsche Regierungssystem. Die Europäisierung von Institutionen, Entscheidungsprozessen und Politikfeldern in der Bundesrepublik Deutschland*, 2nd edn, VS-Verlag, Wiesbaden.

Tewdwr-Jones, M. and D. Williams (2001) *The European Dimensions of British Planning*, Spon, London.

Van Deth, J. (2003) 'Measuring Social Capital: Orthodoxies and Continuing Controversies', *International Journal of Social Research Methodology* 6, 79–92.

Van Waarden, F. (1995) 'Persistence of National Policy Styles: A Study of their Institutional Foundations', in: B. Unger and F. van Waarden (eds) *Convergence or Diversity?*, Avebury, Aldershot, 333–73.

Walter, R. (1995) '50 Jahre Planungskultur in den Niederlanden: veränderte Leitthemen der Raumordnung seit 1945', *DISP* 122, 24–28.

Wentz, M. (1992) 'Sozialer Wandel und Planungskultur', in: M. Wentz (ed.) *Planungskulturen*, Campus: Die Zukunft des Städtischen 3, Frankfurt/ Main, 10–19.

Williams R.H. (1996) *European Union Spatial Policy and Planning*, Paul Chapman Publishing, London.

Yaro, R.D. (2007) 'The Role of NGOs in Regional Planning. A Case Study on Regional Plan Association', in: U. Altrock, H. Hoffmann and B. Schönig (eds) *Hoffnungsträger Zivilgesellschaft? Governance,*

Nonprofits und Stadtentwicklung in den Metropolregionen der USA, Reihe Planungsrundschau H.15, Berlin, 155–62.

Chapter 3
En Route to a Theoretical Model for Comparative Research on Planning Cultures

Joerg Knieling and Frank Othengrafen

Urban and regional planning are strongly rooted in and restricted to the cultural contexts or traits of a society, or as Sandercock (1998a, 30) stated: 'Local communities have experiential, grounded, contextual, intuitive knowledges, which are manifested through speech, songs, stories, and various visual forms […], rather than the more familiar kinds of planning "sources" […]'. As consequence, urban and regional planning are understood and practiced differently depending on their constitutional settings and cultural roots that vary significantly across countries and regions (Friedmann 2005, 29; CEC 1997).

Referring to Gullestrup (see his contribution in this volume), planning culture can be understood as aggregate of the social, environmental, as well as the historical grounding of urban and regional planning (Young 2008, 35) plus the material and immaterial results of these foundations. Against this background urban and regional planning is influenced by culture through manifestations in history or by contemporary developments and via tangible and intangible ways. Or as Gullestrup (2006, 21) recognised, culture is subtle and complex in nature and its concepts are fluid and abstract. But at the same time these characteristics describe the difficulty of analysing the role culture has in the context of planning practices.

When analysing and comparing urban and regional planning in different countries, the respective cultural contexts have to be taken into consideration (see also Fürst's contribution in this volume), i.e. the particularities of history, attitudes, beliefs and values, cognitive frames, interpretations of planning tasks and responsibilities, political and legal traditions, rules and norms, different levels of market integration, and different institutional structures of governance (Keller et al. 2006, 279–80; Sanyal 2005b, xxiii). However, at least two questions remain:

- How are urban and regional planning approaches and their practical implementation shaped through different cultures of legal, administrative and economic traditions (Breulliard and Fraser 2007a,

208), as well as shared cultural practices that inhere communities and their 'ways-of life' (Williams 1966, 16)?
- Which techniques and approaches are adequate to analyse the impact of culture on planning practices? What are the methodological requirements to use culture as an organising concept for urban and regional planning (Young 2008, 71) or as 'analytical tool' for the evaluation of planning practices (Avruch 2002, 9)? How may culture be defined and made coherent concerning urban and regional planning?

It is therefore the intention of this chapter to outline a systematic approach for accessing and incorporating culture in urban and regional planning and thereby enable us in turn to identify differing cultural roots. To consider the 'rules of the game' (Triandis 2004, 17) on how culture affects planning practices, this chapter first introduces a definition of the term planning culture, based both on the concept of culture (see also Gullestrup's contribution in this volume) and the different approaches to planning culture (see also Fürst's contribution in this volume). Second, it will be shown that the contemporary comparative studies in the field of urban and regional planning more or less lack the concept of culture, even if this could contribute to explaining their research subjects (Triandis 2004, 35) and although these kind of study, especially cross-cultural studies, are important to improve (mutual) knowledge about planning practices (Breulliard and Fraser 2007b, 1). To indicate how culture resides in each and every place (Young 2008, xv), how it affects planning processes and how it can be used as analytical tool to analyse and compare planning practices, a culturised theoretical concept for comparative research on urban and regional planning will be developed in the final step, on the particular basis of Gullestrup's semi-static model (see also Gullestrup's contribution in this volume).

Planning Culture as Expression of Culturised Planning Practices

The Concept of Culture

To understand and analyse the enduring role of culture and its impact on contemporary planning procedures and practices it is necessary to explain the concept of culture first (see also Gullestrup's contribution in this volume). Among the key concepts in social sciences, the concept of culture is perhaps the subject of the largest variety of definitions or interpretations, ranging from very narrow and specific definitions to broader and more imprecise ones.[1] It

---

1 In 1952 and 1963 Kroeber and Kluckhohn identified over 140 or rather 160 different definitions of the term 'culture', including, for example, 'the human-made part of the environment' (e.g. Triandis 1994) or the 'collective programming of

covers a wide range of meanings, from objects and tools manufactured by humans to values, ideas, world conceptions, language and philosophy and ways of relating to animate and inanimate subjects and objects (Thomas 2003, 21).

The English anthropologist E.B. Tylor is seen as having first defined the concept of culture in 1871:

> Culture is that complex whole which includes knowledge, belief, art, morals, law, custom, and any other capabilities and habits acquired by man as a member of society. (Tylor 1871, 1, in Harris 1989, 20)

The essential core of culture consists of traditional ideas, ideologies and the values attached to them. Culture consists of the derivatives of experience, more or less organised, learned or created by the individuals of a population (socialisation), including images or decodements and their interpretations or meanings, as well as the forms of discourse transmitted from past generations, from contemporaries, or formed by individuals themselves (Holden 2001, 21; Avruch 1998, 17; Scollon and Scollon 2001, 140). In line with this discussion and rationale, Gullestrup (2006, 57) defines the concept of culture as follows (see also his contribution in this volume):

> Culture is the world conception and the values, moral norms and actual behaviour – and the material, immaterial and symbols results thereof – which people (in a given context and in a given period of time) take over from a preceding 'generation', which they – possibly in a modified form – seek to pass on to the next 'generation'; and which in on way or another make them different from people belonging to other cultures.

The Concepts of Planning and Planning Culture

Culture is never homogeneous, but heterogeneous. Because of its subtle and complex character, or as Avruch (2002, 18) put it, because no population

---

mind' (e.g. Hofstede 2001). No doubt there are even more definitions in use today. Furthermore, culture has different meanings in different languages in Europe (Holden 2002, 21): The German term 'Kultur' and the Finnish term 'kulttuuri' strongly suggest 'the intellectual side of civilization and society' (highbrow culture), but without the negative connotations of snobbery as it is used in English society. By contrast, the Russian word 'kultura' has no trace of inverted snobbery and, like the term 'culture' in other languages, it also embraces a scientific meaning, referring to a milieu propagating micro-organisms, for example. Additionally, the concept of culture is used in its 'broad anthropological and ethnographical meaning, as seen for instance in Danish, Chinese or American culture, modern industrial culture, women's culture or the hunting culture in Greenland, etc., etc.' (Gullestrup 2006, 32).

can be adequately characterised as a single culture, it is rather a collection of different subcultures. These subcultures may exist among occupational groups, social classes, genders, races, religions, professions, corporations, and social movements. Decisive for the existence of subcultures is a relatively stable, homogeneous and consistent system of values, beliefs, norms and rules, signs and symbols, traditions and other factors that members of a group, an organisation, or a nation have in common (Holden 2002, 27) and which result in 'easy positive interaction among individuals' (Triandis 2004, 19).

In this context, the planning profession might also be considered as a subculture of urbanists, planners, geographers, developers and other actors involved in planning processes which are producing and sharing cognitive frames, practices, knowledge, beliefs, norms and rules, values and codes (see also Hansen 2003, 42). In other terms, planning culture can be considered as a specific subculture because all actors involved in planning processes are conditioned by the system of planning they act in, including the acceptance of rites and power structures etc. (see also Fürst's contribution in this volume).

But what is planning about, then? In general it refers to a process of formulating objectives and developing plans for future activities (Alexander 1992, 69–70). When thinking of urban and regional planning it refers to the methods which are used in order to influence the built environment, especially the future distribution of people, activities and resources in cities and regions by public and private measures and activities as well as the coordination and control of interdependent activities like housing, land-use planning, transport, water management etc.

In this context, planning is understood both as controlling and restricting development, consisting of a kind of drawing or mapping of future land use policies (control of land use via a statutory spatial plan), and as an activating process or methodology for urban and regional development (Greed 2000, 2; (Alexander 1992, 70–73; Young 2008, 33). The latter function refers to strategic planning and consists mainly of assessing environmental and social impacts of proposed development projects, as well as of motivating endogenous potentials and coordinating public and private interests (Gleeson 2003, 25). But both functions of planning have in common that they have to be seen in the context of urban or regional cultural contexts. In other terms, planning is embedded in a specific cultural framework, which is composed of interactive processes among involved actors, their cultural cognitive frames and the particular planning procedures and instruments. In this sense, planners and planning systems need to be responsive to their cultural contexts. Against this background, Huxley (2000, 369) argues that it is important to expand the methods of studying planning by emphasising 'the importance of listening to planners' views of their worlds; tracing the forms of communication they use among themselves and with their publics' to understand the cultural contexts which are affecting their planning practice.

To summarise, the concept of planning culture is not easy to define due to the broad tasks and fields planning is involved in, as well as its different purposes and diffuse research approaches, which Fürst describes (see his contribution in this volume). But according to the concept of culture, planning culture might be understood as the way in which a society possesses institutionalised or shared planning practices. It refers to the interpretation of planning tasks, the way of recognising and addressing problems, the handling and use of certain rules, procedures and instruments, or ways and methods of public participation. It emerges as the result of the accumulated attitudes, values, rules, standards and beliefs shared by the group of people involved. This includes informal aspects (traditions, habits and customs) as well as formal aspects (constitutional and legal framework).

Analysis of Planning Models and Practices – The Need for an Understanding of Planning through Culture

As has been shown in the first part of this chapter, planning, development processes and decision-making are influenced by the cultural context of (groups of) people and society. Urban and regional planning and development are understood and practiced differently depending on their constitutional and cultural settings, which vary significantly across countries and regions. As a consequence, planning culture includes more than planning instruments and procedures – it is determined by several framing factors and is embedded into political-administrative and institutional structures as well as in socio-economic and cultural models and traditions which differ across Europe. Thus, each planning culture is affected by political, legal and administrative traditions and current developments, economic and technical practices, and demographic development, as well as societal traditions, values, attitudes and contemporary societal movements or changes (e.g. Sanyal 2005b, 13).

But despite the increasing awareness to achieve a better understanding of the relationship between cultural contexts (Young 2008; Breulliard and Fraser 2007b, 1) and urban and regional planning as the operative fields of territorial policy, planning as well as planning theory have mostly disregarded the principles of culture, in particular the reflection of diversity and of various differences in the social, historical, environmental and ecological circumstances of any certain place, community, or culture. Recent research has shown that the emphasis of planning culture lies on planning systems (CEC 1997; Newman and Thornley 1996), planning styles (Innes and Gruber 2001), planning phases or periods, and planning perceptions (Keller et al. 2006 and 1993; Selle 1999; Albers 1993; Sanyal 2005b). But irrespective of the desire for a systematic comparison of planning cultures (Friedmann 2005; Sanyal 2005a; Faludi 2004) culture is addressed in a conceptually fragmented, ad hoc or frequently opportunistic way (Young 2008, 5); a rigorous methodology for

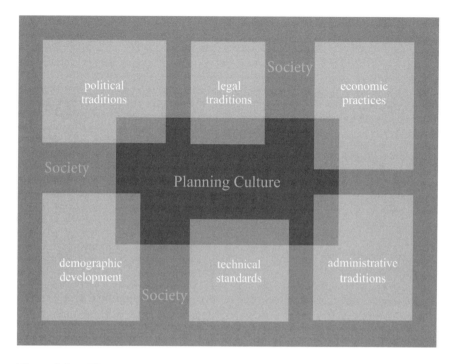

Figure 3.1   The embeddedness of planning culture

Source: authors' own illustration.

comparative studies is still lacking. In other terms, planning culture, depending on the methodology and reflection of the analysis, refers to a collection of various planning characteristics but not to a systematic approach or a common conceptual framework for discussing the role of culture for planning practice (see Fürst's contribution in this volume).

The EU *Compendium of Spatial Planning and Policies*

One of the first comparative studies on planning cultures in the European context was generated by the European Commission with the *Compendium of Spatial Planning Systems and Policies* (CEC 1997). The Commission recognised territory as well as spatial planning and development as key factors in the context of social, economic and territorial cohesion. But experiences with cross-border, transnational and interregional cooperation had shown that different cultural and political-administrative contexts complicated cooperation because of the 'ignorance' of each partner about other structures and traditions (see also contribution of During et al. in this volume). In terms of the *Compendium* the European Commission mainly aimed at improving the mutual knowledge about each planning system across the EU member states.

The *Compendium* analyses the planning systems and contexts of 15 EU member states by means of a determined structure. This comparative structure mainly consists of (see also contribution of Stead and Nadin in this volume):

- the traditions of spatial planning (scope of the system, extent and type of planning at national and regional levels, locus of power, relative roles of public and private sectors, nature of the system of law, constitutional provisions and administrative traditions, maturity or completeness of the system, distance between expressed objectives and outcomes;
- the context and principles of spatial planning (constitutional law, government structure and responsibilities for spatial planning, legal framework); and
- the emerging trends and the impact of the European Union (central-local government relations, flexibility and certainty in decision-making, government structure, impact of EU on planning systems) (CEC 1997, 33–45).

As a result, the *Compendium* identifies four major trends of spatial planning each of the member states can be attached to (CEC 1997, 36–7; see also Map 3.1):

- the regional economic planning approach, which pursues social and economic objectives, especially in relation to disparities in wealth, employment and social conditions between different regions and which is provided by central government and public sector investment (e.g. France and Portugal);
- the comprehensive integrated approach, where spatial planning is conducted through a very systematic and formal hierarchy of plans which coordinate public activities across different sectors and where the focus is more on spatial coordination than on economic development (e.g. The Netherlands, the Nordic countries, Germany and Austria);
- land use management, where planning is associated with the task of controlling the change of use of land at the strategic and local levels (e.g. United Kingdom, Ireland and Belgium); and
- the urbanism tradition, which has a strong architectural focus, including urban design, townscape and building control and where various laws and regulation exist without a coherent system or general public support (e.g. the Mediterranean countries).

With regard to comparative studies on planning cultures the *Compendium* provides a profound basis for comparisons of planning systems, including constitutional and political-administrative structures. But at the same time

Map 3.1   The four major trends and traditions of spatial planning in Europe

Source: authors' own illustration.

the exclusive focus on the formal structures of planning cultures is one of its major criticisms: The concentration on institutional structures does not allow a more dynamic and including analysis of planning cultures. The emphasis of the comparison seems to be too static, it neglects the role of cultural traditions, values, habits and semantics, and furthermore it does not consider, that planning systems are subject of constant change (Farinós Dasi and Milder 2006, 8): New challenges and tasks arise which need to be dealt with on the urban or regional level, and the EU itself is responsible for adoptions that national planning systems have to undertake by its Community initiatives, guidelines, and laws. The second criticism refers to the limited capability of the *Compendium* to explain planning practices in each of the member states. In many cases, the *Compendium* illustrated the planning system with its legal background and its structure as well as the planning instruments but

Map 3.2   The five legal and administrative planning families

Source:Urban Planning in Europe, Peter Newman and Andy Thornley ©1996, Routledge. Reproduced by permission of Taylor & Francis Books UK.

it cannot explain specific spatial developments across the EU member states which are due to different traditions, tangible or intangible cultural elements and experiential, grounded, contextual, and intuitive knowledge (Sandercock 1998a, 30). This, for example, refers to the question why some countries follow planning specifications easily and others reject requirements of spatial plans? Why do some countries pursue a more flexible approach to spatial planning and others not? Or – on a more specific level – why are summer cottages and their spatial consequences an important subject in some countries but not in others?

Further Comparative Studies on Planning Culture

But the criticism mentioned is not only related to the *Compendium* but also to other comparative studies on planning culture (e.g. Newman and Thornley 1996; Balchin and Sykora 1999). In these studies, planning culture refers to a collection of various planning characteristics, depending on the methodology and reflection of the analysis, and not to a systematic approach or a common conceptual framework for discussing the role of culture in planning practice. Furthermore, these studies 'only' or mostly focus on constitutional or institutional elements like central-local relations, political and administrative structures, forms of state organisation, kinds of state-society relationships and their impacts on the spatial planning system (e.g. Loughlin 2001; Newman and Thornley 1996; Balchin and Sykora 1999).

Other studies with regard to planning cultures are mostly based on surveys by concerned planners (Keller et al. 1993 and 2006) or on reports of specific planning practices in one or two countries (Sanyal 2005a; Duehr 2005; Hovey 2003). Keller et al. (1996, 42), for example, use a hermeneutical approach (see also Fürst's contribution in this volume) to describe how planning culture is related to fundamental beliefs and values, administrative structures and interpretations of tasks and objects of planning. Their aim was to describe and identify current trends planning was facing in Germany, France, Italy and Switzerland at that time. Therefore an expert discourse was initiated intending 'to listen to other's arguments and to try to understand prior to systematic ordering or evaluation' (Keller et al. 1996, 42).

Surveying these studies it becomes obvious that feedback between the micro level (experiences of planners) and the macro level (institutional and social context) is missing, as well as a more systematic comparison. By bringing together the micro and macro levels and the 'parallel universes of planning and culture' (Young 2008 6), a culture-based planning paradigm could be developed to understand planning practices on the basis of a critically viable and applied approach.

Where Culture Already Matters: Culture and Organisations

There are other fields where a culture-based paradigm has already prevailed. These are the management and organisational sciences as well as the cross-cultural sciences (e.g. Hofstede 2001; Hofstede and Hofstede 2005; Trompenaars and Hampden-Turner 2005; Schein 2004; Hoecklin 1995; Harris et al. 2004). All these approaches have in common that they emphasise the significance of culture for international companies and international managers which have to operate on a number of assumptions at any given time. These assumptions 'arise from [the managers] culture of origin, the culture in which they are working and the culture of the organisation which employs them' (Trompenaars and Hampden-Turner 2005, 3). But beliefs, values, attitudes, norms and rules which are different from one's own can lead to misunderstandings and even to business failures; the 'management-by-objectives schemes, for example, have generally failed within subsidiaries of multinationals in Southern Europe because managers did not want to conform to the abstract nature of preconceived policy guidelines' (ibid., 2).

In the management or organisational sciences, the concept of culture is recognised to adapt a business or an organisation to specific local or national characteristics. In this context, the concept of culture is used to increase the 'cultural sensitivity' (Harris et al. 2004, 21) as a kind of 'competitive advantage' (Hoecklin 1995, 15). Hence, culture is used in a systematic way to figure out differences in preferences, values, norms, rules and attitudes and to manage these (cultural) differences successfully:

> What happens in organizations is fairly easy to observe; for example, leadership, failures, marketing myopia, arrogance based on past success, and so on; but in the effort to understand why such things happen, culture as a concept comes into its own. (Schein 2004, xi)

> Perhaps the most intriguing aspect of culture as a concept is that it points out to the phenomena that are below the surface, that are powerful in their impact but invisible and to a considerable degree unconscious. (ibid., 8)

To figure out these 'phenomena that are below the surface' (see also Gullestrup's contribution in this volume) several theoretical and systematic approaches of how to arrange or systemise the values and preferences, the communication styles and hierarchical patterns and the practical orientation have been elaborated by various authors (e.g. Hofstede 2001; Hofstede and Hofstede 2005; Trompenaars and Hampden-Turner 2005).

The most widely known research dealing with organisational culture or behaviour and the comparison of national cultures is Hofstede's (2001; Hofstede and Hofstede 2005). He describes culture as the 'collective programming of the mind' (Hofstede 2001, 4) which consists of the two 'poles' of human nature on one side and the individual personality on the other (see Figure 3.2). Related to this understanding, Schein developed a similar model to describe culture and to analyse organisational culture via '(1) visible artefacts, (2) espoused beliefs, values, rules, and behavioural norms, and (3) tacit, taken-for-granted, basic underlying assumptions' (Schein 2004, 59; see also Figure 3.3). Both approaches have in common that they aim at developing a theoretical and systematic model to explain the cultural 'phenomena that are below the surface' of an organisation.

Hofstede identified five dimensions of 'work-related value differences' (Hoecklin 1995, 27) which have important effects for organisations operation across (cultural) borders. These five dimensions are (Hofstede 2001):

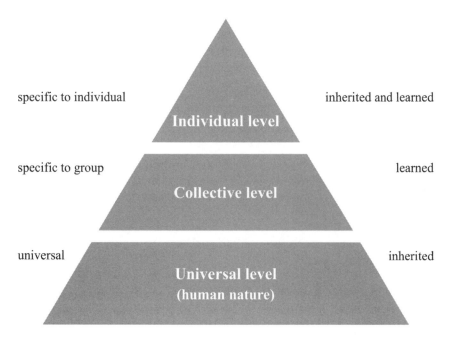

Figure 3.2　The different levels of the mental programme

Source: *Cultures and Organizations: Software of the Mind*, Geert Hofstede and Gert Jan Hofstede, 2005, McGraw-Hill, 4.

1. power distance, which refers to the extent to which the less powerful members of organisations and institutions accept and expect that power is distributed unequally (Hofstede and Bond 1984, 419, quoted in Gudykunst 2000, 299);
2. individualism versus collectivism, which describes the relationship between the individual and the collectivity, e.g. the emphasis on individual goals versus societal achievements;
3. uncertainty avoidance, which is the 'lack of tolerance for ambiguity and the need for formal rules' (Hoecklin 1995, 31), i.e. the extent to which a culture programmes its members to feel either uncomfortable or comfortable in situations which are novel, unknown or different from usual;
4. masculinity versus femininity, which refers to the distribution of emotional roles between the genders (with regard to value orientation, e.g. solidarity versus competitiveness, focus on performance versus focus on balance etc.);
5. long-term versus short-term orientation, which means the extent to which a culture programmes its members to accept delayed gratification of their material, social, and emotional needs.

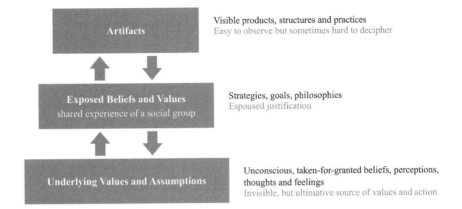

Figure 3.3   The levels of culture

Source:Organizational Culture and Leadership (3rd edn), Edgar H. Schein © 2004, Jossey-Bass/Wiley. Reprinted with permission of John Wiley & Sons, Inc.

Similar to Hofstede's cultural dimensions, Trompenaars and Hampden-Turner (2005) developed five comparable dimensions:

1. universalism versus particularism: societal versus personal obligation;
2. individualism versus collectivism: personal versus group goals;
3. neutral versus affective relationships: emotional orientation in relationships;
4. specific versus diffuse relationships: degree of involvement in relationships;
5. achievement versus ascription: legitimation of power and status.

All these approaches or dimensions draw on related or similar criteria and have in common that, in a systematic and comprehensive way, they use the concept of culture to highlight some of the most important aspects in which culture differs and how those differences generally affect organisations and institutions. In this sense, the introduction and adoption of the concept of culture into planning might be able to contribute to valuable outcomes with regard to comparative studies about planning in different countries.

The Cultural Turn and Planning Theory

Despite the recognition of the concept of culture in organisational sciences, planning practice and planning theory have 'remained alarmingly diffuse and unfocused in relation to the cultural turn', and have 'failed to address the issue of culture in direct terms' (Young 2008, 43). This, at least, refers to a systematic and comprehensive model to increase the integration of culture as an organising principle of planning to be able to produce generalising outcomes regardless of the cultural diversity of the postmodern world.

Postmodern (planning) theories might function as a basis for the development of a systematic theoretical model for comparative research on planning that integrates planning cultures. They recognise differences (Allmendinger 2002, 164; Sandercock 1998a, 197; Soja 1996, 87) and emphasise the value of cultural diversity as well as the importance of space explaining that each area or region has its own culture, its specific institutional context, as well as its own traditions, values, and attitudes which are different from other places (Dear 2000, 2).

Postmodern Social Theory

The modernist approaches of the universal theories and master-narratives with their comprehensive explanations and prescriptions (Lyotard 1984) as well as the modernist norm of a 'homogeneous public' (Sandercock 1998a, 197) have been criticised for their 'blindness' considering local contexts and cultures. Although these master-narratives present 'themselves as providing answers [...] in reality they mask many different truths' (Allmendinger 2002, 164). As a consequence, postmodern theories have tried to develop a framework to involve key issues of differentiation, such as diversity, openness and flexibility. Following Young (2008, 45), the

> dismissal of master-narratives and [Lyotard's] argument for the incommensurability of values and discourses is relevant to evaluating the implications of cultural diversity and the juxtapositions of diverse values, ethnicities, sexualities and lifestyles that is commonplace in cities today [...].

This also refers to the role of power and the ways in which a society controls and reproduces itself (Allmendinger 2002, 166). In that context, postmodern theories aim at a culturally pluralist ideal which provides 'mechanisms for the effective recognition and representation of the distinct voices and perspectives' of different groups (Sandercock 1998b, 182) which cannot be 'socially equal unless their specific experience, culture, and social contributions are publicly affirmed and recognised' (Young 1990, 174). The principles of diversity, openness and flexibility are used for understanding and encouraging social reality, i.e. to introduce new concepts of social justice, to establish new forms of power and dominance, and to improve citizenship, ethnic and racial tolerance (Soja 1997, 245; Sandercock 1998b, 182).

Challenges for Postmodern Planning Approaches: Culture as Organising Principle?

Urban and regional planning is often linked with rational forms of societal organisation, rational modes of thought and the dominance of instrumental or scientific rationality (Allmendinger 2002, 157; Sandercock 1998a, 27). These attributes mainly correspond with modernist approaches of the universal theories and master-narratives in terms of using rational decision-making processes with regard to a 'homogeneous' public interest, applying comprehensive planning approaches and processes, and using scientific and quantitative methods (see also Fischer's contribution in this volume).

But, based on this self-conception, it seems nearly impossible for urban and regional planning to consider local and regional cultural contexts. Thus, to assure and reflect planning approaches, urban and regional planning have to be reflected, 'to be more aware of power relations and more sensitive to local needs and demands' (Allmendinger 2002, 168). Soja (1997, 245) argues in a similar way when explaining that a postmodern planning theory

> must be built upon an epistemological openness and flexibility that are suspicious of any attempt to formalize a single totalizing way of knowing, no matter how progressive it may appear to be. Second, it must make this openness a means of understanding ambiguity, fragmentation, multiplicity, and difference, for these are the material social realities of the contemporary world. This means not only tolerating difference but encouraging what can be described as the disordering of difference (as opposed to the modernist search for order and stability).

Following this argumentation, openness and flexibility can be described as characteristics of postmodern planning approach, aiming at including or integrating the various groups and interests into the planning process. Additionally, the principle of diversity is emphasised to recognise differences and multiple public interests to reflect the cultural and institutional context, meaning the physical conditions as well as social traditions, values and attitudes, of any area or region. These specific cultural contexts are 'the basis for determining planning responses and emphases' urban and regional planning has to take into consideration (Young 2008, 51).

As shown above, postmodern (planning) theory, as a reaction on modernist theoretical approaches, includes the concept of culture. But there is no general and systematic framework to integrate culture as an organising principle into planning in order to analyse similarities and differences of cities, regions and nations. Thus the 'loss of the big picture', which accompanies postmodern thought (Eagleton 1996, 70), has become a real challenge for the further development of planning and planning theory:

The postmodern challenge is hence not to produce small stories describing difference, but stories in which authors highlight both those things that are novel/different and those that are similar to other parts of other small stories. (Oranje 2002, 182)

This leads to some critical considerations concerning postmodern approaches. If urban and regional planning and planning theory only focuses on 'small narratives' and the uniqueness of local cultures, this might lead to a neglect of similarities which are of mutual concern among local cultures, and which, as a consequence, might result in the conclusion that there are no similarities at all between local cultures (ibid.). Hence postmodern planning theory is challenged to develop a theoretical model which is based both on the unique local cultural contexts or specifics of place (micro-level), as well as on more abstract concepts to figure out differences and similarities of local cultures and to draw (theoretical) conclusions between them (macro level).

The framing or development of such a (culturised) planning model can be found in the context of 'new' systemic (postmodern) planning approaches which are trying to include the complexity of planning processes (Schönwandt 2002, 30; Byrne 2003) without becoming 'classical rational planning approaches' again. Culture, in this context, refers to specific local or regional contexts but also functions as an organising principle for planning research to be able to produce valuable and comparable outcomes regardless to the cultural diversity of a postmodern world. Such a model, which will be discussed in the following section, might increase the integration of culture into planning in two ways:

1. by strengthening the emphasis that planning is embedded in political-administrative structures, socio-economic contexts, and societal traditions and values (culture as organising and connecting principle); and
2. by reducing the distinction between planning practice and planning theory which, due to the plurality and uniqueness of local cultures, seems to be a problem of the postmodernism (culture as a bridging principle) (Oranje 2002, 181; Young 2008, 46; Sanyal 2000, 322–4.).

Framing a 'Culturised Theoretical Model' for Comparative Research on Spatial Planning

The cultural theory Gullestrup describes (see also his contribution in this volume), the theoretical approaches of the organisational sciences and the postmodern theoretical approaches give the basis for a common conceptual framework or analytical tool to explain the relations between cultural values, rules and attitudes and their integration into spatial planning and development. The following section presents a conceptual framework that may allow a more systematic discussion about functional structures and mechanisms, planning systems and planning styles with regard to the cultural context of different countries and societies.

For Gullestrup, culture consists both of 'shared meanings' as they are conceptualised in the basic philosophy of life and values among a group of people, and of the way in which these shared meanings are visualised or manifested in people's social interactions, as well as in the results of those interactions (see Gullestrup's contribution in this volume, but also Hofstede 2001 and Schein 2004).

Therefore, the concept of culture differentiates between two perspectives: the participants' point of view (emic descriptions), and the observers' point of view (etic descriptions) (Harris 1999, 31). In other words, etics cover the more universal elements (ideas, behaviour, items and concepts) that are observable to outsiders, whereas emics refer to more specific elements known only by insiders (Triandis 1994, 67). The combination of these two perspectives allows the generation of scientific generalisations about relationships among variables and small narratives or local cultures (etics) and, at the same time, the deepening of the knowledge and understanding by integrating the specific local cultural contexts (emics) (Gullestrup 2006, 26; Triandis 1994, 67).

Theoretical modelling follows the objective to decode the cultural phenomena of planning and to identify and analyse functional structures and mechanisms, planning systems and planning practices with regard to the cultural and institutional context of the specific countries and societies in a logical, developmental sequence. By this, the 'culturised' (Young 2008, 9) planning model aims to enable scientists and practitioners

- to analyse what the role of culture in planning and development processes is and to find out if there are core cultural traits or phenomena which differentiate planning models and practices in different countries or regions; and
- to define planning culture conceptually and to operationalise it in a practical sense for planning. This will indicate that it is possible to develop a workable system to increase the reliable integration of culture into planning and which is able to produce beneficial outcomes for understanding planning practices in different contexts.

An outline of how to approach the enduring phenomenon of culture and its impacts on contemporary spatial planning and development practices is shown in Figure 3.4. It refers to both Gullestrup's concept and Schein's model that the underlying assumptions and values, which are more difficult to observe, will appear when immersing in a foreign culture (Gullestrup 2006; Schein 2004; see also Holden 2002; Hoecklin 1995). For the investigation of planning cultures, this also implies that there are elements which can be easily recognised and understood because they refer to 'planning artefacts' such as urban structures and urban master plans, or to planning institutions and further public or private actors involved in planning processes. At the same time there are cultural values, traditions, attitudes and habits which have a significant influence on planning structures, processes and outcomes but are not obvious immediately. These cultural assumptions and values can be divided into two dimensions: the 'planning environment' and the 'societal environment'.

The 'planning environment' refers to assumptions and values that are specific for actors being involved in structures, processes and products of spatial planning (e.g. urban and regional planners, urbanists, geographers etc.). The taken-for-granted assumptions, frames and values of this group comprise, among others, the objectives and principles planning is aiming at (such as the provision of equal living conditions, sustainability etc.), traditions and history of planning, the scope or range of planning (comprehensive planning versus planning by projects) and political, administrative, economic and organisational structures. The knowledge of the different administrative traditions, for example, is important for analysing planning cultures. Local self-government is one of the basic principles of the Scandinavian constitutions. In contrast, the Socialist states were highly centralised. Since the early 1990s each Eastern European country 'has been developing its local administrative and electoral systems and although there are different approaches there is a common tendency to react against this highly centralised past and adopt very decentralised approaches' (Newman and Thornley 1996, 36) by increasing participation in local decision-making. Thus the knowledge of these backgrounds is essential to understand the planning culture as well as the planning practices of a country or region, i.e. the scope of the planning system, its components, principles and sub-levels, the involved actors etc.

The 'societal environment' describes underlying assumptions which are more difficult to perceive but which affect urban and regional planning by forming the specific societal background. These unconscious, taken-for-granted societal norms, beliefs, perceptions, thoughts and feelings contain, amongst others, the (self-)perception of planning, people's acceptance of planning, but also different concepts of justice, impacts of socio-economic or socio-political models on planning as well as the consideration of nature (see Figure 3.4). Looking at the latter aspect, especially at the orientation towards environmental protection, Inglehart (2003, 257) has shown that there are different perceptions of the necessity and the public support for environmental protection between the Germanic and/or Scandinavian 'group' on the one side, and the Latin 'group' on the other side. This affects the individual planning cultures by various means, for example, by the exposure to territory as part of the environment, the way of planning (urbanism versus suburbanism etc.) and the priorities planning is aiming at (economic competitiveness versus environmental protection etc.).

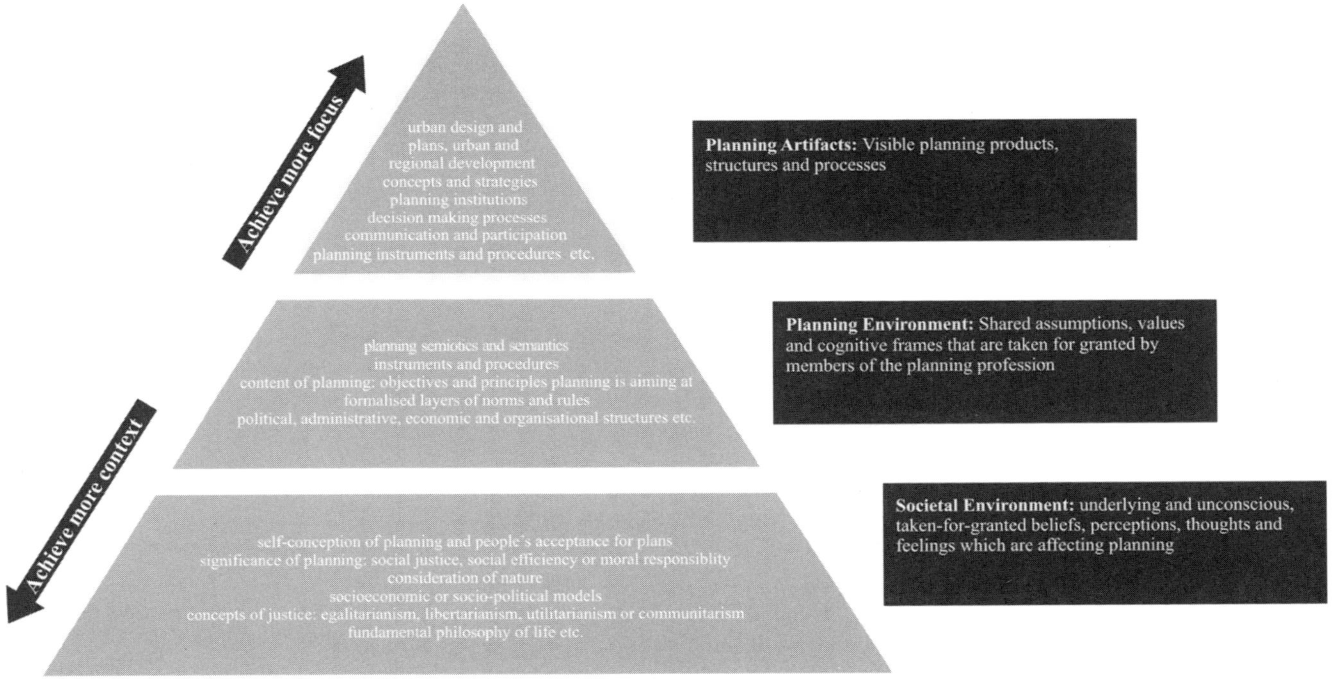

Planning Artifacts: Visible planning products, structures and processes

- urban design and
- plans, urban and
- regional development
- concepts and strategies
- planning institutions
- decision making processes
- communication and participation
- planning instruments and procedures etc.

Planning Environment: Shared assumptions, values and cognitive frames that are taken for granted by members of the planning profession

- planning semiotics and semantics
- instruments and procedures
- content of planning: objectives and principles planning is aiming at
- formalised layers of norms and rules
- political, administrative, economic and organisational structures etc.

Societal Environment: underlying and unconscious, taken-for-granted beliefs, perceptions, thoughts and feelings which are affecting planning

- self-conception of planning and people's acceptance for plans
- significance of planning: social justice, social efficiency or moral responsibility
- consideration of nature
- socioeconomic or socio-political models
- concepts of justice: egalitarianism, libertarianism, utilitarianism or communitarism
- fundamental philosophy of life etc.

Achieve more focus →

Achieve more context →

Figure 3.4 The 'culturised planning model': the exposure of culture and its impact on spatial planning and development practices

Source: authors' own illustration.

The figure indicates a distinction between a horizontal and vertical level of planning (Gullestrup 2006; see also his contribution in this volume). Again, the assumption is that, with regard to the analysis of planning cultures, there are elements which occur immediately, as well as elements which belong to the underlying norms of morality and social structures being more difficult to observe. The figure furthermore assumes that the territorial structures, planning documents, planning institutions and their political-administrative embeddedness, planning laws, and planning strategies and instruments can be observed without difficulty. In this sense, the elements belonging to the 'planning artefacts' might serve as the horizontal level of the common conceptual framework. The elements or categories can be interpreted as horizontal because they are manifested at the same level and because they are all of equal importance to understand the cultural impacts on urban and regional planning. Furthermore, they represent obvious cultural categories which might easily be discovered and analysed (first impressions that are visible but nevertheless sometimes difficult to decode).

The dimensions 'planning environment' and 'societal environment' belong to the vertical level of planning culture and represent the more 'hidden' assumptions and values of culture which are difficult to perceive but have strong impact on the specific occurrence of cultural manifestations in planning models and practices. These 'invisible parts' of planning culture are more difficult to figure out and so far have rarely been part of the theoretical discourse about planning systems, planning traditions and planning cultures. But the relevance of these invisible structures and traits is important for the observation and comparison of planning cultures. They are emphasised by Hoecklin (1995, 4) who argues that

> the essence of culture is not what is visible on the surface. It is the shared ways groups of people understand and interpret the world. These differing interpretations that cultures give to their environments are critical influences on interactions between people working and managing across cultures.

Conclusions

The outlined culturised planning model follows the aim to consider and decode cultural phenomena concerning planning not only on the visible surface but also on a 'hidden' level. By introducing the (analytical) dimensions of (1) 'planning artefacts', (2) 'planning environment', and (3) 'societal environment' the model allows the systematic and comprehensive analysis and comparison of planning cultures. These analytical dimensions can be useful to identify the relation between culture and planning at any one region or area in a more systematic and structured way to increase the knowledge about planning practices. Additionally, the culturised planning model contributes to the operationalisation of the concept of planning culture (see also Fürst's contribution in this volume) by identifying functional structures and mechanisms culture implies for planning in a more abstract way. But still some open questions remain to be discussed:

- Are there further, maybe conflicting, theoretical approaches in the field of (anthropological) cultural studies or organisational sciences? Which influence or impacts could these approaches have for the shape of the model?
- How can the model contribute to the broad field of postmodern planning theories? If postmodern theories reject the idea of comprehensiveness and 'big narratives' in spatial planning, which role can the model play? How can postmodern cultural theories be connected with postmodern planning theories?
- Is the model feasible for practitioners? What can it achieve in practice? Can it improve the communication between practitioners and lead to a better understanding of planning cultures?

Nevertheless, the model and its (analytical) cultural dimensions describe elements for a culture-based planning paradigm which provides a framework for the analysis and description of planning practices and cultures in the following case studies that represent the cultural variety of countries and regions throughout Europe. The cultural paradigm which is the basis of the culturised planning model will be valuated by each of the case studies so that they provide the final chapters of this volume with an empirical fundament for summarising the usability of the model, including its potentials and strengths as well as weaknesses and restrictions.

Bibliography

Albers, G. (1993) 'Über den Wandel im Planungsverständnis', *RaumPlanung* 61, 97–103.

Alexander, E.R. (1992) *Approaches to Planning. Introducing Current Planning Theoreis, Concepts and Issues*, 2nd edn, Gordon and Breach Science Publishers, Yverdon.

Allmendinger, P. (2002) *Planning Theory*, Palgrave, Hampshire.

Avruch, K. (2002) *Culture and Conflict Resolution*, United States Institute of Peace, Washington.

Balchin, P.N. and L. Sykora (1999) *Regional Policy and Planning in Europe*, Routledge, London.

Breulliard, M. and C. Fraser (2007a) 'Preface', in P. Booth, M. Breuillard, C. Fraser and D. Paris (eds) *Spatial Planning Systems of Britain and France, A Comparative Analysis*, Routledge, London, xiii–xv.

Breulliard, M. and C. Fraser (2007b) 'The Purpose and Process of Comparing British and French Planning', in P. Booth, M. Breuillard, C. Fraser and D. Paris (eds) *Spatial Planning Systems of Britain and France, A Comparative Analysis*, Routledge, London, 1–13.

Byrne, D. (2003) 'Complexity Theory and Planning Theory: A Necessary Encounter', *Planning Theory* 2(3), 171–8.

Commission of the European Communities – CEC (1997) *The EU Compendium of Spatial Planning Systems and Policies*, Regional Development Studies, Office for Official Publications of the European Communities, Luxembourg.

Dear, M.J. (2000) *The Postmodern Urban Condition*, Blackwell, Oxford.

Duehr, S. (2005) 'Spatial Policies for Regional Sustainable Development – A Comparison of Graphic and Textual Representations in regional plans in England and Germany', *Regional Studies* 39(9), 1167–82.

Eagleton, T. (1996) *The Illusions of Postmodernism*, Blackwell Publishing, Oxford.

Faludi, A. (2004) 'Spatial Planning Traditions in Europe: Their Role in the ESDP Process', *International Planning Studies* 9(2–3), 55–172.

Farinós Dasí, J. and J. Milder (2006) 'Evidence of Convergence towards a Common Model of Styles of Planning in Europe', Annex to the Final Report of the ESPON Project 2.3.2 Governance of Territorial and Urban Policies from EU to Local Level, ESPON Coordination Unit, Luxembourg.

Friedmann, J. (2005) 'Planning Cultures in Transition', in B. Sanyal (ed.) *Comparative Planning Culture*, Routledge, London, 29–44.

Gleeson, B. (2003) 'The Contribution of Planning to Environment and Society', *Australian Planner* 40(3), 25–30.

Greed, C. (2000) *Introducing Planning*, The Athlone Press, London.

Gudykunst, W.B. (2000) 'Methodological Issues in Conducting Theory-Based Cross-Cultural Research', in H. Spencer-Oatey, (ed.) *Culturally Speaking: Managing Rapport through Talk across Cultures*, Wellington House, London, 293–315.

Gullestrup, H. (2006) *Cultural Analysis, Towards Cross-Cultural Understanding*, Aalborg University Press, Aalborg.

Hansen, K.P. (2003) *Kultur und Kulturwissenschaft, Eine Einführung*, 3rd edn, A. Francke Verlag, Tübingen.

Harris, M. (1989) *Kulturanthropologie, Ein Lehrbuch*, Campus Verlag, Frankfurt.

Harris, M. (1999) *Theories of Culture in Postmodern Times*, Sage Publications, London.

Harris, P.R., R.T. Moran and S.V. Moran (2004) *Managing Cultural Differences, Global Leadership Strategies for the 21st Century*, 6th edn, Elsevier Butterworth-Heinemann, Oxford.

Hoecklin, L. (1995) *Managing Cultural Differences*, Strategies for Competitive Advantage, Addison-Wesley Publishers, Harlow.

Hofstede, G. (2001) *Cultures Consequences, Comparing Values, Behaviors, Institutions, and Organizations across Nations*, 2nd edn, Sage Publications, Thousand Oaks.

Hofstede, G. and G.J. Hofstede (2005) *Cultures and Organizations, Software of the Mind*, 2nd edn, McGraw-Hill, New York.

Holden, N. (2002) *Cross-Cultural Management, A Knowledge Management Perspective*, Pearson Education, Harlow.

Hovey, B. (2003) 'Making the Portland Way of Planning: The Structural Power of Language', *Journal of Planning History* 2(2), 140–74.

Huxley, M. (2000) 'The Limits to Communicative Planning', *Journal of Planning Education and Research* 19(4), 369–77.

Inglehart, R. (2003) *Human Values and Social Change: Findings from the Values Surveys*, Brill, Leiden.

Innes, J.E. and J. Gruber (2001) *Planning Styles in Conflict at the San Francisco Bay Area's Metropolitan Transportation Commission*, Working Paper 09/2001, Institute of Urban and Regional Development, University of California, Berkeley.

Keller, D.A., M. Koch and K. Selle (1993) *Planungskulturen in Europa, Erkundungen in Deutschland, Frankreich, Italien und der Schweiz*, Verlag für wissenschaftliche Publikationen, Darmstadt.

Keller, D.A., M. Koch and K. Selle (1996) '"Either/Or" and "And": First Impressions of a Journey into the Planning Cultures of Four Countries', *Planning Perspectives* 11(1), 41–54.

Keller, D.A., M. Koch and K. Selle (2006) 'Verständigungsversuche zum Wandel der Planungskulturen. Ein Langzeit-Projekt', in K. Selle (ed.) *Zur Räumlichen Entwicklung beitragen: Konzepte, Theorien, Impulse*, Planung Neu Denken, Bd. 1, Rohn-Verlag, Dortmund, 279–91.

Loughlin, J. (2001) *Subnational Democracy in the European Union, Challenges and Opportunities*, Oxford University Press, Oxford.

Lyotard, J. (1984) *The Postmodern Condition, A Report on Knowledge*, Manchester University Press, Manchester.

Newman, P. and A. Thornley (1996) *Urban Planning in Europe: International Competition, National Systems, and Planning Projects*, Routledge, London.

Oranje, M. (2002) 'Planning and the Postmodern Turn', in P. Allmendinger and M. Tewdwr-Jones (eds) *Planning Futures, New Directions for Planning Theory*, Routledge, London, 172–86.

Sandercock, L. (1998a) *Towards Cosmopolis, Planning for Multicultural Cities*, Wiley, Chichester.

Sandercock, L. (1998b) 'The Death of Modernist Planning: Radical Praxis for a Postmodern Age', in M. Douglas and J. Friedmann (eds) *Cities for Citizens – Planning and the Rise of the Civil Society in a Global Age*, Wiley, Chichester, 163–84.

Sanyal, B. (2000) 'Planning's Three Challenges', in L. Rodwin and B. Sanyal (eds) *The Profession of City Planning, Changes, Images, and Challenges 1950–2000*, Rutgers, The State University of New Jersey, New Brunswick.

Sanyal, B. (2005a) 'Preface', in B. Sanyal (ed.) *Comparative Planning Culture*, Routledge, London, xix–xxiv.

Sanyal, B. (2005b) 'Hybrid Planning Cultures: The Search for the Global Cultural Common', in B. Sanyal (ed.) *Comparative Planning Culture*, Routledge, London, 3–25.

Schein, E.H. (2004) *Organizational Culture and Leadership*, 3rd edn, Jossey-Bass, San Francisco.

Schönwandt, W.L. (2002) *Planung in der Krise? Theoretische Orientierungen für Architektur, Stadt- und Raumplanung*, Kohlhammer, Stuttgart.

Scollon, R. and S.W. Scollon (2001) *Intercultural Communication, A Discourse Approach*, 2nd edn, Blackwell Publishing, Oxford.

Selle, K. (1999) 'Neue Planungskultur – Raumplanung auf dem Weg zum kooperativen Handeln?', in K.M. Schmals (ed.) *Was ist Raumplanung?*, Dortmunder Beiträge zur Raumplanung, Bd.89, Universität Dortmund, Dortmund, 210–26.

Soja, E.W. (1996) *Thirdspace, Journeys to Los Angeles and Other Real-and-Imagined Places*, Blackwell Publishing, Oxford.

Soja, E. (1997) 'Planning in/for Postmodernity', in G. Benkoand and U. Strohmayer (eds) *Space and Social Theory, Interpreting Modernity and Postmodernity*, Blackwell, Oxford, 236–49.

Thomas, A. (2003) 'Kultur und Kulturstandards', in A. Thomas, E.-U. Kinast and S. Schroll-Machl (eds) *Handbuch Interkulturelle Kommunikation und Kooperation, Band 1: Grundlagen und Praxisfelder*, Vandehoek&Ruprecht, Göttingen.

Triandis, H.C. (2004) *Culture and Social Behavior*, McGraw-Hill, New York.

Trompenaars, F. and C. Hampden-Turner (2005) *Riding the Waves of Culture, Understanding Cultural Diversity in Business*, 2nd edn, Nicholas Brealey Publishing, London.

Williams, R. (1966) *Culture and Society, 1780–1950*, Penguin, London.

Young, G. (2008) *Reshaping Planning with Culture*, Ashgate, Aldershot.

Young, I.M. (1990) *Justice and the Politics of Difference*, Princeton University Press, Princeton, NJ.

PART 2
Planning Cultures in Northwestern Europe

Chapter 4
How German Is It? An Essay in Epistemological Eclecticism

Friedhelm Fischer

The persistent push of the European Union towards harmonising planning legislation is rapidly changing the practice of planning in all member states. Yet much of what at surface level appears like shared common positions and interpretations is sometimes understood in divergent ways in the context of different planning cultures and traditions. The fact that the scope for misunderstanding is often wider than meets the eye can become quite a sensitive issue in international cooperation projects. Seemingly straightforward comparisons of international case studies can be misleading if the particular cultural and institutional background is not sufficiently appreciated.

To mention just one of many fields of 'benign confusion' (Bullock, in Larkham 2004, 75) between English and German architects and planners: Nick Bullock, an expert on international comparisons (Bullock 1985), reminds us that 'the English are fascinated by the German housing reform movement and their social housing structure', but that this cannot easily be transferred to an English context. 'Likewise the Germans are fascinated by building societies and misunderstand them' (Bullock 2004, 75). This indicates that it can be more than helpful to develop a grasp of the different institutional arrangements in their historical evolution and also of the interaction of various actors over time.

Further sources of misunderstanding and complication in the communicative process lie in the differences in intellectual style in which research and discussions are conducted (Galtung 1996). Thus, German straightforward bluntness can clash uncomfortably with English diplomatic reservation, while on the other hand, what is 'perceived as a typically German approach to planning with precision' can form a smooth synthesis with 'Dutch spontaneously-flexible ways of acting' (Stadt Duisburg 2008).

Observations of this kind touch on quite complex issues. As the above examples indicate, the subject matter with which we are dealing ranges from the twilight zone of clichés to something as structured and palpable as the legal and administrative frameworks of planning in different planning cultures. It is at this end of the spectrum, i.e. where we are dealing with the level of formal planning, that we can find a substantial body of work which can help us understand differences and to work across borders.

In this respect, one of the most useful introductions to the European context is Peter Newman's and Andy Thornley's book (1996) *Urban Planning in Europe, International Competition and Planning Projects*, referred to several times in this volume. For the German situation, a similar introduction is provided by Sven Patrick Marx in his 'Europäisches Planungsrecht' (2002). Based on the work of Newman and Thornley, it presents an additional angle on the planning families and focuses on German case studies in the field of public-private partnerships.

Considering the effects of the ongoing harmonization of planning laws at the European level, one might be tempted to attribute little more than historical relevance to the evolution of the European families of planning and administration. But the fact that this would be shortsighted is demonstrated not only by the case studies in these books. Anybody who has worked in an international context will have found that the processes of international cooperation and learning from each others' experience can be further enhanced by understanding more about different planning cultures than what is enshrined in formal frameworks. Another important dimension is 'intellectual style', as the Norwegian sociologist Johan Galtung has pointed out in an essay on 'structure, culture, and intellectual style ... comparing saxonic, teutonic, gallic and nipponic approaches' (Galtung 1981, 817).

The term 'intellectual style' relates to the ways in which 'intellectuals' think, pursue their research, construct their hypotheses, theories and paradigms and also to the way in which they communicate about these in publications and academic discussions. Galtung points out that the remarks in his essay are limited to the field of social science. But to an extent they are undoubtedly valid beyond that realm – even more than 25 years after publication of his essay. Galtung confirms that there does seem to be something 'typical' in the ways Germans behave, interact, organise their lives and their bureaucracy and in their approach to science, as opposed to representatives of other European and certainly non-European cultures.

The present chapter starts off using Walter Abish's novel *How German Is It?* as a reference, and takes a look at the role of clichés about Germany, then employs Galtung's observations to cast a spotlight on what planning history might identify as typically German features of planning culture and, finally, looks at specific German traditions which have left their traces on attitudes as well as on institutional and physical features of the environment – from the Prussian virtues to Ernst Neufert's *Architects' Data*, from the clashes between modernism and traditionalism in the early twentieth century to post-war reconstruction and its repercussions in the recent wave of reconstructions in the twenty-first century.

How German Is It? – A Postmodern City Novel

Let us begin with a consideration of clichés, because this is what is addressed in the somewhat absurd title of *How German Is It?* While the exclamation 'this is typically German!' is a complaint uttered by international tourists competing for a place on the beach as much as by Germans complaining about red-tape bureaucracy, it does not of course make sense to make enquiries as to the degree of just how German something might be.

Figure 4.1   Typically German?

Source: Beach Beds illustration by Hector Breeze, *The Guardian*, 21 June 2003.
© Guardian News and Media Ltd., 2003.

In fact, the title of this essay is derived from Walter Abish's PEN/Pulitzer prize-winning novel of 1982, *How German Is It?* (Abish 1982) At first glance, the book appears to be about life in typical post-war German cities, their glittering glass facades and modern inner-city highways – manifestations of the post-war 'economic miracle'. The cover blurb promises 'an icy panorama of contemporary Germany' and the novel confirms the expectations of many a reader. Yes, yes, by the late 1970s, which is the period in which the novel is

68 *Planning Cultures in Europe*

Figure 4.2 **Front cover of *How German Is It?***

Source: *How German Is It?*, Walter Abish (Penguin Books, 2004). © Walter Abish, 1979, 1980

set, the former omnipresence of moustached wearers of lederhosen, policemen with *pickelhaube* and buxom, blonde Brunhildes, or, in the words of the cover text, 'the tradition of order and obedience, the patrimony of the sabre and the castle on the Rhine' had obviously given 'way to an indiscriminate fascination with all things American'. The clichés could hardly be laid on more thickly. The title of the novel might as well be 'how German can you get?'

Post-war Germany is epitomised in the new town of Brumholdstein. Efficiently modern, glossy, yet imitative, the town appears to be a successful compromise between tradition and modernity. Its steel and glass architecture – though regrettably by no means a 'return to the experimentation of the Bauhaus' – reflects both the blue German sky and 'those clusters of carefully reconstructed buildings that are an attempt to replicate entire neighbourhoods obliterated in the last war' (Abish 2005, 3). However successful the reconstruction may look, Brumholdstein, a metaphor for post-war Germany, stands on shaky ground. It is built on the remains of a concentration camp and one day, as sewerage repairs cause a main shopping road to cave in, a mass grave is revealed, though the reader is left uncertain as to the identity of the corpses exposed – Jewish inmates? German soldiers? American prisoners?

Similar incongruities between surface appearance and what may or may not lie below feature throughout the novel. The celebrated city architect, Helmuth Hargenau, and his rich, trendy friends lead lives as one-dimensionally superficial as any mirrored in the postmodern/super-realist mode – all glossy surface, pure magazine cover stuff. The magazine shots of his life and of his glass buildings mirroring each other are but endless reflections with no real content at all.

The theme is familiar in postmodern fiction and postmodern art alike. The mirror theme and the glossiness equal that in many paintings of Edward Hopper, Richard Estes and Ralph Goings. It is the dazzling, sunny glare which in some of Van Gogh's later paintings almost hurts the eye, and which is associated with schizophrenia.

The mode of representation is not accidental. Literary criticism and psychology have pointed out the parallels between the syndromes in literary fiction, art and pathology and, like a red thread, the theme of split consciousness also weaves through the history of German reconstruction, both in the novel and in the reality of the post-war planning culture; for beneath the upward mobility, beneath the success of an allegedly inexplicable economic miracle were the nightmares buried beneath a layer of silence. As planning historians have become increasingly aware since the 1980s, the pattern of the new Germany was determined long before the end of war, amidst the rain of bombs and bullets – behind the facade of German detachment, to put it in the terms implied by the novel.

The theme of schizophrenia, though employed by many postmodernists for reasons of little relevance for the analysis of the reconstruction period, suggests itself as a descriptive category when dealing with the spirit in which the reconstruction of Germany was conducted. This applies to the psychological repression of the past, to the seeming contradiction between a deeply-felt rejection of the National Socialist past on the one hand and a surprising continuity of the old 'enemy images' (*Feind-Bilder*) on the other (for instance in the realm of anti-urban hostility), and to the connection between construction and destruction. The observation that Albert Speer held both the position of Hitler's Minister of War and that of his Minister of Reconstruction easily lends itself to associations of a pathologically split consciousness.

In the book, the final pages reveal that the protagonist is not who he claimed to be all along. Hargenau is not the son of a famous member of the Stauffenberg group. He has no idea who he really is, and the reader is back at page 1, left to re-evaluate all the information given in the book. That is the point at which it can no longer be overlooked that the book is not primarily about Germany but about the ambiguity and unreliability of labels, about clichés in general.

That blue German sky evoked by the novel exists primarily on tourist posters rather than in a country that has nine months of winter and three months of non-summer (at least before climate change). The novel is peopled by men and women with a curious predilection for black leather and by the archetypal 'German blonde in high heels, a white face, and a shrill, ear-piercing laughter' – obviously the imagined equivalent to the mythical SS girls. Their male companions do not shout *swinehund* and *dummkoff* any more (as they were supposed to do in the war years), but still suffer occasional outbursts of unmotivated violence. Finally, the Liebfraumilch wine which everybody is drinking in the novel would be hard to find in Germany, because it is in fact a product essentially made for export.

Abish, who had not visited Germany before writing the novel, lays the clichés on so thickly and recreates German names in such obvious allusion to the American/British comedy tradition *à la* 'Hogan's Heroes', that none of his readers could take any of this at face value. Or could they? Surprisingly perhaps, a great number of the early reviews recommended the novel to its readers as 'an introduction to the new Germany' and, as late as 2008, the book was still 'hailed for its complex portrait of modern German society' (Barnes and Noble 2008).

While, in essence, the novel can be described as a skilful postmodern play with clichés – which is one of the reasons it received the PEN/Pulitzer prize – it does address unresolved conflicts and traumata characteristic of Germany. Among these is the contrast between apparent perfectionist thoroughness and a tacit substructure of problems with which German society has not fully come to terms even 60-odd years after the end of war. The trauma of the large-scale destruction of German cities in World War II coupled with a guilt-induced 'inability to mourn' (Mitscherlich 1967) in the aftermath of National Socialism caused massive ruptures of identity. This experience has been dealt with in curiously selective ways until the present.

Reconstruction amidst Resounding Silence

For a long time the impression prevailed that the principles of German reconstruction had been the products of a fundamentally new beginning. Thus, one of the early investigations on reconstruction speculated:

> German reconstruction did not have the benefit of early planning during the war. Plans are said to have been prepared by the Nazi organisation of General Speer ... but they must have been based on assumptions as to Germany's future that exploded with military defeat, and the plans were confiscated by the Allies. Some day, when the archives are opened, scholars may find it interesting to reconstruct the Nazi's image of future cities. Meanwhile, this material was unavailable to postwar planners, and there was a great deal of change in planning personnel. (Grebler 1953, 70).

Only in the 1980s did the revelations by Werner Durth and Niels Gutschow spark a wave of research on the continuities and ruptures in planning (Durth 1986; Durth and Gutschow 1988). As it turned out, there had been far less 'change in planning personnel' than assumed. Many of the planners of the National Socialist era had again been in charge of post-war reconstruction. Their skills were very useful in the new situation, because well before the end of war, the experience of the bombardments had shifted 'the Nazi's image of future cities' away from a focus on the well-known megalomaniac architecture to a type of modern urban planning at the height of the international practice (Fischer 1990b).

Breaking the silence surrounding the continuities across the mythical 'zero hour' kept planning historians busy through the 1990s (von Beyme et al. 1992). But then, around the turn of the millennium, the public became aware of quite a different 'realm of silence'. As the scholar and writer W.G. Sebald claimed, German writers had failed to explore the wartime suffering of their own population out of guilt over the horrors committed by their country. There had been 'a tacit agreement ... that the true state of material and moral ruin in which the country found itself was not to be described ... a kind of taboo like a shameful family secret' (Sebald 2003, 10). While close scrutiny showed that there had in fact been literary treatments of the bombings (Hage 2003), the point was that they had found no readership. 'No one wanted to hear of the pain, the destruction, the death. The trauma, though touched on by some authors, was too much, if not for words, then for readers' (Denham 2005, 1).

In a culture which had been totally absorbed, perverted and 'instrumentalised' with all its traditions, institutions and symbols by National Socialism, almost every single concept has had to be re-invented, reclaimed, salvaged and cleaned of its 'brown' connotations – from 'heimat' to marching music and national anthems – or to be discarded as 'ideologically contaminated' beyond repair.

This has been a Tantalus task, which has always born a number of risks such as offending sensibilities, getting applause from the wrong side and equating the incomparable, as became evident in the 'historians' dispute' of 1986 (Fischer 1990c). When, in 1950, the German soccer team entered the stadium for their first international match after the war, there was a minute of silence, because a new German national anthem had not yet been found. Following the omnipresence of the national chauvinist symbols of the Nazi era, Germany was then a country without an anthem or a flag and moreover at a loss which other symbols to use. Silence at very different levels thus seems to have been a recurring feature in post-war Germany.

(Don't) Mention the War

The dynamics of dealing with this dilemma entered a new phase following German unification in 1989. This event is seen as having contributed to a commemorative turn (Niven 2002, 2; Horstkotte 2006, 1) characterised by a renewed interest in discussing perspectives on National Socialism and by 'a great swell of public memory and remembering' (Denham 2005, 1). What was once perceived as a reluctance of Germans to talk about the war – lampooned in the comedy series 'Fawlty Towers' by John Cleese's famous constant admonition 'don't mention the war' – seems to have turned into an eagerness of discussing themes such as war, history and national identity. Recent exhibitions and publications have addressed topics such as 'German Angst' (Bode 2006) and 'German Symbols'. More specifically in the field of architecture, a 'Foundation for Architecture and Building Culture' was founded in 2006/7 as a joint initiative of federal and professional institutions and business. Its task is to 'raise public awareness of the concerns and possibilities of building culture and better highlight the level of proficiency of German planners nationally and internationally' (Lütke Daldrup 2007).

Identity through Reconstruction?

The most visible expression of an altered way of dealing with history is the very recent wave of reconstructing destroyed German monuments. Among the best-known examples of this recent practice are the Frauenkirche in Dresden, the 'reconstruction' of the castle in Braunschweig as a shopping centre, the planned reconstruction of the Berlin castle and the debate on the recreation of a complete 'Altstadt' district in Frankfurt. What is less well-known is that there are more than 100 similar reconstruction projects in all parts of Germany. (Altrock et al. 2008) With respect to this order of magnitude, the reconstruction of buildings and urban structures destroyed a long time ago is a unique phenomenon in the Western half of Europe. It is also to an extent

Figure 4.3 Against sauerkraut and marching musik. Poster for a demonstration against right-wing tendencies

Source: Landesjugendring Hamburg, with permission.

puzzling. This is what motivated the German Federal Ministry for Transport, Building and Urban Development to hold an interdisciplinary conference on this theme in October 2008 and to ask what was behind the desire for recreating harmonious, coherent townscapes through re-construction. Is it an expression of an anti-modern, politically regressive (or even revisionist) reflex? Or is it an appropriate expression of a legitimate interest to re-create *Heimat* – 'where home is'? Behind these questions is a rather heated debate about classic questions of architecture and conservation. How legitimate is the reconstruction of long-destroyed buildings? To what extent is it an attempt to alter a past that is both highly idealised and 'altered to "improve" it' (Lowenthal 1985, 332)? Would modern designs without nostalgia be more appropriate? And who is to decide? Professionals? The 'broad public'? International scholars have noted a 'fierceness of the discussion and a rigidity of opposition between the supporters of restoration and those concentrating on the present and the future, with neither of these extremes offering a satisfying solution' (Vees-Gulani 2005, 14).

Figure 4.4 **Invitation for conference on the reconstruction of lost buildings and spaces 2008**

Source: reprinted with the kind permission of the conference organisers.

While the solution is not going to be found on the following pages either, they are going to try to cast some light on the specific combination of, design and planning issues as well as the political connotations which make up this intellectual discourse and its emotional undercurrents. To this end, we have to go back in the sometimes curious history of German planning culture. In order to discover what may be the distinguishing features of the German debate, let us first allow an outsider, a sociologist, to cast a spotlight on the connections between culture and intellectual style in an internationally comparative perspective.

Johan Galtung on 'Culture and Intellectual Style'

Based on Galtung's previous research on Eastern Oriental and Western civilisation, his essay examines ways of thinking at the level of sub-civilisations. (The reason Galtung refers to Saxonic, Teutonic, Gallic and Nipponic approaches instead of English, German, French and Japanese is that the respective realms of these cultures extend well beyond the associated national borders.) In this sample of cultures, he describes distinctly different ways of thinking, doing research and engaging in discussion – a matter that is likely to be of consequence for intercultural cooperation and for comparative observations on planning cultures in general. Here, the focus will be restricted to the question just which peculiarities might be specific for German culture.

Galtung observes that the Western type of epistemology seems to proceed 'in terms of an atomistic conception of reality combined with a deductive approach to understanding', while

> in the Orient these two approaches mix and blend with a more holistic approach to reality and a more dialectic approach to understanding. Thus the point is made that in the Occident, in extremis, the way of obtaining valid knowledge is by subdividing reality into a number of small parts, obtaining insights about a low number of them at a time, and then linking these insights together to form often highly impressive, deductive pyramids. (Galtung 1981, 819)

Among these pyramids of thought and theory formation, the Germanic or Teutonic pyramid is the biggest, the most solid. 'Teutonic theory-formation is above all purely deductive ... If one has accepted the premises and certain rules of inference, then the conclusion follows ... The teutons are masters of building such pyramids. Mathematics are based on this, so mathematisation may tend to bias the intellectual towards the teutonic style' (ibid., 829). Walter Christaller, who published his central place theory with its mathematically based formulae in 1933 and Ernst Neufert, whose influential 'Architects Data' has been capturing the world of building in precise figures since 1936, would probably agree.

The Saxon intellectual's approach is, by contrast, more oriented towards empirical evidence, less strong at the deductive level. 'The British penchant for documentation is proverbial, as is the US love of statistics.' These are features of a kind of scholarship which is less susceptible to 'faiths and beliefs'. They are not likely to produce 'sweeping theories [or] grand perspectives ... One could even surmise that an average saxon researcher would fall prey to vertigo if a theoretical pyramid rose five centimeters above the ground' (ibid., 828).

Galtung visualises such intercultural differences in a set of figures. The most striking contrast is that between the big Teutonic pyramid and the range of small Saxonic pyramids. As for the Gallic intellectual style, this is characterised

76   *Planning Cultures in Europe*

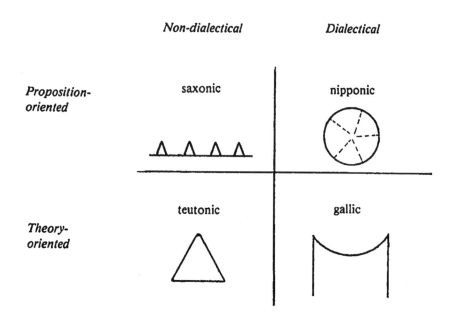

Figure 4.5   Figures of thought, theory formation and communication

Source: Galtung, 1981.

by a dialectic juxtaposition of arguments, 'a stringing-together of words' in an artistic fashion involving 'the use of bonmots, double entendres, alliterations and various types of semantic and typographic tricks such as the reversal of sentences' (ibid., 830).

> The underlying figure of thought would be ... two pylons and between them a hammock suspended. The body comes to rest when the stringing-together of words is suspended between the two opposed poles, with a balanced tension. ... There is a totality to things, a balance rather than a centre ... But the totality cannot be shown through rigorous deduction. It has to be hinted at, one has to dance around it and view it from many angles until in the end its rests suspended between the two poles. (ibid., 831)

A more holistic view reflecting a very different cosmology underlies the Nipponic approach. It leads to a looser way of 'chaining data together [leaving room for] 'inconsistency, ambiguity, [and] contradiction' (ibid., 833, 839). They are represented by the Buddhist wheel.

'The four figures ... should certainly not be taken too seriously' (ibid., 839) But they are useful for clarifying specific features of the four intellectual styles. Again, the focus here is going to be on the Teutonic intellectual style, for which the underlying figure of thought is the pyramid,

> perhaps the steeper the better, even with a basic 'contradiction' on top. Thus, the contradiction between labour and capital for Marx, between Id and Super-Ego for Freud and between Aryans and Jews for Hitler were such key principles, from which an enormous number of conclusions were more or less rigorously deduced. The basic postulate for all three was that the contradiction had to be overcome for the system to 'mature', by labour controlling capital in a mature socialist society, by Super-ego and Id producing an Ego in balanced command of either, and by the Aryans overcoming the Jews, by expelling and exterminating them. From one basic principle very many conclusions were drawn, some of them highly dramatic. (ibid., 839)

As these examples show, 'teutonic theory formation is based on strong and strict dichotomies, and is highly unambiguous. But it puts reality into a straight jacket' (ibid., 829). Sometimes the reality for which the Teutonic intellectual with his strong deductive bias is looking is 'a more real reality free from the noise and impurities of empirical reality' (ibid., 828) Let us now see how these observations can help to cast a light on aspects of German planning history.

Germany's 'Special Path' between Prussian Virtues and Reconstruction

In order to develop an understanding of the 'special path' Germany has taken, we have to go back in history to a point well before the foundation of the modern German state, at least to the Thirty-Years' War (1618–1648). By the mid-seventeenth century, 30 years of war had destroyed more than the economic and physical basis of the state. It had led to almost ubiquitous anarchy and the destruction of the very basis of society. In that seemingly hopeless situation, the state of Prussia adopted strategies for which it was later to become famous among the German states. Designed to pull Prussia, as it were, out of the swamp by its own hair, these strategies included the deductively-derived formulation of the famous 'Prussian virtues', which were later assumed to be German virtues. These included perfect organisation, punctuality, modesty, diligence, rule of law, obedience to authority, reliability, tolerance, thriftiness, thoroughness and others. Myths developed around each of these, each with more than a kernel of truth, and therefore helpful for understanding elements of planning culture. But myths can also be a source of misunderstanding and inappropriate generalisation:

> Since Prussia, and in particular the capital of Berlin, acted as nuclei for the emergence of a German state, characteristic features of Prussia, including its myths, have often been assumed to be typical for Germany as a whole, overlooking the more liberal tendencies in Southern Germany and the completely different traditions in the Rhineland. Similarly, many of the specific features of urban development, planning and architecture in Berlin were assumed to be equally valid for other German cities, particularly from the nineteenth century on. To an extent, this was a result of the sheer volume of publications which dominated the German planning discussion, and explains many a prejudice in the origins and development of urban planning and planning culture in Germany. (Fischer 1990a, 86)

Dealing with these myths of Prussian virtues can entail other risks, too – for instance, if they are taken as absolute principles irrespective of the social context in which they are applied. While the virtues of reliability, thoroughness, efficiency and obedience to authority were to a large extent an expression of a society striving for solidarity following the experience of emergency, they proved equally useful for the expulsion of Polish subjects from Prussia in the 1880s and even for the punctual and orderly dispatch of the trains to Auschwitz. As 'secondary virtues' they lend themselves to be exploited and abused for all sorts of primary purposes, including criminal ones.

Building Big Pyramids of Thought: From 'Gesamtkunstwerk' to 'Total Architecture'

Thoroughness, efficiency and deductive thinking have shaped the German scientific system leaving less room for rule-of-thumb approaches than the Anglo-Saxon system. In the realm of spatial planning, one of the manifestations of thoroughness is the notion of a method of registration and planning for which the term *flächen-deckend* has been coined. There is no short translation or equivalent in other languages for this term. 'Surface-covering' would be the literal translation. It refers to an area-wide, spatially inclusive and comprehensive kind of recording and deduction-based planning.

Walter Christaller's central place theory, Heinrich von Thünen's concept of the rings of agricultural land use and August Loesch's trade centres' model are cases in point. Employed as analytical concepts, which can assist spatial planning, these concepts have proved very useful, and they have developed into cornerstones of regional science. Applied with fundamentalist rigor, however, these tools, like many others, can prove harmful. National Socialism exploited them to plan for a *flächen deckende* 'Germanisierung des Ostens' ('Germanification of the East). The idea was to develop a scientifically based, all-encompassing new pattern of German settlements in the conquered lands east

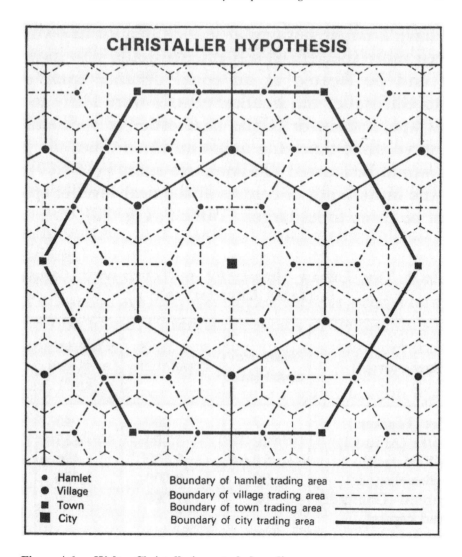

Figure 4.6 Walter Christaller's central place diagram

Source: James H. Johnson, *Urban Geography, An Introductory Analysis*, Pergamon Press, London, 1972, 102.

of Germany designed to replace the historically-grown structures – including the undesired indigenous population (cf. Gutschow *Ordnungswahn* 2001).

Much damage was also done in the Territorial Planning of the former GDR, which left traditional settlements to decay while new prefab centres designed for new monoculture agricultural compounds were implanted in deductively-derived, 'scientifically correct' locations in the name of 'Scientific Socialism'.

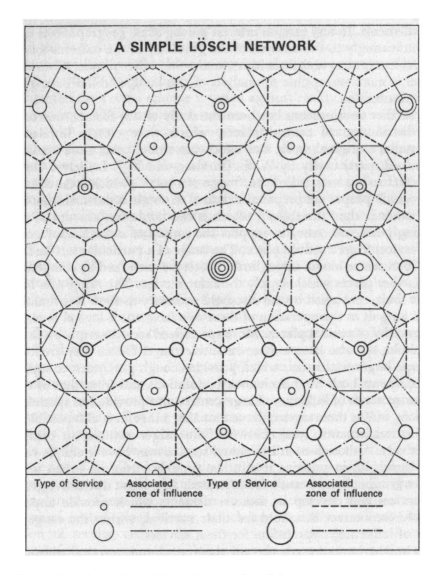

Figure 4.7 August Loesch's trade centres' model

Source: James H. Johnson, *Urban Geography, An Introductory Analysis* (Pergamon Press, London, 1972), 103.

The German inclination towards thorough, comprehensive conceptual constructions – big pyramids in Galtung's sense – is also evident in the notion of the *Gesamtkunstwerk* popularised by Richard Wagner in 1849, which has been influential internationally ever since. In this context, Bruno Taut and Walter Gropius produced their concepts of 'Total Architecture' in the 1920s, aiming

How German Is It? An Essay in Epistemological Eclecticism

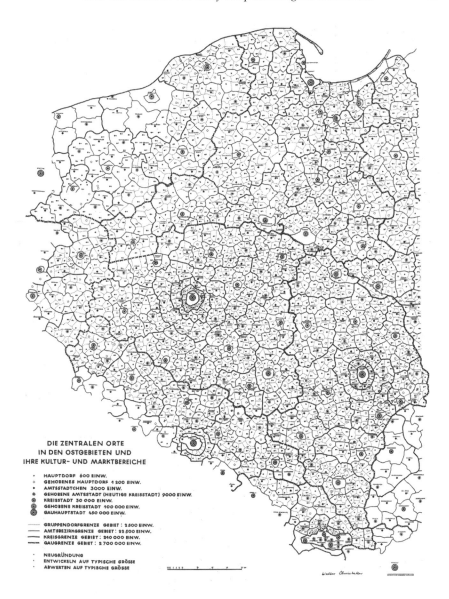

Figure 4.8 Walter Christaller's Central Place Diagram applied to re-plan conquered Poland

Source: W. Christaller, *Die Zentralen Orte in den Ostgebieten und ihre Kultur-und Marktbereiche. Struktur und Gestaltung der Zentralen Orte des Deutschen Ostens*, Vol. 1 (K.F. Koehler, Liepzig, 1941).

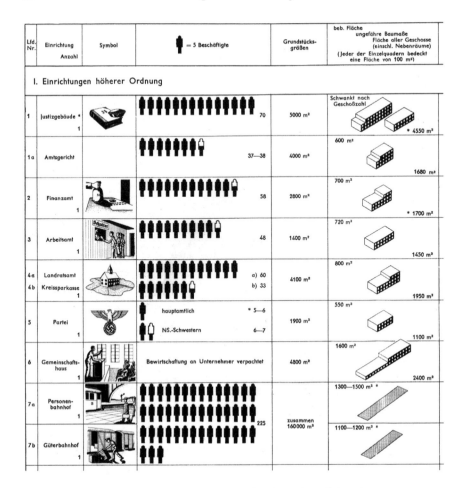

Figure 4.9   Total design for the mass production of traditional towns

Source: Die Neue Stadt, Gottfried Feder © 1939, J. Springer. Reprinted with permission of the publisher.

for a synthesis of all the arts and crafts in a new architecture comprising the whole range of 'objects' from simple tools right through to entire cities. While the term 'total' lost its attraction and relative innocence in Germany after having been used in the context of 'total war', Gropius published his *Scope of Total Architecture* in the USA in 1955. (By the late 1960s, the term was used again in Germany, with less inhibition, e.g. in a book by Fritz Haller entitled *Totale Stadt* (Haller 1968).) The desire for thoroughness and for 'total', area-wide, 'surface-covering' recording as a basis for comprehensive, 'total' design also shaped Gottfried Feder's compendium on mass-producing traditional small cities, 'Die Neue Stadt' (Feder 1939) and, most notably, Ernst Neufert's 'Architects' Data' ('Bauentwurfslehre' Neufert 1936/1970 ... 2008).

By the post-war years, solid foundations were thus laid for the formulation of the norms of Social Housing. However well-intentioned and useful they were, they frequently contributed to uniformity, limited usability (e.g. of balconies opening out to inner-city highways) and unimaginative design (though clearly no unique features in post-war European social housing). In 1956, the strict insistence of the Berlin building administration on the prescribed room ceiling heights drove Le Corbusier to despair in the process of building his 'Unité d'Habitation' in Berlin. In his view, the reason why lower ceiling heights were not acceptable to the German authorities was obvious: they still used to go to bed without taking their *pickelhaube* off.

The way in which Ernst Neufert's *Architects' Data* has been adopted as an essential tool for architects in all parts of the world is an indication for the fact that the underlying systematic thoroughness and the desire to design a world in complete accordance with one unifying set of criteria is by no means restricted to Germany, however influential the German contributions may have been. Nor is the existence of control freaks restricted to the Germany. Their scope of action has increased worldwide since industrialisation, the machine age and the advent of modern science and technology. In Germany, it came to particularly problematic fruition during National Socialism. Much later, the planning euphoria of the post-war decades became a phenomenon that left its traces not only on German cities and thoroughly modernised landscapes (Ipsen 1991) but in most industrialised countries. The potential unlocked by the computer led to unprecedented visions of 'control and planning' (McLoughlin 1973), and urban development as 'a repetitive, industrialised sequence mass production process' became a wide-spread ideal of the planning culture of the 1970s (Fischer 1989, 183). Obviously, building 'big pyramids' is not restricted to the Teutonic realm, although the attempt of applying these constructs to thoroughly shaping a whole world is a different matter.

How German Is It? – Dichotomies behind the 'German Werkbund Dispute'

The increasing uniformity imposed upon the environment by modern society has been recognised to be partly an almost unavoidable consequence of the industrialised production processes and partly the result of conscious design decisions of intentionally repeating the same patterns all over. This was a concern of design and planning culture all through the twentieth century, and a central theme of the 'German Werkbund'. The conflicts between the development of norms and types (*Typisierung*, i.e. stylisation, later sometimes interpreted as standardisation) and the role of artistic freedom, of individual, creative crafts-type elements to be retained in the production process were articulated most acutely in the famous 'Werkbund dispute' between Hermann

Muthesius and Henry Van der Velde at the 1914 building exhibition in Cologne (Mallgrave 2005, 234).

The dispute was embedded in a highly problematic and specifically German discourse on tradition, modernisation and politics during the nineteenth and twentieth centuries. Industrialisation and capitalism were seen to be destroying the natural and built environment as much as the familiar social patterns. In the course of the nineteenth century, criticism of this development, which began with German Romanticism, became increasingly dichotomous in nature, one strand concerned with issues of environment, local culture, tradition and a yearning for the imagined stability of the political systems of the past, the other fighting for social issues and democracy in a socially just society without exploitation.

While the French Revolution had led to liberalisation, industrialisation and a rapidly growing economy, the members of the bourgeois classes profiting from this were also frightened by the violence associated with it. Deeply disturbed by the all-encompassing transformation of virtually every aspect of the social and physical environment, the conservative segments of German society preferred alliances with the established feudal powers instead of running the unknown risk of rapid democratisation. As an early specifically German reaction to this, the movement of German Romanticism, (which developed relatively late compared to its English counterpart) had tried to negate these consequences by looking to the Middle Ages as a seemingly simpler, more integrated period, in which society and the environment had supposedly existed as an 'organic totality'. A new synthesis of art, philosophy, and science were therefore to be combined into a kind of total *Gesamtkunstwerk*. Democracy, by contrast, was seen in this view as an 'impractical theory' leading to a complete 'slackening and degeneration of the nation' (Riehl in Sieferle 1984, 149). The notion of egalitarianism was creating fear among the bourgeoisie. For them, progress and democracy did not simply mean liberation and liberty. They could mean the loss of status and a threat to established societal identities. Rapid industrialisation in the face of agrarian restoration politics spawned an ever growing wave of harsh criticism against any emancipative tendencies; a wave that was clashing hard with the endeavours of Social Democracy and the trade unions.

By contrast, the social interests of 'the Left', their demands for a transformation of traditional structures, for modernity and technical progress as a basis for social change were diametrically opposed to the claims of 'the Right'. In the course of the nineteenth century, 'the social question' had become a cause of 'the Left'. Its members criticised social injustice and political repression and pursued modernity as a synthesis of enlightenment, egalitarianism, science, technology and industry. Concentrating on the social and political realm they were blind to the destruction of nature through industrialisation, the disappearance of a plethora of regional traditions and cultures, the loss of *Heimat*.

Figure 4.10   Slogans of the conservative party of the post-war years: 'Against depersonalisation' in the working class districts and 'Individual home ownership as a bulwark against bolshevism'

Source: © FischerVerlage. Reprinted with kind permission.

What the criticism of the Left was ignoring, was central to the campaigns of the right. The conservative wings of society were in defence of the 'organic' unity of nature and society, community and the individual. To them, social emancipation and industrial mass production meant the end of craftsmanship and quality. They would inevitably lead to *Vermassung* (depersonalisation). This was another key word of the German debate. It meant the loss of personal identity and individual character by the sheer crowding of 'the masses' in the evil urban agglomeration – a notion which lived on well into the post-war period.

While anti-urban sentiment was by no means restricted to Germany (Lees 1985), this tragic dichotomy – the division of attention and priorities between Left and Right in relation to what were in fact the common, joint problems of the transformation of society and environment – was a particular feature of the German discussion. It found particular expression in architecture, urban design and planning. Both parties were critical of the products of nineteenth industrialism such as unscrupulous speculative urban development and in particular of mass-produced stucco facades. These historicist manifestations of the industrial age were most vigorously attacked, on moral grounds too, by the Austrian architect Adolf Loos in his famous essay on 'Ornament and Crime'.

While the modernist avant-garde was projecting deductively derived, logical, and rationalist norms for the cities of a future new society, the traditionalists were looking backwards to the medieval purity of the crafts (like the English Arts and Crafts movement). Both parties developed ideal concepts for the design of their 'ideal' cities. While one party was designing cities of the future – geometric, orderly, functionalist – the other was striving to re-create the traditional European city – organically structured, historically unique, creating *Heimat*. Another feature was common to both: Their concepts were deductively conceived urban designs of an 'ideal type' nature, part of a planning culture that did not seem to take account of any actors in the process of planning and development except for the god-like architect-creator. They were designs of a city unaffected by their economic and political functionality, a city without chaos and dirt, aggression, corruption and speculation – in Galtung's words (1981, 828), products of 'a more real reality free from the noise and impurities of empirical reality'.

'A More Real Reality Free from the Noise and Impurities of Empirical Reality'

These juxtapositions became even more momentous in the precarious situation of the newly founded, crisis-shaken Weimar Republic. The accelerated concentration of the economy and party political confrontation turned the old schools from mere academic groups into robust lobbies fighting for their share of market and capital.

The process of designing a new, socially just world for a new civilisation grew, in Galtung's terms, into an increasingly 'impressive, deductive pyramid'.

How German Is It? An Essay in Epistemological Eclecticism 87

Figure 4.11   Ludwig Hilberseimer: investigations into the modern city (1927)

Source: © Bauhaus Archiv Dessau. Reprinted with kind permission.

One of its essential components was the new modern architecture, 'das neue bauen' – spelled in small letters as part of the spelling reform, which was another part of a comprehensive reform concept designed to shape every aspect of life – 'total architecture'.

In an absurd culmination of ideological conflict termed 'the war of the roofs', the flat roof became a major focus of the clashes of interest between the opponents. Modern architecture was attacked as 'un-German' and subversive, a sign of the 'Decline of the West'. Almost as 'The Internationale' as a musical piece represents communism, the flat roof became a symbol of socially progressive Social Democratic or Socialist positions, much as *Zeilenbau*, the linear row housing type of urban development, did in urban development. The traditional steep pitched roof, by contrast, was seen as a sign of patriotism, of *Heimat*, and of being 'rooted in the soil' (Miller-Lane 1968).

Typical strategies in this war of images included the juxtaposition of pleasantly familiar traditionalist designs with unfavourably photographed modernist buildings insinuating that the latter were but artistically flawed intrusions upon familiar German townscapes. The depiction of the model development of the Werbund International Building Exhibition of 1927, the Weissenhof Estate, as an Arab village, and of those who could not relate to modernist architecture as over-fed bourgeois living fossils of the Wilhelminian era, were signs of a building culture which was resorting to increasingly aggressive means.

88 *Planning Cultures in Europe*

Figure 4.12   The 'Weissenhof Siedlung' estate after completion. Stuttgart 1927

Source: Stuttgart City Archive. Reprinted with kind permission.

Figure 4.13   Attack and counter-attack: cartoons lampooning the 'Weissenhof Siedlung' estate as an Arab village

Source: Stuttgart City Archive. Reprinted with kind permission.

How German Is It? An Essay in Epistemological Eclecticism 89

Figure 4.14   … and exposing its critics as over-fed bourgeois fossils of the pre-war era – 'Nichts fürs Gemüt'

Source: ManfredFuhrich et al., Neue Heimat, Hamburg VSA 1983 s. 72. Reprinted with kind permission.

The notion that the architecture of modernism was causing undesirable disturbances of established German identities and of *Heimat* was then further exploited by the 'blood and soil' ideology of the National Socialist Era. As a consequence, the notion of *Heimat* became a term fraught with reactionary connotations until today (Boa; Palfreyman 2000). This is what the Luxemburg architect Léon Krier was referring to when he pointed out: 'In Germany since the last war, it has become indecent to speak of Heimat. And yet we all come from somewhere and always long to be somewhere. Only when coming from *somewhere* and longing to be *somewhere* can we speak of having a home' (Krier 1984: 101).

Heimat is one of the notions referred to above which has had to be cleansed of its 'brown' connotations. What the architectural face of the new pieces of *Heimat* should look like remains a matter of the ongoing cultural discourse. The rigidity of the connections between architectural form and ascribed political content was a specifically German phenomenon, which persisted for several decades after World War II. By now, it seems to have lost most of its significance. But the underlying structure of argument still reverberates in discussions about *Heimat*, tradition and modernism and the role of planning culture in this context. This takes us back to the questions posed early in this essay in connection with the recent wave of re-construction projects in Germany.

Back to Galtung: Where Do We Go from Here?

In the sense of Galtung's typology, this chapter has tried to construct a couple of smallish pyramids, a bit in the Saxon manner, well aware of the fact that only a few spotlights could be set on a complex matter. By way of discussion – not so much of what has been said as to potential modes of discussion – I would therefore like to let Johan Galtung point out more basic qualities of intellectual style in a comparative manner.

> The saxonic style fosters and encourages debate and discourse. The general spirit is that intellectuals constitute a team, that togetherness should be preserved, that there is a gentlemen's agreement to the effect that 'we should stick together and continue our debate in spite of our differences'. The first discussant will open his/her speech with the usual comment to the effect that 'I greatly enjoyed listening to Mr X's presentation, but ...'.
>
> More likely than not there will be a complimentary, congratulatory point at the end ...The general idea is that very different convictions should be brought together in a debate, be confronted with each other, and ultimately perhaps produce something that is more than the sum of the parts. The other person should be built up, not put down.
>
> Not so in teutonic and gallic discussions. There will be no complimentary introduction even among friends, and certainly not if there is the slightest discrepancy of opinion. Also, nobody will go out of their way to try to find that little nugget, that little element of hope on which to build – on the contrary, the discussants will go straight for the weakest point. That weakest point will be fished out of the pond of words, brought into the clearest sunlight for display, so as to leave no doubt, and for dissection, which is done with considerable agility and talent. Probably most of the debate will be devoted to such aspects, and there will be few if any soothing comments towards the end to put the defendant together again as a human being; no attempt will be made to mop up the blood and put wounded egos together. As opposed to the saxonic exercise in humour and back-slapping on such an occasion, gazes would be somewhat cold, faces somewhat stiff, and a slight element of scorn and derision might emerge from the corners of the eyes. ...The teutonic intellectual simply believes what he says, something his gallic counterpart would never really do. The teutonic intellectual might even come to the point where he believes that his pyramid is a good model of empirical reality and act accordingly ... The gallic intellectual would

consider his model as a metaphor, shedding some light on reality but not to be taken too seriously ...

And thus ends the story: The Teutonic intellectual may become an extremist because he takes his own theory seriously. The Gallic intellectual may prefer a good lunch, with beautifully ornamented conversation as an accompaniment to a splendid French meal. (Galtung 1981, 840)

Isn't it beautiful that we can learn from each other?

Bibliography

Abish, W. (2005) *How German Is It?*, Penguin Books, London.
Altrock, U., G. Bertram and F. Fischer (2008) *Wieder-Aufbau, Stadtidentität und Rekonstruktion im Forschungsprogramm 'Baukultur'*, Final Report to the Ministry for Transport, Building and Urban Development, Manuscript, Kassel.
Bausinger, H. (2000) *Typisch deutsch: Wie deutsch sind die Deutschen?*, Beck, München.
Beyme, K. v., W. Durth, N. Gutschow and W. Nerdinger (eds) (1992) *Neue Städte aus Ruinen*, Prestel, München.
Boa, E. and R. Palfreyman (2000) *Heimat. A German Dream. Regional Loyalties and National Identity in German Culture 1890–1990*, Oxford University Press, Oxford.
Bode, S. (2006) *Die deutsche Krankheit – German Angst*, Klett-Cotta, Stuttgart.
Böhme, H. (1987) 'Städtebau als konservative Gesellschaftskritik', *Die Alte Stadt* 1, 1–27.
Bullock, N. and J. Read (1985) *The Movement for Housing Reform in Germany and France 1840–1914*, Cambridge University Press, Cambridge.
Chadwick, G. (1977) *A Systems View of Planning*, Pergamon, Oxford.
Christaller, W. (1941) *Die Zentralen Orte in den Ostgebieten und ihre Kultur-und Marktbereiche. Struktur und Gestaltung der Zentralen Orte des Deutschen Ostens*, Vol. 1, K.F. Koehler Verlag, Leipzig.
Collett, P. (1993) *Foreign Bodies. A Guide to European Mannerisms*, Simon&Schuster, London.
Craig, G. (1982) *The Germans*, Putnam, New York.
Durth, W. (1986) *Deutsche Architekten: biographische Verflechtungen 1900–1970*, Vieweg, Braunschweig.
Durth, W. and N. Gutschow (1988) *Träume in Trümmern: Planungen zum Wiederaufbau zerstörter Städte im Westen Deutschlands 1940–1950*, Vieweg, Braunschweig.

Feder, G. (1939) *Die Neue Stadt. Versuch der Begründung einer neuen Stadtplanungskunst aus der sozialen Struktur der Bevölkerung*, Bauwelt-Verlag, Berlin.
Fischer, F. (1989) 'Canberra: Myths and Models', *Town Planning Review* 60 (2), 155–94.
Fischer, F. (1990a) 'Berlin: Myth and Model. On the Production of German Planning Ideology in Berlin', *Planning Perspectives* 5, 85–93.
Fischer, F. (1990b) 'German Reconstruction as an International Activity', in M. Diefendorf (ed.) *Rebuilding Europe's Bombed Cities*, Macmillan Press, Houndsmill/Basingstoke/Hampshire/London.
Fischer, F. (1990c) 'Der Historikerstreit und seine Relevanz für die Planungsgeschichte', in F. Lüken-Isberner (ed.) *Stadt und Raum 1933–1949. Beiträge zur planungsgeschichtlichen Forschung*, AG Stadtbaugeschichte, Kassel.
Galtung, J. (1981) 'Structure, Culture, and intellectual Style. An Essay Comparing Saxonic, Teutonic, Gallic and Nipponic Approaches', *Social Science Information* 20(6), 817–56.
Grebler, L. (1965) 'Europe's Reborn Cities', *Urban Land Institute Technical Bulletin* 28(3) Washington DC.
Gropius, W. (1955) *Scope of Total Architecture*, Harper, New York.
Gutschow, N. (2001) *Ordnungswahn. Architekten planen im ‚eingedeutschten Osten' 1939–1945*, Birkhäuser, Gütersloh.
Hardtwig, W. (ed.) (2003) *Utopie und politische Herrschaft im Europa der Zwischenkriegszeit*, Oldenbourg, München.
Haller, F. (1968) *Totale Stadt*, Olten, Homberg.
Ipsen, D. and T. Fuchs (1991) 'Die Modernisierung des Raumes', *1999 – Zeitschrift für Sozialgeschichte des 20. und 21. Jahrhunderts*, Hamburg, 13–33.
James, H.(1990) *A German Identity 1770–1990*, Weidenfeld and Nicolson, London.
Krier, L. (1984) 'Architectura Patriae or the Destruction of Germany's Architectural Heritage', *Architectural Design*, 54, 101–2.
Larkham, P. and J. Nasr (2004) *The Rebuilding of British Cities: Exploring the Post-Second World War Reconstruction*, Working Paper Series, no. 90, Faculty of the Built Environment, School of Planning, UCE Birmingham, Birmingham.
Lees, A. (1985) *Cities Perceived: Urban Society in European and American thought 1820–1940*, Columbia University Press, New York.
Lowenthal, D. (1985) *The Past is a Foreign Country*, Cambridge University Press, Cambridge.
Mallgrave, H. F. (2005) *Modern Architectural Theory: A Historical Survey, 1673–1968*, Cambridge University Press, Columbia.
Marx, S.-P. (2003) *Europäisches Planungsrecht und Public Private Partnerships im Städtebau*, Universität Kassel, Kassel.

Miller-Lane, B. (1985) *Architecture and Politics in Germany 1918–1945*, Harvard University Press, Harvard, MA.
Mitscherlich, A. and M. Mitscherlich (1967) *Die Unfähigkeit zu trauern. Grundlagen kollektiven Verhaltens*, Piper Verlag, München.
Mitscherlich, A. and M. Mitscherlich (1975) *The Inability to Mourn. Principles of Collective Behavior*, Grove Press, New York.
Newman, P. and A. Thornley (1996) *Urban Planning in Europe: International Competition, National Systems and Planning Projects*, Routledge, London.
Neufert, E. et al. (1936/.../2008) *Bauentwurfslehre*, Bauweltverlag/Vieweg, Berlin/Wiesbaden.
Niven, B. (2002) *Facing the Nazi Past: United Germany and the Legacy of the Third Reich*, Routledge, London.
Schmidt, S. (2007) *Hegels System der Sittlichkeit*, Akademie Verlag, Berlin.
Sieferle, R. P. (1984) *Fortschrittsfeinde? – Opposition gegen Technik und Industrie von der Romantik bis zur Gegenwart*, Beck, München.
Vees-Gulani, S. (2003) *Trauma and Guilt: Literature of Wartime Bombing in Germany*, Walter de Gruyter, Berlin/New York.
Vees-Gulani, S. (2005) 'From Frankfurt's Goethehaus to Dresden's Frauenkirche: Architecture, German Identity and Historical Memory after 1945', *The Germanic Review*.

Internet-based References

Barnes and Noble (2008) Synopsis of Walter Abish's novel *How German Is It?*, <http://search.barnesandnoble.com/Eclipse-Fever/Walter-Abish>, accessed 2 December 2008.
Denham, S. (2005) 'Review of Vees-Gulani, Susanne, Trauma and Guilt: Literature of Wartime Bombing in Germany', *H-Net Reviews* (published online January 2005), <http://www.h-net.org/reviews/showrev.php?id=10111>, accessed 7 December 2008.
Horstkotte, S. (2006) 'Werden die Deutschen endlich normal?', *IASLonline* (published online 2 October 2006), <http://iasl.uni-muenchen.de/rezensio/liste/Horstkotte1902459377_1543.html>, accessed 7 December 2008.
Lütke Daldrup, E. (2007) 'Federal Foundation for Building Culture Starts Work' (published online January 2005), <http://www.bmvbs.de/-,1913.994051/Luetke-Daldrup-Federal-Foundat.htm>, accessed 7 December 2008.

Chapter 5
Planning Culture in Austria – The Case of Vienna, the Unlike City

Jens S. Dangschat and Alexander Hamedinger

Introduction

Parallel to the intensification of globalisation processes and ideologies the bigger cities are competing increasingly. However, there are different causes, driving forces and reinforcement processes behind theses unifying dynamics which are impacting the material basis of the cities on the one hand as much as the blueprints and cultural orientations on the other hand. Freedom of capital transfers, enlarged information networks, lowered transport costs, deregulation of former protectionist trade barriers and establishment of free trade and tax zones led to the fact that value-added chains are not linked to specific places anymore but can be decentralised and newly organised. For this reason the selection of the ideal place for every step within the value-added chain can be chosen.

As the former partitioned markets are increasingly open, flexible speculative capital is directed to those places expecting high returns. In the perceptions of the national states and the cities, these cash flows are foreign direct investments, which serve as indicators for international competitiveness (see also contribution of Prehl and Tuçaltan in this volume). The challenge for the cities is to draw as much foreign direct investment as possible in operation within its own boundaries. Cities, therefore, are following an increasing strategic orientation, which is part of the discourse and practice of new urban governance. This results in new strategies for competitiveness by which information, knowledge and interests become integrated and optimised to form 'territorial capital' (Camagni 2007). Strategies are aimed at reaching two main goals: the extension of economic competitiveness on the one hand and social cohesion on the other. Both goals were consistent as social market economy in high Fordism, but seem to become contradictory under post-Fordist regulation conditions.

In this chapter we analyse the development of Vienna, the capital of Austria, which is eagerly looking for a 'third way' of modernisation in these times of rapid changes. Vienna is trying to reconcile its social democratic orientations and values, which are deeply inscribed in its political structures, with an increasingly competitive strategy. Vienna was always 'unlike' the mainstream, either as a latecomer compared to other European capitals or late in its trends as the capital of Austria, very often forming general trends into specific 'Austro'-styles.

Before we analyse the recent planning structures and processes we shall shed some light on the historical past of the recent political-administrative system as much as on economic and social structures the city is facing in the period of the shift to strategies explicitly dedicated to meet the challenges of globalisation. We conclude with a preliminary assessment of the Viennese way of modernisation, particularly summing up the planning approaches.

Fordist 'Red Vienna'

Up to now, the city has been marked by a strong continuity of social democratic governance, which emerged first in the 1920s. In that time, the Social Democratic Workers Party started an enormous and ambitious housing programme as well as social reforms particularly to stimulate the local industry which was in deep economic crisis after World War I. Between 1924 and 1928 local government expenditure was higher than that of the central government (Becker and Novy 1996, 11). The Social Democratic Workers Party invented 'Red Vienna' as a local, ideologically-framed project and social movement, which was completely contrary to the conservative national political strategies. Red Vienna mainly relied on a local form of Austro-Keynesianism and on the establishment of strong links between the party, civil society and the city administration (e.g. via a territorial based party structure).

After World War II, Austria entered the 'golden age' of Fordism (Novy et al. 2001). Austria's form of Fordism was mainly supply-side driven and based on exports to other West European countries. In this period, the Austrian form of cooperatism, called the *Sozialpartnerschaft* ('social partnership'), which shaped policy making in Austria and Vienna up to the 1990s, was created.[1] From the 1960s the economic base of the city changed dramatically. Besides the de-industrialisation process (losses in favour of the regional periphery and the western part of the country) Vienna lost parts of its status as a centre of finance and commerce. The city also lost its status as a centre for commerical headquarters. Nevertheless, economic growth was considerable, thus enabling Social Democrats to rely on the strategy of delivering services of general

---

1 The Austrian form of cooperatism refers to the regulated cooperation of employers and employees' representations in preparing and implementing political decision-making. It is an influential network comprising unions, Chambers of Work, Chambers of Commerce, the Federation of Austrian Industry and the Austrian Chamber of Agriculture.

interest to the public. These strategies and programmes strengthened the already existing clientelism (Becker and Novy 1996).[2]

The 1970s mark the beginning of slight changes in planning concerning urban development goals, organisation and implementation of projects and the relationship between the public and municipal planning (implementing elements of participation). Additionally, the city embarked upon the Viennese way of 'gentle' urban renewal. This is a model which became famous under the heading 'soft urban renewal' implementing urban renewal offices in relatively deprived urban areas.

These developments in urban planning are reactions to the profound economic and social changes emerging at the beginning of the 1970s. But also the ecological crisis and the fact, that also in Vienna first citizens´ initiatives showed up which questioned urban development projects, induced changes in planning policies.

Post-Fordist Restructuration

Economic Restructuration

Austria's entry into the European Union (1994) and by this into the European Single Market has further strengthened the already existing close economic relations with EU member states (most of all with Germany). Moreover, the break-down of state socialism in Eastern Europe changed the geopolitical and economic position of Vienna. Particularly, Viennese firms reacted to the changes in Austria's neighbouring countries by foreign direct investment within the Central European countries. Considerable investments have been made in manufacturing and specialised services (e.g. banking) (Altzinger 1998).

Since 1995, the Viennese economy has shown a more or less modest economic development, which is mainly based on an increase in the service sector. Compared to other cities, Vienna shows a relatively high GDP per capita (€26,500 in 1998, €41,500 in 2005, Austrian average: €31,100[3]). Vienna's

---

2 Clientelism is one of the main features of the Austrian and Viennese political culture. After World War II, Austrians have defined themselves or have been defined as members of the two large people's parties (SPÖ – the Social Democrats, and ÖVP – the Conservative Party) as well as of their at arm-length interest representation organisations (e.g. via obligatory membership in the Chambers of Work or of Commerce). Within these tight structures an exchange relationship of loyalty and allocation of life chances between the public and the representatives of the political system was established. In this way, a really strong system of dependencies and patronage (the patron being the representative of a political party) has been created (Gerlich and Pfefferle 2006, 2004; see also Vettoretto's contribution in this volume).

3 http://www.magwien.gv.at/statistik/daten/grafik/bruttoregional.gif, accessed 30 November 2008.

relatively good economic performance and output is also fostered by a (slightly decreasing) inflow of foreign direct investment (nearly 50 per cent of the national total in 1999) (Giffinger and Wimmer 2005, 97).

In the last 20 years, Vienna's economy has mainly been challenged by the process of industrial restructuring. Firms with high spatial requirements (e.g. metal goods, textiles) closed down; simultaneously, the relocation of firms to the city's periphery – especially the neighbouring districts in Lower Austria, which have displayed high growth rates in manufacturing – and the relocation of parts of the service sector to Lower Austria, changed Vienna's economic structure tremendously. However, some high-tech industrial subsectors and various parts of private or public services remain in the city (e.g., Mesch 1989; Reiterlechner and Schmee 1995; Mayerhofer and Palme 1996).

These developments are mirrored in employment development by economic sector. Between 1981 and 1991 the secondary sector lost nearly 23 per cent of its jobs, whereby the tertiary sector won 20 per cent. The share of people employed in the service sector increased to 81 per cent until 2001, which is again relatively high compared to other European cities. The fundamental job losses in the secondary sector could only be partially compensated by the good development in the tertiary sector. Therefore, the unemployment rate increased, particularly from 5.8 per cent in 1990 to about 9.8 per cent in 2004 (Giffinger et al. 2008, 74).

Social Restructuration

In 1918 the number of inhabitants in Vienna peaked at 2.24 million inhabitants (Bobek and Lichtenberger 1987, 31), which was never reached again in the recent past. After a post-war increase in population, the number of inhabitants had already decreased from the late 1950s – the loss until 1991 was about 250,000 inhabitants, down to 1,540 million. Since then the number of inhabitants has started to improve slowly, speeding up later, between 2001 and 2007 the figures increased by more than 100,000 up to actually 1.678 million inhabitants. The growth is mainly due to international migration resulting in an increase in the proportion of foreigners from 16.1 per cent (2001) to 19.4 per cent (2007).

Moreover, since 2004 the population growth has been due to natural increases – Vienna is the most dynamic region of Austria. The demographic prognosis emanates from a further increase of some 100,000 inhabitants until 2015; in about 30 years the 2 million threshold will be reached again (MA 5 2008).

As one third of all citizens have a migration background, the high migration rates are challenging the integration capacity. The urban administration and the local politicians are still arguing for 'Vienna as a melting pot', which the city had been at the beginning of the twentieth century. Contrary to the ideologies, Map 5.1 shows clear concentrations alongside the western part of the circular road 'Gürtel' and in the 2nd, 3rd, 5th, 10th, 11th and 20th district, which were enlarged and became more intensely populated over time.

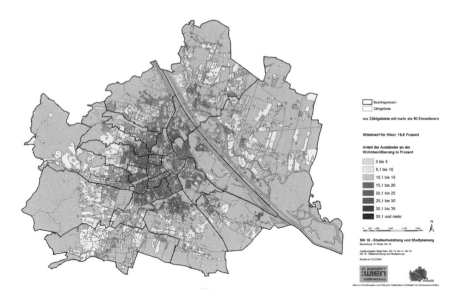

Map 5.1 Spatial concentrations of non-Austrians, Vienna 2008

Source: Kleinräumige Bevölkerungsevidenz 2008, MA 18, Grundkarte: MA 14, MA 41; Datenbasis: OMR (31.10.2008), MA 62.

As result of a regulation of the EU the city reluctantly gave up its policy of excluding non-EU citizens from its communal housing sector[4] in 2006. This is one of the reasons of the concentrations of non-EU households in the less attractive, privately rented old housing stock in the least desired areas. In 1986 about 11 per cent of the Austrian households lived in category D dwellings (without bathroom, toilet and central heating), while some 70 per cent of the Turkish and former Yugoslav households live in these categories. In 2000 this relation was 6 per cent to 41 per cent (Giffinger and Wimmer 2003).

---

4   The communal housing stock – the city of Vienna owns little more than 220,000 dwellings – was originally reserved for Austrians with lower incomes. The earning capacities, however, are checked only at the very beginning of the tenancy and never again. Moreover, the right of abode can be handed down along the direct kindred line without checking the earning capacity of the beneficiary.

Current Approaches to Planning and Urban Development Policies

Political Structures and the Organisation of Planning – Austria and Vienna

Austria The competencies in spatial planning are strongly split between the federal state, the federal provinces and the municipalities concerning legislation and application.

The Federal Constitutional Law (Bundes-Verfassungsgesetz) regulates the allocation of rights and duties between the federal state, the federal provinces and the local municipalities. In Austria no general planning law exists on the federal level. Legal regulations concerning spatial development are laid down in many different legal texts (e.g. Forest Law, Water Right, Federal Transport Network Law, Mining Law). The federal state intervenes in spatial developments mainly by sector planning:

The federal provinces are responsible for the legislation in terms of spatial planning in the strict sense; every province makes its own law (provincial spatial planning law).[5] The application of these laws lies in topics concerning the supra-local level in the field of functions of the province. In topics concerning planning at a local level, the local municipalities are responsible.[6] Important planning instruments on the level of the federal provinces are the regional development plans which are 'comprehensive plans for a region with a[n] [optional] regulation and development policy element' (Schindegger 1999, 199). These plans can be made for the whole province or for subregions only. They may define general guidelines (optional) as well as detailed definitions of environmental protection zones, zones reserved for recreation, agricultural use or mining (obligatory).

On the local level, the implementation of spatial planning lies within the autonomous competence of the municipal authorities, like Vienna. The autonomy is restricted by superior provincial laws concerning planning (regional development plan) and sector planning (federal state and province). Spatial plans of local municipalities are controlled by the state government, which is the supervisory authority. The central planning regulation instruments solely in the hands of the municipalities are the land use ('zoning plan') and building regulation plans. In the land use and building regulation plans the specific utilisation of lots is defined (for housing etc.) after political decision making within local parliament. These plans are crucial elements in the concrete implementation of local and supra-local development plans.

---

5 Bundes-Verfassungsgesetz, Art. 15 Abs.1, (Federal Constitution, Art. 15), http://www.oesterreich.com/deutsch/staat/b-vg_4.htm, accessed 27 June 2003.

6 Bundes-Verfassungsgesetz, Art. 118. (Federal Constitution, Art. 118), http://www.oesterreich.com/deutsch/staat/b-vg_4.htm, accessed 27 June 2003.

Vienna As mentioned above, the political-administrative system of Vienna is deeply marked by the strategies of the ruling party, which – since the 1920s – has been the Social Democratic Party. The Social Democrats received well above 50 per cent of the votes in local elections up to the 1980s. Despite a process of political de-concentration, which hit the Social Democrats in 1991, they won back the absolute majority of seats in City Council Elections in 2001. This situation was continued in the elections to the City Council in 2006.

Vienna is in a unique position as it maintains the status both of a federal province (there are nine in Austria) and a municipality divided into 23 districts. Thus, the Viennese state, represented by the Mayor, the City Senate (City Government) and the City Council consisting of 100 elected members, has considerably wider powers, especially concerning planning, than other municipalities.

Changes in urban governance Mainly as a reaction to an increasing fiscal and legitimation crisis, which started at the beginning of the 1990s, Social Democracy began to modernise and restructure the political-administrative system according to new urban governance: efforts towards new urban governance mainly comprise measures to reform the political-administrative system ('new public management') and strategies to involve the public in planning processes (see Vettoretto's contribution in this volume).

The process of reforming the administration was started at the end of the 1990s. At that time, an administrative group elaborated the specific 'Vienna path' of modernisation, which today mainly relies on the conclusion of contracts ('contract of performance') between the respective City Councillor and the Chief Executive on the one hand and a department on the other hand (as contractor). The main characteristics of this approach are stronger outcome-orientation, decentralised responsibility of resources and controlling (Astleithner and Hamedinger 2003). Today, the Coordination Unit 'Strategy and Communication' of the Chief Executive Office of the administration is in charge of accompanying, coordinating and promoting the reform process.

In addition, outsourcing strategies were carried out in order to improve the fiscal situation of the city (e.g. outsourcing of the 'Wiener Stadtwerke', a formerly state-owned energy supply company in 1999). Concrete nodal forms of this new form of governance are also decentralised planning institutions like the WWFF (Vienna Business Agency) and the WBSF (Vienna Land Procurement and Urban Renewal Fund), which were both founded in the 1980s; furthermore, recently the social agendas of the local state were handed over to the 'Fonds Soziales Wien'. The mission of the WWFF and the WBSF is to manage the rapid utilisation of land and to organise cooperation between the actors of urban planning, especially between private investors, urban planners and citizens. (Novy et al. 2001). Their structures are strongly influenced by the Austrian neo-corporatist tradition.

Participation Since the beginning of the 1980s, an increasing number of participation processes has been implemented, particularly in the context of urban renewal and planning. Primarily, the Viennese experience has been marked by successful endeavours under URBAN I. Although models of direct citizen participation did not come as something completely new to the Viennese administration, the first URBAN programme provided the impetus to experiment with a comprehensive neighbourhood advisory council model for the first time (see also Vettoretto's contribution in this volume). The project ('Grätzlmanagement Yppenplatz') was focused on a central but run-down neighbourhood within the programme area. It involved citizen groups (among them many immigrants) in a mediated development process that produced a neighbourhood development concept covering social, economic and infrastructural aspects.

After the end of the URBAN I programme, the positive experience was carried over into the follow-up project 'Target Area (Zielgebiet) Gürtel' (which receives no EU co-funding), where a citizen advisory council was installed for a much wider part of the city covering even more than the initial URBAN I-designated area. It is composed half of representatives of public authorities and half of representatives of the local inhabitants. Thus, in this particular case, an EU area-based programme has helped to create a new network between public authorities, community representatives, private business and social partners. The programme created the nucleus for further participatory arrangements after the end of URBAN I. For Vienna, the Gürtel advisory council truly represents a new form of grassroots and voluntary sector participation. Oddly, Vienna failed to translate this experience into URBAN II and Objective 2 programmes that are situated in different parts of the city (Wolffhardt et al. 2005). Additionally, current participation efforts can be found in the course of implementing Local Agenda 21 in nine districts.

Resurgence of Strategic Planning

In the 1990s cities began to compete and cooperate strategically ('co-opetition'). As the easternmost Western metropole, Vienna has the edge as the capital and dominant Austrian city/urban region adjacent to the new emerging markets of the Central European and new EU member states.

After a period of concentration on large-scale urban development projects, urban development policies started to favour more comprehensive and strategic approaches to urban planning in Vienna. This is in tune with changes in urban planning also emerging at the beginning of the 1990s in many European cities: integrated, comprehensive, more process-orientated and city-wide strategic planning concepts have experienced a revival in planning at that time (Hamedinger et al. 2008, 14). In Vienna, particularly, the urban development plans of 1994 and 2005 (MA 18 1994, 2005) and the

Strategy Plans for Vienna of 2000 and 2004 (MA 18 2000b, 2004) underline a 'resurgence of strategic planning'.

Urban Development Plans   In the mid of the 1980s the phase of a more strategic planning was established in Vienna. The Urban Development Plan 1984 (STEP 84) was followed by the Urban Development Plans of 1995 (STEP 95) and 2005 (STEP 05) (MA 18 2005), augmented by respective Transport Master Plans and The Green Belt Vienna Programme (1995), defining the forest and meadow belt, agricultural areas, recreational areas and park protection areas.

The Urban Development Plans have no legal binding character. Nevertheless, they are important instruments for steering economic and socio-spatial developments of the city. STEP 1984 was designed by a working group out of all parts of the administrative groups and mirrors the moral background of the early 1980s very well. The first version was discussed and had to integrate more than 3,000 comments before it was exhibited in the Vienna Fair where some 25,000 people were informed. The headline of the plan was 'More quality of life – venturing more democracy'. The plan was predominately concentrated on social development like improvement of the quality of life, social justice, solidarity, richness of urban culture, urban design, cooperation and self-determination (Pirhofer and Stimmer 2007, 73–4). The spatial impact was defined by the topic of 'healthy environment'. Economic and labour market policies – as they dominate the recent planning documents in Vienna as well – only played a minor role and were met predominantly by big infrastructure projects like the underground construction.

At that time, urban renewal was a field where new ideas and instruments had been developed, laying the ground for the 'smooth urban renewal strategy' for which Vienna became well respected (and won some 'best practice' prizes). Settlement growth was said to be restricted to the main axes and within them to the sub-centres which, however, failed, as the instruments were too weak and more pertinently the political will was absent to control the 'freedom of the mayors' of suburbia.

During the next few years new elements were integrated into urban planning, such as housing subsidies and urban renewal, which became increasingly dominant in Vienna. Even though the city started growing again and the culture of urban planning and local state policies changed towards modernisation, competitiveness, deregulation and liberalisation, the city tried to continue the goals of social inclusion and environmental protection.

New commissions were established, such as the Commission for the Urban Development Areas in 1991 ('Beirat für die Stadtentwicklungsbereiche'), the Infrastructure Commission (1994), the Estate Commission ('Grundstücksbeirat' – 1995) and new forms of interest balance were implemented. On the basis of a broad analysis of the traffic situation, an international expert group was established for the Transport Concept.

The Urban Development Plan of 1994 (STEP 94) was a continuation of the dominant traditional value system of the 1960s, with only arguments for environment protection and the development of infrastructure networks (as sustainable cities) added. In its strategic orientation, the Urban Development Plan of 1994 mainly reacted to the new-geopolitical situation of Vienna after the fall of the 'Iron Curtain' and to the assumption that Vienna would grow considerably in the near future. For the first time in urban planning, this plan pictures a planning approach, which is strategic, flexible and conceptualised in order to be open for new conditions in social and economic terms.

This was altered, however, by the Urban Development Plan of 2005 (STEP05) which is not only the result of an increased management orientation, but also a reaction to the European competition which is driven by same means and aiming for the same goals – namely that of finding its own unique selling proposition. The Urban Development Plan of 2005 continues and fosters some of its predecessors. Central strategic goals of STEP05 are: strengthening Vienna's position in international city marketing, developing cooperation in the expanding Vienna region, increasing the share of public transport, and stabilising as well as advancing quality of life in Vienna.

A major invention concerns its spatial strategy: urban development axis building the central point of departure for all planning projects and the backbone of urban development, are supplemented by so-called 'key areas of action'. In the new plan 13 key areas are delineated, because they are seen as hot spots of urban development in the upcoming years. Development programmes, which are tailored for solving the specific problems of these areas, should be elaborated in close cooperation with local citizens and business owner representatives. Hence, for the first time, urban development policy should be more area-based and, consequently, integrative as the work envisaged for the areas will cross administrative boundaries.

Another innovation concerns the process of developing the new urban development plan. Whereas STEP94 was mainly elaborated within the planning administration, the development of the latter relied on the involvement and consultation of citizens, representatives of the private sector, experts and different policy actors. Not surprisingly, also one of the principles mentioned in this plan refers to the idea of participation. Other principles are gender mainstreaming and diversity.

Strategy Plans of Vienna   The Strategy Plans of Vienna are new, explicitly process-orientated, cross-departmental and open plans, which should disclose new development goals and work as motor for innovation and economic development. The general vision should be realised through implementing certain flagship projects of urban development. Furthermore, it should contribute to integrate the various goal systems, measures, instruments and projects in Vienna.

The process of developing the first Strategy Plan for Vienna (MA 18 2000a) started in 1997 under the guidance of the first City Councillor for planning, who was not socialised within the tight networks and structures of the Social Democrats. Broadly speaking, this conservative politician explicitly favoured more business orientated approaches to urban planning. He was one of the main initiators of administrative reforms, which the city embarked upon in 1999. The 'rhetoric' of the Strategy Plan for Vienna clearly pictures his ideological backgrounds: the title of the plan is 'Quality and Innovation'; its main goal is to improve the economic position of Vienna, particularly through changing the image of Vienna. 'However, the economy rises in rank into the changing value system as an equal pole (besides society and environment; note by the authors)' (Pirhofer and Stimmer 2007, 155 [authors' translation]).

The first strategy plan was elaborated in a long participation process, in which all strategic groups of the city administration, institutions of the corporatist network and external experts (also from different universities) were involved. The first draft of the plan was discussed in so-called 'city talks' and in an international symposium with a wider public.

The subsequent Strategy Plan for Vienna (MA 18 2004) was aligned with the strategic lines set out by its predecessor. At the same time, some new strategic goals emerged (e.g. housing, social security). The new focus was also flagged up in the title, 'Strategy Plan in an Enlarged Europe'. A certain 'European turn' and the topic of modernising the administration clearly prevailed in the strategic outline, which indicated that Vienna should be aiming for the development of a dynamic, customer-orientated and efficient enterprise (Hamedinger 2008, 165). Basic strategies which were gone into in more depth were: sustainability, regional cooperation, gender mainstreaming, proactive locational policy and participation. Additionally, the plans' bias towards implementing flagship projects (42 in total) was further strengthened, as it was recognised that some projects mentioned in the 2000 plan had not been realised.

Contrary to the development process of the first strategy plan, the new plan was mainly drawn up within the narrow confines of the city administration, without consulting the public or establishing cross-departmental working groups. Also in contrast to the first plan, the final product was decided on by the city senate in order to raise its legitimacy and to strengthen its importance for the work of all municipal departments.

The advent of area-based, more integrated approaches to urban renewal Since 2000, Vienna has experimented with new approaches to urban renewal, which should be more area-based, participatory and integrative. As a result of an evaluation on the work of the urban renewal offices, carried out in the course of the 25th birthday of urban renewal offices in Vienna, a serious reorientation process started concerning the organisation, tasks and competences of these offices. As a first step towards enforcing new public management measures in urban renewal, a small project of local area management was established in the district of Ottakring. Furthermore, the internal discussion process to reconfigure urban renewal offices was continued. In 2001, new urban renewal offices were founded, which are in charge of especially accompanying and supporting council-owned residential houses.

In 2002, these debates were strongly influenced by EU Regional Policies as, for the first time, two relatively deprived urban areas in the second and 20th district of Vienna became eligible for funding within the EU Objective 2 programme. These areas were selected as they showed a high population density, high unemployment rates and a large share of low-income jobs. In these areas the number of non-Austrians (38 per cent) was considerably above the Viennese average.

In the course of implementing the EU programme two local area managements ('Grätzlmanagement') were set up. These pilot projects were closely linked to the strategy of modernising the administration (top-down modernisation), simultaneously they were based on local mobilisation, participation and self-organisation (bottom-up). One aim was to realise integrative bottom up planning processes involving various actors, from individuals to investors, municipalities and other organisations. Hence, both local area managements aimed at renewing the urban areas using the endogenous potentials and resources of the areas (GB 2, GB 20 2007, 19).

The organisational structure of the local area managements was new compared to other urban renewal approaches, because the Vienna Business Agency (WWFF) was responsible for managing and implementing the programme. Additionally, a local area advisory council was established as a supervisory board, consisting of representatives from the municipal departments, the City Planning Bureau, the district chairman, local area managers and elected citizens (up to 50 per cent of the full members).

The Objective 2 programme provided some possibilities for network-building (especially through the concept of local areas management, which creates some participation opportunities for the local inhabitants), but so far has not lived up to the expectations of prospective project carriers and interested non-governmental organisations and citizen groups. It seems that the main causes for this failure to use the current area-based programmes to extend participatory structures are a lack of interest in the governance potential (as the area-based EU programmes are seen rather as a financial opportunity), a cumbersome departmental structure that prevents a clear leading role of one administrative unit, and the delegation of key operational tasks to an arm's-length institution (WWFF) that regards EU programmes as a sideline to its overall agenda.

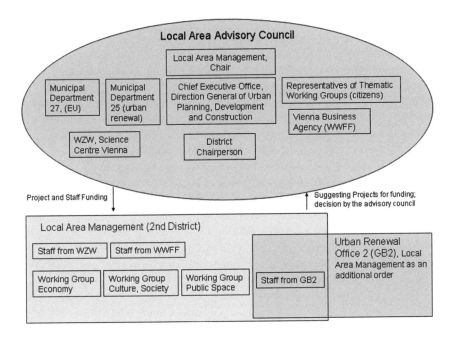

Figure 5.1   Organisation of the 'Grätzlmanagement Volkert- und Alliiertenviertel 2004'

Source: Grätzlmanagement Volkert- und Alliiertenviertel 2004 (authors' translation).

Regional Planning

Vienna as a municipality and a federal province has had a delicate relationship with the suburban municipalities of Lower Austria ever since and therefore has never developed a profound and long lasting culture of urban-suburban cooperation.

Without having established a proper, politically high ranking authorised urban-suburban policy, Vienna –a city at the very edge of Western Europe – was the driving institution to engage at the turn of the century for a more far reaching regional model on European scale. Vienna became the 'capital' of the Central European Core Region (CENTROPE), which is the only one in Europe that covers parts of four European national states (as well as Austria, it also covers the Czech Republic, Slovakia and Hungary) where the major cities are Bratislava (SLK), Györ (HUN), Brno (CZ) and St Pölten, the capital of Lower Austria (A). CENTROPE was officially established on 22 September 2003 under the headline 'A growing togetherness – together we are growing'. The main – some say the only – aim is the strengthening of the economic region on the basis of the urban network – the term 'co-opetition' is explicitly used in STEP 05. Officially it is said that this region might develop regional models – de

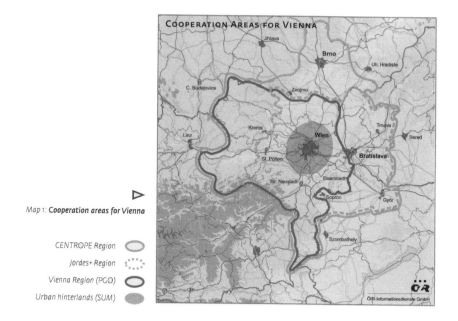

Map 1: **Cooperation areas for Vienna**

CENTROPE Region
Jordes+ Region
Vienna Region (PGO)
Urban hinterlands (SUM)

Map 5.2   Vienna's different Planning Regions

Source: MA 18 2005b, 18 (Stadtplanung Wien) Urban Development Plan Vienna 2005, Short Report, Vienna.

facto, however, Vienna tries to benefit as much as possible from the emerging markets of the new member states, as their economic strength is developing in the capital regions and in the border regions to the older EU member states.

The backbone of CENTROPE is the twin city relation between Vienna and Bratislava, which the Austrian capital clearly wants to dominate. Therefore, transport infrastructure, the relation of the economic centres, the R&D potentials and the way to open up the respective labour markets[7] are the most important subthemes. Other themes are cultural heritage and the protection of natural resources. A further aspect of interest to Vienna is to strengthen the urban labour markets against the suburban markets, which became strong in the past through large concentrations of shopping malls, office parks, logistic and entertainment centres.

Another aspect is that, not only does cooperation within the single urban regions need to be improved, but also cooperation between the three federal provinces Vienna, Lower Austria and Burgenland (together they formed the Vienna Region) to define national interests, which had always been over-

---

7   The relations of the levels of salaries between Vienna and Bratislava are about 4:1 with some differences between the branches, but with a slight convergence.

estimated. The infrastructure systems in particular, traditionally separated due to the political blocks, needed integrating. This was done much more quickly on the side of the new member states than on the Austrian side.

One effect of the integration strategies on the European level has been the establishment of two city-suburbia management institutions (SUM North-East, SUM South) formed between the border districts of Vienna, the micro-regions and municipalities in Lower Austria, the Regional Management of Lower Austria and the Planning Community East (PGO). SUM North-East is of most interest as, in this subregion, future developments will be allocated linking Vienna and Bratislava. SUM South's main interest is to keep green and open land in the densely suburbanised area.

The main planning goals in CENTROPE are particularly orientated to controlling suburban sprawl (stopping it entirely is believed to be unrealistic) in suburban centres at the intersections of the high-ranking transport lines and to safeguard public green and open spaces. The organisation should be based on flexible forms of inter-municipal agreement processes, including joint development companies and the re-orientation of umbrella institutions and financing systems like housing subsidies, high-ranking infrastructural development (like motorways, TEN etc.), land division policies and financial balance.

Conclusion: Is Vienna Really Different?

Red Vienna developed a certain political culture in the 1920s which has continued to shape urban governance up to the present day. The core of the political culture was based on clientelist relationships between local government and citizens, the high concentration of decision processes in the administration and within the extended structure of the ruling party (stretching to banks, insurances, construction firms, etc.), the Austrian form of cooperatism ('Sozialpartnerschaft') and the provision of services of general interest to the public (close to 70 per cent of the population live in publicly-supported forms of housing, of whom nearly half live on council housing estates). Clientelism is a slowly altering but still dominant force in Viennese political culture. In particular, it is an 'invisible' obstacle for establishing participation processes in Vienna. The 'Sozialpartnerschaft' has lost importance in policy making due to the above-mentioned processes of economic, social and political restructuring. But conflict avoidance and consensus building, which are important features of the Viennese political culture rooted in this partnership, still have some influence on planning procedures and planning strategies, too. So, these characteristics are still very prominent on the political agenda.

The shift from government to governance, therefore, is a complex and contradictory process because of the existence of these deeply rooted habits and practices (Novy et al. 2001, 131). The urban government/governance still is state-centred (see also the contribution of Serraos et al. in this volume). In spatial planning, simultaneous forms of 'old' government and new governance can be detected as top-down planning approaches interwoven with bottom-up integrated area development. Planning procedures are very selective and they still do not use the full creative potential of participation. The Social Democrats are avoiding more open planning procedures and the unlocking the system to allow participation of more actors, as this could mean that they would partially lose control over the development of the city.

However, particularly in the new strategic urban development plans, the advent of more integrated and more area-based approaches in urban renewal and efforts to foster participation processes as well as to strengthen regional cooperation (CENTROPE) indicate certain shifts in urban planning. These shifts mainly embody:

- a strategic re-orientation in planning concepts, predominantly taking account of the need to increase the city's competitiveness and to modernise the administration, and at the same time, referring to the need to improve social cohesion;
- new ways of incorporating citizens and business representatives into planning procedures (albeit very reluctantly); and
- the emergence and use of more cooperative instruments in urban renewal and regional development.

Bibliography

Astleithner, F. and A. Hamedinger (2003) 'Urban Sustainability as New Form of Governance: Obstacles and Potentials in the Case of Vienna', *Innovation* 16(1), 51–75.

Altzinger, W. (1998) 'Austria's Foreign Direct Investment in Central and Eastern Europe: "Supply Based" or "Market-Driven"?', Department of Economics, Vienna University of Economics and Business Administration, Working Paper No. 57, Vienna.

Becker, J. and A. Novy (1996) 'Territorial Regulation and the Vienna Region: a Historical-Geographical Overview', *IIR-Discussion* 54, Vienna University of Economics and Business Administration, Vienna.

Bobek, H. and E. Lichtenberger (1987) *Wien – Bauliche Gestalt und Entwicklung seit der Mitte des 19. Jahrhunderts* 1, 2nd edn, Schriften der Kommission für Raumforschung der Österreichischen Akademie der Wissenschaften, Vienna.

Camagni, R. (2007) 'Towards a Concept of Territorial Capital', paper presented at the joint 47th ERSA-congress and ASRDLF (29 August–2 September 2007), Paris.

Gebietsbetreuung Leopoldstadt and Gebietsbetreuung Brigittenau (2007) *Grätzlmanagement in Wien – ein Erfahrungsbericht*, Vienna.
Gerlich, P. and R. Pfefferle (2006) 'Tradition und Wandel', in H. Dachs, P. Gerlich, H. Gottweis, H. Kramer, V. Lauber, W.C. Müller and E. Tálos (eds) *Politik in Österreich*, Manz, Vienna, 504–11.
Giffinger, R. (1999) *Wohnungsmarktbarrieren und Stadtentwicklung*, Birkhäuser, Basel.
Giffinger, R. and H. Wimmer (2003) 'Kleinräumige Segregation und Integration', in H. Fassmann and I. Stacher (eds) *Österreichischer Migrations- und Integrationsbericht*, Drava Verlag, Klagenfurt, 78–86.
Giffinger, R. and H. Wimmer (2005) 'The Meaning of City-to-City Cooperation: Lessons from Vienna', in R. Giffinger (ed.) *Competition between Cities in Central Europe: Opportunities and Risks of Cooperation*, ROAD, Bratislava, 89–107.
Giffinger, R., J.S. Dangschat, A. Hamedinger, M. Krevs, N. Pichler-Milanovic, D. Djordjevic and S. Subotic (2008) 'Challenges of Urban Governance: Planning Efforts, Cooperation and Participation', *Territorium* 8, Belgrade, 66–100.
GM VAV (2004) *Grätzlmanagement Volkert- und Alliiertenviertel: Grätzlentwicklungskonzept Volkert- und Alliiertenviertel*, Vienna.
Hamedinger, A. (2008) 'Strategieorientierte Planung in Wien', in A. Hamedinger et al. (ed.) *Strategieorientierte Planung im kooperativen Staat*, VS Verlag für Sozialwissenschaften, Wiesbaden, 151–77.
Hamedinger, A., O. Frey, J.S. Dangschat and A. Breitfuss (eds) (2008) *Strategieorientierte Planung im kooperativen Staat*, VS Verlag für Sozialwissenschaften, Wiesbaden.
MA 5 (Stadt Wien, Statistik) (2008) Bevölkerungsentwicklung, -struktur und -prognose-Statistik, <http://www.wien.gv.at/statistik/daten/pdf/beventw-struk-prog.html>, accessed 24 November 2008.
MA 18 (Stadtplanung Wien, MA18) (1994) *Stadtentwicklungsplan 1994*, Wien.
MA 18 (Stadtplanung Wien, MA 18) (2000a) *Stadtregion Wien*, Werkstattberichte, Band 33.
MA 18 (Stadtplanung Wien, MA 18) (2000b) *Qualität verpflichtet – Innovationen für Wien. Strategieplan für Wien*, Werkstattberichte, Band 39.
MA 18 (Stadtplanung Wien, MA 18) (2001) *Urban Development Report 2000 – Contributions to Update the Vienna Urban Development Report*, Werkstattberichte 38A.
MA 18 (Stadtplanung Wien, MA 18) (2004) *Strategieplan Wien 2004*, Vienna.
MA 18 (Stadtentwicklung Wien, MA 18) (2005a) *STEP 05 – Stadtentwicklung Wien 2005*, Vienna.
MA 18 (Stadtplanung Wien, MA 18) (2005b) *Urban Development Plan Vienna 2005*, Short Report, Vienna.

Mayerhofer, P. and G. Palme (1996) 'Wirtschaftsstandort Wien: Positionierung im europäischen Städtenetz', Studie des WIFO im Auftrag der Bank Austria AG, Wien.

Mesch, M. (1989) 'Beschäftigungsentwicklung- und struktur im Raum Wien 1970 bis 1989', *Wirtschaft und Gesellschaft* 15(3), 349–88.

Novy, A., V. Redak, J. Jäger and A. Hamedinger (2001) 'The End of Red Vienna: Recent Ruptures and Continuities in Urban Governance', *European Urban and Regional Studies* 8(2), 131–44.

Pirhofer, G. and K. Stimmer (2007) *Pläne für Wien. Theorie und Praxis der Wiener Stadtplanung von 1945 bis 2005*, <http://www.wien.gv.at/stadtentwicklung/planungsgeschichte/index.htm>, accessed 18 November 2008.

Reiterlechner, K. and J. Schmee (1995) 'Die Entwicklung der Arbeitsstätten und Beschäftigten im Raum Wien', *Materialien zur Wirtschaft und Gesellschaft*, No. 56, AK Wien.

Schindegger, F. (1999) *Raum.Planung.Politik. Ein Handbuch zur Raumplanung in Österreich*, Böhlau, Vienna.

Wolffhardt, A., H. Bartik, R. Meegan, J.S. Dangschat and A Hamedinger (2005) 'The European Engagement of Cities – Experiences, Motivations and Effects on Local Governance in Liverpool, Manchester, Vienna, Graz, Dortmund and Hamburg', in A. Antalovsky, J.S. Dangschat and M. Parkinson (eds) *European Metropolitan Governance. Cities in Europe – Europe in the Cities*, Europaforum, Vienna, 65–109.

Chapter 6
Visualising Spatial Policy in Europe

Stefanie Dühr

Introduction

The conceptualisation of the territory through spatial images is an integral part of spatial planning. The illustration of spatial policy options through maps and other cartographic representations can be very powerful both in the planning process and in communicating the key messages of planning strategies. The product of the planning process – the final key diagram or policy map – can help to raise awareness for certain spatial issues and stimulate action at lower tiers of government, or within the private sector. During the planning process, the communicative power of policy maps can support the discussion by revealing different parties' priorities for spatial strategies (Healey et al. 1997). Cartographic representations can help to set the agenda and shape discourses, but they can also be used to manipulate other participants in the process by distorting or highlighting certain facts (Pickles 1992; Neuman 1996, 2000). The decision of what should be 'put on the map', and how it is going to be presented, can empower certain interests over others and influence decision-making.

In most traditions of spatial planning, planning policy documents involve a symbolic representation of the territory in the form of icons, diagrams and maps. Yet, the style and content of cartographic representations of spatial policy varies considerably across Europe. These differences in visualising spatial policy have over the past years regularly contributed to controversial discussions among EU member states when discussing joint spatial development frameworks for transnational territories (see Dühr 2007). The visualisation of spatial policy is deeply rooted in a planning culture and much of planning practice in relation to mapping therefore remains unreflected.

Against the background of ongoing territorial cooperation in Europe, the focus of this chapter is on analysing the differences in visualising strategic spatial policy in the Netherlands, Germany and England. The chapter concludes with a discussion of the importance of planning traditions of visualising spatial policy for future cooperation processes on transnational spatial planning in Europe.

Spatial Planning and Cartographic Representations

The planning literature has only recently given more attention to the role of spatial images (e.g. Dühr 2007; Jensen and Richardson 2004; Healey 2007). This is surprising as maps are powerful instruments in planning processes, but it reflects the traditional understanding of planning as a rational process with maps providing objective and unbiased representations of reality. The communicative turn in planning has, however, also prompted a recognition that the style of spatial images may be key to understanding spatial planning traditions as they 'are forms and crystallizations of the thought of ... planners as they go about their work' (Söderström 1996, 252).

In the cartographic literature, the discussion on the socially-constructed rules and the way in which they affect map-making has been strongly influenced by the work of J.B. Harley (1989). He argued that maps consist of two power structures: the 'internal' power of maps refers to the cartographic process of information selection, generalisation and schematisation, and thus the power that cartographers have over what is depicted. The 'external' power, according to Harley (1989), is the power of non-cartographers over cartographers. It relates to the institutional aspects of map production, the question of who has commissioned the map and who is involved in the process of producing it. There are many largely unspoken rules about map production that reflect the values of the culture within which the map has been produced (such as positioning of the territory in the centre of the map) as well as power structures and political interests that influence the cartographic process. Only by 'deconstructing the map' (Harley 1989) and a deeper analysis of spatial images can such relationships be revealed.

Pickles (1992), in a similar vein, proposed to treat maps as being constructed of two interrelated structures: one being graphical, the other linguistic. Whereas the graphical structure of the map and the effective use of symbols and graphic variables has been subject to extensive study over the last decades, the linguistic components (or the context in which the map was prepared) have been largely ignored by cartographers and geographers alike until more recently. However, according to Pickles (1992), the graphical and linguistic structures of a map are almost inseparable from each other, with the linguistic elements being embedded within the image. This reflects an understanding that maps 'do not communicate so much as provide a powerful rhetoric, and therefore can be critically examined as texts themselves' (Crampton 2001, 238). It implies that it is impossible to separate the 'technical' procedures for the preparation of cartographic representations from the social and political uses to which those representations are put in the outside world (see also Gullestrup's contribution in this volume). This view acknowledges the persuasive power of representations in winning over public opinion and to coordinate action by using a certain commonly accepted code of representation that communicates the legitimacy of planning policies or intended actions (Söderström 1996).

Maps are thus by no means value-free and unbiased representations of reality. Rather, cartographic representations of spatial policy are expressions of political interests that may or may not be easy to identify. Moreover, Söderström (1996) has pointed out that the principle of zoning and the planning techniques available since the 1920s had an important (and largely unreflected) side effect on planning cartography as

> what resisted graphic treatment would be slowly pushed into the background, so that the diffusion of zoning ... corresponded to the elaboration of a form of urban planning which essentially depended upon visualizations. This does not mean that urban planning was limited to dealing only with the visible forms of the city, but it does mean that the elements dealt with by urban planning would be taken into account all the more readily if they could be visualized. The passage through graphic representation became a condition of entry into the urban planner's laboratory. (Söderström 1996, 266)

Many of the factors that influence the design and use of cartographic representations in planning are thus historically rooted and have evolved over time, and many aspects of map production in spatial planning in Europe therefore remain largely unreflected (see also Fürst's contribution in this volume). An important role play the dominant professions in planning, which are influenced by the organisation of planning and likewise shape planning practice, as they influence the ability of a planning tradition to 'think spatially'. For example, the use of cartographic representations is well established at most or all levels of planning in member states that follow a comprehensive integrated approach to planning (CEC 1997) as – it could be argued – there is a strong emphasis on streamlining and clarifying information for lower levels of planning. Emphasis is also usually put on cartographic representations in those member states which follow the 'urbanism' tradition that is dominant in the Mediterranean countries. This could be explained through the dominance of architects in the planning domain.

Healey (2006) also attributes great importance to the historical and geographical context to explain a planning tradition's 'spatial consciousness'. She argues that in the mid-twentieth century, planning policy cultures in Europe were intellectually dominated by concepts of urban form and physical structure, but the capacity of these concepts to 'travel' and interrelate with wider policy cultures and political assumptions varied between countries. A spatial consciousness informed by physical planning concepts was strongly developed in the Netherlands, underpinned by geographical and technical necessities and a strong multi-level state. Within France and Germany, notions of settlement hierarchy and regional identity were sustained by the longstanding cultural recognition of local territorial identities. In the UK, planning was focused on the defence of the countryside.

However, the force of sectoral policy development and the growing influence of neoliberal economics in national politics and administration has undermined the traditional 'spatial consciousness' associated with planning (sse also contributions of Tynkkynen and Serraos et al. in this volume). Planning practices in the 1970s and 1980s moved increasingly away from plans and strategies to focus on projects and regulations, and traditional spatial concepts were sealed in governance processes, often without a legitimising intellectual discourse to support or refresh them. Healey (2006) argues that this lack of explicit spatial consciousness was particularly strong in highly fragmented states where individual property owners were privileged, as in Belgium, or in highly centralised states, such as England, where in addition public policy has been strongly shaped by the commercial and financial sectors. Recent efforts to re-awaken a spatial consciousness in such contexts have been problematic. For example, in Flanders, Albrechts (2001) has highlighted the enormous political effort needed to create a momentum behind a capacity to 'see' the Flanders region/state in spatial terms.

The spatial concepts used and the approach of a planning tradition to visualising spatial policy are thus historically rooted, yet have over time also strongly been shaped by the wider geographical, socio-economic and political context (see also contribution of Knieling and Othengrafen in this volume). What emerges in contemporary spatial plans, thus, may be a combination of the traditional 'core' of a planning culture, complemented by more recent changes to the understanding of planning and planning responses and instruments.

The Visualisation of Spatial Policy in the Netherlands, Germany and England: A Comparative Perspective

There is considerable variation in how strategic spatial planning is organised in different European countries, and these differences are also reflected in the design, content and use of policy maps (Dühr 2007). In this chapter, strategic spatial policy maps at regional levels in the Netherlands, Germany and England are analysed with a view to identifying differences in the planning traditions' approach to visualising. Following a brief introduction to the three planning systems and the strategic planning instruments at regional level, the graphic and linguistic structure of spatial policy maps in statutory regional plans are analysed in a comparative manner.

Undoubtedly, the scope of a planning system affects the themes covered by planning instruments and ultimately determines how comprehensive and integrated policy maps are (Dühr 2007). While the Dutch and German planning systems have traditionally sought to achieve spatial integration (albeit through different mechanisms), the English planning system has for many years been much more sectoral in focus.

Spatial Planning in the Netherlands, Germany and England: A Brief Introduction

The Netherlands is a decentralised unitary state, and planning is conducted at the national, provincial and local levels. Supra-local spatial plans are indicative and non-binding on citizens and generally also on public authorities, although national government funding ensures a considerable level of control over planning at sub-national levels of government (Kragt et al. 2003). National framework legislation identifies the planning instruments at different levels and the procedures for their preparation, but prescribes little in terms of content of spatial policy or cartographic representation.[1] National Spatial Strategies have been prepared since the 1960s and provide the comprehensive conceptual and policy framework for provincial and local-level plans. The *Streekplannen* of the 12 Dutch provinces give a vision of the future spatial development of the territory, and contain a policy map (usually in scale 1:50,000 or 1:100,000) as well as an explanatory text with the results of the analysis and policy statements.

The German approach to spatial planning reflects the federal system and is more regulatory than planning in the Netherlands (see also Fischer's contribution in this volume). Supra-local spatial planning in Germany, *Raumordnung* ('spatial ordering'), is understood as comprehensive planning aimed at coordinating the spatial impacts of various policy sectors. The *Bund* (federal level) has limited competences for planning and spatial policy is therefore set out in non-binding 'guidelines' that are devised jointly by the federal government and the *Länder* (federal states) (see BMVBS 2006). The planning system thus mainly operates at the level of the *Land* and below, where *Landesentwicklungsprogramme* or *Landesentwicklungspläne* (*LEPros/LEPs*) (state development programmes or plans) are prepared. In some *Länder* there are also provisions for *Regionalpläne* (regional plans) for sub-territories of the federal states. Spatial plans at *Land* level normally contain broad statements of development intentions covering issues such as population projections, settlement hierarchies and priority areas. Federal legislation regulates the content of *Länder* and regional spatial plans and that these have to be presented on a topographic map base, although there is flexibility with regard to the symbolisation. The *LEPs/LEPros* comprise concrete spatial and sectoral objectives for the entire *Land* illustrated at a scale of usually 1:200,000–1:500,000. *Plankarten* ('plan maps') at this level are binding on lower-level public authorities. They are not site-specific but should

---

1   The revision of the Spatial Planning Act, which came into force on 1 July 2008, makes provisions for replacing the existing spatial planning instruments at national and provincial levels with 'spatial visions'. At the time of writing (August 2008) the implementation of the reform was underway. This chapter therefore refers to the planning system and instruments prior to July 2008.

rather provide a guiding framework and leave lower planning tiers (sectoral planning and development planning) enough scope for specification. The map is supported by an explanatory text (which is usually non-binding).

The United Kingdom (UK) is a unitary state, but it includes four countries (England, Wales, Scotland and Northern Ireland) and three legal systems. There is no written constitution for England or the UK, and rights or duties in relation to spatial planning are thus defined by laws that can be changed relatively easily. The overriding comparative characteristic of the English planning system is that of discretion in decision-making: national and regional guidance and local policy instruments are the primary consideration, but are not legally binding. In the late 1990s, a major reform of the planning system aimed at establishing a more comprehensive spatial planning system. Policies and guidance at national level, set out in *Planning Policy Statements* (*PPSs*), however still provide a largely non-spatial framework. There is no national spatial plan for England, and the system is – despite devolution efforts – still centralised. The eight English regions have to prepare integrated *Regional Spatial Strategies* (RSSs). RSSs identify the scale and distribution of provision for new housing and priorities for the environment, transport, infrastructure, economic development, agriculture, minerals and waste treatment and disposal. The preparation of integrated spatial strategies has not been easy in many regions as sectoral demarcations are strong, and there has been criticism that the new regional plans may fall short of expectations (Counsell et al. 2006).

Spatial planning professionals in the Netherlands and Germany come from a wide variety of disciplines, including law and economics. Nevertheless, the importance attached to 'planning maps' in statutory spatial planning in Germany means that mechanisms for producing these are well established and offer little scope for variation and experimentation. In contrast, the Dutch system has more flexibility for experimenting with new cartographic techniques and different planning approaches. In England, planning is more strongly institutionalised than in other European countries, with the 'Royal Town Planning Institute' (RTPI) playing a strong role in ensuring coherence in planning education and practice. In the absence of a strong regulatory framework, the professional judgement of planners is crucial for the operation of the English planning system.

There is ample use of spatial concepts in both Dutch and German planning, many of which, such as the Randstad (city ring) and Green Heart in the Netherlands, have been in use for several decades. The concepts of central places and development axes are still cornerstones of German planning, even though they have been criticised for relying on outdated theoretical assumptions and proximity considerations. In England, there has traditionally not been much attention to spatial analysis or 'mapping' in planning education in England, and there have been few spatial concepts in use (with the exception of the well-known example of 'Green Belts' around major urban areas). The reform of the English planning system towards more integrated spatial strategies at regional and local levels has, however, prompted more interest in spatial concepts and cartographic illustrations. For English planners, who have for many years worked within a non-spatial and policy-led planning system, this requires some considerable adjustment.

The Graphic and Linguistic Structure of Cartographic Representations in Regional Spatial Plans in the Netherlands, Germany and England

Comparing regional-level plans across Europe implies certain methodological challenges, as there is variation in how 'regions' are defined and differences in how spatial planning is organised. However, in trying to identify traditions of visualising spatial policy, the statutory regional plans may still offer a more promising route than single national-level strategies or informal regional planning instruments, which tend to vary considerably in their visual language.

In order to identify similarities and differences in planning traditions' approaches to the visualisation of spatial policy, two regional-level spatial plans from the Netherlands, Germany and England each were analysed and compared. For the Netherlands, these were Streekplan Noord-Holland Zuid (Provincie Noord-Holland 2003) (Map 6.1a and b) and Streekplan Noord-Brabant (Provincie Noord-Brabant 2002). Due to the indicative nature of Dutch *Streekplannen*, much effort is spent on presenting attractive and convincing documents. There is a wide variety of styles, sizes and layout, and the plans are presented in a highly professional way. There is generally extensive use of illustrations, covering the range from photographs, sketches, more digital-cartography-oriented representations of spatial policy in the actual *Plankaart* (policy map), and analytical maps presented on a topographic map base.

For Germany, the *Landesentwicklungsprogramm III Rheinland-Pfalz* (Staatskanzlei Rheinland-Pfalz 1995) (Map 6.2) and *Landesentwicklungsplan Hessen* (HMWVL 2000) were analysed. Federal law (as set out in the federal Spatial Planning Act) ensures a high level of coherence among *Landesentwicklungspläne- and programme*, which are detailed both in content as well as cartographic expression.

Regional Spatial Strategies (RSSs) for the North East (GONE 2008) and the East of England (GOEE 2008) were selected for analysis (Map 6.3). In line with national guidance, the key diagrams are all strictly diagrammatic and schematic in style to avoid clear locational references. The legend of the key diagram includes a cross-reference to the written statement of policies.

A number of criteria were defined for the analysis of the 'graphic' and 'linguistic' structures of spatial policy maps based on the theoretical discussion above. These criteria will be explained in the following sections alongside the analysis results.

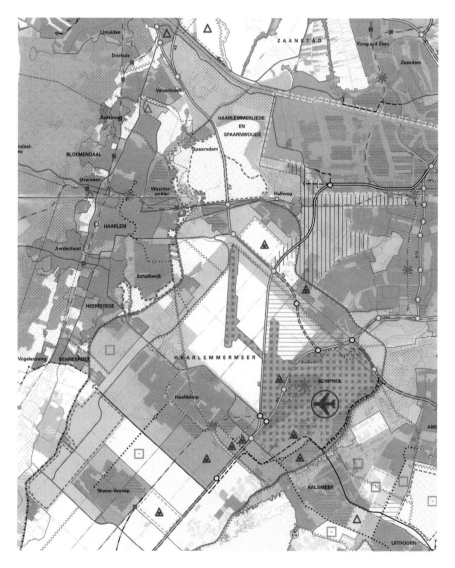

Map 6.1a   Streekplan Noord-Holland Zuid – Streekplankaart (extract)

Source: Provincie Noord-Holland 2003 (separate plot, original size 96 × 60 cm).

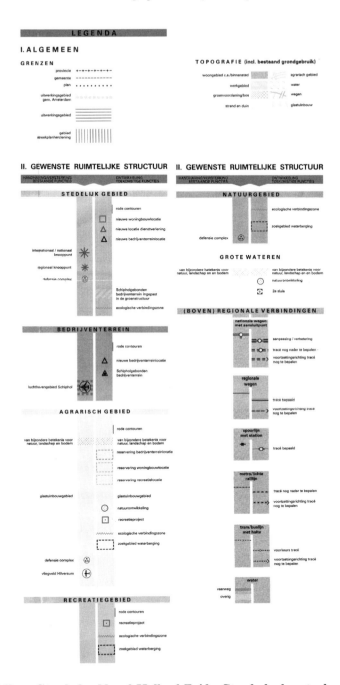

Map 6.1b   Streekplan Noord-Holland Zuid – Streekplankaart – key

Source: Provincie Noord-Holland 2003.

122 *Planning Cultures in Europe*

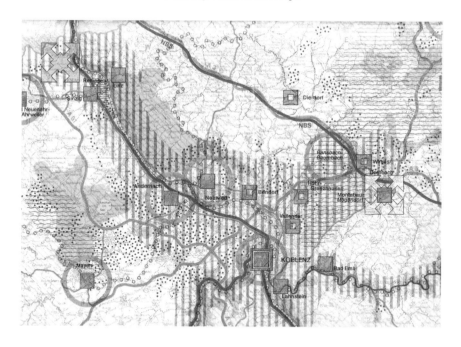

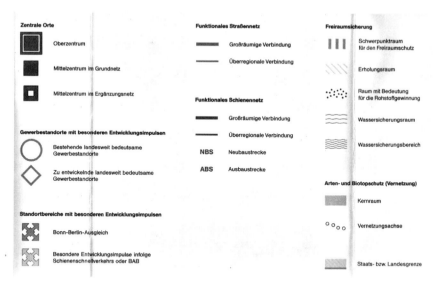

Map 6.2   Landesentwicklungsprogramm III Rheinland-Pfalz (extract)

Source: Staatskanzlei Rheinland-Pfalz 1995 (separate plot, original size 91 ×114 cm, scale 1:200,000).

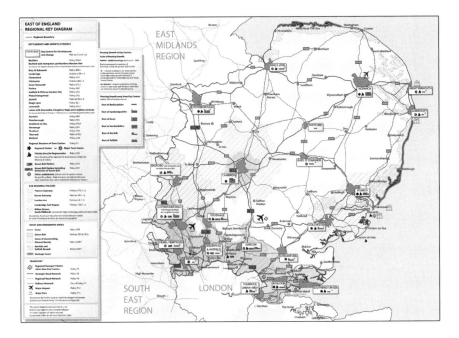

Map 6.3   East of England Regional Key Diagram

Source: East of England Plan, GOEE 2008. Crown Copyright, 125.

The Graphic Structure of Cartographic Representations in Strategic Spatial Plans in the Netherlands, Germany and England

For the cross-national comparative analysis of the graphic structure of visualisations in regional plans in the three countries, the level of abstraction and the level of complexity are analysed. The level of abstraction reflects the underlying view on the reliability and binding character of planning policy (Dühr 2007). Where the graphic structure shows a high degree of abstraction and generalisation, it is more clearly communicated that the content of the plan is 'tentative' and negotiable (a guiding principles approach). Is the graphic representation in contrast very detailed, site-specific and strict, possibly presented on a topographic map base, then policies are presented as irrevocable and the information contained in the plan as reliable, trustworthy and 'scientific' (a regulatory approach).

The cross-national comparison of the level of abstraction of the cartographic representations in Dutch, German and English strategic spatial plans is shown in Figure 6.1. The different functions of the plans are reasonably well communicated through the level of abstraction of 'policy maps' in different countries, although the approach is not universally consistent. Cartographic representations in Dutch and English strategic spatial plans are considerably more varied than in German plans. Nonetheless, the indicative nature of Dutch spatial plans is evident in comparison to the binding nature of German *Länder* plans. The key diagrams in English RSSs are significantly more diagrammatic and abstract than binding German plans and overall even than indicative planning instruments in the Netherlands.

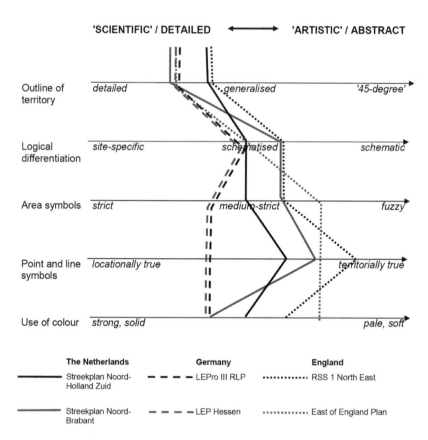

Figure 6.1 Cross-national comparison of the level of abstraction in Dutch, German and English strategic spatial plans[2]

Source: author.

---

2 While the criteria on the outline of the territory and the use of colour should be self-explanatory, the other three criteria are defined as follows (based on Junius 1991a, b):
- logical differentiation, ranging from site specific (relatively clear orientation at topographic elements or land use boundaries), to schematised (rough orientation at topographic elements or land use boundaries) and schematic

There are also differences in the complexity of cartographic representations in strategic plans in the three countries, in terms of the number of symbols and cartographic layers. German *LEPs/LEPros* and Dutch *Streekplannen* are overall considerably more complex than key diagrams in English RSSs (see Maps 6.1–6.3). In the *Streekplannen* for Noord-Holland and Noord-Brabant, a series of analytical and thematic maps are developed over the course of the document, which are then represented on an integrated and therefore complex *plankaart*. In Germany, federal planning law sets out the topics to be covered by *Länder*-level plans, and all planning policy is combined in one integrated map.

The Linguistic Structure of Cartographic Representations in Strategic Spatial Plans in the Netherlands, Germany and England

The criteria for analysing the 'linguistic' structure of cartographic representations in strategic spatial plans relate to the role and comprehensiveness of policy maps in the plan document, and the attention given to the wider planning context. The rationale behind these criteria derives from the assumption that only a map that contains the same policies as the written statement will play an equally central role in the planning process. Table 6.1 shows the link between the written and the visual expression of spatial policies in Dutch, German and English strategic spatial plans. The information in the table is organised under generic policy headings as promoted in European spatial planning debates (CSD 1999).

Table 6.1 confirms that Dutch and German strategic spatial plans are overall more comprehensive than English RSSs in the representation of spatial policies in comparison to written policies. Some of the gaps in the table can be explained by themes or spatial concepts of a planning tradition that are not used in other countries, such as the German system of central places or the English Green Belt concept.

These differences in the understanding of planning aside, it is notable that there are important commonalities with regard to what is represented in strategic spatial plans in all three countries. First and foremost, policies for urban areas are extensively discussed in all plans and are also depicted without exception. This is much less so for policies on rural areas, which – although

---

  (no orientation at topographic elements or land use boundaries, hence spatially vague);
- graphic differentiation of area symbols, ranging from strict (area contour delineated by line symbol), to medium-strict (coloured area symbols with little colour contrast adjoining) and fuzzy (indication of continuous transition);
- graphic differentiation of point and line symbols, ranging from locationally true (exact location of an object) to territorially true (approximate location of an object).

Table 6.1 Cross-national comparison of policy aims in text and graphical expression in regional-level statutory spatial planning documents in the Netherlands, Germany and England

	Policies and instruments	Streekplan Noord-Holland Zuid	Streekplan Noord-Brabant	LEPro RLP	LEP Hessen	RSS 1 North-East	East of England Plan
Polycentric spatial development and a new urban-rural relationship	Strengthen urban networks and/or cross-border connections						
	Improve cooperation between cities and towns						X
	Urban areas in Germany including: system of central places (centres of higher, medium and lower order)	X	X	X	X	X	
	Promote mixed-use development and multifunctional land uses	X	X			X	
	Containment of urbanisation and urban sprawl/promotion of brownfield development	X	X	X		X	
	Preservation of open space within surrounding urban areas for leisure and recreation uses	X	X				
	Safeguard Green Belts					X	X
	Improve liveability and performance of rural areas/promote rural diversification				X		
	Strengthen agriculture	X	X		X		
	Provision of housing land	X					
	Promote recreation and tourism/sports and recreation facilities	X	X				
	Provision of retail facilities/retail development						
	Economic regeneration areas/strengthening of business clusters	X		X		X	
	Conversion (military sites, industrial areas) to strengthen the regional economic structure						X

Policies and instruments	Streekplan Noord-Holland Zuid	Streekplan Noord-Brabant	LEPro RLP	LEP Hessen	RSS 1 North-East	East of England Plan
Parity of access to infrastructure and knowledge						
Safeguard main infrastructure/transport corridors			X	X	X	
Improve accessibility and transport infrastructure in and between urban networks	X					
Road infrastructure network	X	X	X	X	X	X
Rail infrastructure network	X	X	X	X	X	X
Airports	X	X		X	X	X
Ports and waterways	X	X		X	X	X
Freight transport		X		X	X	
Modal shift/reduce traffic impacts						
Public transport	X	X			X	
Cycling and walking						
Traffic management and parking						
Information communications technology (ICT)/improve conditions for research and higher education					X	

Policies and instruments	Streekplan Noord-Holland Zuid	Streekplan Noord-Brabant	LEPro RLP	LEP Hessen	RSS 1 North-East	East of England Plan
Wise management of the natural and cultural heritage						
Integrated water management (including groundwater)	X	X	X		X	
Integrated Coastal Zone Management/coastal protection						X
River policies and prevention of flood risk	X	X	X	X	X	
Nature and landscape protection	X	X	X	X	X	
Ecological and biotope connections			X	X	X	
Forestry and woodland					X	
Increase use of renewable energy/energy efficiency/location for wind turbines			X	X		
Waste management and treatment/sewage treatment						
Minerals and aggregates					X	
Air quality and emission protection						
Redevelopment of contaminated land						
Protection of cultural heritage				X	X	
Others						
Define and strengthen sub-regions/sub-areas					X	X
Defence and military sites	X	X				
Technical infrastructure (oil, gas, pipelines)						

X = represented on 'policy map'.

▓ = discussed in policy text (written statement).

Source: author.

discussed in the majority of plan documents under study – are hardly ever visualised. Besides this urban bias, there is also a clear dominance of linear transport infrastructure (road, rail and waterways) on all 'plan maps', which is often defined as structuring device for the territory (e.g. development axes) but nonetheless reflects the understanding that accessibility equals economic competitiveness. Despite current concerns about the 'network society' and its effects on the use of space, the use of information and communications technology (ICT) and its impact on the spatial structure are virtually ignored on the policy maps. Likewise, while water, landscape and nature protection areas are visualised on the majority of the key diagrams, there is significantly less attention given to the protection of cultural heritage.

There are significant differences in how surrounding areas are represented and linkages and connections are visualised in the planning maps from the different countries. In most plans, the wider planning context including the European, cross-border or national dimension is represented on a separate diagram. The *North East of England Plan* (RSS 1) in this respect challenges traditional representations by showing that the distance between the North East and Cornwall is longer than between the North East and the Netherlands (Map 6.4).

However, there is little acknowledgement of functional interdependencies on the actual 'plan maps'. In Dutch planning, the surrounding territories are usually represented, either through a topographic map base or by showing a continuation of land uses. Many spatial concepts that are in use in the Netherlands aim at an integration of spatial impacts, though there is also much use of 'zoning' instruments (such as red contour) in some of the plans. The 'connections' that are referred to frequently (ecological connections, development axis, urban networks) are often represented through arrow symbols. This means that zoning instruments and more network-oriented ideas currently co-exist in many Dutch plans, which inevitably raises questions about the effective combination of these two different conceptions of space (see also Healey 2006).

In comparison, while in statutory German plans the surrounding territory is at *Länder* level represented through a topographic map base, there is no acknowledgement of spatial interdependencies with neighbouring areas on the actual 'plan map', thus strictly reflecting the planning competences which end at the administrative boundary. The dominance of traditional and static spatial planning concepts leaves little room for the consideration of relational aspects. The only possible exception is the *LEPro RLP* (Map 6.2) which identifies areas with development impulses following the Bonn-Berlin compensation. Arguably, planners may have given a little more thought to the underlying spatial structures, and how this could be visually represented in this respect, and thus, within the regulatory framework, have begun to deviate from their established 'scientific' representation of policies.

130 *Planning Cultures in Europe*

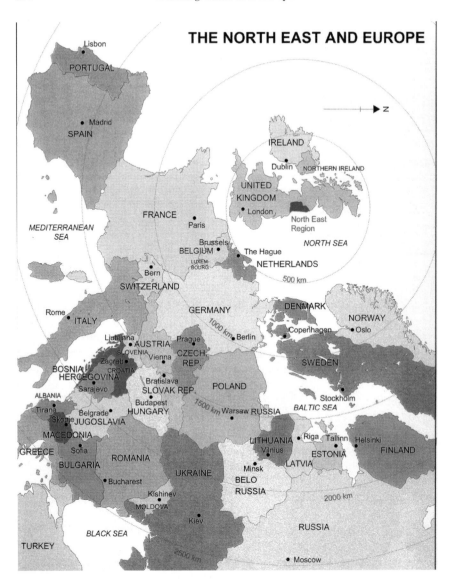

Map 6.4   North East and Europe

Source: The North East of England Plan. The Stationery Office, London.
   Reproduced under the terms of the Click-Use Licence.

There is variation in the representation of surrounding territories in the English RSSs, although mostly the planning territory is represented as an 'island map' (with surrounding territories left white) or merely some vague depiction of neighbouring areas. Furthermore, the illustrations in English key diagrams primarily focus on the representation of designations or certain locations, with little evidence that any consideration has been given to the cartographic representation of functional relationships.

Thus, while overall functional interdependencies and networks are given increasing attention in policy text, the style of cartographic representations in strategic spatial plans in the three countries has to date not been significantly affected. There are certain elements identified in the cartographic representations which depict spatial relations or networks, but the overall impression is that of 'scientific' but rather traditional policy maps in the German plans, and of generally not very comprehensive and elaborated key diagrams in the majority of the English RSSs. The Dutch plans show an interesting ambiguity in this respect, with on the one hand an obvious interest in experimental and innovative ideas for spatial development (expressed through integrated spatial connections and concepts), yet on the other hand – at least in some of the plans – an insistence on the (subconscious) belief in the 'objective' and 'unbiased' map by using remote sensing data and geographic information systems (GIS).

In terms of the users of these plans one can assume that the planning instruments in Germany and England are predominantly directed at lower planning tiers and other sectoral departments, i.e. other professionals, and not necessarily to the wider public. The obvious differences in style can then be explained through the function of this planning instrument in the system, rather than different user groups. Whereas the German approach in many respects seems to fulfil its requirements by providing a 'scientific' representation (see also Fischer's contribution in this volume), which prompts confidence in the trustworthiness of the plan contents through a certain standardisation and thereby gives planning certainty for lower levels, the cartographic representations in English key diagrams seem somewhat less well prepared for their role. The flexibility and discretion in the English planning system, and the strong emphasis on communication and consensual planning would ideally find their visual expression in an indicative and somewhat fuzzy representation, but one which is nevertheless informative, attractive and convincing. That many RSSs seem to fall short in this respect can be explained through the relatively new requirement for preparing strategic regional plans in England, and possibly also through the notable absence of mapping and visualisation in planning education. In this respect, English planners could learn much from other countries about the 'mapping' of spatial policies. Although indicative in nature, Dutch plans are besides a professional audience clearly directed at the wider public, and are therefore generally presented in a highly attractive and professional format.

Conclusions: Planning Traditions of Visualising Spatial Policy in Europe

There are significant differences in the understanding of planning in different European countries, and this also affects the content and design of 'policy maps'. The role of a plan in the system as well as the underlying planning concepts determine both what is visualised as well as how it is visualised. The analysis showed that spatial policies are overall more comprehensively visualised in the German and Dutch spatial plans, thus giving certainty to lower planning tiers, although the two countries rely on different mechanisms to achieve conformity. The German planning system is hierarchical and regulative, with a 'scientific-rational' approach to mapping, whereas the Netherlands rely on the power of consensus, persuasion and 'golden reins' of national government funding. Evidently, this leaves more room for different visualisation techniques from complex GIS-based mapping to more 'artistic' representations in Dutch spatial plans. In comparison, although all English plans are required to contain a key diagram, this is often merely an instrument to highlight future road improvements, show natural protection areas and allocate regional policy funding, rather than an attempt to visualise the complex spatial interrelations facing the territory. Hence, there is a much stronger emphasis on the written statements in English plans, which give more general guidance on principles for territorial development in the region. The maturity of a system also affects the approach to visualising, as demonstrated by the new agenda for regional planning in England and the emerging cartographic representations. Furthermore, the still largely sectoral approach to spatial planning in England may also at least partly explain a certain reluctance to visualise the interaction of different policies on the territory. However, in a planning tradition which is primarily based on communication and consensus, one would expect a somewhat more sophisticated use of powerful communication tools such as key diagrams. This, and the wide variety of approaches to visualisation in RSSs indicate the relatively new and inexperienced use of planning instruments at this level.

Above and beyond these differences that relate to the organisation of the planning system, there are some observations on the basis of the analysis which apply more generally. First, there is a structural distortion in favour of urban areas, infrastructure and designations (for example for environmental protection or economic development). Spatial structures and themes that are not so easily depicted, such as rural areas, tend to be underrepresented on policy maps. Second, the scope of European planning systems is expanding to include ever more policies without a clear territorial reference, such as ICT or social cohesion issues. Clearly, the cartographic representation of their spatial impact is a very difficult task, possibly requiring new approaches to visualisation. Structural distortion in favour of objects with clear territorial delimitation is already evident in the plans analysed for this chapter, and the widening scope of spatial planning in many European countries implies a challenge for an integrated and comprehensive representation of spatial policies. Third, there is an indication that the content and message of policy text and policy map in recent plan documents is increasingly drifting apart. While current planning discourse pays much attention to the 'network society' and the increasing functional interdependencies across the territory, there is not much evidence that these changing conceptions of space have had much effect on planning cartography yet. Cartesian cartographic representations still appear to dominate the planning approach in the three countries under study. Planning theory and practice, thus, will have to move on to consider more relational approaches to the visualisation of spatial policy. This would require a discussion of many of the underlying principles of spatial planning, such as proximity as the guiding principle for many spatial concepts, and implies a focus on 'connectivity' aspects.

The differences in visualising surely to an extent reflect the shared understanding of the content and purpose of spatial planning in the countries studied, and thus represent 'planning traditions of visualising'. However, this notion requires some further reflection. There have been far-reaching planning reforms in many countries over the past years and a partial convergence of planning systems has been observed (Adams 2008; PRP and UWE 2002). Nonetheless, the analysis has shown that the cartographic representations of spatial policy appear to remain largely unaffected from this evolution and continue to carry forward traditional approaches. Cartographic techniques and styles may thus be an even more reliable indicator of a planning tradition than policy text and planning discourse. It appears that policy maps do not change as quickly and sometimes carry planning ideas forward over several generations of plans, thereby preserving traditional planning principles. This, however, also presents many risks as planning debates move on to take on new themes and different paradigms, such as the network society, which are not easily mapped. Surely maps and policy text in a spatial plan should convey the same messages, namely that of the envisaged spatial future of the territory-to-be-planned, yet increasingly there seems to be a mismatch between the two media, with policy text becoming ever more encompassing and policy maps locked in their traditional paths.

One explanation for the different trajectories of planning texts and maps may be found in the production process of cartographic representation of spatial policy. Many planners do not have much cartographic experience, and this can result in communication problems through what Forester (1989) has called the 'legitimate division of labour'. In most planning traditions the cartographic aspects are dealt with in another department than the preparation of planning policy text, and while this *per se* does not have to present a problem it raises questions about the education of planners with respect to cartographic communication and the experience with mapping and map-reading. Also, there are certain technical limitations through existing GIS and mapping systems, which for instance do not easily allow the representation of fuzzy phenomena (see Veregin 1995). Lastly, spatial information on new planning topics or functional relations are often not readily available and thus present restrictions for the phenomena and topics that can be mapped.

There may be two main areas of influence of planning traditions' approaches on the visualisations used in transnational initiatives on spatial development. One refers to the agenda for cooperation and supra-national spatial policy, which is often a result of 'uploading' national and regional planning issues (Börzel 1999; Dühr 2007). The other is about the preference for certain styles of cartographic representation of planning policy, which range from a more 'scientific' spatial analysis-based approach to a more design-led, qualitative approach to cartography. In some planning traditions, there seems to be a deeply rooted acceptance of certain cartographic styles that are considered 'scientific' and seen as communicating reliability and trustworthy 'evidence' for policy-makers, lower planning tiers and the public. Such a rational-scientific planning cartography can lead to serious misunderstandings at transnational level, where competences for spatial development are usually shared and policy is indicative and non-binding. Breaking through these underlying assumptions to raise the awareness that every cartographic representation is just a selection and merely an interpretation of reality, thus that cartography is always subjective, will require much effort. The increasing interest in preparing informal planning strategies in many European countries over recent years, which often include a more qualitative and design-led approach to the cartographic representation of spatial policy, might contribute to a more open discussion of the communicative potential of plan maps and more appropriate styles of representation at transnational level. But again there is a task for planning education across Europe to place more emphasis on the visual aspects of strategic spatial planning.

Bibliography

Adams, N. (2008) 'Convergence and Policy Transfer: An Examination of the Extent to which Approaches to Spatial Planning have Converged within the Context of an Enlarged European Union', *International Planning Studies* 13(1), 31–49.

Albrechts, L. (2001) 'How to Proceed from Image and Discourse to Action: As Applied to the Flemish Diamond', *Urban Studies* 38(4), 733–45.

BMVBS – Bundesministerium für Verkehr, Bau und Stadtentwicklung (2006) *Leitbilder und Handlungsstrategien für die Raumentwicklung in Deutschland, verabschiedet von der Ministerkonferenz für Raumordnung am 30.06.2006*, Berlin.

Börzel, T.A. (1999) 'Towards Convergence in Europe? Institutional Adaptation to Europeanisation in Germany and Spain', *Journal of Common Market Studies* 37, 573–96.

CEC – Commission of the European Communities (1997) *The EU Compendium of Spatial Planning Systems and Policies*, Office for Official Publications of the European Communities, Luxembourg.

Counsell, D., P. Allmendinger, G. Haughton and G. Vigar (2006) 'Integrated Spatial Planning – Is It Living Up to Expectations?', *Town and Country Planning*, 243–46.

Crampton, J.W. (2001) 'Maps as Social Constructions: Power, Communication and Visualization', *Progress in Human Geography* 25(2), 235–52.

CSD Committee on Spatial Development (1999) *European Spatial Development Perspective (ESDP): Towards Balanced and Sustainable Development of the Territory of the European Union*, Office for Official Publications of the European Communities, Brussels/Potsdam.

Dühr, S. (2007) *The Visual Language of Spatial Planning. Exploring Cartographic Representations for Spatial Planning in Europe*, Routledge, London/New York.

Forester, J. (1989) *Planning in the Face of Power*, University of California Press, Berkeley/Los Angeles/London.

GOEE – Government Office for the East of England (2008) *East of England Plan. The Revision to the Regional Spatial Strategy for the East of England*, May 2008, The Stationery Office, London.

GONE – Government Office for the North East (2008) *The North East of England Plan. Regional Spatial Strategy to 2021*, July, The Stationery Office, London.

Harley, J.B. (1989) 'Deconstructing the Map', *Cartographica* 26(2), 1–20.

Healey, P. (2006) 'Relational Complexity and the Imaginative Power of Strategic Spatial Planning', *European Planning Studies* 14(4), 525–46.

Healey, P. (2007) *Urban Complexity and Spatial Strategies. Towards a Relational Planning for our Times*, Routledge, London/New York.

Healey, P., A. Khakee, A. Motte and B. Needham (eds) (1997) *Making Strategic Spatial Plans. Innovation in Europe*, UCL Press, London.

HMWVL Hessisches Ministerium für Wirtschaft, Verkehr und Landesentwicklung (2000) *Landesentwicklungsplan Hessen 2000*, HMWVL, Wiesbaden.

Jensen, O.B. and T. Richardson (2004) *Making European Space. Mobility, Power and Territorial Identity*, Routledge, London/New York.

Junius, H. (1991a) 'Analysierung und Systematisierung von Planinhalten', in ARL Akademie für Raumforschung und Landesplanung (ed.) *Aufgabe und Gestaltung von Planungskarten,* Forschungs- und Sitzungsberichte 185, ARL, Hannover, 30–82.

Junius, H. (1991b) 'Zur Gestaltung der planerischen Aussage von Festlegungskarten', in ARL Akademie für Raumforschung und Landesplanung (ed.) *Aufgabe und Gestaltung von Planungskarten,* Forschungs- und Sitzungsberichte 185, ARL, Hannover, 147–54.

Kragt, R., B. Needham, G. Tönnies and G. Turowski (2003) *Deutsch-Niederländisches Handbuch der Planungsbegriffe. Duits-Nederlands Handboek inzake Planningsbegrippen,* ARL/DGR, Hannover/Den Haag.

Neuman, M. (1996) 'Images as Institution Builders: Metropolitan Planning in Madrid', *European Planning Studies* 4(3), 293–312.

Neuman, M. (2000) 'Communicate This! Does Consensus Lead to Advocacy and Pluralism?', *Journal of Planning Education and Research* 19, 343–50.

Pickles, J. (1992) 'Text, Hermeneutics and Propaganda Maps', in T.J. Barnes and J.S. Duncan (eds) *Writing Worlds. Discourse, Text and Metaphor in the Representation of Landscape,* Routledge, London/New York, 193–230.

Provincie Noord-Brabant (2002) *Brabant in Balans, Streekplan Noord-Brabant 2002,* Provincie Noord-Brabant, Hertogenbosch.

Provincie Noord-Holland (2003) *Streekplan Noord-Holland Zuid, Vastgesteld door Provinciale Staten van Noord-Holland op 17 Februari 2003,* 29, Provinciaal Bestuur van Noord-Holland, Haarlem.

PRP Planning, University of the West of England, Bristol (2002) *European Planning Systems Update,* Department for Transport, Local Government and the Regions, London.

Söderström, O. (1996) 'Paper Cities: Visual Thinking in Urban Planning', *Ecumene* 3(3), 249–81.

Staatskanzlei Rheinland-Pfalz (1995) *Landesentwicklungsprogramm III,* Staatskanzlei Rheinland-Pfalz, Mainz.

Veregin, H. (1995) 'Computer Innovation and Adoption in Geography: A Critique of Conventional Technological Models', in Pickles, J. (ed.) *Ground Truth. The Social Implications of Geographic Information Systems,* The Guilford Press, New York, 88–112.

PART 3
Planning Cultures in Eastern Europe – Between Breakup and Tradition

Chapter 7
Remarks on the Features of Lithuanian Planning Culture

Eugenijus Kęstutis Staniūnas

Introduction

I can probably not go wrong saying that in these latter years attention has cumulatively been drawn to the study of legal systems of territorial planning in European countries. The comparative analysis of law regulations is worthwhile; however, it is no less challenging or relevant to approach the planning from a broader perspective, incorporating the milieu of a country's social mentality, its traditions and a system of values wherein the legal systems come into existence and start to operate. I presume that the mental environment wherein a legal planning system has come into being, the territorial planning and its product – the development of regions and towns – can be understood as the country's planning culture.

A legal planning system cannot emerge from nothing (see Knieling and Othengrafen earlier in this volume). Even if it could be 'imported', a country's life practice would interpret it in its own manner by steering a prevailing social perception into the required direction. This is not a theoretical assumption but the reality of life for EU countries. The countries' legal systems of planning are not covert – EU ideas and directives, for example, merge into the countries' own systems. The cultural environment plays its own role – the comprehensive flow of ideas and documents is sought to be taken 'impartially', according to the established norms of social life in a country. Cultural coherence encourages one to consider that, when countries wish to deepen their cultural knowledge, it is more productive to move towards questions on planning through the whole planning culture rather than analysing its separate elements.

Territorial planning culture is the fact which can be examined (as can many other cultural features such as language, ceremonies, custom, etc.), when seeking to facilitate the communication between various nations or simply in the name of general understanding of the world. I assume that an anthropologist would be able to investigate the countries' planning cultures; however, territorial planning is not a common element of social culture but one of self-government instruments. Therefore, when considering my country's planning culture, I do not wish to provide a thorough and comprehensive description of it, but rather endeavour to analyse the efficacy of this instrument. To put it differently, I am interested in those cultural features which exert influence over the country's rapid and harmonious development.

I am not going to consider all the methods and possibilities of evaluating the efficacy of the culture of planning. I believe that several elements exist which constitute the specific 'genetic code' of the planning culture. The whole logic of planning culture 'construction' mainly depends on these elements. These 'genetic' elements are the position and brightness of the planning in the country's worldview and the conception of the essence and meaning of planning as well as on how proactive the social attitude is towards it. These are the features of the Lithuanian planning culture which I wish to draw attention to in this chapter.

In what follows, I am assuming, without entering into the argument, that the status of a contemporary Lithuanian planning culture is likely to be close to that of the neighbouring Baltic countries – Estonia and Latvia – which have been through the same history. For decades Baltic countries lived according to the scenario of Soviet life in which the public played a major role. After the restoration of independence, the Baltic countries headed towards a market economy. It is quite natural that the Baltic countries were directed towards the market system which their people knew and envisaged. It might be too daring to claim that their knowledge was not very profound, but the fact is that it incorporated less scientific or market experience than those countries with a long market history. It became evident that individual proprietorship assumed a new and very important position; however, the public role was not clearly defined. This world outlook embracing the importance of an individual and the undefined public role has now 'pictured' the whole country's life as well as the territorial planning culture. It is not hard to understand that the questions such as 'Why do we have to deal with planning?', 'Who has to deal with the planning?', 'What objectives does one have to pursue?' and 'Why does one have to pursue these but not the other objectives?' are not easily answered in a post-Soviet society. Oriented towards the West, it may try to copy the indigenous planning system, but without answering these questions the 'copies' of planning systems do not operate properly. That is precisely why I am more concerned about the 'foundation' of the planning system – the answer to the key questions regarding the planning existence and its meaning (as I believe) – rather than its facade.

I have left some room to present a precise description of the above-mentioned planning culture's most important 'parameters'. After describing them, I shall try to 'measure' Lithuanian planning culture according to each of them. It is possible to 'measure' something, in logically modelling the consequences of the culture of planning; something can be revealed, comparing Lithuanian planning culture with that of other countries.

Concerning the Essential 'Parameters' of the Planning Culture

Referring to history, it is obvious that the perceived canvas of human activity alters. To make a comparison, not long ago the same specialist was able to work as both a hairdresser and a doctor. It was a fairly common social phenomenon that in the Renaissance period the same specialist worked as, for example, a painter, a sculptor, a builder, a constructor of war machines and a planner of cities and their fortification. The Egyptian architect Senmut, who lived during the reign of Hatshepsut (a pharaoh of Ancient Egypt), thought that in general 'from the beginning of time' nothing existed he did not know (Николаев 1984, 32). The differences in a world outlook can be observed on a geographical plane. For instance, nations living in the north have more attributes to denote various conditions of snow than those living in the south. The distinction of phenomena (I would think that the spheres of activity can be identified among them) and the establishment of new connections between them take place mainly due to the abundance of knowledge which can no longer be 'fitted' into the former classification 'frames'; it also happens because, in deepening our cognition, the nature of the phenomena seems to be different from the previous one; moreover, some people treat these very phenomena as important, others as less important. While comparing the expression of a sphere of activity in various cultures, I am encouraged to examine them, for 'sticking' to an activity in terms of a timeworn world outlook will not create favourable preconditions for its sustainable development.

When speaking about the national peculiarities of the conception of the essence and meaning of planning, I imply that the meaning of planning can be perceived differently in different countries. Understanding the meaning of an activity can differ not only in its content but also in its profundity. In our life we encounter a myriad of activities which we perform without reflecting deeply on them. In some countries it is common to greet people by shaking hands, or to nod if you express confirmation. One hardly stops to think why someone does it. We perform some actions in this or that way because 'other people do it' or because 'we've always done it' and the like. I think that it may concern not only separate actions but also the spheres of activity. The concept of the meaning of planning (in terms of content and profundity) is 'the root' of the culture of planning. Here the logic creating the planning culture emerges. Even an irrational model of activity may not be of great concern, provided the society is active and self-critical, i.e. tries to analyse, verify and, when necessary, adjust its activity. Therefore, I would ascribe a society's active participation to the essential features of the culture of planning.

I do not think that an absolute 'evaluation' of the above-mentioned features of the culture of planning is possible. Yet, we can compare them with analogous features in other countries. This comparison is not considered to be an evaluation of the planning culture; however, it urges us to reason, to review our own culture of planning, model its consequences and possibly develop a deeper understanding of it. It may even encourage us to re-organise it.

What does the contemporary Lithuanian planning culture look like from the following perspectives?

The Face of Planning Activity in the Lithuanian World Outlook

In Lithuania, the law on territorial planning is working and the documents of territorial planning are prepared; however, there is no space for the planning profession in comparison to many other countries. No professional organisation of planners has formed in Lithuania. Lithuania is not a member of the European Association of Planners. There are not and cannot be any planning institutions, for there is no such discipline in the Lithuanian classification of studies.

The documents of planning are prepared by people with education in architecture, engineering or geography. Although the specialists who come from various professions work in this domain, Lithuanian architects believe that planning is a branch of architecture. This is shown by the fact that the urban committee functions under the auspices of the Lithuanian Architect's Association – the only formation uniting specialists working in the sphere of planning in Lithuania. It is the Association of Lithuanian Architects which certifies the managers of territorial planning projects.[1] At the time of writing, the architects' community is preparing an architecture law which seeks to implement the following objectives of the planning activity: 'to determine the competences of the institutions of city planning and architecture' and 'to regulate the relations emerged in the process of an architect's professional activity while creating (urban and territorial planning) objects, and the like.[2]

Perhaps when accepting planning, Lithuanian architecture incorporates not only the practice of this activity or the reward for the work done but also a natural amount of the planning-related knowledge? This can hardly be said to be the case. The classification of Lithuanian study fields and disciplines

---

1 Architektų atestavimo, atestatų galiojimo sustabdymo arba jų panaikinimo tvarkos aprašas (Lietuvos Respublikos aplinkos ministro 2007 m. lapkričio 20 d. įsakymas Nr. D1-616), *Žin.* 2005, Nr. 93-3466 [Schedule of the Procedure for Architects' Assessment, Certificates' Validity Suspension or their Abolition (Order No. D1-616 of the Minister of Environment of the Republic of Lithuania from 20 November 2007, *Official Gazette Valstybės žinios*, 2005, No. 93-3466)].

2 Lietuvos Respublikos architektūros įstatymo koncepcija. Projektas. 3.1., 3.3 [The Concept of the Law on Architecture of the Republic of Lithuania. Project. 3.1., 3.3], http://www.architektusajunga.lt/LT.php?Id=470&content=page.

ascribes architecture to the field of art studies.[3] Practice shows that Lithuanian architecture institutions firmly adhere to this classification with an attempt to protect architecture students from obtaining the knowledge unrelated to art. It is quite natural that architects exceed the traditions of art while carrying out their planning practice, but in Lithuania people do not like to acknowledge it.

There are certain circumstances that prevent the planning activity in Lithuania from being developed. The first deals with a clear sectoral thinking. The essence of the spheres of activity seems to be permanent and therefore rigid and self-perpetuating. The reality of the planning activity does not correspond to a system of work distribution which is considered to be 'sacred'. All this means that practitioners tend not to see the planning or to 'section it off' and force it into the common frames of work distribution. That is why the 'normalised' planning (mentioned above) in most cases becomes architecture.

A comparatively small labour market is one more factor influencing the development of the planning profession. Planning activity in Lithuania develops with huge time intervals: only a few country general plans and a couple of town master plans have been prepared in the last 18 years. From 2007 to 2008 a 'burst of activity' occurred – the plans of almost all Lithuanian towns and regions were ordered simultaneously. This activity has subsided; it has become possible that there is nothing for planners to do in the next 20 years. Such a situation does not encourage specialists – even if they were given an appropriate professional preparation in the sphere of planning – to remain in a country where they can obtain a job only every 20 years.

The main reason for the planning standstill is that the public does not see its meaning. I have mentioned before that the features of the planning culture discussed above constitute the 'genetic code' that creates that culture. I think that the conception of the essence and meaning of the planning is its essential part.

---

3 Bendrasis studijų sričių ir krypčių, pagal kurias vyksta nuosekliosios universitetinės ir neuniversitetinės studijos Lietuvos aukštosiose mokyklose, klasifikatorius ir pagal šias studijų kryptis suteikiamų kvalifikacijų sąrašas (Lietuvos Respublikos Vyriausybės nutarimas Nr. 107, 2007-01-31, *Žin.*, 2007, Nr. 15-550 [General Classification of the Fields and Disciplines of Study whereby Consistent University and Non-university Studies Introduced in Higher Education Institutions of Lithuania and a List of Qualifications Acquired in Compliance with these Fields of study (Resolution of the Government of the Republic of Lithuania No. 107 of 31 January 2007, *Official Gazette Valstybės žinios*, 2007, No. 15-550], http://www3.lrs.lt/pls/inter3/dokpaieska.showdoc_l?p_id=291953&p_query=Studij%F8%20sri%E8i%F8%20ir%20kryp%E8i%F8%20klasifikatorius%20&p_tr2=2, accessed 2 March 2007.

The Peculiarities of the Lithuanian Search for the Meaning of Planning and their Consequences

The conception of the meaning of the existence of planning is a baseline of planning culture. The whole 'construction' of the planning culture emerges from the answer to the question: 'Why do we need planning?' Here are the roots of our present planning culture – its 'genes'.

In everyday Lithuanian life there are two different ways of looking for the meaning of the planning culture which lead to similar conclusions. The first mental way is indispensable to the general public taking an active part. Lithuania is a market country. A market system (as it is interpreted in Lithuania) is a system wherein the key agent is an individual and freedom is the greatest value. The less it is constrained, the better. As planning is a sort of interference with individual freedom, it follows that it would be better if it did not exist.

The second way of thinking is inherent in some of my colleagues (architects). As mentioned before, Lithuanian architects are inclined to regard territorial planning as a branch of architecture; however, according to these architects, the position of territorial planning in the domain of architecture is contradictory. Many specialists working in the sphere of architecture believe that territorial planning is a specific field of architecture which differs from the rest in the arrangement of vast spaces. The larger the spatial structures, the fewer possibilities exist for these structures to enter in the field of aesthetic interpretation, and the stronger the role of the economic, social and ecological aspects of their subsistence start to play (Daunora 2000, 66–8). The apparently inevitable conclusion drawn from such a way of thinking is that territorial planning is a branch of architecture wherein there is no art and therefore no architecture. Hence the position of planning under the aegis of architecture is rather complicated. On the one hand, architecture formally seems to accept planning; on the other hand, architecture is constantly seeking to dispose of it or 'remedy' it, i.e. to transform it into architecture 'in the full sense of the word'.

To sum up, I can say that a national feature of the conception of the meaning of planning is that we do not see the meaning. I am not sure whether Lithuanian territorial planning would exist at present if it were not for a prominent factor: Lithuania compares itself to the world's developed countries in which territorial planning exists.

Accordingly, the question of planning existence is obviously contradictory: we see no meaning for contradiction, but it lies in the fact what we would want to copy. Perhaps it is possible to resolve this contradiction in various ways. Such a situation is favourable for expanding the planning fiction. After all, we can live in the way we understand, i.e. without planning, so as to resemble other Western nations, to present the planning 'facade', without influencing social life practically. It would be 'right' and Western-like.

There are certain features that should be indispensable to the fiction of planning. Those mentioned above must be among them.

In a fictitious, 'facade' planning culture, laws could exist but their language must be equivocal, for instance, extremely 'scientific'. This is very convenient, for laws could be read at any time when necessary or in the way people want to be read. Legal acts must be ambiguous or, better, contradictory. The 'advantage' is the same – they can be read in the way people 'want' to read them in a concrete event. The preparation of plans must be postponed: we could create an image of a law-based country, but we would not do what is 'not acceptable' as long as possible.

Eventually, it would be possible to start to prepare plans, but it would be efficient that these plans be prepared by specialists not 'spoilt' by Western education (the situation would be as it is in the West, but those specialists could be directed in the way they could make plans more effective).

It would be possible to include words popular in Western countries at the beginning of planning documents, for instance, 'sustainable development', 'ecological equilibrium', 'social balance'. This presents a lovely image of an advanced country. Yet, in this case it would be better that the solutions bore no relation to these phrases. It is not very hard to do – the explanatory writings are sometimes fairly long and people quite often have no time to study them with much attention. It would be great if the ideas denoted in plans were only to be named ... named – and that is al. To name is not so complicated, naming does not imply anything special. If we still have to designate a regulation in a plan, it would be acceptable that a lot of possible activities should be indicated in a plan – in the future we will choose the activity which is most needed. The plan will generally undertake nothing. The regulation on territorial planning can be objective. Then we have to note that this regulation specifies only the priorities. The implication is that all the spheres of activity are practically permitted, in other words, the plan commits to nothing.

We ought to be tolerant, not to be at odds with one another when the construction starts without plans being prepared. Plans can be prepared in succession. If we plan before construction, then it is more rational to begin with the detailed plans. The master plans can be prepared subsequently. It is better to prepare municipality master plans first and only then draw up regional plans. To put it frankly, when we bind municipality master plans, we get a regional plan – the system of planning is present and there is a great deal of work to do.

I am not in a position to go into here how deeply our planning system culture is 'immersed' in terms of these features, but I assume that some features are likely to be observed in the planning culture.

I cannot generally assess all the language of legal acts regulating Lithuanian territorial planning, but there are certain intricate instances of that language incorporated into the legal acts. For example, it is not easy to understand what society stands for according to Lithuanian law. The principal state law differentiates the interests of the public from that of an individual, i.e. it treats the public and an individual separately; however, the Law on Territorial Planning states that the public is groups of natural and legal entities and even separate persons.[4] The Law on Territorial Planning commits to establishing preconditions for maintaining and restoring an ecological equilibrium of a landscape;[5] however, it does not indicate the type of a landscape (planet, country, region, and town or land plot). The law does not define the concept of 'an ecological equilibrium'. Instead, Lithuanian law introduces two different definitions.[6] These and similar aspects of a law-based 'climate' create favourable prerequisites for endless interpretations and discussion.

In Lithuania general planning has been proceeding very slowly to date. The development was mainly controlled by detailed plans that often included one land plot and were prepared on a private person's initiative, using his or her own funds.

I cannot evaluate all the regulations of the detailed plans prepared in Lithuania, but I consider that some of their details correspond to the above-mentioned features.

The Comprehensive Plan of the Territory of the Republic of Lithuania presents a classification of country towns as centres of a settlement system; however, that classification involves neither obligations nor restrictions. We could not maintain that the stated classification does not imply anything at all – some decisions are sometimes sought to be grounded on the basis of that classification – but its meaning can be understood differently. The politicians of Vilnius' county municipalities did not approve of the draft Comprehensive Plan of the Territory of Vilnius County as long as it was written in its discourse that all the regulations indicated in the said draft are only of a guideline-related nature. The consequences became evident. The county administration cannot make decisions whether the drafts of the plans of municipalities correspond to the provisions of the county plan. Considering that the planning bears no meaning, we are in an advantageous position: authorities and planners reason and discuss, while the construction works are taking place in a territory.

The Comprehensive Plan of the Territory of Vilnius city has presented the zoning of the town territory until the year 2015, according to the activity allowable in it. The boundaries of territory categories provided in a document are quite broad. For instance, a subgroup of non-urbanised territories, 'forests

---

4 Lietuvos Respublikos teritorijų planavimo įstatymas (*Žin.*, 1995, Nr. 107-2391) 2 str., 49 [The Republic of Lithuania Law on Territorial Planning, *Official Gazette Valstybės žinios*, 1995, No. 107-2391, Article 2, 49[.

5 Lietuvos Respublikos teritorijų planavimo įstatymas (*Žin.*, 1995, Nr. 107-2391) 3 str., 1 [The Republic of Lithuania Law on Territorial Planning, *Official Gazette Valstybės žinios*, 1995, No. 107-2391, Article 3,1].

6 The first is presented in the Law on Protected Areas; the second, in the European Landscape Convention.

and woodlands', indicates that for agriculture, the building of residences can be developed apart from forests, as well as allowing the objects of engineering infrastructure to be built, mineral to be mined and the like.[7] Other categories are very similar.

In Lithuania it is not common to pursue programme-related parts of plans. Although the Lithuanian Law on Territorial Planning requires the analysis of the need for investments necessary for the implementation of plans and preparation of programmes on the realisation of solutions of master plans,[8] actual practice does not abide by this. Plans are simply approved without considering whether it is possible to realise them.

What are the consequences of the planning fiction? If there are valuables which an individual is incapable of producing, and if the territorial planning is one of the instruments of creating those valuables, the planning fiction does not create the valuables which could be created with the help of planning, or creates less than it really could. In other words, such a peculiarity of the planning culture leads to country's stagnation. Do people notice? Lithuania is not densely populated; the process of urbanisation has not been rapid in recent years; therefore, the planning culture described has not led to serious ecological consequences (although descriptions of the construction work taking place in the most picturesque and fragile territories of nature are evident in newspapers). In my view, the social consequences of the planning culture are the most striking. Lack of confidence in the authorities has assumed a typical character the country. The people's confidence in municipalities is below 30 per cent, confidence in government, 12 per cent, in the Seimas, 7 per cent, in political parties, 5 per cent. The country is losing its social capital.

How Active is the Lithuanian Public Attitude towards Planning?

Lithuanian residents demonstrate a strong reaction to construction. The public easily accepts the preparation of plans and more easily accepts the discussed planning culture in general. It is not ignored. In 2008 more discussions concerning a system of Lithuanian territorial planning took place and the topic has been debated by the government. It must be admitted that other countries' have a more active awareness of planning. I notice that, apart from several conferences in Lithuania, we only have the fact of the law on territorial

---

7 Vilniaus miesto teritorijos bendrasis planas iki 2015 metų. Bendrojo plano pagrindinio brėžinio reglamentų lentelė (http://www.vilnius.lt/bplanas/download.php?file_id=256) [The Comprehensive Plan of the Territory of Vilnius City until 2015. A Chart of Regulations of the Main Scheme of the Master Plan].

8 Lietuvos Respublikos teritorijų planavimo įstatymas (*Žin.*, 1995, Nr. 107-2391) 10 str., 7 [The Republic of Lithuania Law on Territorial Planning, *Official Gazette Valstybės žinios*, 1995, No. 107-2391, Article 10, 7].

planning, post-statutory acts and the preparation of plans. All legal documents are acceptable to the public, but here, unlike some other European countries, there are no comments or explanations of any laws and post-statutory acts; moreover, there are not even any studies of planning practice. 'White books' related to the problems occurring during planning are not being prepared and in Lithuania we cannot find any websites or publications with good or bad examples of planning. Although the Law on Territorial Planning requires implementing the monitoring of plans,[9] it is not performed.

To sum up, at present Lithuania is a country with a vague view on the culture of planning. Unfortunately, the result of the above-mentioned features is associated with a vibrant fervency observed in the public, social tension and a receding social capital, i.e. the respect which residents pay to the country and the will to work for it. One of the main reasons deals with a small amount of work done in the sphere of planning; therefore, the collaboration of countries (especially small ones), an exchange of experience and thoughts constitute a possibility to observe planning not intermittently but constantly, to expand the boundaries of knowledge, to encourage the public to express an active attitude towards the self-government instruments and to rationalise the 'technology' of public life, i.e. development resources.

Bibliography

City Municipality of Vilnius (2006) *Vilniaus miesto teritorijos bendrasis planas iki 2015 metų, Bendrojo plano pagrindinio brėžinio reglamentų lentelė*, http://www.vilnius.lt/bplanas/download.php?file_id=256>, accessed 7 December 2008.

Daunora, Z.J. (2000) *Architektūra, urbanistika, teritorijų planavimas: disciplinų sampratos ir tikslesnio sąvokų vartojimo, Urbanistika ir architektūra* 22(2), Technika, Vilnius, 66–8.

Николаев, И. (1984) *Профессия архитектора*, Stroyizdat, Moscow.

Lietuvos Respublikos architektūros įstatymo koncepcija (1995), Projektas 3.1., 3.3, http://www.architektusajunga.lt/LT.php?Id=470&content=page, accessed 4 September 2008.

Lütke Daldrup, E. (2007) 'Federal Foundation for Building Culture Starts Work' (published online January 2005), http://www.bmvbs.de/-,1913.994051/Luetke-Daldrup-Federal-Foundat.htm, accessed 7 December 2008.

Ministry of Environment of the Republic of Lithuania (2007) *Architektų atestavimo, atestatų galiojimo sustabdymo arba jų panaikinimo tvarkos aprašas*, Žin. 2005, Nr. 93-3466.

---

9 Lietuvos Respublikos teritorijų planavimo įstatymas (*Žin.*, 1995, Nr. 107-2391) 10 str., 7 [The Republic of Lithuania Law on Territorial Planning, *Official Gazette Valstybės žinios*, 1995, No. 107-2391, Article 10, 7].

President of the Republic of Lithuania (1995) Lietuvos Respublikos teritorijų planavimo įstatymas, *Žin.*, 1995, Nr. 107-2391.

Seimas (Parliament) of the Republic of Lithuania (2007) *Bendrasis studijų sričių ir krypčių, pagal kurias vyksta nuosekliosios universitetinės ir neuniversitetinės studijos Lietuvos aukštosiose mokyklose, klasifikatorius ir pagal šias studijų kryptis suteikiamų kvalifikacijų sąrašas*, Nr. 107, Žin. 2007, Nr. 15-550, <http://www3.lrs.lt/pls/inter3/dokpaieska.showdoc_l?p_id=291953&p_query=Studij%F8%20sri%E8i%F8%20ir%20kryp%E8i%F8%20klasifikatorius%20&p_tr2=2>, accessed 7 December 2008.

Chapter 8
Planning Rationalities among Practitioners in St Petersburg, Russia – Soviet Traditions and Western Influences

Veli-Pekka Tynkkynen

Introduction

In this chapter I will examine how planning discourse has changed in St Petersburg after the collapse of the Soviet Union by analysing practitioners' views in St Petersburg.[1] My analysis will shed light on the planning objectives and practices that are prioritised in St Petersburg planning, but also in Russian planning, since many of the above-mentioned planners have practised their profession in several Russian cities. In addition to describing and analysing planning both in St Petersburg and more generally in Russia, I will also show how these objectives and priorities are related to Western planning theory and practice.

While analysing the planning discussion, I use a methodology of discourse analysis, keeping in mind the physical, cultural and political geography of the locality. For example, the specific geographic location of the St Petersburg region does have a particular effect on the way local knowledge and thus discourses are produced. Especially in post-Soviet St Petersburg, Russian and Soviet ideas have been linked with European influences much more than in many other Russian regions, owing to the specific geographical position of the city as 'the window to Europe'.

This kind of research on Russian urban and regional planning is not widespread – neither in Russia nor in the West. Gaining access to the roots of planning goal-setting is difficult even in the West (e.g. Flyvbjerg 2003, 325), so it is not a surprise that research of this type is marginal in Russia. Moreover, Russian planning research is interested in purely theoretical questions, such as the optimal forms of physical land-use planning and theorising on

---

1 I have analysed planning discourse in St Petersburg by following the professional planning discussion through interviews and statements outlined in strategic planning documents. My empirical material comprises 14 thematic interviews, which I undertook in St Petersburg between December 2003 and March 2004 among local and regional planning professionals (9), researchers (3) and NGO representatives (2).

sustainability indicators (e.g. Brade et al. 2000; Dem'yanenko 2000; Kaz'min and Kalinin 2000; Lappo 1997; Makarov and Pegov 2001; Maslov 2003). This perspective leaves political goal-setting totally outside the focus of planning research. This illustrates the fact that in Russia both planning and planning studies resemble Soviet times: the gap between theorising and Realpolitik remains wide.

Next I will frame present planning in St Petersburg by describing the paradoxes of Soviet urban and regional planning. Furthermore, I will highlight the changes in planning discourse from the Soviet years, through the 1990s till the 2000s. I concentrate on the role of expertise and the self image of the planners, which I compare to the theoretical findings of planning research. Finally, I shall give an informed view on the future direction of Russian urban and regional planning, taking into account the ongoing amalgamation of the Soviet style and Western neoliberal planning perspectives.

The Paradoxes of Socialist Planning

In the Soviet Union the perspective on regional planning was system-centred: urban regions were first and foremost considered as functional entities (Brade et al. 2000, 21). General plans of the cities were formulated by state and city officials (Chant 1999, 310–12), and a very small circle was aware of their content. These secret plans were drawn up for 20 years, and their formulation was based on the assumption that experts know what is best for the society (Ruble 1995, 105–7; Lappo 1997, 458).

Plans were based on large amounts of statistical data, with the help of which the socially and economically optimal urban structure was supposed to be gained. The problem with these precise plans was that they departed from context reality (Lappo 1997, 458), when the danger of formulating unrealistic plans grew. For example, concentration of industry and urban growth was uncontrolled, because reactions to changes in the environment were slow (Ruble 1995, 106). Soviet planners believed in expertise and had an ultra-rationalistic worldview (Chant 1999, 310–16), but they cannot be blamed for all the problems. One central problem was the lack of optional plans, which was a result of prioritising the political goals of the Communist party over other more rational ones (Lappo 1997, 458).

Political goals, many times distorted by gigantomania, had departed from the aims of laypeople, but also from the goals of planners, which tried to enhance the common good. Another central obstacle to enhancing the common good in planning was the greater importance of quantitative aims in relation to qualitative in Soviet politics (Shaw 1999, 132). For example, vast dam construction projects were carried out, despite the negative effects on the environment and local communities, because electricity production and heavy industry dependent on it were prioritised before local socio-economic priorities (Brade et al. 2000, 24; Lopatnikov 2004, 214).

Based on literature (e.g. Brade et al. 2000) and interviews, there were two main problems in the system of Soviet urban and regional planning. First, the approved land-use plans were only requesting, not legally binding. In practice plans were not followed and their rational goals – seen even from today's viewpoint – were not followed partially or, in the worst cases, totally ignored. Secondly, the extreme sector form of the Soviet governance system made the comprehensive approach weak. There were over 60 sector ministries, which constructed industrial areas, housing and service infrastructure for their workers, confined by the narrow goals of the sector. In practice there were two overlapping planning systems in the Soviet Union. Despite the fact that in principle sector planning was supposed to be subordinate to comprehensive land-use planning, in reality this was many times the opposite (Brade et al 2000, 22–3; Lappo 1997, 459–60). Corruption and unofficial social networks, which made it possible to deviate from the comprehensive plans, also played a central role in creating problems in Soviet planning.

Socialist planning was thus full of paradoxes. In a planned economy there was not supposed to be competition, but in practice state enterprises and sector ministries were rivals, which made urban planning almost as controversial as in the West (Chant 1999, 324–5). Especially the enlargement of rapidly growing industrial cities led to an uncoordinated concentration of factories and residential areas, which turned communities into 'industrial villages'. Without legal protection, urban green and recreational areas outlined in general plans, important for the quality of the living environment, were watered down under the pressure of expanding industrial areas (Pertsik 1980). The problem was made worse by the fact that industry lacked an incentive to use the land effectively, since there was no officially announced real estate value for the land (Lappo 1997, 460).

Planning Discourse in the 1990s – Do We Need Planning in the Market Economy?

As the Soviet Union and its vast planning system collapsed, the meaning and importance of planning – in a society on its way towards the market economy – has changed totally. As one interviewee, Shitinskij, described the situation:

> After the fall of Soviet Union, very little attention was devoted to planning. This was because the change affected the whole society, and especially the principles of planning and funds directed to … Instead of one owner, the state, there were now a great number of owners, like the local government and the private sector … In a changing society there appeared a need for new regional planning legislation, which was to be created from scratch.

Russia was thus unavoidably becoming a society, which was starting to function according to the laws of the market, which were difficult to understand. With the change also came libertarian ideas and the appreciation of the need for planning decreased drastically. Some wondered if planning was needed in the first place, and what planning means in a market economy:

> In the planned economy everything was planned, including the production of soap and needles. If there was a malfunction in the system, you could not find soap in the whole country ... During the 1990s everything disappeared in a moment, all planning. Nothing was to be planned ... everybody said this. 'What should we plan? If we start to plan again, a new depression will come, everything will vanish again ... Nothing should be planned. Let things evolve as they will. (Nazarov)

Everything reminiscent of Soviet governance, including urban and regional planning, was regarded as bad especially in the eyes of the lay people, but also among regimes that seized power on the local and regional level after the collapse of the Soviet Union. Another reason was the almost total seizure, during the early 1990s, of state funding for planning, which previously was the sole monopoly of the state. Moreover, public planning lost its prestige and position also because of the lack of understanding among newly established power regimes – or then the ambiguous societal situation was used by these regimes to enhance private interests:

> During the first years, people that gained power in cities through elections didn't understand the necessity of urban planning. People gained power through random political turmoil – and sometimes with the help of criminal money. These [people] were only concerned about their own interests. (Shitinskij)

Lack of prestige and diminishing public work has greatly reduced the number of planners. Public planners are afraid that the expertise accumulated during the Soviet years has been lost:

> Urban planning and construction stopped immediately after the fall of the Soviet Union ... Now, for example, a new general plan is being formulated in St Petersburg. But I must admit that in this work collective there are no people under 40 – maybe two ... The potential of the profession has been radically lost. And my son is an architect, and like his colleagues, he doesn't want to become a planner. (Berezin)

However, planning did not stop in Russia. After the socio-economically harsh years of the mid-1990s, planning activity began to grow as new constructions sites were opened. Enterprises buying substantial tracts of land were not influential in land use before the mid-1990s. Since then the situation has changed, as Petrovich remarks: 'Especially after 1998 enterprises owning land began to challenge state authorities on land-use questions. They begun to formulate demands and brought forward their goals.'

The scale of planning has been very small, since developer firms have been interested only in planning land use on the neighbourhood level. These firms have bought the most talented young planners to do the job, as Maslennikov concludes: 'This [situation] enables corporations to buy experts, which master project planning and its bureaucratic and political hindrances ... The city doesn't have money to buy these experts.'

The public planning that has remained seems to continue along the Soviet style trajectory. As during the Soviet era despite the officially stated comprehensive and integrative planning approach, in practice these goal-settings, problem definitions and rationalisations were and still are subordinate to the goals and needs of different sectors of the local economy and private enterprises. The sector approach in planning has been easier to sustain, firstly because also during the Soviet era this perspective was strong, and secondly since the strongest Soviet sector ministries have kept their power and importance in national governance even after the regime change. The following quotations clearly show that planning today is strongly affected by the paradoxes and inertia of the former Soviet system:

> I don't know if the general plan matches the objectives of city strategy, but it definitely matches the development plan of the metro line ... Similarly, in Russia we don't have a development strategy for the whole country, but certainly a development strategy for the nuclear branch up until the year 2050. There's your planning! (Karpov)

> Rather this plan [of the Vyborg district] consists of strategies and projects of different branches and enterprises, not of spatial plans where things would be put together regionally. This kind of development planning is done effectively. (Maslennikov)

> And this strategic plan [of Sosnovy Bor] was absolutely horrible, because in practice all the construction objectives of investors and the state were just summoned up – without any critical analysis. (Fedorov)

In light of these views and the resulting changes, Russian urban and regional planning resembles planning in the USA. Peter Hall's (2002, 202) description about the US local level planning resembles in some respects the Russian counterpart because in both the sector approach dominates over an integrated, comprehensive one, and in both systems the developers have a strong position vis-à-vis the local public administration. However, the biggest difference is that in Russian local governance, the urban planning committee, with a comprehensive approach, has de jure a decisive position in land-use planning (Gradostroitel'ny kodeks Rossijskoj Federatsii 2004), whereas in the USA a body resembling urban planning has even officially a subordinate position compared to road construction or public infrastructure authorities (Hall 2002, 202), for example.

Return of Planning in the 2000s – Why Has it Become Necessary Again?

Public urban planning is increasing, partly inspired by international examples (Tynkkynen 2004; Leontief Centre 1998; Vakhmistrov 2002; Zhikharevich 2003). Another reason is the stronger role of the federal state, in guiding and controlling the development especially on the regional level, which is the direct outcome of former President Putin's centralisation politics. The stronger role of the state in guiding the development of Russian regions and cities is also clearly stated in the new Urban Planning Codex (Gradostroitel'ny kodeks Rossijskoj Federatsii 2004).

The changes in the federal power regime and legislation naturally affect the way the interviewees define present planning. Planners speak about the revitalisation of planning on the city and urban regional level, despite the fact that still only a few leaders on the local level find it necessary, as Zalegaller said frankly: 'Practically speaking plans don't exist ... Most of the regions don't have a plan guiding their land use.' Furthermore, Shitinskij pointed out that:

> These kinds of spatial plans, you see ... do not have a direct connection to these practices [guiding land use], and that's why until lately these plans haven't been actively formulated. And literally only during the last couple of years ... have progressive governors initiated plans of this kind.

The initiatives of these governors are viewed as progressive, since at the same time part of the power planners used to have during the Soviet years is returning, although that power enjoyed was more illusionary than real because of the primacy of sector objectives. Naturally, 'the new coming' of land-use planning strengthens the self-esteem of the profession.

Nonetheless, is the formulation of planning documents and standardisation of a land-use planning procedure just a way to legitimise the actions of power regimes in Russian cities and regions without making any changes in the prioritisations of land-use objectives? In addition, are we seeing Russian urban planning turning from one that was illegal and fulfilled the narrow goals of the regimes in power, as in the 1990s (see e.g. Tynkkynen 2004), to one that uses these same narrow objectives as the basis of planning documents, thus legalising this action? One experienced planner, Nazarov, gave an example from his experience: '[The Governor of St Petersburg] Matvienko needs a general plan for four years to carry out her policy. And if I make a plan till the end of her term, why would it be necessary for her? And for a person coming after her it definitely isn't useful anymore.' Zalegaller added:

> The directors of districts don't see the benefits of strategic plan formulation, because their time-perspective is short, maximally extending an electoral term ... Without the help of professional planners, land use becomes unclear; that's when construction permits are distributed among friends, and problems accumulate.

In the light of these reports, I understand that plan formulation is a way to legitimise the actions of the power regime towards both the state and the civil society. Professional planners draw plans exactly as the leadership of the community or region demands, leaving the role of expertise and rational, integrated planning spurious. In this view it is dubious to claim that Russian planners would form the fourth power axis in land-use planning, as described by Beauregard (1989, 392–3) and Klosterman (1985, 12), in addition to state, capital and population, as they do in Central Europe and the Nordic countries.

Defining Planning: An Idealistic Perspective vs Realpolitik

An interesting feature in the planning discourse of this society, which is moving towards a market economy, is the way planning itself is defined. In many interviews a very narrow planning perspective was emphasised, where the political struggle over decisions was not mentioned. This came up when the interviewed planners commented on the role of private sector in the planning process. For example, Nazarov explained:

> These [enterprises] don't affect planning itself. But on spatial structures they do have a rather strong influence ... Construction corporations, predominantly. They do what they want ... Try then to tell them that not to build houses like these, but like these. They won't listen.

Furthermore, Zalegaller elaborated on the process:

> And, instead what [blueprints] we have done, these [enterprises] can have connections to state leadership ... we say that a blueprint has to be made in the desired area. And they invest money in this, and get permission from the Governor. We then start to formulate planning documentation with the help of [this] external financing.

This definition leaves the planner in the role of a mechanical formulator of blueprints and construction permits. The political planning process with different interest groups is thus not planning. According to this interpretation, goal-setting is something shadowy and is thus not part of the planners' job description, which is thus defined as placing a project, decided elsewhere, in space in a rationally argued way. It should be noted, however, that also in Soviet planning, strategic goal setting was out of reach of the regional level planners – it is not a surprise that planners of 'the old Soviet guard' see it this way.

But then again, a young expert, Kurikalov, also internalises planning as technical land-use planning, although during the 1990s and the beginning of the 2000s the (re)construction of St Petersburg plot by plot has been dictated by private developers (Pavlov 2003; Tynkkynen 2004; Vakhmistrov 2002):

> Do you understand? Corporations don't have a particular role in planning, because actual planning has not taken place ... [E]nterprises have got their will through regarding individual sites – this is not planning ... Developers buy plots and only after this do they start to think about what they can and should do.

There is also planning when construction proceeds plot by plot, dictated by developers. We are thus discussing incremental planning practice and paradigm. However, urban reconstruction has not been fully dictated by developers, but the Governor's office has divided construction permits according to a plan, which is held back from the public (e.g. Tynkkynen 2004).

Conceiving planning this way will not promote a more realistic comprehension of Russian urban planning, which is permeated by strong economic and political conflicts of interests, that is, Realpolitik. Despite the rhetoric, planners, like Nazarov, are well aware of the linkages to power: 'Well, tell me which enterprise I should contact? According to whose interests [should the general plan be formulated]?'

Power is central in Russian planning, which is explicit when planners reflect on the financing of planning, which in practice means not only paying for the formulation, but also purchasing a beneficial land-use decision, as Berezin hints here:

> Yes, they [municipalities] do have the right to plan their territory, but another thing is financing this ... Peripheral districts don't have enough capital to do any kind of planning. Only if the federation or the region [*oblast*] agree to financing, then they can.

The self-governing districts and municipalities, outside St Petersburg, for example, are not actually responsible for conducting integrated planning.

Zalegaller, but also other interviewed planners, clearly link developers to plan formulation:

> The situation is as follows: the districts don't have money. In the Primorsk district a harbour company made a plan with their own finances ... We just approve the blueprint, and see that it fits to the general structure.

Thus, financing planning means that you must be able to purchase or rent the land, be able to invest in and build on it as indicated in the plan. In practice this means that plans are not made to guide and control future land use, but instead that individual construction projects steer land-use planning and plan formulation.

The Role of Expertise

It is understandable that planners defend those rationalities, which justify their central position in planning. A more central role for planners in the process is legitimised, for example, with views about the weaknesses in local political governance:

> In regional planning there are many subjective approaches ... Because the general plan of Russian regional structure has been made according to the principle 'do as you feel best', a common approach is impossible to establish. The system should be strictly defined and the main objectives confirmed. (Zalegaller)

This comment demonstrates a preference for an extreme expert-centred approach and a Soviet-style general plan for the whole country. According to this view, goal-setting that emerges from regional political reality harms the regional development of the country. Thus, this discourse claims that objectives should not be formulated by democratically elected regional bodies, but by undemocratically chosen experts that serve the bureaucratic system.

The idealisation of planning expertise seems also to bring with it an illusion that professionalism abolishes conflicts and power struggles from planning. In fact, this illusion of an objective perspective, a value-free rationality conceals conflicts from the public. A planner representing the state, Shitinskij, clearly demonstrates the permanency of this impression, which is so typical for planners of the modern era (see Scott 2003, 131–2):

> The state should say to the regions: here are my interests, and here I want to act like this, and elsewhere you can freely carry out your interests. In other words, activities should be coordinated, balanced, so as to avoid conflicts. This approach is the right one.

Expert-centrism is naturally rationalised by claiming that planning needs special, professional skills and knowledge, which lay citizens, businesses or politicians do not possess. Even a person, representing the civil society, Karpov, has adopted and internalised this view: 'And correspondingly the civil society cannot act as an initiator, because it lacks professional knowledge and financial possibilities.' Furthermore, Perelygin argues along the same lines, but his tone reflects his position as a state official: 'These are issues that only planners see and understand. But now those that win in elections are in power, and not those that are the most professional.'

On the other hand, expert-centrism is argued by over-emphasising the role of norms in planning. In a situation of normative dictatorship, as many of the interviewed planners see the essence of Russian planning, only experts possess the knowledge to take part in planning, and thus others have no role in it. Berezin notes:

> Although residents have the right to express their views while formulating [land use] zones, many objectives guiding planning have been decided in advance in the form of state norms, so it's pointless to discuss them, and decisions should be made only by the experts.

Bureaucratic governance is thus seen as a better way to carry out planning than both the representative democracy and direct participation of residents. However, these views are understandable for people, who were in a much more important position during the Soviet expert-centred planning system.

At the same time, this is a view that is intertwined with the project of the modern, which was also an elementary ideological thought of Soviet state communism (Pursiainen 1999, 77-8; also Scott 2003, 131-2). Planning bound to the thought of the modern presupposes that from the society can be found a common objective, shared by all, which is recognisable with the help of planners' professionalism. As defined by Russian scholars, one indicator of good and sustainable planning is a lower level of political activity of citizens, because it is assumed to mean a more firm trust in politicians and officials (Pokrovskij 2001, 14). This stems from the idealism of rationalist planning where conflicts are avoided because of the skilful work of professionals. In addition, it is related to a problem created by Habermasian idealism, which entails that conflicts can be evaded by society through open discussion (see e.g. Fainstein 2000; Healey 1996, 220-221).

Postmodern planning rejects this conflict-free ideology (e.g. Beauregard 1989, 391-2; Campbell 1996). The postmodern critique is exceptionally waspish in the case of Russia and St Petersburg: urban planning is not conflict-free, and taking inhabitants as a community sharing common objectives is not justified during times of ever growing socio-economic differences. If the modern planning tradition of the Soviet Union is kept alive, it means that places important for city dwellers are undervalued in planning (cf. Pavlov

2003). Direct participation is not valued or included, as Kurikalov defines the hardest tasks in formulating the St Petersburg general plan:

> Primarily this has been done by professionals using classic Le Corbusier style planning, which has its roots in the Soviet years of the 1980s. The hardest task has been to decide which agricultural lands should be built and which saved.

Also in a new political situation, when regimes do not want to formulate strategies and plans extending over the electoral period, but to proceed with planning in an incremental manner plot by plot, professional planners do have a role to play. As Nazarov points out:

> There you have a state official, possibly an architect; he knows where you can build and where not. Why should you write it down somewhere in advance?

This view about the planning process, promoted by Nazarov, is even more problematic than the synoptic, expert-centred planning. Planners do possess significant power in comprehensive planning, which is doubtful from the viewpoint of local democracy. However, in planning that is represented as integrative-comprehensive on a rhetorical level, but in practice proceeds incrementally according to the goals of the regime in power, the planner has even more hidden power in relation to the citizens.

In integrated planning, the general plan, even in present-day Russia, is a public document, which sets out the goals formulated by planners and the administration for public criticism. For transparency and legitimacy of planning, the worst situation would be one where land use is controlled without public planning documentation, as in St Petersburg in the 1990s, but at the same time claiming that planning is made rationally by professionals; choices made by the regime in power are rationalised by appealing to planners' expertise.

A Mixture of Eastern and Western Planning Ideas

Work done by Western governments and NGOs in Russia has had an effect on Russian planning practice. Russian planners were not very aware of the development of Western planning discourse in recent years, but they seem to have clung to contemporary issues. For example, strategic planning has become popular in St Petersburg and Northwest Russia due to Western contacts (Leontief Centre 1998; Tynkkynen 2004; Vakhmistrov 2002; Zhikharevich 2003).

There are, however, significant differences in the way strategic planning is understood and internalised in St Petersburg and in the Nordic countries;

for example, St Petersburg borrowed many central themes and processes for its 1998 strategic plan from the city strategy of Barcelona (Leontief Centre 1998; Zhikharevich 2003). Also due to Western aid and financing of the St Petersburg strategy-work, many democratic components were asked from the strategy process. However, the process was far from democratic or 'soft strategic', which would include stakeholders on a wide front taking part in the definition of the issues and agenda. Whereas, the St Petersburg strategy formulation resembled much more 'hard strategic', since only the voice of the elite – key politicians, officials and business circles – was heard, and they formulated the goals of the strategy (Tynkkynen 2004; Zhikharevich 2003).

Karpov describes these new trends in Russian and St Petersburg planning:

> Then came structural perestroika, reorganisation, and then our Western soul mates decided to lend a helping hand and brought with them their progressive planning methods.

And Perelygin continues:

> Regional planning has developed in Russia along two lines: Western regional planning ideas and the principles of Soviet planning. These ideas live side by side and their fusion brings to life something new and interesting. I think that these ideas will be of global importance.

Despite these sarcastic and messianic views, the fusion of Western and Soviet planning principles could result in good planning. A hopeful view on the future of Russian planning is that a normative approach is borrowed from the Soviet comprehensive tradition, whereas from the more incremental, yet democratic Western tradition a more central role for civil society and the private sector in goal-setting would be incorporated. This makes it possible to keep the goals of social amenities and environmental quality on the agenda, enabled by 'the Soviet normative and comprehensive perspective', while abandoning the definition of an expert-centred, objective common good, which is contested in the 'the Western incremental and postmodern perspective'.

On the other hand, it is as possible that planning will be diverted even further away from the goal of common good. If the expert-centred goal-setting of the Soviet times is emphasised in the planning discourse, but at same time in practice giving the private sector a special position in planning and decision-making, in relation to public administration and the civil society, as in Western and especially US planning, the outcome can be a setting described by Flyvbjerg (2003, 320–21): goals of the coalition of enterprises and public government, the regime in power, are formulated by planners in a rationalisation process to stand public review. Planning expertise will thus be used to validate the planning process and make it look professionally ground and justified, despite the fact that decisions benefit by large the public-private elite in power.

Furthermore, there is evidence that on some occasions the regime in power does not even need this rationalisation process, but relies on the naked use of power. This danger has been well understood by planners, as Perelygin states here:

> With good planning we can avoid the mistakes of Western urban planning. But we want to step on the rake twice; we proceed according to the Western doctrine: the initiatives of the private actors take us where they want and the state becomes the loser.

The planners emphasise the importance of the Soviet planning tradition – the disappearance of the socialist bloc has not eradicated the objectives of socialist planning. As Polishchuk emphasises:

> What is happening now is convergence, reversion to the old ... We begin to realise that solely market-steered governance does not take us in the right direction ... And now it seems that we who have known and mastered all this are walking away from this, whereas the West is striving towards it.

Perelygin continues along the same lines:

> In my view, Soviet planning was the best ... In the West planning was started 30 to 40 years ago, whereas in the Soviet Union planning was there from the beginning ... And Vernadsky's system-approach on planning was a central element of the Soviet urban planning school ... And these (principles) are simply copied now. We even joke: Gosplan has moved to Europe.

However, when planners evaluate the functionality of previous Soviet and present-day Russian planning systems, the influence of Realpolitik in the planning outcome is not fully understood, despite the fact that planners, as Perelygin, are aware that Realpolitik does play a vital role:

> Another thing is that the party apparatus, the Soviet power, was not the best mechanism to realise, execute plans, but the principles of planning were good.

Here then is the core problem of contemporary Russian planning discourse: there is an illusion that the principles of planning, ideology, can be separated from practical planning without again producing plans that diverge from context reality. The next comment by Perelygin confirms the diehard nature of this fallacy:

> The main differences between Western and Russian planning are the basic objectives: in the West the power of the private sector is diminished by buying property, whereas in Russia land is mostly in the hands of the state. The setting is totally the opposite, so the objectives of planning must be also.

The objectives of Russian and Western planning are not, however, so different; according to the officially uttered goals, both strive for the common good and regional development by controlling land use (Gradostroitel'nyj kodeks Rossijskoj Federatsii 2004). The fact that most Russian land is still owned by the state does not relieve land-use planning from conflicts and power struggles in present day Russia. Power struggles have not taken place so much between private enterprises, the state and the civil society as in the West, but more between different sectors of the state administration, as especially during Soviet times, and between regional power regimes formed by the corporate circles and the regional and local administrations (Chant 1999, 324–5; Tynkkynen 2004).

Conclusion – The Elite's Goals are Rationalised by Planners

I argue that the 'planning paradigm' promoted by the practitioners in St Petersburg is very problematic from the viewpoint of the common good. The planning discourse maintained by practitioners seems to borrow from the Soviet paradigm the idea of overarching instrumental rationality, which grants a superior position to professionals in defining planning goals and practices.

Beauregard (1989, 389–90) and Klosterman (1985, 10), representing the postmodern view in planning theory, emphasise that expert-centred and comprehensive planning of the modern era runs the risk of ignoring both the competitiveness requirements of the private sector and the important life-world places of the city-dwellers. However, because of the potential for corruption arising from the association of the St Petersburg city administration and the corporate world, this equation leaves only concerns that the life-world of citizens and 'the city of places' are on the losers' side as the present planning discourse in St Petersburg admits that de facto urban planning is led by powerful developer corporations in an extremely incremental manner.

Furthermore, the traditional view of Western planning theory, perceiving planners as the fourth political power (Beauregard 1989, 392–3; Klosterman 1985, 12), seems to be in St Petersburg the case only in a marginal sense. As I highlighted in my analysis, the setting seems to be more of a kind where the regime in power, the elite, uses professional planners to promote policies based on their own agendas by appealing to planners' expertise in formulating the common good.

This raises concerns that although planning is in reality dictated by public–private regimes, an idealistic planning discourse is being deliberately kept up. This is an even more troubling discovery when one considers that all of Northern Russia, and even beyond, follows the examples of the westernised 'Northern Capital' in their pursuit to search for solutions to the planning tasks ahead (e.g. Zhikharevich 2003).

Bibliography

Beauregard, R. (1989) 'Between Modernity and Postmodernity: The Ambiguous Position of US Planning', *Environment and Planning D: Society and Space* 7, 381–95.
Brade, I., E. Pertsik and D. Piterskij (2000) *Rajonnaya planirovka i razrabotka shem rasseleniya – Opyt i perspektivy*, Mezhdunarodnye otnosheniya, Moscow.
Campbell, S. (1996) 'Green Cities, Growing Cities, Just Cities? Urban Planning and the Contradictions of Sustainable Development', *Journal of the American Planning Association* 62:3, 296–312.
Chant, C. (1999) 'Cities in Russia', in D. Goodman and C. Chant (eds) *European Cities and Technology. Industrial to post-industrial city*, Routledge, New York, 301–27.
Dem'yanenko, A. (2000) 'Sotsial'no-ekonomicheskaya geografiya i upravlenie: vozmozhnye napravleniya vzaimodejstviya', *Izvestiya Rossijkogo Geograficheskogo Obshchestva* 132:1, 38–44.
Fainstein, S. (2000) 'New Directions in Planning Theory', *Urban Affairs Review* 35:4, 451–78.
Flyvbjerg, B. (2003), 'Rationality and Power', in S. Campbell and S. Fainstein (eds) *Readings in Planning Theory*, 2nd edn, Blackwell, Oxford, 319–29.
Gradostroitel'ny kodeks Rossijskoj Federatsii (2004) *Ofitsial'nyj tekst*, deistvujushchaya redaktsiya, Ekzamen, Moscow.
Hall, P. (2002) *Urban and Regional Planning*, 4th edn, Routledge, London.
Healey, P. (1996) 'The Communicative Turn in Planning Theory and its Implications for Spatial Strategy Formation', *Environment and Planning B: Planning and Design* 23, 217–34.
Kaz'min, M. and J. Kalinin (2000) 'Problemy i perspektivy kottedzhnogo stroitel'stva v Moskovskom regione', Vestnik Moskovskogo Universiteta, *Seriya Geograficheskaya* 6/2000, 44–8.
Klosterman, R. (1985) 'Arguments for and against Planning', *Town Planning Review* 56:1, 5–20.
Lappo, G. (1997) *Geografiya gorodov*, Vlados, Moscow.
Leontief Centre (1998) *Strategic Plan for St Petersburg*, St Petersburg.
Lopatnikov, D. (2004) *Postindustrializm i ekologicheskaya perspektiva*, ABF, Moscow.

Makarov, O. and S. Pegov (2001) 'Ekologicheskaya politika, ustojchivoe razvitie i ekologicheskaya bezopasnost', *Regional'naya ekologiya* 9:1, 6–12.
Maslov, N. (2003) *Gradostroitel'naja ekologyja*, Vysshaja shkola, Moscow.
Pavlov, N. (2003) 'Peterburzhtsy mogut vliyat na gradostroitel'ny protsess', Konserzh 15 December 2003, St Petersburg.
Pertsik, E. (1980) *Gorod v Sibiri: problemy, opyt, poisk reshenij*, Moscow.
Pokrovskij, S. (2001) 'Sostoyanie geosistem i ustojchivost' regional'nogo razvitiya', Vestnik Moskovskogo Universiteta, *Seriya Geograficheskaya* 1/2001, 11–15.
Pursiainen, C. (1999) Venäjän idea, utopia ja missio, Ulkopoliittisen instituutin julkaisuja 6, Gaudeamus, Helsinki.
Ruble, B. (1995) *Money Sings: The Changing Politics of Urban Space in Post-Soviet Yaroslavl*, Cambridge University Press, New York.
Shaw, D. (1999) *Russia in the Modern World. A New Geography*, Blackwell, Oxford.
Scott, J. (2003) 'Authoritarian High Modernism', in S. Campbell and S. Fainstein (eds) *Readings in Planning Theory*, 2nd edn, Blackwell, Oxford, 125–41.
Tynkkynen, V.-P. (2004) 'Venäläisessä kaupunkisuunnittelussa tuulee lännestä', *Idäntutkimus – The Finnish Review of East European Studies* 11:1, 3–10.
Vakhmistrov, A. (2002) 'Pyat let strategicheskogo planirovaniya v Sankt-Peterburge', in B. Zhikharevich et al. (eds) *Territorial'noe strategicheskoe planirovanie. Pervye uroki Rossijskoi praktiki*, Vypusk 2, Leont'evskij tsentr, St Petersburg, 16–17.
Zhikharevich, B.S. (2003) 'Strategicheskoe planirovanie v gorodah Rossii', in S. Vasilev (ed.) *Territorial'noe strategicheskoe planirovanie pri perekhode k rynochnoi ekonomike: opyt gorodov Rossii*, Leont'evskij tsentr, St Petersburg.

Interviews

Berezin, M., Freelance architect and urban planner, 10 December 2003.
Fedorov, A., Chairman, Environmental NGO 'Centre for Environmental Initiatives', 7 March 2004.
Kalinkina, O., Regional Architect (Zelenogorsk District), Committee of Cultural Heritage of St Petersburg, 1 March 2004.
Karelina, I., President, Leontief Centre, 9 December 2003.
Karpov, A., Chairman, Association of Naturalists of St Petersburg, 28 February 2004.
Kurikalov, J., Juridical expert, Administrative Council of the City of St Petersburg, 6 March 2004.
Maslennikov, N., Professor of Architecture, St Petersburg School of Economics, 12 December 2003.

Nazarov, V., Director, Urban Planning Enterprise 'ZAO Peterburgski NIPIgrad', 3 March 2004.
Perelygin, J., Scientific Director, Strategic Research Centre of Northwest Russia, 6 March 2004.
Petrovich, M., Department Head, Urban planning enterprise 'ZAO Peterburgski NIPIgrad', 15 December 2003.
Polishchuk, V., Deputy Director, Committee of Urban Planning and Architecture of St Petersburg, 17 December 2003.
Shitinskij, V., Director, state urban research and planning institute 'Urbanistika', 28 February 2004.
Zalegaller, V., Expert, Urban Planning Committee of Leningrad oblast, 6 March 2004.
Zhikharevich, B., Deputy Director, Leontief Centre, 18 December 2003.

Chapter 9

The House of Many Different Ages

Violeta Puşcaşu

Introduction

In Romania's third millennium the term 'planning' still has a bad image in its general usage. After almost 50 years of centralised decision-making, delivered as economic planning, family planning (an obligatory birth rate) and especially planned systematisation of localities (enforced demolition), any new idea relating to planning could become a failure. That is why, after 1990, it was necessary to find different syntagms to relate to what Europe calls spatial planning. In this chapter we try to draw up a planning history as a way to look into the dimension of planning culture.

But how do we begin a difficult and risky enterprise such as outlining the history of planning in Romania, when the concept itself is unclear and insufficiently substantiated in the country?[1] The need to set the contemporary activity of planning and arrangement of the territory within a process equally evolving as compared to itself and to other systems, raised the questions, how old are the actions that can be attributed to Romanian planning and to what external evolutions can they be compared? Relating to the writings belonging to this type of analysis from other cultures, we were tempted to search for the same elements in Romania that are considered roots of planning actions in other countries: urban plans, specialised laws and organisms, data and brands, etc. During our research we confirmed to ourselves that it was about a difference of content rather than a temporal difference (as we might have been tempted to believe), which was understood *a priori* due to the general and specific contextual diversity that is at work on the level of large systems such as the national planning systems.

The simplistic dichotomy between stages of organic evolution and planning periods measurable in terms of norms, institutions and actions is inadequate in the case of complex systems. Nevertheless, the need for arranging and staging is included in the logic of understanding any spatial phenomenon. Therefore, we shall use statistics and synopses as arguments to support our correlations and extrapolations in order to outline the edifice of the Romanian planning.

---

1 The Romanian equivalent of the term planning is *urbanism and territorial planning*, dating from 1991, which replaced the phrase 'territory and settlements systematisation' introduced in 1974.

The Historical Context

The Emergence of the Romanian City

A number of works about city history and urban planning, along with those from the viewpoint of geography, anthropology and/or sociology, allow us to put forward the idea that organising inhabited territory by an urban community is an action intrinsically and implicitly derived from the human spirit, manifested since age-old times. These works, as well as others, convey the idea according to which the rule/law functions in particular (actually, we believe that it simply functions) at reduced territorial scales, in small, self-controllable communities through their examples and case studies. To put it differently, planning is more a self-regulation when it emerges naturally in closed and limited territorial systems and becomes an institution when the areas in question go beyond those boundaries and the implications of the action have wider application. This has been verified by looking at the territory in the Carpathian Mountains, the Danube River and the Black Sea. The analyses of historical works, studies and essays undertaken by various authors regarding the organisation of the social and economic life of cities and villages, and of the political and ideological context in which they functioned, show that the small settlements represent the depositories of the first nuclei of planning, even more so if these settlements were urban, but the planning institution appears only once the unitary national framework is created. The city is one of the media, but not the only one and not enough to enable us to consider that the beginnings of spatial planning lie within urban planning.

The history of the Romanian city has a few features of its own which differentiates it from the history of Western European cities.[2] This observation is important for understanding the differences between planning systems in the modern period. The Romanian city is an economic and political phenomenon which chrystallised at the same time as the establishment of the feudal states, unlike Western Europe which, preserving an urban network inherited from the declining Roman empire, also displays a difference in development between

---

2 Before the middle of the fourteenth century (a somewhat conventional chronological landmark, connected to the constituting period of the two Romanian principalities neighbouring the Carpathians), the cause-effect ratio between central political authority and the developing urban area had a spontaneous nature, in the sense that the formation of the incipient settlements, starting from the fortified centres in which such authorities had their headquarters, took place independently of any special steps taken by these authorities (as not all fortified centres became cities in this manner). Being situated within the boundaries of the same political formation (principality) and lacking the internal forms of organisation specific to cities, they were under the discretionary authority of the local voivodes (local rulers or officials) (Matei 1997, 13–15)

the state and the city in favour of the city in terms of the establishing of feudal political and administrative structures (Matei 1997). The territories to the north of the Danube lost the urban skeleton almost entirely; the majority of Romanian medieval cities being the result of self-organising mechanisms.[3]

The aspect is not without relevance for the nature of the relationship between urban planning and spatial planning: Western cities developed their state administration from a bottom-up relationship. Meanwhile, the Romanian city experienced a simultaneous emergence with its state feudal administration, generating a top-down relationship.

East and West – National and European Gradient

After their formation, the historical provinces of the present Romanian territory were predominantly under external administrative influence and restrictions. This aspect is the second major observation that must be taken into account when comparing Eastern and Western Europe. Moldavia and Wallachia (the Romanian country) were under constant Turkish threat, whilst Transylvania was under Hungarian and Austro-Hungarian influence and even administration for a long period of time. In the eastern and southern parts of Romania as a Turkish vassal, the Sublime Porte[4] imposed the economic and foreign status and policy, leaving the home affairs, however, including law and institutions, to the local prince. But long and close contact with Ottoman rules translated into a specific attitude towards city organisation. This fact had several ramifications: it ensured the pre-eminence of the central ruling/ authority in its relationship with urban communities, but it introduced and made permanent a cultural difference in the manner of thinking about space and its exploitation (Matei 1997). The need to organise the security system coincided, chronologically speaking, with the period when the cities located in the Carpathians reached a level of maturity that would have permitted regime of freedom (like in Western Europe) as a premise for certain forms of incipient urban planning. The cities did not have the status of autonomy (for instance, 'republic' or 'league') to enable them develop their own planning systems.

---

3   The forming of the medieval Romanian cities beside the Carpathians is related to political factors (the feudal residences and in succession the royal ones become nuclei of the polarisation of commercial and crafts activities in the eighteenth and nineteenth centuries and only on a secondary level economic ones (centres of production and trade). Transylvania is the only province where the cities acquired the function of defence, becoming fortresses as well ,and where colonisations with Saxons and Szeklers took place, a fact which brings the urban structure closer to the specificity of central Europe. The church/cathedral did not contribute to an urban genesis (as compared to the West) as long as it did not have a local ecclesiastical hierarchy autonomy towards the ecumenical patriarchy from Constantinople.

4   The open court of the Turkish sultan during the Ottoman Empire.

Historians of the mediaeval period supply us with few relevant facts of the territory layout at macro-regional scale and of the administrative and political units (province, duchy, voivodship and kingdom). On the other hand, the territorial level at which references start to be made is the domicile, that of monasteries and of boyar properties which enforce their own rules of organisation and layout with temporal coherence and projection.

As a matter of fact, the beginnings of spatial planning in Romania can be identified with the first feudal regulations regarding the land use. Colonisation in the Middle Ages was accompanied by regulatory measures regarding the use of the colonised lands, waters and forests. It was only much later that the first determinations of dwelling places were set up for some rural settlements, mainly in Transylvania and Oltenia during the Austro-Hungarian occupation (the first half of the eighteenth century).

The great laic feudal property, the 'host' of the urban centres, appeared precisely from the feudal residency/urban centre relationship (Matei 1997), divided as it was into free rural property, boyar property, the royal domain and the church domain. The prerogatives of the central administration remained limited, which explains the absence of a unique system of land-use regulations, on the one hand and, consequently, the absence of a unitary morphology, on the other.

Three great fields of organising the property, private property, the state's domains and the church domain, represent the intermediary operating frameworks, at an infra-state level which experience the regional cultural influence.

As state domains and private property are well known active constants in all planning systems, we shall only dedicate a few explanatory lines to the church domain, which constitutes a particularity of the Orthodox culture within the Romanian space, especially as it re-emerged after a tradition of centuries and a temporary absence after 1990.

The Church Domain – a Territorialised Unit of Strength in the Tradition of Territorial Organisation

Being more often than not the result of a royal or boyar decision, monasteries and their surrounding lands were endowed either from the beginning or later on and represent an exercise in *sui generis* planning. The location for the construction of the church itself was chosen according to events, premonitions, isolation/accessibility from/to the main roads, purposes adjacent to the religious one (defence, leisure, form of investment and accumulation, especially through the domains under administration, etc.). The general rule was that of 'planning without pencil'.[5] The spatial planning decision within the domain

---

5 The locations and configurations of the areas in question are exclusively narrative in chronicles or written references, unaccompanied by blueprints or plans. As

belonged to first of all the Father Superior and to the rightful owner, the king or the boyar. In the internal organisation of the monastery one can recognise an archetypical functional division into zones with the 'centre' represented by the church, surrounded by monastic residences (cells), guest rooms (rarely) and outbuildings, and the agricultural lands or the forests closely placed, almost according to the von Thunen model.

This major level of social and territorial organisation reached its peak in the seventeenth and eighteenth centuries when the church owned almost one-third of the land fund of the Romanian Principalities. The monastery domains would receive a hard blow through Prince Cuza's decision to secularise the wealth of monasteries in 1863.

In the twentieth century, after an era of maximum laicisation of society, monasteries as an institution were reactivated after 1990, regaining lands for new projects of their own spatial planning and organisation, albeit on a much smaller scale, within a regulated framework which limited the specific local decisions. Against the background of social bewilderment, of urban de-regularisation or at least sub-regularisation, public approval and the administrative disorientation in the last decade of the last century, the monasteries tried to rebuild a position which they would find it difficult to achieve in modern society.

The other type of informal territorial territorialised unit, the parish, functions only as a social institution, without its own domains, having only a weak role as a consultative local organism, regained after 1990 as a symbolic image of a local collective authority in recovery. The urban shapes that embody the parish – settlements, churches, buildings with a social function, etc. – are subordinated to the new planning structures.

These partial conclusions emphasise a cultural framework marked by a modest urbanity, with a patient/obedient rural society displaying faith in the spiritual matrix of the community, which would make it malleable and mimetic at the same time in relation to external influences.

Institutions and Administrative Levels

The beginnings of Romanian planning belong to the nineteenth century, a century of great dynamics at European level, which brough about major transformations of an economic, social, political and administrative nature. The common chronological landmark is the reign of Prince Alexandru Ioan Cuza (1859–1866) during which the first noticeably consistent actions for the future of Romanian planning take place. Although many of these cannot be easily separated from the modern administrative ensemble which had begun to

---

a matter of fact, the practice of accompanying ownership documents with blueprints, maps or plans did not exist until the twentieth century.

take shape, the main directions in which planning operated can be identified: the secularisation of clerical wealth, agricultural reform, the reformation of the administrative system and the law of the communes. Through these, the first step towards a unitary planning system was taken – the replacement of small and medium territorial cells, organic and non-related, with a local planning of the self-regulatory type, with the unitary system, centred on the state territorial ensemble, which was already an institution. We therefore witness a gradual crossing from the local, domestic institution, with mixed attributes, to the decisional specialisation of the first administrative organisms of the large territory, conceived as sectoral structures with supervision over permitted evolutions and insertions.

From this moment on, the institutions and the levels of administration were ranked, starting from the national level to the local one, continuously functioning during each historic and political stage, such as before World War I, between the wars, after World War II (Communist era) and post-December 1989.

In the west of the country, under Austrian administration, the institutions were even older and imposed a sense of order on the space and on its inhabitants, as well as on public property which even today still distinguishes the western from the eastern regions.[6]

During the period 1918–1944, spatial planning became a preoccupation of general interest in the context of administrative unification following 'The Great Union' of 1918 (due to the Law of Administrative Unification of 1925). Forums of approval and guidance for urban and territorial systematisation were created (the Superior Technical Council in 1919) as well as the first specialised bodies in the field (the Urbanism Institute of the City Union) and the first specialised publications come out: *The Monitory of the City Union of Romania* (1924–1931) and *Urbanism* magazine (1932–1943).

After 1948, due to political changes, economic planning overshadowed physical and social planning through a dogmatic system in which the relationship between politics and control was predetermined by a legally compulsory plan (the 'Five-Year Plan'). The State Committee of Planning became a national operational body with ministerial status in order to apply a unique ensemble of social and economic decisions in all local administrative units. Public consultation, although regulated, was only formal.

---

6   Two hundred and fifty years ago, structured and coherent architectural urban plans existed, based on which an entire generation of buildings was constructed in Timisoara. In 1776 there was already an Architecture Office of the Administration Chamber which supervised the construction of all new buildings, as well as the restoration of old ones; it also indicated the buildings that were to be demolished the following year. The so-called 'magistrates' ensured that the regulations were observed and that the demolitions were done on time, even before the existence of the Architecture Office.

Table 9.1 Institutional competence coverage (selection)

Year	Relevant ministry	Related committees, ministries
1859–1952	Ministry of Public Works	
1952	–	State Committee for Architecture and Constructions
1953	*between 1953 and 1957, the Ministry of Communal Households and Local Industry	State Committee of Planning (≈ Ministry of Economy)
1974		Central Party and State Committee for Territory, Urban and Rural Settlements Systematisation
1978	–	Council of Economic and Social Organisation
1989 (December)	–	Ministry of Economy
1990	Ministry of Public Works, Transportation and Land Planning	
1991	Ministry of Public Works and Land Planning	
1996	Ministry of Public Works and Land Planning	Committee for European Integration
2000	Ministry of Public Works, Transportation and Residence	Ministry for European Integration
2004	Delegation for Public Works and Land Planning	Ministry of Transportation, Constructions and Tourism Ministry of Agriculture, Forest and Rural Development
2007	Ministry of Development, Public Works and Residence	

After 1990, ministerial responsibilities were redistributed at every governmental change, spatial planning being associated with various other actions and directions. Strictly speaking, urban and spatial planning are carried out through the activity of more than 20 committees and commissions specialised in urbanism, construction and architecture, which interact with the development, investments, tourism or transportation infrastructure.

In the National Plan for Development, spatial planning is increasingly correlated with the regional development policy (developed in parallel after 1998) which imposed the adoption of the NUTS system.

The administrative levels related to regional planning and development activities are the national level – the reference framework for the entire planning and development policy through the National Development Plan, and the infra-national levels – the county, the city and the commune. As an elementary administrative level (NUTS 4), the commune represents a stable mark of Romanian organisational and administrative conception introduced in the middle of the nineteenth century and preserved until today. It represents an administrative level that unites two or more villages whose are considered too small for a spatial planning and funding decision. The idea of conferring power to local administrations by means of a legally acknowledged association meant an avant-garde move which would be similar to French inter-communality which emerged almost 100 years later.

The other two administrative levels – the county and the region – still worked simultaneously for short period of time at the beginning of the 1950s but, after 1990, as well as taking some elements from the French model of spatial planning and development, an intermediary regional level, i.e. the development region, was reintroduced between the central administrative level and the local county and communal one. This territorialised unit is not a legal entity which does not represent a territorial collectivity but it is a level of zonal spatial planning.

Planning Objectives

The institutional actions translate into transforming the landscape through physical planning along two major themes: infrastructure (and later, during the communist era, heavy industry) and urban transformation.

The actions oriented towards the transportation infrastructure are unquestionably the first and least equivocal insertions explicitly manifested in physical planning. They are followed by urban transformation and modernisation.

Since the first railroad constructions which, due to political and military conditions, developed for a while within the framework of two separate networks (one in the old Romania and another in Austro-Hungary) the task of building them was given to foreign consortia, and was followed by the system of tunnels and bridges. Today, the articulations of the European transportation network TEN-T are in direct line with Romanian spatial planning, which became one of the instruments of the mutual language of connecting the Romanian planning system to the European one.

The urban interventions include:

- creating new cities and radically restructuring the existing ones, especially at the level of those with a harbour function, expanding the existing cities by parcelling off various sizes and regular expansions or transforming the existing cities through modifications/rectifications of the street line;
- aligning the streets and correlating the buildings with this;
- drawing up new major axes of traffic (Bucharest boulevards) and partially applying the Haussmann model;
- modifying the parcelling – adapting it (through dimensions) to urban functions; parcelling the great land properties – the emergence of

neighbourhoods (parks), based on the physical model of garden-cities, accompanied by construction rules, as was the case with the first cheap residential neighbourhoods;
- unifying the urban organism (intramural zone with the extramural one), by demolishing the fortifications in the cities of Transylvania and applying the principles of the Viennese ring in a limited and partial manner;
- planning public leisure spaces (parks, gardens); combining classic principles of composition with landscaping principles;
- modifying the urban image by partially replacing the previously built stock and by putting street facades in order.

The partial conclusions show that, institutionally speaking, spatial planning was launched through public works, the main preoccupation being the infrastructure. The urban-architectural component was less forthcoming and copied the French, the German or the English model. Economic development from the middle of the 1950s was politically dictated and privileged the industry-city relationship, displaying a tinge of centralised planning control. After 1990, spatial planning focused on the infrastructure-settlements relationship. The administrative framework of implementation is stable at the extreme levels – national and local – and adaptable at the intermediary level, mezzo-territorial, the new aspect being represented by the region. However, there is no institutional correspondent responsible for regional planning.

The Normative Component

An inventory of the laws adopted in Romania from modern times to the present day has revealed that the normative beginnings of planning are related to the transformations brought about by the political changes of 1848.

If English urbanism is related to the first reports of the British Royal Commission (1885) and of the London County Council (1900), simultaneously displaying a strong social and hygienist tinge, and in the France of the Second Napoleonic Empire the transformation of Paris meant major works of urban planning, in Romania, the regulation of rural property (1864), the expropriation for cause of public utility (1864), the law of communes (1865) or the administration of the state domains (1872) are legislative orientations which seem to suggest that planning at a national scale was at least simultaneous with if not anterior to urban planning preoccupations. The primary explanation resides in the absence of an urban crisis of the Western type caused by the Industrial Revolution, in the non-existence of urban outskirts which would need restructuring and ultimately in a different value of the density of proletarian population. The capital, Bucharest, the only city which could have had a metropolitan evolution due to its function, was far from this experience although it copied the urban-architectural elitist behaviour of Paris on a smaller scale (Cristea and Lascu 1988). The problem of residences, though not as acute as in the Western world, did not remain unregulated; it benefited, as was the contemporary trend, from two complementary laws in 1910.

If we consider the urban plan (the master plan) a normative document specific to the twentieth century, it should be stated that it would not be implemented before centralised planning, although the initiative of a 'super-urbanistic plan' (1919) appears in the works of one of the precursors of Romanian urbanism, Cincinat Sfinţescu, influenced by the European urban trends.

Urban modernisation became the task of the local eligible administrations; the main instrument of controlling the urban development were the various urban, architectural and, after 1900, systematisation plans (Timişoara, Braşov, Bucureşti). The urban models applied were the Western ones in the Old Kingdom and the Central-European models (as before) in Transylvania.

Starting in 1929, spa/watering cities and urban centres had to make their own guiding and systematisation plans according to local administration law. Contests for obtaining the most interesting solutions for systematisation in some maritime settlements and in some zones of the cities became a practice that contributed to the selection and promotion of the most valuable ideas in the field of urbanism (Cristea and Lascu 1988).

World War II and the following decades were marked by major political, administrative, economic and social transformations, which profoundly affected the continuity of spatial planning concepts and activities specific to the previous period.

If the first years after the war are characterised by processes of recovery after the destruction generated by the great conflagration, starting with the sixth decade, territory organisation and settlement development were gradually subordinated to the political and ideological interest of the Communist Party, becoming an instrument of 'transformation' of Romanian society under the label of 'systematisation'. Law no. 58/1974, regarding territory and settlements systematisation, opened the way for radical and brutal interventions both in the territory and inside the settlements.[7] The content of the laws in the

---

7 The purpose of systematisation is to judiciously organise the territory of the country, counties and communes and of urban and rural settlements, to functionally divide them into zones according to the way the land is used, to establish the height and density of buildings, as well as the density of population and green and leisure spaces, providing social and cultural facilities, ensuring technical and public utility works and ways of communication and transportation, to preserve and improve the environment, to value the historic monuments, works of art and historic places, to enhance the economic and social efficiency of the investments and the continuous improvement of working, living and resting conditions for the entire population. Systematisation should ensure the restriction of the building perimeters of settlements to the bare necessity

Communist period reveal a switch in favour of heavy industry, a declared purpose in Party policy, and the social planning accompanied the aberrant ways of society control and guidance by means of decisions regarding demography or nourishment.

It may seem surprising that, partially, the principles and objectives circulated in the Law 58/1974 are to be found in the texts of some European documents, which confirms once again how sensitive the distance between conservative liberalism and extreme leftism is.

Table 9.2   Legislative synopsis

Stage	Normative act	Reveals
1859 – 1900	The Law of Communes (1863), Regularisation of Rural Property (1864),	Crystallisation
Pre-war	Building Healthy and Cheap Residencies (1910)	Internal adjustment
Post-war	Constitution (1923), Encouragement to Build Residencies (1927), The Law of Free Zones (1929), The General Administration of State Fisheries and the Improvements of the Floodable Region of the Danube River (1929), Organising Bucharest Municipality (1939)	European adjustment
Communist	The Law regarding Territory and Settlements Systematisation (1974)	Centralised planning
Democratic	The Law regarding Regional Development (1998), The Law of Urbanism and Land Planning (2001)	European re-adjustment

Centralism was replaced with market economy and the documents was adapted to the new context. The National Development Plan (NDP) (2007–2013) is the document of strategic planning and multi-annual financial programming. It stimulates the economic and social development of the country in accordance with the principles of EU Cohesion Policy, similar to the programming done by the member states for the 'convergence' objective of the structural funds. At an internal level, it is an instrument for prioritising public investment in development. The NDP undertakes a multi-annual planning of the economic and social development of the country, sectoral and regionally integrated on the basis of the national sectoral development strategies, the

---

and the optimum use of land, which is an important national treasure. Territory and settlements systematisation is going on according to prognoses and on the basis of the provisions of the unique national plan of economical and social development of the country and contributes to the harmonious development of the entire territory, to the superior exploitation of the material and human resources and to the rational and balanced distribution of the production forces aiming at an organic union of the economic efficiency criteria with the social ones (art. 1, Law no. 59/1974).

national regional development strategies and the strategic orientations at the European level, in direct connection to the national spatial planning strategy (from 1997).

The NDP's balanced regional development strategy is in full concordance with the principles stated in the European Spatial Development Perspective (ESDP) which refer to the expansion of urban networks and the improvement of cooperation between cities and adjacent rural zones, as an engine of economic growth. The strategy emphasises the catalytic role that urban centres play in economic growth and in the creation of workplaces.

The strategy also accords with the European Commission document 'The Sustainable Urban Development in the EU – An Action Framework'. The NDP's regional strategy seeks to identify the synergies between rural and urban areas (for instance, with regard to promoting tourism at the local level), in concordance with the EU approach. From this perspective, it is worth mentioning that the development regions in Romania have ideal geographic dimensions in order to allow urban and rural development to compliment each other.

We conclude that, from a normative point of view, there are two stages in Romanian territorial planning. The master plan (urban plan) introduced after 1991 as a compulsory document for all settlements, whether rural or urban, is a new task for local communities and quite often they are either obsolete, or are evaded because they imply an untried action: the bottom-up decision. Strategic spatial planning (national level) is more coherent for at least two reasons: a national experience cannot be lost even if the doctrine changes and the development strategy preserves the top-to-bottom component, which is so well-known (and even occasionally convenient) to the Romanians.

Politics, Ideology and Models

Romanian intellectuals have always been oriented towards the European West, more towards France than Germany. England is out of the question. Socialist doctrine does not come late in the list of Romanian principalities, even if the local industrial environment was far from the European evolutionary level and if planning contained a 'leftist' ingredient, and the offspring of the socialist ideology within the Romanian space is represented by the Scăieni-Prahova Phalanstery in 1835.[8] As we do not have the continuation of Diamant's

---

8 Theodor Diamant established a Fourieristic colony on the land of Emanoil Bălăceanu who, shortly after, found the political and economic context inadequate. The colony was dissolved, due particularly to the fact that its initiator left the experiment at the first sign of difficulty. The form of organisation of the new society was in Fourier's opinion the 'phalanx', a group of 1,500–2,000 people split into 'series' and 'groups' according to their inclinations towards certain types of activity. The 'phalanx' members

planning adventure, we can place it in a relationship with any of the pioneering forms of the early models: the social city or Howard's garden-city. This would be done to show that we have 'traditions of utopian urban planning'. Let us not deceive ourselves, though. If urban manifestations of the socialist-Marxist doctrines, anarchic or liberal, worked and produced urban effects, it is because they faced city-industry tension. These appeared in Romania as well, already resolved in the shape of the functionalist city, introduced by the same Marxist doctrine, politically 'improved' from a Stalinist viewpoint, bringing the models of large circulation of the collectivist cities, neighbourhoods of blocks of flats, functional zoning, the priority of the economic principle, etc. The inter-war liberal democratic time-out made room for indigenous ways of urbanisation, which were in fact eclectic copies, as we already said, of some models and trends of the time, as the period was too short to be able to generate a specific Romanian urban style.

The Communist ideology was politically installed all over Eastern Europe after 1945 and standardised projects advanced under the umbrella of equality and social equity. The confusion arising in deciphering the differences between Eastern and Western Europe appears when the label of social and economic principle is attached to any project of spatial planning in the West, and the results achieved are visibly different from the Romanian ones. This is why contemporary society suffers from a bizarre mixture of nostalgia for total planning and the temptation of planning liberty according to needs. Even more amazing (and difficult to conceptualise ideologically) is that world-scale planning is experiencing a paradigmatic change (the globalisation of transition) which brings into debate the opportunity for comprehensive planning and its replacement with communicative actions. For Romania, which is barely (re)enforcing the comprehensive system from a perspective different from the centralist one, there are two alternatives: either consuming and assuming the model rapidly as a compulsory stage in the growth of the planning experience whilst it is still applicable, or bypassing this stage and entering communicative planning directly, in which case there are two other ramifications – non-planning or chaos planning (because there is less a culture of communication and more a culture of execution), or a surprising flexible adaptation, which could be called the Romanian 'miracle'.

External Influences of Proximity

The cultural interferences that derive from Romania's geographical centrality have historically determined regional identities and different spatial behaviours. From a stylistic point of view, the fact that Transylvania, Banat and Bucovina

---

were to live in a central edifice called 'falanster'. Nevertheless, the body functioned for a while, temporarily counting up to 80 people, according to Balaceanu's statements, member of the Academy and heir of the project's sponsor.

belonged to the sphere of central-European cultural influence ensured a natural assimilation of the architecture of the nineteenth century and a greater attention to order and detail on the social level. In the south and east of the country, under the influence of the Balkan and Slavic-Russian cultural melting-pot, there was an inflow of colour and improvisation. Improvisation is actually a cultural mark that suits adaptive planning.

On top of these influences there were opposable stratified influences from the East and from Europeanised West (Europeanisation becoming a kind of local globalisation) The algorithm is apparently the same: a non-native model that works theoretically, transmitted along specific channels, political and intellectual, towards a defined proximity. Both bring about a type of a plan-based development, despite the difference between them – the top-to-bottom direction of action as compared to the bottom-up – out of which specific instruments emerge.

Weak Local Theory

The disjunction between practice and synthesising theory is a handicap that applies to planning as much as to other disciplines. Action prevailed and 'pulled' theory, theory which was observing and analytical more often than progressive and projective, behind it. In fact, this type of commentary suits those systems that developed a school of planning, such as the English, German, Dutch or French. Romania did not have the time or experience for a free theory. The assertion that there was too little time in which a local theory might have manifested itself is completed by the reference according to which there were too few people with initiative as far as theory was concerned. Among them were Cincinat Sfințescu,[9] Florea Stănculescu and Gustav Gusti, the first being the author of a vast theoretical work, the second distinguishing himself through his preoccupations with rural space, while Gusti advanced the theory of the relation between architecture and systematisation (Gusti 1974).

At this point we should emphasise the fact that the profession of planner has never been included in the Romanian job inventory. Professions that permit a specialisation in this direction are mainly technical, construction engineers and, of course, architects. As long as urban decisions are made within a political structure where no individual or group has total knowledge or power, the decision-making process spells out political obedience or populism. As a matter of fact, the latter reappeared vigorously after 1990. It was the perfect moment for the Lindblom statement according to which 'the entire rational and comprehensive system of urbanism has almost nothing to do with what

---

9   Sfințescu introduced the notion of a 'superubanistic plan', the equivalent of national territory spatial planning (comprehensive master plan) and suggested the making of regional plans for a series of zones with significant development potential (north of Bucharest, Prahova Valley and the Black Sea shoreline).

the real process of development policy is: a mixture of values and analyses, a mixture of means and purposes, an ignorance towards alternatives and an avoidance of theory' (Lindblom 1959, 80). Since the contemporary scene of urbanism and planning exclusively comprises architects and construction engineers, where the former lost the battle against the political machinery at some point, which preferred the engineers who build roads, because they focus on expertise and small objectives, other professionals (geographers, sociologists, environmentalists, etc.) hardly penetrate and operate without practical success, with short-term theoretical vision and apprehensive about interdisciplinary cooperation, though not transdisciplinary. The encounter between traditional specialists (architects) and those from the new wave (planners with an urban geography or engineering background) is, if not in conflict, at least in competition.

Before 2004 the urban architects had exclusivity in designing urban plans, following the tradition that urbanism equals physical planning and 'spatial' requirements, were treated with a ruler or, more recently, with a global information system (GIS). It was the time when geographers had their moment. The professional category that enlisted competences in the echelon of planning after 2000 were geographers who specialised in spatial planning, through the prism of territorial dynamism (the cultural landscape), of the interrelation between living and changing, although the city was not totally unknown to them. Geographers are those who compensate for the lack of theory, the 'firm ground' being the system and the region (Ianos 2000). Theoretician engineers (almost a contradiction in terms) are engaged in histories of technology but not in paradigmatic debates. In such a situation, the nature of spatial planning is far from being interpreted via holistic models. The language is backward compared to other cultural areas and the recovery is slow, via corridors of compatibility: the Cluj school is especially open to German literature and, through its Hungarian component, to the American world, while Bucharest and Iaşi are traditionally connected to the French world, although the Anglo-Saxon system is not foreign to the intellectual elite of the architectural school.

Conclusions

Romania both has and does not have a planning system. It has a system of institutions, rules, customs and freedoms, an eclectic compound which constantly rearranges itself, like a house which was built over several generations. One can live in it. It is, though, different from the consecrated models which sell well or which are copied successfully. On a good foundation there are different compartment structures, as many as administrative systems have passed. But nowadays, in a unique national system, these local cultures work quite invisibly, only in the sense of property, the sense of regulation and the sense of aesthetic aspects. Reconstruction is oriented towards Europe. The challenges are multiple: to accommodate the overwhelming roof with the fragility of the compartments, to breathe identity-lending personality (as depicted in Figure 9.1) and 'go well' with the surrounding area. And this without having planners!

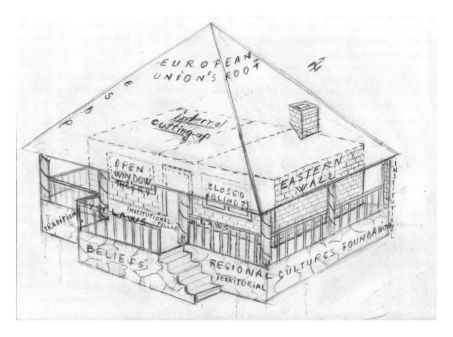

Figure 9.1 The house of many different ages – a metaphor for Romanian planning

Source: author's own illustration.

Bibliography

Cristea, D. and N. Lascu (1988) 'Istoricul sistematizării teritoriale din România', manuscript, UAIM library.

Dolman, P.M., A. Lovett, T. O'Riordan and D. Cobb (2005) 'Designing Whole Landscapes', in B. Stiffel and V. Watson (eds) *Dialogues in Urban and Regional Planning*, Routledge, London.

Gusti, G. (1974) *Forme noi de aşezare. Studiu propectiv de sistematizare macroteritorial*ă, Tehnică, Bucureşti.

Hall, P. (1999) *Orasele de maine. O istorie intelectuala a urbanismului in secolul XX* [*Cities of Tomorrow An Intellectual History of Urban Planning and Design in the Twentieth Century*], Ed. All, București.

Ianos, I. (1987) *Orașele și organizarea spațiului geografic. Studiu de geografie economică asupra teritoriului României*, Academiei, București.

Ianos, I. (2000) *Sisteme teritoriale*, Tehnică, București.

Lindblom, C.E. (1959) 'The Science of "Muddling Through"', *Public Administration Review* 19, 79–88.

Madiot, Y. (1996) *Aménagement du territoire*, 3rd edn, Armand Collin, Paris.

Matei, D.M. (1997) *Geneză și evoluție urbană în Moldova și Tara Românesca*, Iasi, Helios.

Pușcașu, V. (2005) *Planificarea sistemelor teritoriale*, Didactica si Pedagogica, Bucuresti.

PART 4
Planning Cultures in Southern Europe

Chapter 10
Planning Cultures in Italy – Reformism, Laissez-Faire and Contemporary Trends

Luciano Vettoretto

Planning Cultures and Planners' Cognitive Frames

A planning culture cannot be reduced to what planners say about planning. A planning culture is not only a professional culture (or ideology), but the way in which, in some historical moments, a (situated – national, regional or urban) society has institutionalised planning practices and discourses; in other words, values, ways of defining problems, rules, instruments, evaluation criteria, professional/expert roles and knowledge, and relations between institutions and actors, and among state, planners, and civil society (see also contributions of Gullestrup and Knieling/Othengrafen in this volume).

This definition of planning culture is particularly significant for the Italian case, where, unlike other situations in which an influential national 'planning culture' is consistent with social, political, and administrative cultures (such as the Dutch case; see Faludi 2005), we can observe, differently located in space and time, significant gaps between planners' intentions and planning outcomes, exemplary and ordinary planning practices, and planners' cognitive frames and political and administrative cultures and practices. Thus, the field of planning cultures in Italy appears multifaceted and highly problematic. But, because of the intertwining of social and economic changes at a national and global level and widespread acknowledgement of failure and inappropriateness of certain administrative and planning models and practices, this field also shows substantial experimentation and signs of innovation, which are redefining working planning cultures.

Planning Cultures in Italy, as They are Depicted from the EU Point of View

The EU *Compendium of Spatial Planning Systems* and policies recognises four planning traditions in the European Union, according to a set of criteria (CEC 1997). In Italy, as in the other Mediterranean countries, a tradition of 'urbanism' seems to prevail, which means a frame of mind for urban design, townscape and building control. In such a planning culture or tradition, regulation through rigid zoning and codes seems to be the distinctive feature. At the same time, despite a multiplicity of laws and control procedures, planning systems seem to be quite weak and ineffective, and 'have not commanded great political priority or general public support' (CEC 1997, 37). According to this interpretation, the Italian planning culture is depicted as quite different from other European cultures and traditions, which are more informed by rationality, effectiveness, responsiveness, social support and acceptance.

Such an outline of the Italian tradition is quite correct, yet it does not help us to understand why it survives and, above all, to understand the multiplicity of planning cultures and their contemporary transformations.

As regards the Italian case, unlike other European situations (the Dutch or French, for instance), it is not possible to identify a national planning culture, not only because of the contemporary plurality of professional and academic approaches to planning, but also because of the multiplicity of political and social practices and cultural frames in which planning practices are embedded. As it is well known, social, economical and cultural differences among Italian regions are significant. Different levels of institutional effectiveness and of social and institutional capital and policy-making styles are the result of historical social and political heritage and traditions (Putnam et al. 1999). So, 'ordinary' planning practices and their working cultures vary significantly, in a way, among regions (the institutional setting of spatial planning) and among communities of practice. This fact helps to understand the gap between intentions (defined by laws and professional ideologies) and actual practices and their outcomes, which depends both on deeply rooted social, political and administrative cultures and practices and on the appropriateness of the mainstream planning culture.

Hygienists, Town Planners and Architects: Fighting for the City

The institutionalisation of planning took place between the end of 1800 and the beginning of 1900. In such a period, that of planning was a domain contended above all by three professional figures, each of them bearing a specific culture and perspective (Zucconi 1989; Palermo 2004, 99).

Hygienists were significant actors, with a specific positivist perspective on modernity and cities, strong emphasis on extensive surveys and analyses, and a set of techniques for urban modernisation. The 'ingegneri municipali' (civil engineers employed in town offices) were more similar to the British town planners, practitioners particularly skilled at applying techniques of city organisation and development (housing and demographic surveys, zoning as an instrument for urban management, relations among land uses, infrastructures, facilities and building types as a scientific and technical foundation of urban plans), management of the relations between public institutions and private interests as a condition for feasibility of urban policies in the specific legal culture, and economic and financial evaluation. The architects proposed another stance, focused on reflection on the aesthetics and the history of the city, and were particularly interested in urban design of new developments and conservation of historical town centres. In their proposals, planning issues (such as those mentioned above) became less significant. Their position, for many reasons (Zucconi 1989), like the Fascist regime's will to formally re-imagine the city, prevailed, and the profession of the town planner/urban designer was ranked within educational programmes in architecture.

Such a historical process of institutionalisation of the planning profession and of the academic field greatly affected plan-making styles. Ordinary planning practices were directed towards long-range statutory design, with no particular consideration given to the social and political nature of planning (see also contribution of Serraos et al. and Puşcaşu in this volume). Issues such as management and implementation were, for a long time, inadequately taken into account (apart from a few significant exceptions).

In any case, even if the architectural perspective (and culture) on cities has been dominant and is still pervading major schools with urban design, the planning orientation amenable to the 'ingegneri municipali' tradition has not disappeared, and, since the Second World War, has constituted one of the roots of a very significant 'reformist' planning practice and culture (Palermo 2004).

Planning and Administrative Cultures

Italian planning cultures are embedded within a specific administrative and legal system and culture belonging to the 'Napoleonic family' (Newman and Thornley 1996). From the legal point of view, this tradition tends to be founded on an abstract legal norm and on a strong emphasis on public regulation and control. As in the French case, among others, the regulation of land property rights is particularly significant for planning, which is rooted in Roman law. In such a legal culture, 'property is inviolable and sacred' (Booth 2005, 275), and can be violated only by formally defined laws that legitimise interventions by the state and local governments. Thus, on one hand, laws identify the limits to the 'right to govern', which usually need strong social and political legitimacy (ibid.); on the other hand, private land ownership is sovereign. Italian accounts of planning history are often narratives of very frustrating struggles for increasing the public capacity of regulations and control of land through the law and 'grand reforms', which is obviously a very sensitive political issue, looking at British or Dutch experiences (the classical Amsterdam plan has long been an exemplar).

From the administrative point of view, relationships between the centre and peripheries have been conditioned by the historical development of the Napoleonic organisational model (despite a long history of local self-government), with significant power of the 'communes', but within a hierarchical structure of power and relationships between the state and the communes. However, significant innovations have arisen, particularly in the last decade with the devolution of various powers (especially for spatial policy) to the regions. Changes in the local election system (with the direct election of the mayor in a majority system, which significantly affects decision-making and local planning processes) were established, as well as the introduction of formal and informal policy and planning instruments on many levels (state, regions, provinces, communes, etc.), based on negotiations and agreements between public and private actors, and among public actors, with the aim of increasing efficiency. Moreover, the very strong pressure towards a kind of federalist organisation of the state will possibly change the administrative (and planning) cultures towards a more entrepreneurial administrative style even further.

These changes are not dissimilar to those observed in other situations, like the French one. Reasons are quite familiar: progressive horizontal, sectional and functional segmentation in public organisations that require different forms and models of coordination, competition among cities in a situation of limited public funding and new roles of private investments, transformations in local democracy, Europeanisation processes that affect local cognitive and cultural frames, etc. Such transformations are also to be associated with increasing awareness of the weak efficiency and effectiveness in the ordinary practices of planning and policy-making, which significantly challenge the legitimacy of public domain and its regulative and control practices.

So, even if some continue to support a demand for stronger regulation and control and for essentially statutory planning, in the last decade there has been significant reframing towards a more process-directed, dynamic, strategic and participative planning style. Cultures are changing, because of a complex intertwining of transformation in the political sphere, administrative styles and planning approaches and practices.

The Reformist Planning Culture. Public Interest and the Planner as its Hero

The reformist planning culture, which emerged after the Second World War, was essentially dominant till the 1980s. It was very consistent with the administrative traditional culture mentioned. The main planning instrument, formally defined in the first national planning law in 1942, was the Piano Regolatore Generale, a legally binding master plan for the communal level, mainly focussed on land-use regulation.[1] This culture, and its discourse, was organised according to a number of basic values and cognitive frames related to politics and society.

---

1 For a synthetis, in English, of the institutional and legal framework regarding this phase, see Bardazzi (1984).

The situation was that of post-war reconstruction and, subsequently, of heavy impacts, on cities, heritage and the environment, with serious housing conditions, and shortage issues, due to massive internal migration because of the 'economic boom'. No urban and regional policy existed at national level (see also contribution of Serraos et al. in this volume), apart from a few significant housing programmes in the 1950s and 1960s, and appreciable experiences of national economic planning, particularly for Southern Italy. This latter experience significantly contributes to the acknowledgment of the importance of economics (and other social sciences) in the field of planning. Basic values of urban and regional planning culture did not change, but a kind of 'modernisation' in planning discourses, cultures, and practices occurred at last, because the field of planning began to include different kinds of expertise that often produced conflicting interactions among professional figures (particularly between architects/planners and social scientists). At the same time, the increasing importance of often a-spatial economic and sociological approaches, particularly in the 1960s and the 1970s, lessened attention towards issues like place-making, the quality of built environment and of landscape and spatial social practices.

Worthy of note is the fact that, during the 1960s and the 1970s, planning (and more generally that of urban and regional policy) was not a homogenous field. As in the beginning of the last century, different cultures and practices were at work. They included a traditional urban design approach to planning; innovative perspectives on city design, supported by internationally acknowledged theories on the interpretation of urban morphology and its evolution;[2] ideas and practices related to planning as a social process and to the role of participative events (as in the experiences of the famous Italian architect Giancarlo De Carlo in the 1960s[3]); a more classical reformist culture and practice of urban and regional planning (which will be described below); and, lastly, a critical political economy approach (Palermo 1992; 2004).

In any case, like in a number of other European countries, reformist planning practices (and their culture), in such a period, constituted the hegemonic discourse on planning.[4] The first Italian school of planning (detached from educational programmes in architecture), based on the reformist planning culture and promoted by the leading figure of Giovanni Astengo,[5] was established in Venice in 1973. Such a reformist culture was founded on a number of basic ethical and political values and images of society, on a professional ideology focused on the importance of scientific and

---

2 Perhaps the most internationally known contributions are those by Aldo Rossi and Carlo Aymonino.

3 See De Carlo (2005). The original essay was written in 1970.

4 For an Italian planning history from the reformist point of view see Campos Venuti and Oliva (1993).

5 For a short account on Astengo, in English, see Mazza (1991).

technical approaches to planning, and a set of planning and design techniques. It was basically informed by a pessimistic vision of society and of the political system, which were considered incapable of reproducing the extraordinary richness of Italian cities, the cultural heritage and the landscapes, and of achieving objectives of spatial social equity and fair distribution of resources and opportunities.

This culture was essentially rationalistic and pedagogical in character. Reformist planners strove for a clear and hierarchical system of statutory plans, consistent with the various administrative levels, the primacy of public institutions and public interest (where technicians should have an important role), and pressed for efficient administration and management of the plan in a systemic-like vision of the planning process. Scientific analysis and techniques (including, during a phase, mathematical models of analysis, simulation and evaluation) were not only instruments aimed at increasing rationality of decisions, but also a practice intended to make the too often opaque political processes of decision more transparent, public, and rational. Planning was essentially intended as an activity performed by public institutions, strongly supported by the planners' expert knowledge, and basically directed towards regulation and control (see also contributions of Fischer and Tynkkynen in this volume).

The most interesting practices, during such a phase, were those of planners, mainly professionals, who worked in an organic style with leftist local governments, with a strong social and political commitment. Their role was not only to design land-use plans (this was intended as a function of the local administration, to be accomplished by specific 'planning offices') but, above all, to assist local governments and administrations in their implementation, to support and educate local bureaucracy, and to negotiate with private landowners' and developers' urban projects, with the objective of maximising public interest in terms of acquisition of public spaces and affordable housing. So, alongside an official professional ideology and basic ethical values, those practices developed a more pragmatic working culture, made up of a combination of: advocacy of the less privileged (particularly for housing, public facilities, and transportation), strategies for the acquisition of public spaces, an attitude towards the architectural and social reproduction of the vibrant character of historical centres, and negotiating and mediating skills with private interests seeking social equity. Such a practice has deep roots in political and social cultures, from the social catholic solidarity to the domestic version of a light 'socialist city', established on social equity and redistributive justice accompanied by particular consideration of the physical city, not only as a material artefact, but also as reproduction, at the same time, of a vivid and vibrant historical-social and material city, whose quality should be extended to new developments.

A well-known example is the experience of Bologna in the mid-1970s. Kostof, in his history of city shaping, defines such a case as 'unusual' with regard to international practices. 'New housing would no longer be built at the city edge alone: the best undeveloped lands inside the city were acquired through eminent domain, and new housing was raised on them for the working class. Most revolutionary was the concept that conservation should encompass social as well as physical structure' (Kostof 2004, 303–4). It was a culture (and a practice) that mixed social equity, place-making, and planning.

Such a culture, which required efficient and socially-oriented local governments and administrations, was seriously challenged, in the late 1960s and in the 1970s, by a more radical political economy approach, which brought forward the question of the capacity reformist planning had of pursuing social equity in economic capitalist regimes. Such an approach was not only academic, but was also associated with the generation of social movements and related practices, particularly in conflicts over housing and urban services. In parallel, epistemological critiques on the assumed scientific and methodical rationality of planning seriously challenged one of the basic values and sources of legitimacy of reformist planning (Palermo 1992). Planning began to be intended as a political process (technically supported and mediated), which required different ways of legitimating and particular consideration to such complex socio-political processes of plan making and implementation.

Societal and Administrative Cultures and Ordinary Planning Practices

Above are described the noblest and most socially-sensitive practices or cultures of reformist planning. But Italian cities and regions are the ground for thousands of ordinary planning practices. Such practices occurred within administrative bureaucratic cultures, and in a quite particular welfare regime.

It is widely acknowledged that organisational cognitive cultural frames usually have strong influence on behaviour. Bureaucratic models, unlike the entrepreneurial ones,[6] imply the recognition of authoritative forms of organisation and relations as the most appropriate way to arrange social interaction and organise public life, mainly through laws and regulations. Such organisational cognitive frames are obviously associated with larger institutional and political cultures, and contribute to defining a number of policy styles. In several situations such bureaucratic cultures are associated with 'patronage' (*clientelismo*), as a practice of 'exchange of services provided by the state in return for support of political parties', which 'may also include the failure to enforce regulations' (Allen et al. 2004, 104). Patronage, thus, distributes services according to particularistic and/or personalised logic, rather than the depersonalised and universalistic logic associated with Weberian bureaucracies in modernist welfare states' (ibid.). Such practices are well known to be differently distributed among Italian regions, which, even

---

6   For this distinction see Gruber and Innes (2001).

within the same legal and administrative frame, show significant differences in policy styles and institutional effectiveness depending, according to Putnam, on the social capital and on the historical links among cultural, social, civic and even religious cultures and practices and social-economic development (Putnam et al. 1999).

Despite the considerable differences among Italian regions, ordinary planning practices, as practices institutionally embedded in such contexts, have tended to become bureaucratic, even when intentions were noble. The consequences have been that, in some cases, planning, rather than evolving through imaginative design, social and organisational learning and creative management and implementation, has become a formal obligation, where social interactions have been reduced to formal ones defined by laws and regulations and/or have been affected by patronage negotiations.

Ordinary planning practices are embedded in another social and cultural character of the welfare state, (more or less) shared with other European Mediterranean countries, which concerns the role of the family, in a broad sense, as a 'nexus of affectively significant networks extending through a wider kinship circle and into the neighbourhood and locality' (Allen et al. 2004, 112) in the provision of social services and facilities, and in particular, for matters of spatial planning, housing and (at least partially) public transportation. Obviously enough, such a custom does not only depend on limited public investment in housing and transportation, but also has deep cultural roots. Concerning the planning domain, such an attitude, consistent with patronage, has hampered the constitution of a modern public sphere, at least in the less developed regions.

Patronage and familism are often associated with the establishment of urban coalitions including politicians, developers, landowners, professionals, etc. seeking to maximise urban rent through benevolent land-use planning (see also contribution of Dangschat/Hamedinger in this volume). This is often technically legitimated by overestimated population growth and legally supported by discretionary interpretations of laws, frequent and ad hoc changes in land-use regulation and zoning, along with practices of corruption aimed at supporting the costly local political system, and a widespread tolerance towards massive illegal building activity particularly in Southern Italy. Such practices involve both cities (like Rome and Naples in the 1950s and 1960s) and smaller towns, and are quite diffuse, nationally (Campos Venuti and Oliva 1993; Scattoni 2004).

Thus, despite the fact that even small towns were obliged to design and implement land-use plans after the Second World War – at least for new developments – and a new planning law according to the reformist planning culture has significantly increased the power of public authorities at all administrative levels since 1977, 'the critical issue is that the actual implementation of these rules has been rather weak with a significant amount of development going ahead contrary to, rather than in conformity with, planning regulations' (Padovani and Vettoretto 2003). Urban planning 'has been marked by a laissez-faire attitude, offering the maximum of direct incentives to promote housebuilding, and the minimum of controls on the release of land for development' (ibid.). Because of patronage and familistic attitudes and practices, land-use planning, in certain situations, has become more a powerful instrument for political and electoral consensus building and a means to significantly enlarge home-ownership than an instrument for regulation. From the point of view of its impacts on urban geographies, such practices, particularly in rural communes or peripheral areas, have significantly reduced the cost of land and of houses. Starting from the 1970s they have produced massive low-density urban regions and sprawl, as well as negative externalities that have been lessening sustainability and economic efficiency of spatial systems.

A diffuse individualistic attitude has contributed to the developing of a sceptical attitude towards planning. In ordinary practices, consensus for planning tends to be acquired through negotiations and exchanges in small 'privatistic' arenas, and social interactions and/or deliberative efforts are minimised. In some regions, anyway, (particularly the Northern and Central ones), a more sympathetic and cooperative culture, historically, was working (rooted in social-democratic or social-catholic worldviews), which was more open to public intervention, ideas of 'common good' and urban planning. But even in such, more advanced, situations, which began to face globalisation processes and competitive situations, critical awareness of the weak effectiveness of a merely regulative planning practice and culture emerged.

Such processes have challenged the cultural basis of the reformist planning practices. On one hand, the impact of administrative bureaucratic cultures and styles, and a familist and patronage practice have made urban and regional planning quite inefficient and ineffective in achieving objectives of spatial functional organisation, social equity and sustainability. On the other hand, the more advanced situations found such a rigid and technocratic model of planning inappropriate with respect to changes in the political sphere, the rising demand for more local democratic processes, and globalisation and Europeanisation processes.

Reframing Planning Cultures

At the beginning of the 1980s, critical observations significantly contributed to the reframing of planning cultures. The focus was mainly on both the effectiveness of ordinary planning practices and the appropriateness of the professional ideologies (Balducci 1991). Bernardo Secchi, in particular, considered urban and regional planning scarcely effective in organising cities and regions, acknowledging a significant role in the promotion of the real estate sector and in the structuring of local political power (Secchi 1984).

So, while a number of planners kept demanding more laws and regulations, innovations and some kind of reframing of planning cultures were emerging from practices and debates.

Plans and Projects

In the 1980s, a significant debate took place on several important urban projects (particularly in Milan and Turin), mainly on vacant urban industrial areas (see in particular Dente et al. 1990). Such projects did not usually observe the zoning regulations, but were considered very meaningful urban transformations and innovations, for meeting the rising need for urban competition on a European and global scale. Such projects were realised through some kind of negotiation between private developers and local governments, essentially outside the normative enclosure of the general land-use plan (which, in many cases, was extremely outdated).

Orthodox reformist planners negatively interpreted such practices as the Italian version of the Thatcherite deregulation. As a matter of fact, these practices radically challenged the appropriateness of an essentially rational-synoptic, comprehensive and solely state-driven planning practice. A starting point was not only real estate pressure, but also a more or less founded critique on some essential elements of reformist planning, particularly its efficiency and effectiveness in a situation of fast urban transformation and competition. From these experiences, the most interesting results for the planning cultures were a less ideological opinion of the public-private relationships, hypotheses on how to improve the formal-architectural urban structure combining land-use plans and urban projects, and practices of management of urban transformations within a more flexible and strategic planning frame (Palermo 2004). Such practices contribute to reframing the idea of planning essentially as regulation and control over issues of urban economic development, real effectiveness of urban policies, and urban governance. At the same time, relations among urban actors began to change, with the rise of urban policy networks including economic and political actors and a wider public sphere and open debate.

Europeanisation

Europeanisation processes can be intended as 'processes of construction, diffusion, and institutionalisation of formal and informal rules, procedures, policy paradigms, styles, 'ways of doing things', and shared beliefs and norms which are first defined and consolidated in the making of EU public policy and politics, and then incorporated in the logic of domestic discourse, identities, political structures, and public policies' (Radaelli 2003, see also contribution of Waterhout et. al in this volume).

Such processes are quite influential on reframing administrative and planning cultures. The programming of Structural Funds, and experiences of European programmes like URBAN, INTERREG or LEADER have in some way challenged administrations and practitioners. Different habits and practices have been experimented, with significant impact on the institutional and organisational learning: constituting and managing a partnership, accounting, evaluating, interacting with foreign partners and responsiveness. Rhetoric of the European programmes, made up of keywords such as sustainability, participation, integration and diariness, has been incorporated into the planning discourses. But, because of the actual differences among Italian regions (which are in charge of the management of Structural Funds), administrative cultures are changing in a different way and intensity; the constitution of a 'community of practices' can be recognised, including planners involved in European programmes, in a metacultural European spatial planning and policy frame.

Such community of practice has not been generated only through European programmes and policy-making, since Europeanisation is a complex process of horizontal and vertical interaction and learning. Significant experiences were already at work in Italy, particularly in the field of local economic development, where pioneering scientific contributions to the studies of industrial districts have been essential in innovating a policy discourse and culture (particularly on relations among public regulation, self-regulation and self-organisation, and economic development). Experiences of local economic development policy, founded on the consensus of local actors and formalised through the so-called 'territorial pacts' (or other similar instruments) had been experimented since the mid-1990s while, since the beginning of the 1990s, some kinds of integrated programmes for urban regeneration had been implemented, mainly on the initiative of the state (for a discussion on these experiences see Palermo 2004 and Cremaschi 2005). In parallel, from the administrative point of view, worthy of notice are two national laws (142/1990 and 241/1990) that introduced formal procedures for negotiation among public institutions and for constituting partnerships among local governments and other public bodies mainly for increasing efficiency in the implementation of urban projects and policies.

From these events, quite a significant innovation has emerged, for both the administrative and the planning culture. Its basic values are efficiency and effectiveness; the focus is on governance and action, rather than on hierarchy and command; policy styles tend to be directed more to strategic thinking and consensus building, attentive not only to design but also to management and implementation. In such a frame, in some administrations (or in some departments within the same administration) a more entrepreneurial culture and practice arose, formed by learning and creative adaptation, openness to change, intelligent improvisation, informality, and pragmatic negotiations. A new form of public legitimacy has emerged, founded more on deliberative practices and transparent negotiations than on command and authority, or patronage.

Many examples could be quoted, as the 'Integrated territorial project' for the allocation of Structural Funds in Objective 1 Regions (Palermo, 2004, among others), the experiences of rural development programmes like LEADER (Vettoretto 2006) or URBAN programme. If we examine the URBAN I experience alone, for the sake of brevity, analysis on the whole of the Italian experiences has shown the impacts of the URBAN projects, which include the changing of cognitive frames related to urban policy, the acknowledgment of these practices as examples and good practices (that have inspired succeeding experiences), the learning of how to manage complex situations which, at the same time, involve physical intervention, local economic development, networking and partnership building (Palermo 2002). During such processes, a new model of urban governance has been experimented (sometimes with significant participation), with positive influence on administrative and organisational cultures, which seem increasingly directed towards a more entrepreneurial style (see also contribution of Dangschat/Hamedinger in this volume).

However, such a new cultural frame cannot yet be considered as hegemonic. At times, administrative learning and openness conceal essentially opportunistic practices of fund raising, without any appropriate political vision or project. On the other hand, the making of urban strategic plans in many cities seems much more like a symbolic policy, than the (more or less) consensual building of a long-range strategy or vision for the city and a substantial set of concrete actions. Moreover, partnerships for local development, which in many cases produce networking and social capital, often do not generate significant effects in terms of development and employment (Palermo 2004).

Local governments, mainly for urban projects and policies, have promoted many participative practices. Analyses of such practices show a certain degree of uncertainty and ambiguity as to their inclusiveness, effectiveness and appropriateness, compared with the vibrant self-organised mobilisation of citizens for urban and environmental issues. But cultural reframing is on the way, and is becoming more and more influential on institutional and professional practices and on educational programmes.

Innovations in Regional Planning Laws

With the devolution of competences to regions (stated by amendments to the Constitutional Charter in 2001 and 2005), in the last years, many of them have introduced new planning laws. The first and perhaps most significant experience was that of the Tuscany Region. In such laws, the nature of urban plans changed with respect to the old legally binding land-use urban master plan. Plans are indicative and structural at communal or intercommunal level, and operative-regulative at local level (in quite a British style). Regional interpretations of such distinctions are apparent (for instance, Tuscan law, at its structural level, emphasises issues of local identity, and the structural element of the material and cultural heritage as an element of a 'territory charter' that should wisely and consensually guide spatial transformations within a frame of environmental sustainability[7]). Moreover, according to the recent regional planning laws, planning should be participative and collaborative. Such laws, albeit differently, codified frames and practice already at work, particularly for new relations among strategic, structural and regulative elements of spatial planning, recognising the idea of planning as a political process and the role of participation. Interpretations and ordinary practices are, however, still uncertain because of the persistence of traditional administrative and professional cultures.

Moreover, because of the legal restrictions on property rights (which are defended by the Italian Constitution) and the political and legal difficulties in compulsory land purchasing, a number of experiments on the transfer of development rights has been tried (and procedures have been codified into the Regions' planning laws), quite successfully, at times.

From the point of view of ordinary planning practices the present situation is often a sort of hybridisation of mere old regulative styles and new perspectives. Ambiguity and uncertainty characterise the making of spatial planning; still unclear is the image of connections among structural, strategic and regulative issues in various planning instruments, and of the actual role of participation, which is often reduced to information and consultation practices. The change is however significant, and more or less defines new social and political condition for planning.

Conclusions

Italian planning cultures are changing, through the combined effects of economic and social transformations, critical assessment of outcomes of local planning practices, experimentation and Europeanisation processes. Reflection on the effectiveness of spatial planning and of the administrative action, impacts of globalisation and Europeanisation processes and the crisis of the traditional representative model of democracy, have triggered a very significant reframing of planning cultures. Such reframing does not depend on professional or academic debates alone, nor can it be intended as the outcome of failure in the traditional administrative (and welfare state) style and culture.

---

7 A very influential contribution was that of Alberto Magnaghi, who proposed a vision on planning and design within a very sophisticated frame structured on a strong idea of the territory, identity and heritage, participation and self-sustainable communities (Magnaghi 2000).

We can observe an intertwining among planning, administration and welfare state, ideas of local democracy, and influence of European practices.

Therefore, critique of administrative cultures and welfare styles, as well as the crucial assessment of planning effectiveness, even in more advanced situations, have influenced planning cultures, and challenged established practices and relations among state, civil society and practitioners. Recognising the deterioration of the territory and of the urban and rural landscape (one of the major economic and cultural assets of Italy) and the causes, despite existing spatial plans at any administrative level, brings forward to question the legitimacy of traditional statutory planning and calls for new horizons.

Current professional discourses and ideologies are certainly plural. Though a traditional planning culture of planning, as essentially a command and control activity, is still vital and influential, quite evident, from the point of view of both the practices and the academic and professional debates, is a significant shift towards a different planning culture that redefines, in a more or less radical way, social relations towards – still uncertain – more deliberative and consensus-building approaches. The key point in the emerging planning culture is the acknowledgement that the traditional authority of the state and of scientific and technical expertise is no longer the only significant source of planning legitimacy. According to this cultural frame, legitimacy has to be achieved by patient interactive processes, similar to the deliberative ones, and by real effectiveness of planning actions giving consideration to management and implementation issues.

But the social impact of such a change is still unclear, and 'new' planning cultures have not yet adequately coped with this issue, which represents a basic element for its legitimacy.

Bibliography

Allen, J., J. Barlow, J. Leal, T. Maloutas and L. Padovani (2004) *Housing and Welfare in Southern Europe*, Blackwell, London.

Balducci, A. (1991) *Disegnare il futuro*, Il Mulino, Bologna.

Bardazzi, S. (1984) 'Italy', in R.H. Williams (ed.) *Planning in Europe*, Allen & Unwin, London.

Booth, P. (2005) 'The Nature of Difference: Traditions of Law and Government and Their Effects on Planning in Britain and France', in B. Sanyal (ed.) *Comparative Planning Cultures*, Routledge, London, 259–84.

Campos Venuti, G. and F. Oliva (eds) (1993) *Cinquant'anni di urbanistica in Italia. 1942–1992*, Bari-Rome, Laterza.

Commission of the European Communities – CEC (1997) *The EU Compendium of Spatial Planning Systems and Policies, Regional development studies*, Office for Official Publications of the European Communities, Luxembourg.

Cremaschi, M. (2005) *L'Europa delle città*, Alinea, Florence.

De Carlo, G. (2005) 'Architecture's Public', in P. Blundell Jones, D. Petrescu and J. Till (eds) *Architecture and Participation*, Spon Press, London.
Dente, B., L. Bobbio, P. Fareri and M. Morisi (1990) *Metropoli per progetti*, Il Mulino, Bologna.
Faludi, A. (2005) 'The Netherlands: A Culture with a Soft Spot for Planning', in B. Sanyal (ed.) *Comparative Planning Cultures*, Routledge, New York, 285–308.
Gruber J. and J. Innes (2001) *Bay Area Transportation Decision Making in the Wake of ISTEA. Planning Styles in Conflict at the Metropolitan Transportation Commission*, University of California Press, Berkeley.
Kostof, S. (2004) *The City Assembled*, Thames and Hudson, London.
Magnaghi, A. (2000) *Il progetto locale*, Bollati Boringhieri, Turin.
Mazza, L. (1991) 'Giovanni Astengo. Memorial Note', *Town Planning Review* 62(1), 107–8.
Newman, P. and A. Thornley (1996) (eds) *Urban Planning in Europe*, Routledge, London.
Padovani, L. and L. Vettoretto (2003) 'Italy', in N. Gallent, M. Shucksmith and M. Tewdwr-Jones (eds) *Housing in the European Countryside*, Routledge, London.
Palermo, P.C. (1992) *Interpretazioni dell'analisi urbanistica*, Angeli, Milan.
Palermo, P.C. (2002) (ed.) *Il programma Urban e l'innovazione delle politiche urbane. Vol. I*, Angeli, Milan.
Palermo, P.C. (2004) *Trasformazioni e governo del territorio*, Angeli, Milan.
Putnam, R.D., R. Leonardi and R. Nanetti (1999) *Making Democracy Work: Civic Traditions in Modern Italy*, Princeton University Press, Princeton, NJ.
Radaelli, C. (2003) 'The Europeanisation of Public Policy', in K. Featherstone and C. Radaelli (eds) *The Politics of Europeanization*, Oxford University Press, Oxford.
Scattoni, P. (2004) *L'urbanistica dell'Italia contemporanea*, Newton and Compton, Rome.
Secchi, B. (1984) *Il racconto urbanistico*, Einaudi, Turin.
Vettoretto, L. (2006) 'Local Development Projects and the Italian Experience of the Leader Community Initiative Programme: Paradoxes, Uncertainties, and Results', in L. Pedrazzini (ed.) *The Process of Territorial Cohesion in Europe*, Angeli, Milan.
Zucconi, G. (1989) *La città contesa*, Jaka Book, Milan.

Chapter 11
Planning Culture and the Interference of Major Events: The Recent Experience of Athens

Konstantinos Serraos, Evangelos Asprogerakas and Byron Ioannou

Introduction

Over the last few decades, planning in Greece has been identified as an essential prerequisite for balanced spatial development and the necessary institutional frame was formed. As a prerequisite for successful application of the related policy, the main peculiarities of the public administration and some old planning culture rigidities had to be confronted. In this framework, the interference of planning in the 'Athens 2004' Olympic Games acquires distinctive importance due to the magnitude and the appeal of the event. The main questions addressed are how the planning procedure for the Games was integrated into general spatial planning and how the policy applied and the infrastructure developed affect the spatial development of the area.

In order to answer the above questions, this chapter initially gives a brief presentation of the planning and the administrative system, identifying the contemporary situation and problems. Thereafter, the basic spatial features of Athens Metropolitan Region are presented, focusing on the most important spatial problems and related policy, illustrated by specific cases of spatial plans on both regional and urban levels. The main planning aspects for the 'Athens 2004' Olympic Games are presented and evaluated. More specifically, the planning policy is analysed, emphasising the implications for the spatial development of the area and the directions for the post-Olympic era. Ultimately, the potential detrimental effects and the unexploited opportunities of Athens and its habitants are evaluated. During the whole process the main characteristics and peculiarities of planning culture in Greece will be revealed.

System of Administration and Spatial Planning in Greece

Administrative Structure

The Greek Constitution defines the relationships among the different powers at national level. The legislature is represented by parliament. Executive power rests mainly with central government and is limited for the President of the Republic. Government is a collective instrument, consisting of the Council of Ministers. Parliament establishes the structure and the procedures of spatial and town planning in the country, through a series of framework acts (laws). Concerning the judiciary powers at national level, a significant role in the Greek system is played by the 'Council of State', the involvement of which is already very important in the spatial planning process, especially in creating judicial standards for the interpretation of domestic, community and international legislation concerning the sustainable development perspective (ESTIA 2000).

The country is divided into 13 state administrative regions for the purpose of planning, programming and coordinating regional development. Each region is headed by a General Secretary, who represents the national government at the regional level, and includes a number of prefectures with elected authorities (second-tier local government). The first tier of local government is constituted by 900 municipalities and 133 communes. The role of municipalities in urban and regional planning remains mostly advisory, with the exception of certain powers delegated to some municipalities (e.g. a number of important municipalities are empowered to grant building permits).

The governmental executive power, in the field of spatial planning, is represented mainly by the Ministry of Environment, Spatial Planning and Public Works (YPECHODE). Other important ministries are Economy and Finance (which controls regional policy), Development (industrial policy), Rural Development and Food (rural development and forests), Transport and Communications, Interior, Culture (archaeological sites, cultural heritage) and Tourism. There are also two 'regional' ministries, the Ministry of the Aegean and the Ministry of Macedonia and Thrace. The responsibility for urban and regional planning in Athens and Thessaloniki metropolitan areas rests with the Organisation for Planning and Environmental Protection of Athens or Thessaloniki respectively. They are autonomous public authorities under the auspices of YPECHODE.

Law 2742/1999 established an advisory council, the opinion of which is required for the approval of the 'General Framework for Spatial Planning and Sustainable Development' as well as for the nationwide strategic 'Special Frameworks' (e.g. which are under elaboration for tourism or industry development). This council consists of representatives from major stakeholders in the public and private sector (Wassenhoven et al. 2005).

Table 11.1 Key institutions of spatial planning

National level	Ministry for the Environment, Spatial Planning and Public Works (YPECHODE)
	Sectoral and 'regional' ministries
Regional level	General Secretariats of Region (13) headed by the Regional General Secretary and a Regional Council (unelected body)
	Athens and Thessaloniki Organisations
Local	2st tier local authorities (54 Prefectures) headed by the Prefect and a Prefectural Council (elected body)
	1st tier local authorities (900 Municipalities and 133 Communes) headed by the Mayor and a Municipal Council (elected body)

Institutional Framework and Planning Instruments

The Greek Constitution contains specific clauses concerning the obligation of the state to plan the structure of the national territory and settlements and to protect the physical and cultural environment. On the national and regional scale, Law 2742/99 concerning 'Spatial Planning and Sustainable Development', which replaced the previous one that had not been implemented since the mid-1970s, aimed at attempting an overall confrontation of territorial issues in Greece, mainly through the institution of spatial plans.

A national plan, known as the 'General Framework for Spatial Planning and Sustainable Development' (GFSPSD), is based on Law 2742/1999 setting specific goals concerning conflicting issues in land-use management, which aim at the sustainable use of land and the minimisation of negative environmental impacts. The same law requires the production of 'Regional' (RFSPSD) and 'Special (sectoral) Frameworks for Spatial Planning and Sustainable Development' (SFSPSD).

Since 1983, and until the late 1990s, the core of urban planning legislation was Law 1337/83 on the extension of town plans and urban development. Its main characteristics were the introduction of a hierarchy of plans (general and local) and of controlled urban zones to direct urban development, the safeguarding of sensitive areas and the restraining of unplanned construction and sprawl. In accordance with this law, general town plans were produced for many municipalities. In 1997, this law was updated by Law 2508/97 on sustainable urban development, which introduced a comprehensive organisational framework for urban renewal, as well as new provisions permitting organised housing development in the outskirts of cities and in areas of secondary and vacation home development.

The two-step planning procedure at the local level consists of two main spatial planning instruments: the 'General Urban Plan' (GUP) and the 'Town Plan Study' (TPS). The GUP has to cover the whole area of the municipality, providing the general guidelines for its spatial development. The local

Table 11.2   The general structure of the Greek planning system

Main spatial planning instruments	
Planning level	Plans
National level	General Framework for Spatial Planning and Sustainable Development (L.2742/1999 – plan in progress)
	Special (Sectoral) Frameworks for Spatial Planning and Sustainable Development (L.2742/1999 – plans in progress)
Regional level	Regional Frameworks for Spatial Planning and Sustainable Development (L.2742/1999)
Local level	Structural Metropolitan Plan (SMP, L.2508/97) concerning Urban regions, Metropolitan areas, Large urban centres.
	SMP Athens (L. 1515/85) SMP Thessaloniki (L.1561/86)
	General Urban Plan (L.1337/83, L.2508/97) concerning Cities, Towns Urbanised areas and Countryside/Rural space.
	Town Plan Study *implemented by* Implementation Plan (L.1337/83, L.2508/97) concerning Cities, Towns, Urbanised areas.

authorities are responsible for the elaboration of the GUP, while it is ratified through ministerial decision. A series of TPS's constitute the second step of the local spatial planning procedure. According to the general guidelines of the GUP, they have to provide detailed and specific land-use and development guidance for certain parts of the urban area. After their approval by the Minister for the Environment, Spatial Planning and Public Works the GUPs become binding, not only for public authorities but also for private individuals, especially concerning street alignments, building lines, land-use designations, as well as building regulations (minimum plot size and plot dimensions, maximum plot ratios and floor-area ratio, etc.). The implementation of the Town Plan Study, which mainly includes property adjustments, is achieved by another special plan, the 'Implementation Plan' (IP) (ISoCaRP 2002).

Comparisons with Other European Countries

Legal, administrative and planning systems in Greece have historically been influenced by French and German models (see also Puşcaşu's contribution in this volume). In recent decades the professional training scores of Greek planners in the UK and USA have added several influences from the Anglo-Saxon tradition (Wassenhoven et al. 2005). However, the Greek system of planning is considered to be less effective than the equivalents in the above countries. One crucial reason for this might be the division of power in Greece between the core and the periphery, which has resulted in the fact that the most significant decisions are made by the central government (Baiba et al. 2005). Thus, the implementations of some decisions do not inspire the regional or local authorities or the people and that could be a reason why they are occasionally directed to an opportunistic behaviour. As a consequence, the implementation of spatial planning is not certain or secured in some cases.

The division of power is important, because spatial planning is actually an act of policy. Although planners only propose while politicians make the decisions, the implementation of a plan is a political action as it incorporates a number of regulations, motives and propositions that influence people's lives. However, people tend to resist when they are forced to do things that do not inspire them. Thus, the stronger the role of central government, the more ineffective spatial planning becomes (see also contribution of Vettoretto in this volume).

European countries such as Germany, Sweden, Denmark, Finland and Austria have, historically, exceptionally balanced systems of power between core and periphery. As a result, most of the spatial problems are solved at the appropriate level and spatial planning is favoured by social support. Finally, the grade of certainty about the implementation of spatial planning is extremely high (Baiba et al. 2005). In between the two contrasting cases mentioned before there are several others. Countries such as Belgium, France and Italy have already managed to transfer power from the central to regional/local governments successfully. The Netherlands, Portugal, France and Greece keep a powerful central government, although the procedure of decentralisation has already begun.

However, in Greece this will not be an easy procedure. When second-tier prefectural authorities were created, substantial powers were devolved to them by the central government, but unfortunately this decentralisation is endangered by the controversial interpretation of the constitution espoused by the Council of State. Moreover, according to Wassenhoven et al. (2005), there is at least some evidence that local authorities may be reluctant to undertake additional spatial planning competences which are rated as harmful for their popularity in comparison, for instance, with infrastructure projects which are more popular (Wassenhoven et al. 2005).

The particular post-war evolution of the Greek society has led to the current spatial development model where Athens is the centre of almost every significant activity, attracting a huge proportion of the country's population. The extravagant approach for developing small ownerships was the only solution to the housing demand and an agent of social justice and political stability as well, explaining the important role of the specific construction industry (Antonopoulou 1991). Thus, a complex set of economic, social and political relationships was created, making it hard to apply any planning action, regulation or intervention (Ioannou and Serraos 2007; compare also contributions of Staniunas and Puşcaşu in this volume).

Table 11.3 Division of power in EU countries

Countries	Central government is the prominent factor in spatial planning system	Balanced system of spatial planning
Austria		✓
Belgium		✓
Denmark		✓
Germany		✓
Greece	✓	
Finland		✓
France	✓	
Ireland	✓	
Italy		✓
The Netherlands	✓	
Portugal	✓	
Sweden		✓
United Kingdom	✓	

The Greek spatial planning system is currently undergoing a process of change, in accordance with international trends and with a major influence from the European Union and its policies. However, there is much to be done in the near future if spatial planning intends to overcome its malfunctioning implementation.

Problems of the Current Administrative and Spatial Planning System

The organisation of Greek territory was accomplished in the first decades after World War II, in the virtual absence of a restrictive regulatory framework concerning spatial planning of productive activities, social facilities and urban development. This had a serious impact on Greek territorial organisation, such as regional and local disparities, a stronger core region to the detriment of the periphery, although this was also the result of other historical reasons, environmental degradation in urban areas and, in some cases, in coastal and island areas, as well as widespread unauthorised development, especially housing. In the 1980s and 1990s, the spatial planning system was strengthened and equipped with more effective instruments, but its potential impact is still weak due to several shortcomings (Serraos et al. 2005; Wassenhoven et. al. 2000):

- planning law is not consolidated;
- the legal and institutional framework is piecemeal and chaotic;
- the administration is not able to formulate consistent, long-term policies addressing an issue or problem and subsequently develop a strategy of policy implementation;
- departures from approved plans are frequent and the gap between official planning and the reality of development on the ground is wide;
- in most cases, plans are simply adjusted to already stabilised situations and do not lead to development;
- plan approval procedures are very slow, especially because of public reaction and political 'realism';
- there is lack of coordination between levels of spatial planning and development;
- effective systems of land registration are still at an early stage of development and control of plan implementation on the ground is weak;
- there is a lack of efficient mechanisms for public involvement in the plan-making process at the local level, as well as an absence of consultation mechanisms with the economic and social partners at the national and regional levels of planning;
- formal, legal, adversarial and closed patterns of interest intermediation have been established, with informal and ad hoc bargaining between regulatory authorities and private interests;
- there is lack of efficient support, control and monitoring mechanisms for the application of the spatial planning policy.

The Involvement of Planning in the Olympic Games of 2004

Basic Spatial Characteristics and Problems of Athens Metropolitan Area.

The metropolitan area of Athens includes the administrative boundaries of the region (*perifereia*) of Attica with an extent of about 2,000 km^2 and a population approaching 4 million. The majority of the population (over 3 million) is concentrated in the basin of Athens with a total extent that does not exceed 500 km^2. We are dealing with an over-populated and densely structured area with a very small proportion of free spaces and green areas and with significant environmental problems that are due to the exceptionally high concentrations of population, activities and built areas. The demographic and building pressures that continue to exist (up to a certain degree) in the metropolitan complex of Athens (with a very reduced pace compared to its recent past), are now defused in the eastern part of Athens, including the area of Messogeia and the new airport. This area (until recently an area of mainly seasonal residence), presents heavy signs of urbanisation with obvious marks of alteration, even mutation, of its recent rural character. In the Athens basin, on the contrary, various tendencies are observed. These include the reduction of the population in overpopulated and undervalued areas of the centre and its near suburbs on the one hand, and a continuing increase in population in other regional municipalities on the borders of the basin on the other, with its total population remaining steady nevertheless (NTUA 2004).

Athens is not classified as a city of global impact according to its international role and its position in the world hierarchy by researches (Beaverstock et al. 1999). This is due to both its geographic position (outside the main global land areas of development), as well as the country's limited economic influence and the great degree of introversion of the Greek economy. Nevertheless, Athens appears to have a powerful potential of performing an international role, especially in sectors such as tourism and culture but also the advertising sector. Furthermore, it appears that a wider dynamic is emerging for cities of global impact which were not included in the territorial zones of international development up to recently (North America, Western Europe, Asian Pacific). Athens is included in this group of cities and is considered to have all favourable potential to play an important role in Europe and the Mediterranean (Taylor 2000).

Athens occupies a dominant position and possesses a sovereign role in Greece thanks to both its population size (over 30 per cent of country's population) and the economic activities that it attracts (more than 30 per cent of Greece's annual gross domestic product (GDP)). Its geographical position is rather crucial (situated in the centre of the country) and it is considered to be the most important urban complex in the region, including the neighbouring Balkans, especially in sectors such as transport, services, industry and commerce. The sovereignty of Athens in Greece is reinforced by the centralised structure of the Greek governmental and administration system which makes the city the absolute decision-making centre of the country. This centralised system has favoured Athens for many decades but has also led to significant problems such as unequal development in the country and the creation of anti-economies of scale, such as environmental pollution and degradation of the quality of life in the metropolitan area (NTUA 2004).

Policy and Actions: The 'Olympic Poles'

Since 1985 planning regarding the centres' structure has become crucial for the Athens Basin (AB), while a completed centre hierarchy was proposed through the 1985 Structural Metropolitan Plan. Since then the proposed centres' structure has always followed emerging development trends (Serraos et al. 2007).

Even though the decisions concerning the placement of the Olympic infrastructure were not directly based on an analysis of the spatial dynamics and the centralities of the Athens Basin (AB) or the wider Metropolitan

Region of Attica (MRA), it is believed that there is an indirect relation between the existing centres of the AB and the decisions about the placement of the 'Olympic Poles' (OP). That is because there is at least one common main agent for both functions; accessibility, i.e. the connections with transportation and the circular network of the conurbation. The development of central urban poles is connected with the transportation network by definition and access to the main road axes, while this same parameter was vital for the functional interconnection of the Olympic venues and therefore for successfully conducting the Olympic Games. Moreover, the OPs were, on purpose, placed in the AB using a scattered model that in some aspects reduced the effectiveness of their influence on the city (Gospondini and Beriatos 2006, 179). Nevertheless, it is generally accepted that these decisions were directed by land availability (Map 11.1).

The Olympic Games were initially presented as a catalyst for a positive intervention in the conurbation, despite the limited margins given for innovative planning policies, while they promoted the strategy for a completed transportation network, a renewed network of urban infrastructure and finally an upgrading of the urban environment (Committee for the Athens 2004 Candidacy 1997). In the last stages of planning and implementing the projects, greater emphasis was put on reinforcing the role of Athens on a regional level, as well as on its position in the hierarchy of the world cities (Zifou et al. 2004).

The Athens Olympic Centre in Maroussi was an existing venue. The poles of Ellinikon/Ag. Kosmas and Faliron had the greater concentration of athletic activities (Map 11.2), while the Olympic Centre in Goudi, an area designated to become a metropolitan park, can be considered a fourth main pole. A number of recent evaluations (Committee for the Athens 2004 Candidacy 1997; Dekleris 2003; Zifou et al. 2004) have shown that these three poles had some crucial characteristics before their inclusion in the programme of the Games:

- they had already functioned as sites of athletic activities, so part of the necessary infrastructure was already available;
- they had access to the existing main circulatory network and they could easily be interconnected by the proposed Olympic Ring and connected with the planned upgraded public transportation system at the same time;
- they consisted of a vast area of undeveloped, empty land, with relatively clear ownership status and a possibility for design and construction without unforeseen obstacles and reactions;
- they were institutionally characterised as areas of metropolitan importance or areas of supra-local uses of recreation, sports or metropolitan parks by the official plans, or they were thought to become institutionally characterised for years.

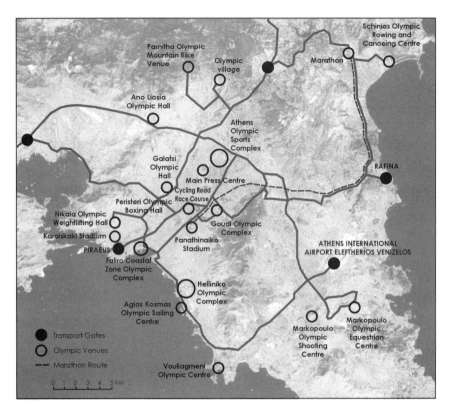

Map 11.1   The Athens 2004 Olympic Venues

In our opinion, their selection as basic poles of hosting the Olympic venues was a choice without alternatives for these reasons, since they were almost the only places in the AB that satisfied the above criteria. The objections from society mostly concerned the management of the environmentally sensitive Faliron waterfront and the designated metropolitan park in the area of the ex-airport of Ellinikon. Nevertheless, the importance of the specific poles for the successful organisation of the Games has eventually led to the fast-forwarding and materialisation of all relevant Olympic planning. Consequently, there was a kind of inflexibility of the Olympic planning alternatives due to the existing conditions already shaped, at least for the specific areas.

Another equally important element derives from the placement of the poles, and is connected with their relation to the main existing central poles of the AB conurbation. Based on the analysis of NTUA (2004) we can conclude that (Map 11.2):

- The Athens Olympic Centre pole of Maroussi lies in an immediate relationship with Maroussi, a developing centre of economic activities and financial headquarters;
- Faliron Gulf neighbours the metropolitan pole of Piraeus and the main centre Kallithea without being functionally tied to them, because of the current structure of transportation and the circulatory network that isolates it from the urban fringe;
- the area of Goudi is on the outskirts of the Athens metropolitan centre area;
- the venues of Ellinikon and Ag. Kosmas are next to Glyfada, which is the most dynamic centre in the southern part of the AB.

Hence, it is proved that the basic Olympic poles were in a direct relationship with the upgrading centres of the AB. The construction and the function of the Olympic venues in the examined areas did not seem to turn over the existing equilibrium in the AB substantially. The north-south development axis was maintained and reinforced, while three of the four main poles were placed on it. The West AB was always in disfavour considering its centrality and its role in the conurbation, putting it outside any significant placement decision. Therefore, the opportunity of balancing the distribution of the development poles by the placement of a main pole in West AB was lost. Several exceptions were the Olympic venues at Ano Liossia, Peristeri and Nikaia (Maps 11.1 and 11.2) which were of less significance compared to the others. What remained to be seen during the years after the Games was the size of the impact of the Olympic interventions and the post-Olympic use for each pole on the area of the immediate influence of the centres (Serraos et al. 2007).

The Post-Olympic Use of the Venues

The post-Olympic use of the Games' infrastructure was regulated by the Law 3342/2005. The 'Olympic Properties SA', a private law-enterprise, had the responsibility of managing a large number of the Olympic sites in almost every specific area (Serraos et al. 2007).

The post-Olympic use of infrastructure was highly related to sports, recreation, cultural and leisure activities in general, which the urban centres of the AB lacked to quite a large extent. The infrastructure facilities were not located in order to serve these specific purposes in the most effective way. This reveals the lack of connection of the Olympic Games interventions with long-term planning procedures.

The uniqueness of this procedure rests on its extended scale in terms of time and space. It also reveals consolidated administrative discontinuities while planning authorities are rather peripheral consultants of this process. This process seemed effective while the Games were successfully organised, but it neither assured the positive post-Olympic use of the venues, nor the

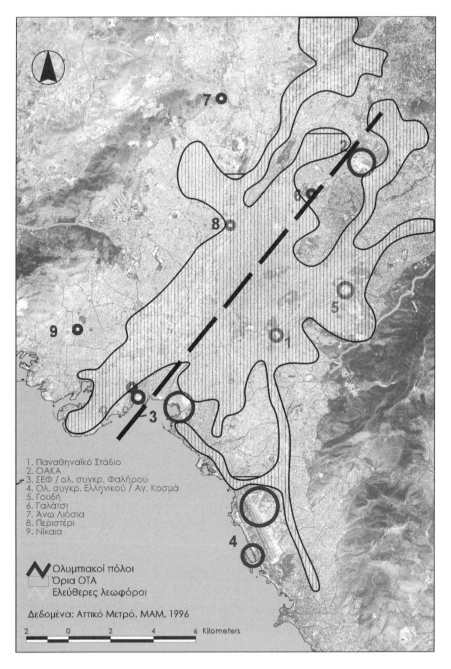

Map 11.2 The spatial correlation of Olympic/post-Olympic poles with the areas of the basic poles of central activities, building density, population density and concentration of places of labour

Planning Culture and the Interference of Major Events 217

Figure 11.1 Ellinikon Olympic Canoe/Kayak Slalom Centre

Source: Olympic Properties SA. (c) Konstantinos Serraces.

Figure 11.2 Faliro Bay Complex

Source: Olympic Properties SA. (c) Konstantinos Serraces.

maximum efficiency of the projects in any term of economic or socially sustainable planning.

Conclusions

In comparison to the rest of Europe, planning in Greece has theoretically been identified quite recently as an essential prerequisite for a balanced spatial development. The necessary institutional frame that covered the gap was formed during the last few decades. The result, however, was a quite complicated and ineffective legislation, rather too weak to control the development mechanisms as this process of planning usually follows development instead of anticipating and defining it. Characteristically enough, the town plans made during the 1980s preceded the plans on regional and national levels, some of which have still not been completed. The problem is partially attributed to the centralisation of public administration, a feature that differentiates it from the corresponding administrative structures in central Europe. Although important reforms are currently imposed, there is still a long way to go, as old planning culture rigidities have to be confronted.

In the existing way planning remains subordinate to land-use control with weak strategic orientation, while some special cases are very occasionally confronted. The plans for the Olympic facilities are a case which was neither conditioned by a wider policy nor officially related to existing regulatory plans (see also contribution of Prehl and Tuçaltan in this volume). However, as the choice of their positioning was determined by objective factors such as accessibility, the new poles created followed the structure of the old or emerging centres without necessarily being identified with them. The north-south axis concerning the development of the centres has been maintained and reinforced. The chance of balancing the distribution of the development poles through the positioning of a metropolitan pole in the functionally downgraded western Attica has been lost.

What was achieved has to do with the complementary nature of the post-Olympic functions of the Games' facilities and their neighbouring urban centres. The new – Olympic – poles do not include uses of trade and services which would compete with the functions of old urban poles. To a great extent, they maintain their athletic, leisure and cultural nature which could not have been developed in the old poles. In this way the infrastructure developed for the Olympic Games can cover current needs and tendencies. The future development of the region around these poles is quite interesting given the possibility of their becoming units for development of new economic activities, probably of metropolitan range.

In any case, the example set by the Olympic facilities proves that a short-term policy related to specific interventions in the urban net and infrastructure building projects can dynamically form new balances in the urban space, particularly when the formal planning system seems to be ineffective. Nevertheless, however successful the function of the new Olympic poles can be considered to be, this case is difficult to generalise from and thus result in a kind of new model. It will always remain an occasional situation of adjusting the process of covering the city's immediate needs to the peculiarities of the Greek planning culture in relation to the administrative and planning system. All in all, the internationalised role that is Athen's target demands substantial and interventionary planning combined with an organisation of those mechanisms that will make its application effective.

Bibliography

Antonopoulou, S. (1991) *The Postwar Transformation of the Greek Economy and the Ekistic Phenomenon 1950–1980* (in Greek), Papazisis, Athens.
Aravantinos, A. (1997) *Urban Planning: For the Sustainable Development of Urban Space* (in Greek), Symmetria, Athens.
Baiba, A. Serraos, K., Tsakiropoulou and Chantzopoulou (2005) 'Study of systems and levels of planning in countries of Europe' (in Greek), Technical Chamber of Greece assignment, February 2005, Athens.
Beaverstock, J.V., P.J. Taylor and R.G. Smith (1999) 'A Roster of World Cities', *Cities* 16(6), 445–58.
Committee for the Athens 2004 Candidacy (1997) *The Athens 2004 Candidacy File*, Vols I, II and III, Committee for the Athens 2004 Candidacy, Athens.
Dekleris M. (2003) 'Athens and the Olympic Projects', *Architektones* 39-B, 73–5.
DEPOS (2002) *Guidelines of Syntax of 'Integrated Local Programs of Sustainable Development in implementation of HABITANT AGENDA'*, YPEHODE, Directory of Ekistics and Housing, Athens.
Economou, D. (2000) 'Rythmistikon Schedion of Athens: Experiences and Prospects', in D. Economou and G. Petrakos (eds) *The Development of Greek Cities* (in Greek), Publications of the University of Thessaly Gutenberg, Volos, 267–309.
ESTIA, INTERREG IIC (2000) *European Space and territorial Integration Alternatives, Spatial Planning Systems and Agencies in Southeast Europe*, Thessaloniki, http://estia.arch.auth.gr/estia/eng/docs/index.htm.
Gospondini, A. and E. Beriatos (2006) 'The Emerging "Local-internationalized" Cityscapes. The Case of Athens 2004', in A. Gospondini and E. Beriatos (eds) *The New Urban Landscapes and the Greek City*, Kritiki, Athens, 168–82.
Ioannou, B. and K. Serraos (2007) 'The New "Faces" of the European Metropolis and Their Greek Version', *International Journal of Sustainable Development and Planning* 2(2), 205–21.

ISoCaRP (2002) *Planning in Greece, Special Bulletin in the Frame of the 38th International Planning Congress*, ed. E. Beriatos, Athens.

National Technical University of Athens (NTUA) (2004) *Strategic Framework for the Spatial Development of Athens – Attica, Research Programme for the Ministry of the Environment, Spatial Planning and Public Works (YPEXODE)*, Scientific Resp. Kleito Gerard, NTUA, Athens.

Serraos K. (1996) 'Kommunalplanung in Griechenland und Österreich', *Schriftenreihe für Städtebau und Raumplanung 'Stadt und Region'*, Vol. 3, Institut zur Erforschung von Methoden und Auswirkungen der Raumplanung der Ludwig Boltzmann Gesellschaft, Technische Universität Wien, Vienna.

Serraos K., E. Gianniris and M. Zifou (2005) 'The Greek Spatial and Urban Planning System in the European Context', in G. Padovano and C. Blasi (eds) *Complessitá e Sostenibilitá, Prospettive per i territori europei: strategie di pianificazione in dieci Paesi, Rivista bimestrale di pianificazione e progrettazione*, anno 02, numero 06, giu/lug 2005, edizioni Poli.design.

Serraos K., B Ioannou and T. Papaioannou (2007) *The Generation of Urban Poles of Interest on the Occasion of Great Events and Interventions. Athens – Hamburg: A Comparative Approach*, Proceedings of XXII AESOP Conference (11–14 July), Naples.

Serraos K. and M. Skortsis (2003) *Urban Planning of Coastal Urban Zones and Relevant Shortcomings: The Case of Alimos (Attica)*, proceedings of international conference on 'Coastal Regions and Cities of Europe' (29–31 May), Herssonissos, Heraclion.

Taylor, P.J. (2000) 'World Cities and Territorial States under Conditions of Contemporary Globalisation', *Political Geography* 19, 5–32.

Wassenhoven L., E. Asprogerakas, E. Gianniris, T. Pagonis, C. Petropoulou and P. Sapountzaki (2005) *National Overview: Greece, Study for the Research Program 'Governance of Territorial and Urban Policies from EU to Local Level'*, School of Architecture, National Technical University of Athens, Athens.

Wassenhoven, L., L. Karka and P. Sapountzaki (2000) *National Overview of Conditions for the Implementation of Sustainability through Spatial Planning: Greece, Research Program 'Sustainability, Development and Spatial Planning: An Examination of the Capacity of Spatial Planning Systems in Europe to Develop and Implement Policy for Sustainability'*, NTUA, Athens.

YPECHODE (1998) *Spatial Planning and Sustainable Development (The Bill on Sustainable Spatial Development)*, Athens.

Zifou, M., B. Ioannou, D. Polychronopoulos, K. Serraos and A. Tsikli (2004) *The 2004 Olympic Games: A Non Planning Paradigm?*, Conference proceedings, AESOP (Association of European Schools of Planning) Congress 'Metropolitan Planning and Environmental Issues' (1–4 July), Grenoble.

Chapter 12

Coping with the Era of Change – Planning and Decision-Making under Globalisation in Turkey: The Case of the French Street Urban Transformation Project, Istanbul

Susanne Prehl and Gül Tuçaltan

Introduction

Since 1980s the world has been facing fundamental economic, political and social changes. Sassen (1991) summarises the growth of the international financial market, the expansion of the international trade in service and the re-patterning of foreign investment as the main attributes in this development towards advanced capitalism. Additionally, in one of his most recent works, *Spaces of Hope*, Harvey (2000) emphasises that the strengthening capital market creates spatial discontinuities directly affecting social relations that increase the disparity between urban poor and the urban rich.

These developments went along with a political restructuring towards neoliberal politics in most countries worldwide. As planners and decision-makers were directly affected by these changes, a transformation of urban planning structures can be observed and thus indicated as a reaction to the era of change. In this regard, Fukuyama (1992) argues in his book *The End of History and the Last Man* that the central role of the state has started to be questioned with the collapse of the Soviet Union and the Keynesian Welfare State system and therewith a new type of liberalism, which takes market mechanisms and individual entrepreneurship as strong welfare creators rather than the nation states, was born (Şengül 2001; see also contributions of Tynkkynen and Staniunas in this volume). Accordingly, the classical hierarchical top-down model of government seems to lose its sufficiency, as the system lacks flexibility to react to the new requirements of the international market.

The response to these transformations differs between advanced capitalistic countries, where the city itself is the main unit of capitalistic relations, and countries where economic development and urbanisation processes are not concurrent. This chapter aims to give momentum to the debate on urban issues after the 1980s in the latter group. For this purpose Turkey is chosen as a case study within the larger consideration of change in ethical and cultural values under the main focal concern of how the perspectives in planning and decision-making in Turkey have altered. In this regard, the argument will be discussed that, influenced by globalisation, Turkey's institutional background as well as its legal and constitutional principles are transformed simultaneously with the Western countries group, i.e. towards (neo)liberalisation, deregulation and privatisation.

The chapter will give a brief overview of the initial situation in Turkey before the political turning point in the 1980s. Later, the ensuing socio-political, administrative and economic restructuring processes will be contextualised. Subsequently, particular attention will be paid to the adjoining spatial restructuring, focusing especially on the issues of urban transformation and decision-making among urban actors. The argument will be supported by the presentation of the urban transformation project of French Street Istanbul. Detailed analysis of private and public actors' contributions to the planning process by reference to their strategies and cooperation will be reflected on under the main focal concern of the changing perspectives on planning and decision-making in Turkey. Finally, the chapter will conclude with a critical evaluation of the case study and the Turkish way of coping with the era of change. Within this context it is not possible to give an exhaustive overview but we aim to illustrate some of the many aspects of contemporary Turkish planning culture.

Turkey before 1980

The Turkish Republic was founded in 1923 under the power of Mustafa Kemal Atatürk CHP (The Republican People's Party) that followed the politically ideas of modernisation and westernisation by governmentally enforced secularisation, rationalisation and enlightenment. Due to the new political attitude, the traditional capital of the Ottoman Empire, which was deeply entrenched in Islam, lost its capital status and its political power to Ankara. The Kemalist model of government was thus a strictly centralised one, based on state control from Ankara not only in the economic sector but also in planning and governing issues.

With the incipient industrialisation favoured by the Marshall Plan, the economic environment started to change from the 1950s. Resulting from the mechanisation of the agrarian sector, huge migration movements from rural to urban areas were the consequence. Şengül defines this rapid urbanisation process between the 1950s and 1980s as the 'urbanisation of labour power' (Şengül 2001, 76). The lack of residential space provision by the state led to the formation of *gecekondu* (a house built in one night) as a residential settlement type unique to Turkey (Şengül 2003, 160). The *gecekondu* development was neither expected nor planned by the state. Therefore, in the atmosphere of rapid urbanisation, the 'State Planning Organisation' (SPO) was established in 1960 and has been responsible for the preparation of Five Year National Plans since then. However, Turkey still does not have a national strategic spatial plan.

Returning to our issue, since they were unfamiliar with the place they had migrated to, the immigrants distributed geographically in the city according to their local origin by moving either to *gecekondu* areas or to abandoned inner-city neighbourhoods. In addition, the lack of provision of formal jobs led to the emergence of the informal sector and clientelistic network relations, based on kinship and local origin, within the immigrants' communities (for 'clientelism' compare also contributions of Dangschat and Hamedinger and Vettoretto in this volume). This type of socio-spatial emergence brought a new type of urban development in which the local communities were confirmed as the base, not the state or the middle class, as Şengül (2001, 77) explains.

The Era of Change: Restructuring Processes in Turkey after the 1980s

Socio-Political, Administrative and Economic Restructuring

In 1980 the military coup destroyed the political ideals of the former periods in Turkey and paved the way for a restructuring of Turkish policy towards neoliberal politics and internationalisation of economic activities. The new Constitution was enacted in 1982. But the subsequent general elections did not take place in a free and competitive setting, as many former political parties were banned. Thus the Motherlands Party (Anavatan Partisi – ANAP), under the presidency of Turgut Özal, came into power in a rather uncompetitive and undemocratic atmosphere.

Özal's perspective for Turkey was neoliberal in economic terms and conservative in social terms. Thus, the idea of replacing the statist import-substitution based economy with the market based export-led policies via deregulation, privatisation and liberalisation policies was followed. To be able to do this it was necessary to transform the bureaucratic structure of the existing system. Consequently, Özal's reforms included the creation of a dual structure within the complete system of Turkish bureaucracy. The urban policy model of 'Metropolitan Governance' was enacted for the three main, most populated, Turkish cities (Ankara, Istanbul and Izmir) as they were on the one hand regarded as serving as showrooms on the 'international stage', but on the other hand were, due to their population density, considered as primary areas to canvass votes for national elections. This model of metropolitan governance, for the first time, and contrary to the former republican model, gave flexibility to local governments without any dependence to the central governments. Unlike in the former republican model, big cities were allowed, to develop, implement and change projects on their own, as the power of the central administration was delegated to the municipal majors.

Populist and rent-seeking politics became common practice. In this way, according to Alev Özkazanç (1995, 1218–24), the state lost its ideological, bureaucratic and legal position in the 1980s and the 1990s, rather than building the necessary background for the technological and industrial transformation.

In the 1990s the harmonisation process towards the EU and the intense relation with global institutions like the IMF (International Monetary Fund) introduced concepts such as democratisation, decentralisation and human rights to the Turkish Republic. Furthermore, concepts such as strengthening of local communities, sustainability, standard of living, equity, equality, citizenship, governance and strategic spatial planning were presented to Turkey at the United Nations' Rio Conference in 1992 and the HABITAT II Istanbul Conference in 1996 (Göymen 2000, 3–5, cited in Gedikli 2004, 94).

Favoured by the economic fluctuation of the Turkish economical crisis in 2001, the Justice and Development Party (Adalet ve Kalkınma Partisi – AKP) came into power in 2002. The economic programme of the AKP confirmed the government's interest in maintaining relations with the European Union, the World Bank, the IMF and other international institutions along the lines of the requirements of Turkish economy and national interests and accepted the important role of foreign capital for Turkey's economic development. Furthermore, privatisation was seen as an important mean for the formation of a more rational economic structure, recognising that the state should remain, in principle outside all types of economic activities. On a general basis, the programme on the one hand favours the three main principles of privatisation, deregulation and liberalisation and, on the other hand, brings a new dimension to the harmonisation process.[1]

The AKP government introduced the law packages of the Public Administration Reform which referred to concepts of 'new public management' and 'good governance'. Through these, new public management has a market-based approach to government. It is a quality- and performance-oriented process within 'institutionalised', 'efficient', 'effective' and 'economic' public service provision and it involves disaggregation, organisational change and competition stimulated by the public sector (Dunleavy et al. 2005). Therewith the Public Administration Reform aims to establish a participatory, transparent, accountable public administration which respects human rights and freedom under the 'devolution' of power from central to local governments.

Recently introduced laws[2] show an increased desire to harmonise policies in the field of public administration with the EU, which can be interpreted

---

1 See the Party Programme of the Justice and Development Party (AKP) for further details.
2 In 2004/05 the Local Administration Reform package was adopted by Parliament. Law No. 5302 (replacing Law No. 3360) for regulating the ongoing organisation of Special Provincial Local Administrations was enacted in 2005. Law

as a desire for public sector modernisation. In addition, it is regarded as problematic that all laws do not specifically determine which services are to be provided, to what extent and by whom. This missing assignment of authority and responsibilities can turn out to be a disaster in a developing country like Turkey. It was inevitable that the public administration system in Turkey was in urgent need of restructuring, but the success of the reform at solving problems is questionable.

Moreover, by favouring reforms for the devolution of authority, the centre lost control over the local. Even if it seems to be a good attempt to allow local decision-making, in the Turkish case the local administration system and the civic organisation types had been very state-centric. For that reason, local decision-making, and because of that counteracting planning traditions, did not work out well.

Newly introduced concepts and planning ideals entered the Turkish planning system in the name of harmonisation with the EU, but an examination of whether they could easily be adopted by the existing system was not submitted. As can be followed from the discussion above, the adoption of these concepts can be followed in the legal regulations subsequently passed concerning both public and urban policy. However, it can be questioned whether, in exchange for immediate change (in favour of local decision-making and EU harmonisation), an integrated approach to the transition to local decision-making would have been more suitable.

Spatial Restructuring: The Issue of Urban Transformation

The city after the 1980s is no longer a complementary unit to other cities, but a competitive unit which is trying to become a gateway to the world. Thus, the allocation of resources gained by privileged cities has become a daydream in which the increasing disparity in global, national, regional, provincial and even district scales is inevitable. The state directs foreign investment to the developed regions as demanded by capital holders under neoliberal perspectives. In the Turkish case, the most profitable area has been Istanbul. Thus, the 1980s created the privileged Istanbul which became Turkey's connection point to the world. The urbanisation of capital in Turkey and the commodification of land (Lefebvre 1991) have created a dual structure in the cities. Capital owners remain wealthy and the urban poor become poorer. In addition to these two poles, a decreasing number of the middle class can be found (Şengül 2001)

Similarly, Turkish cities faced a transformation process that replaced the purpose value of *gecekondu* (as a shelter) by the exchange value (as a

---

No. 5393 (replacing Law No. 1580) for regulating the ongoing organisation of the Municipalities was enacted in 2005 and Law No. 5216 (replacing Law No. 3030) for regulating the ongoing organisation of the Greater Metropolitan Municipality Administrations was enacted in 2004.

commodity). Global and national capital used for investments in mega projects and urban transformation led to a spatial change of the urban space (compare also contribution of Serraos et al. in this volume).

The transformation of *gecekondu* areas[3] via improvement planning, the construction of gated communities and new business districts including highrise office buildings as well as the transformation of historical centres via gentrification (like the French Street example in Istanbul that will be analysed in detail in the next section), became crucial parts of the Turkish urban agenda, even if, due to the fast restructuring processes, Turkish planning often just reacted to the changes rather than controlling them. Thus between 1980 and 2000, several laws and development rights were enacted to favour these objectives: the *Greater Metropolitan Municipality Law*, the *Municipality Law*, the *Development Law*, the *Law for Protection of the Cultural and Natural Assets*, the *Environmental Law*, the *Boğaziçi Law*, the *Law for National Parks* and the *Gecekondu Amnesties* (Ataöv and Osmay 2007). The urban transformations undertaken in the name of these laws marked the 1980s and 1990s and were often legitimised by the promise of *gecekondu* transformation via improvement planning. This action can be claimed to be both a politically and economically profit-seeking, populist action, widely accepted by the middle and upper classes of society. In addition, it gave flexibility to investors in the construction sector and thus advantaged rent-seeking actions as a neoliberal economic strategy.

This tendency was reinforced in the 2000s. The sector of construction gained importance as defined in the urban policy party programme of the AKP.

> The quality of Government in a country and the place of it in the international community is often measured by the quality of cities they construct. For this reason, the issue of urbanisation and housing has a meaning further than its technical content ... The major obstacle facing the issue of urbanisation and housing in reaching contemporary standards is the internal migration ... Improving urban planning in the slum areas of the towns will ease the problem, rather than increase the concentration by revising the building codes in established urban areas and planning in areas adjacent to municipal boundaries shall be accelerated ... Improper and ugly urbanisation shall be prevented. Cities shall be liveable spaces. Inexpensive housing shall be provided for those living in shantytown areas ... Cooperation with nongovernmental organisations shall be developed for the solution of urban problems; the establishment of district organisations shall be promoted ...[4]

---

3 The illegal housing type defined with the Law No. 775 enacted in 1966.
4 See the Party Programme of the Justice and Development Party (AKP) for further details.

Consequently, the main subjects of spatial restructuring appearing in Turkey were municipal mass and disaster housing provision projects and private sector luxury housing provision, as well as the use of historical residential areas as areas of trade. Therefore, oversupply of housing has taken place in this period. When totalling up the number of unregistered housing to the registered supply it can be claimed that 30–50 per cent of the provision is unnecessary (Balamir 2004, cited in Ataöv and Osmay 2007, 69).

In the period of the 2000s, strategic planning and the communicative paradigm gained worldwide importance and started to be discussed in the academic environment. In Turkey, some practical examples can be observed, but still the above-mentioned issues are discussed rather than implemented. Accordingly, when distribution politics gave way to identity politics, the most-discussed issues were democracy and participation. The change in paradigm in the hegemonic literature of the West thus affected Turkish law, order and planning, and hence the concepts of strategic planning, participation and urban transformation. In addition to the package presented, the 'Law Draft for the Urban Transformation Areas' forms a specifically important attempt at legal regulation on the current agenda. It covers the transfer of planning authority to the municipalities in both urban or rural areas for the purpose of renewal, improvement, development or purification where the physical, social or technical infrastructure is insufficient, irrespective of whether there is a development plan and irrespective of whether there are public or charity foundation buildings located on the areas (Uzun 2006, 51–2; Ataöv and Osmay 2007, 70) The transfer of planning authority to the local, seemingly democratic, level reproduces the hierarchical structure on another scale and therewith leads to a monopoly in terms of planning of the Greater Metropolitan Municipalities on the local level.

To close on the issue of the general theoretical overview, the general characteristics of Turkish planning culture after 1980s can be summarised as follows. As a result of the implementation of the metropolitan governance model, planning power was transferred from central government to big cities' municipalities. Newly enacted laws and regulations that cope with the municipal power provision generally have a partial approach rather than an inter-relational perspective that is connected to upper-scale planning activities. Planning guidelines are often missing and binding city development plans have only recently been presented or are still about to be set up. Furthermore, as liberalisation, privatisation and deregulation are an integrated part of the current policy model, a strengthening of the private sector's position in planning and urban development can be highlighted.

Accordingly, attitudes towards planning are manifold and cover the will to implement European ideals such as participation and democratisation as well as networking as an integral characteristic of development structures be it in terms of business associations, political organisations or social activities (Erder 1999, 165).

To summarise, it can be said that Turkish planning has a reactive character to the restructuring processes rather than an active one, which can mostly be attributed to the dynamic socio-economic character of the country.

Case Study: Implementation of French Street Project in the City of Istanbul

The spatial appearance of the urban is the result of both political and social developments. Thus to survey an actual example of urban transformation can provide an interesting insight into the restructuring processes in Turkey, that supports the above arguments, namely that Turkey's institutional background as well as its legal and constitutional principles are being transformed simultaneously towards (neo)liberalisation, deregulation and privatisation.

Therefore the case of the French Street Urban Transformation Project, which covers the revitalisation of one street in the historical core area of Istanbul via gentrification and restoration, has been chosen to demonstrate the planning and implementation process of an urban transformation project in Istanbul under the newly-enacted institutional and constitutional conditions in the atmosphere of the era of change in the largest Turkish city.

Istanbul after the 1980s

Under Özal's Motherlands Party (ANAP) government, Istanbul received a large amount of financial support directly from the state budget and was furthermore able to raise an estimated $900 million in loans from abroad between 1983 and 1989 (Keyder and Öncü 1994, 400). Thus, since the mid-1980s plenty of projects were initiated by the private as well as by the public sector, mainly aiming to transform Istanbul 'from a national primate city, ravaged by rapid immigration, into a newly imagined world city' (Keyder and Öncü 1994, 401) within the larger consideration of Turkey's involvement in the western countries group or in the European Union since 1999. Starting in the 1980s, Istanbul became the new showcase for international and national investment. These developments went along with the creation of new employment opportunities for well-educated individuals, especially in the service industries (Islam 2005, 125–6). Likewise, the new global interconnectedness allowed Istanbul's citizens, especially the newly emerging middle class, to adapt to Western consumption patterns and values. Istanbul was rapidly becoming a city designed for cultural consumption (Keyder 1999, 17; Islam 2005, 121–36).

The occupational and cultural transformation processes were, similarly to cities worldwide, accompanied by the spatial transformation of Istanbul's inner city via gentrification, as the historic centre of 1980s Istanbul hosted much of the dilapidated late nineteenth- and early twentieth-century housing stock with a view of the Bosporus that was most popular for purchase and renovation by the gentrifiers of the new middle class. In addition, it was inhabited by easily relocatable occupants, namely lower-income immigrants who lacked the resources to reinvest in their properties to maintain the buildings (Islam 2005, 121–3). These core areas[5] (Cihangir, Galata and Asmalımescit) were formerly inhabited by different ethnic and religious groups, Muslims and more predominantly, non-Muslim minorities. As, until the 1940s, political pressure in the Turkish Republic compelled most of them to leave Turkey, the prestigious inner-city districts remained temporarily abandoned. The forced decline of cosmopolitanism coincided with the economic boom of the post-1950s and the open borders after the 1980s which attracted an influx of working immigrants from the East Anatolian provinces and later from the Eastern Bloc. Istanbul's population increased rapidly from 2.9 million in 1980 to over 10 million in 2006 [census referring to city borders without independent suburbs]. The newcomers either moved to informal settlements (*gecekondus*) or 'invaded' the abandoned inner-city sites of the non-Muslim population.

One of these neighbourhoods is the area of the French Street Project. It belongs to the inner-city district Beyoğlu, located on Istanbul's European shore. After political and economical restructuring in the 1980s, Beyoğlu became one of the main investment areas for national and international shareholders in Istanbul. Today, the district, especially the area alongside İstiklal Street, is a very prestigious, mainly gentrified part of the city that is carefully promoted to the global world as Istanbul's cosmopolitan, western city centre and attracts thousands of visitors and tourists each day.

The development process of French Street is similar to the above-described gentrification process up to a certain point. The neighbourhood used to be a Greek settlement. Under the Turkish Republic most of the Greek inhabitants left the district. Abandoned houses with open land tenures remained and were informally populated by immigrants, Kurds and Roma who were not able to obtain the buildings formally (Mills 2005, 441–62) Consequently French Street's housing stock visibly degenerated and served as a home for the low-income class until the private developer Mehmet Taşdiken, owner of the real estate agency Afitaş, decided to place his project idea of a 'French Street' in the area of Cezayir Street. At this point the development process of the street turned out to be specific. Initiated by a private investor, French Street was originated without any governmental financial support, but approved by the municipality as a major package (compare also contribution of Tynkkynen in this volume).

Aiming to provide a useful connection of theory part and case study analysis, the following description examines the complex scenario of the project's planning and implementation process by analysing strategies and functions of the involved actors as well as the legal frames that supported the decision-making process.

---

5 Islam (2005) describes three waves of gentrification. The gentrification of Istanbul's inner-city neighbourhoods forms the second wave.

The Case Study of French Street, Istanbul

The case study area of French Street consists of two streets (Cezayir Cikmazi and Cezayir Sokag, meaning Algerian Street and Algerian Alley) with the adjoining 29 three- to six-storied nineteenth-century buildings and a small square. After the project's implementation in 2004 the newly renovated houses mostly housed restaurants and bars that use the street's space for seating. Furthermore there were shops, an art gallery, a hotel and some of the upper floors were still used for living.

The official project report, written by Afitaş, considered the recovery of Beyoğlu's natural connection to European Culture[6] to be the main purpose of the project. It was argued that the French Street project could bring back European (namely French) culture to the district.

> This Beyoğlu Project was called into being to remember French culture. Maybe it is a small area but the practice and the trade in French Street is a very big symbol of Pera. We find a multicultural scene here. (Interview, Taşdiken 2006)

On this note the street was thematically staged according to strict French design motives with 'French flair' pastel-coloured walls, French paintings and furniture as well as with restaurants with French names, playing French music and serving French food (*Cumartesi VATAN*, January 2004). Cultural events take place in several locations on the street. These include small concerts and exhibitions. A street magazine is published which contains articles about fashion, artists and lifestyle, thus catering to the interests of the street's target group, who are, as the street's director Taşdiken explains (interview 2006), 'economically well situated and also culturally interested people'. By implementing a French theme and by offering relatively high prices, the street management attracts this specific group of customers which understands itself as the modern and cosmopolitan elite and thereby underlines the project's economic approach. The concept's idea runs in concord with the common passion for the Islamic and Ottoman past and connects its approach to Istanbul's history as capital of the nineteenth-century Ottoman Empires. By this means a period is chosen as being presentable today, which is known as pro-Western and pro-multi-ethnic.

French Street is small scale but is a representative example that allows us to comprehend the shift in claims of a formerly low-income neighbourhood with

---

6 In Ottoman's Istanbul, Beyoğlu used to be a 'Europeanised' quarter, inhabited by diverse non-Muslim inhabitants, characterised by a wealth of languages and cultural practices and dominated by symbols of modern living such as office buildings, banks, theatres, hotels, department stores, and multi-storey apartment buildings (Bartu 1999; Mills 2005).

Figure 12.1 French Street in 2006, newly renovated buildings house restaurants and bars, coloured awnings and restaurant seating characterise the street's appearance

Source: Prehl 2006.

historical importance to a private sector's development for the economically well situated population of the city. Therewith the project goes along with the common Turkish planning practice of inner-city rehabilitation, namely to 'value' a poor neighbourhood by enlisting private investment and by implementing popular entertainment and culture concepts.

Accordingly, the project was originated and financed by a private investor on the one hand, but supported by the public authorities, on the other. Assisted by a team of architects, artists and scientists the private developer Taşdiken worked out the project's idea (Afitaş 2004) and successfully presented its proposals to the public authorities, who were in charge of the approval of the project. During that time Taşdiken was a consultant to Mayor Gürtuna[7] and therefore held strong connections to the city's municipality.

The project was accepted as one main package – including permission for the renovation, demolition and reconstruction of the buildings and

---

7 Ali Müfit Gürtuna (Virtue Party– Refah Partisi) was mayor of Istanbul in 1998–2004.

licences and work permits for the restaurants. The generally time-consuming process of the approval in the case of French Street took just a few days. As the government and thus the municipality were willing to support private investment in the district (Büyükköksal and Özkan 2005), a new authorisation model was implemented for the French Street project. As *Beyoğlu Idare* (July 2004, 5) reports, it did not comply with the existing legal regulations. But with its implementation a project's concept could be supported that suited the governmental attempt to form a new, 'more modern and contemporary' composition for Beyoğlu by 'protecting and respecting its former identity and carrying its traces of the past' (*Beyoğlu Belediyesi* 2006, 1) The support of Istanbul's city mayor Ali Müfit Gürtuna as a strong political figure who had the power to implement projects also probably accelerated the approval procedure.

> I think that this project [French Street project] will be a very important project for our country on the way to the European Union, especially for Istanbul, which was the capital of the empires, as well as for Beyoğlu district, which has been the window of our city to Europe for centuries in terms of architecture and culture [sic]. (Gürtuna 2002 in an official letter sent to the real estate agency of Mehmet Tasdiken in 2002)

The mayor's statement, shown above, clearly points out that he declares the French Street project to be presentable as it evokes Istanbul's European cultural roots. Alike the incumbent mayor of the district of Beyoğlu stated in the French Street magazine:

> That zone was in need of rehabilitation before, with this kind of a community it became an artistic place ... It's now time for all parts of Beyoğlu for similar projects. (Afitaş 2006, 80)

Thus, since 2005, French Street and its adjoining neighbourhoods have been declared a priority area for renewing the deprived urban fabric by revitalisation, according to Law No. 5366.[8]

On the whole, Afitaş easily implemented its idea of a themed street project. Taşdiken convinced private business partners to invest, bought most of the houses and obtained long-term tenancy agreements for the government-owned buildings. To put the project's idea into practice, most of the former tenants were given notice to leave their flats. In total 48 tenants moved to other settlement areas for low-income population, e.g. Yedikule, Tarlabaşı and Şişhane (Büyükköksal and Özkan 2005). Today the houses are rented

---

8   Law No. 5366: Law for Renewing the Deprived Urban Fabric by Revitalisation/ Yıpranan Tarihi ve Kültürel Tasınmaz Varlıkların Yenilenerek Korunması ve Yasatılarak Kullanılması Hakkında Kanun.

to new tenants who are mostly involved with a restaurant or a bar in the area. Afitaş still influences the everyday street life as owner and through management. Activities in the street are controlled and restricted by specific tenancy agreements, as the street's management stated in an interview in 2005: 'We have prepared a very strict contract that regulates how the places can be decorated and what kind of activity is allowed. We only want establishments that suit our concept' (*The Guide* 2005, 70)

The public discourse on French Street was mainly influenced by Istanbul's municipality, by Mehmet Taşdiken himself and by the national press by predominantly positive statements. But after the *Postexpress* published a critical comment in August 2004 concerning the investor's one-sided concept and the lack of inhabitant's participation and their resettlement, the issue of French Street was publicly discussed.[9]

Evaluation of the Case Study

Advantaged by the political and economic redefinition of Turkey towards liberalisation and deregulation, private enterprises started to influence planning and decision-making after 1980s and thus became an inherent component of urban development strategies (compare also contributions of Tynkkynen and Staniunas in this volume). The analysis of the case study underlines this already-existing strength of the private sector. Interestingly, in the French Street case the complex relationship network of the private investor (to the municipality and to private business partners) seemed to have accelerated and supported the project's implementation. By using its political and personal contacts and financial power, Afitaş was able to put a 'French theme park' into practice in a core area housing neighbourhood. Thus the enterprise was allowed to use nearly the whole area for private commercial and consumption purposes and therefore was able to implement its profit-driven approach. Public authorities participated in the project's development mainly in a supporting role, as they approved the project as a whole, following a newly formulated authorisation procedure. As there were no binding development plans, the municipality flexibly reacted to the private investor's requirements and therewith again demonstrated its willingness to endorse privatisation, as municipality members affirmed (compare also the contribution of Serraos et al. in this volume).

Both public and the private stakeholders used the image of a cosmopolitan and therefore European Istanbul to promote the project. French culture was nostalgically linked to the Ottoman Beyoğlu of the late nineteenth and early twentieth century, being known for its diverse multi-ethnic population. In this way a link was created between the concept and the currently popular Ottoman

---

9   As, at the end of 2006 the project lacked commercial success, Afitaş decided to reduce the French theme and to rename the area.

history. By implementing French cuisine, French lifestyle and French music the local specifics of the place (even if, according to Mills (2005, 441–62), they were somewhat invented) were connected to a pleasurable experience. Consequently the immigrant culture of the neighbourhood was confronted with the planned cultural concept of a glamorous Western lifestyle.

Conclusion: Whereby and How to Cope with the Change – Planning, Decision-making and Ethics

In the Turkish case, the politics of redistribution gave way to the politics of identity after the 1980s. Both society and space became fragmented and socially stratified. Therefore, Turkey's administration was restructured and accordingly Turkish urban planners and decision makers now operate through a variety of rules that are determined by laws under restructuring. Each year new laws are enacted or, as presented in the case study of French Street, new regulations are implemented that are not yet endorsed by existing laws. Most of this legislation has an open part that can be misused – due to the low level of standardisation. The main characteristics in common are the ambiguous articles which do not specifically determine which services are to be provided, to what extent and by whom, which may lead to the protection of some specific group's rights either politically, economically or ethnically. Furthermore, it may lead to a favouring of private and economic interests in decision-making, instead of controlling and coordinating private urban interventions and investments. It appears that Turkey's adoption of principles such as democratisation, decentralisation and devolution of authority – the main ideological beacons of the transformation under the discourses of transparency, accountability, participation, responsiveness and auditing – have so far been rather problematic.

On the contrary, compared to other countries of the Western countries group, it would be wrong to talk about a withdrawal of city authorities from their traditional controlling and coordinating functions. The city's municipality never had these functions. In fact, urban planning was the task of the central government in Ankara. The implementation of the metropolitan governance model in the 1980s first enabled the city's municipality to plan and implement projects by itself. But it has to be asked whether municipalities and local governments are sufficiently able to fulfil these functions, as there is no tradition in doing so and the centre is not able to give adequate attention to each and every single locality. Therefore, when considering the recent emphasis of 'the local' in the Turkish planning system, and when considering the long-lasting central focus of Turkish republican planning, the legal regulations should be taken into account again to provide a proper balance between central government and the local governments and to prevent the interest-seeking acts due to the misuse of the laws.

In the Turkish case, the balance between the local and centre is not set up yet. Planning practices are market friendly as well as being highly incremental and partial (disconnected from the city and its problems) like the French Street case.

When considering planning itself, the hierarchically organised planning and decision-making of the past has been (or has to be) changing itself into a strategic type of planning, which is responsive to the changes occurring in a volatile way, with an interactive approach. Therefore, the question is to what degree the planners and decision-making authorities use the tools to be more democratic, efficient, effective and collaborative and how? They have the laws and regulations, albeit inevitably imperfect, but the use of them is in the hands of the planners and decision-making authorities, either for the benefit of society or not.

Bibliography

Afitaş (2004) *Projects Report*, Afitaş, Istanbul.
Afitaş (2006) 'Fransiz Cezayir Sokağı i dergisi', *Aylık Kültür Sanat ve Magazin*, Eylül 2006, 1.
Ataöv, A. and S. Osmay (2007) *Türkiye'de Kentsel Dönüşüme Yöntemsel bir Yaklaşım, Mimarlık Fakültesi Dergisi* 24(2), METU Press, Ankara, 57–82.
Bartu, A. (1999) 'Who Owns the Old Quarters? Rewriting Histories in a Global Era', in C. Keyder (ed.) *Istanbul between the Global and the Local*, Rowman and Littlefield Publishers, Boston.
Beyoğlu Belediyesi (2006) *Beyoğlu* (Quarterly Magazine of Beyoğlu Municipality), June, Istanbul.
Beyoğlu Idare (2004) French Street Special Issue, July.
Büyükköksal, A. and M. Özkan (2005) 'Gentrification in Cezayir Street', seminar paper, Middle East Technical University, Ankara.
Cumartesi VATAN (2004) 'Fransiz Sokagi nisan sonunda aciliyor', 3 January.
Dunleavy, P., H. Margetts, S. Bastow and J. Tinkler (2005) 'New Public Management Is Dead – Long Live Digital-Era Governance', *Journal of Public Administration Research and Theory Advance Access* 16(3), 467–94.
Erder, S. (1999), 'Where do You Hail From? Localism and Networks in Istanbul', in C. Keyder (ed.) *Istanbul between the Global and the Local*, Rowman and Littlefield Publishers, Boston, 161–72.
Fukuyama, F. (1992) *The End of History and the Last Man*, Palgrave Macmillan, New York.
Gedikli, B. (2004) 'Strategic Spatial Planning and its Implementation in Turkey: Şanlıurfa Provincial Development Planning Case', PhD thesis, Department of City Planning, Middle East Technical University, Ankara.
Guide, The (2005) *Istanbul*, APA Group, Istanbul.

Harvey, D. (2000) *Spaces of Hope*, University of California Press, Berkeley/ Los Angeles.
Islam, T. (2005) 'Outside the Core: Gentrification in Istanbul', in R. Atkinson and G. Bridge (eds) *Gentrification in a Global Context: The New Urban Colonialism*, Routledge, London.
Keyder, C. (1999) 'The Setting', in Keyder, C. (ed.) *Istanbul between the Global and the Local*, Rowman and Littlefield, Boston, 3–31.
Keyder, C. and A. Öncü (1994) 'Globalisation of a Third-world Metropolis: Istanbul in the 1980s', *Review* 17(3), 383–421.
Lefebvre, H. (1991) *The Production of Space*, Blackwell, Oxford.
Mills, A. (2005) 'Narratives in City Landscapes: Cultural Identity in Istanbul', *Geographical Review*, 95(3), 441–62.
Özkazanç A. (1995) *Türkiye'de Yeni Sağ, Türkiye Ansiklopedisi*, 1218–24.
Postexpress (2004) 'Occupation, Exile, Plundering [Isgal, sürgün, yagma]', August.
Prehl, S. (2007) 'Akteurskonstellationen und Lebensstildistinktion im Öffentlichen Raum Istanbuls: Das Beispiel Französische Straße', Masters thesis, Bauhaus – University Weimar, Weimar.
Robins, K. and A. Aksoy (1995) 'Istanbul Rising: Returning the Repressed to Urban Culture', *European Urban and Regional Studies* 2(3), 223–35.
Sassen, S. (1991) *The Global City: New York, London, Tokyo*, Princeton University Press, Princeton, NJ.
Şengül, T. (2001) *Kentsel Çelişki ve Siyaset, Kapitalist Kentleşme Süreçleri Üzerine Yazılar*, Istanbul.
Tuçaltan, G. (2008) 'Dynamics of Urban Transformation via Improvement Plans for Ankara City', Masters thesis, Middle East Technical University, The Department of Urban Policy Planning and Local Governments, Ankara.
Uzun, N. (2006) 'Yeni Yasal Düzenlemeler ve Kentsel Dönüşüme Etkileri', *Planlama Dergisi* 2006/2, Şehir Plancıları Odası Yayınları, Ankara, 49–52.

Interviews

Taşdiken, M. and N. Taşdiken (2006) Istanbul.

PART 5
Interdependencies between European Spatial Policies and Planning Cultures

Chapter 13
The Impact of Europeanisation on Planning Cultures

Bas Waterhout, João Morais Mourato and Kai Böhme

Introduction

This chapter argues that spatial planning in European member states at national, regional and local scale is undergoing an incremental process of Europeanisation. The concept of spatial planning is understood here as the methods or governance arrangements that seek to shape patterns of spatial development in particular areas (Nadin and Stead 2008). Under this definition we can observe a multitude of different spatial planning approaches throughout Europe, such as the French *l'aménagement du territoire*, the German *Raumordnung* and the Dutch *ruimtelijke ordening*. In this chapter, we interpret how these different approaches reflect the particular societal models and cultural contexts from which they have emerged. We also expand on the shaping influence of the 'system' in which these approaches have evolved. By 'system', we refer to laws and regulations, administrative and organisational arrangements as well as discourses and policies, all of these parts of a domestic planning culture. Cultures do not change in a linear way (Shaw and Lord 2007, see also contribution of Gullestrup in this volume). Cultural change is a continuous process and the result of a multitude of intended or unintended top-down or bottom-up influences, both from inside and outside the planner's realm.

The EU is just one of these sources of influence, and only recently can we see it impacting upon spatial planning. This chapter forms an exploration of the question of whether the Europeanisation of spatial planning as such also leads to changing planning cultures in Europe? A further question then would be whether this leads to convergence between planning cultures in Europe and even to a European planning culture?

To answer these questions we should first have a better idea of what Europeanisation of planning amounts to. Because, as Markusen (2003, 702) highlights: 'If it exists how can I see it?' In fact, evidence of Europeanisation in the field of planning has only recently become an object of collection of data and analysis. Aiming for conceptual systematisation, we will discuss both the current usage of the term and recent developments concerning Europeanisation as an explanatory concept. Critically revising interpretations derived from other disciplines, we propose a specific interpretational framework for the Europeanisation of planning. We conclude that, for now, the Europeanisation of planning remains visible only to those who are really looking for it and to those who are actively evaluating these newly-embedded influences and their outcomes.

Europeanisation and Culture Change: What Does It Actually Mean?

Originally a political science concept, in planning, Europeanisation has been mainly used as an umbrella term to describe the pattern of responses of EU member states to what has been termed the European spatial policy environment. Despite its conceptually fashionable and simultaneously contested nature (Olsen 2007, 68), it can be broadly accepted that:

> Europeanisation consists of processes of a) construction, b) diffusion, and c) institutionalisation of formal and informal rules, procedures, policy paradigms, styles, 'ways of doing things' and shared beliefs and norms which are first defined and consolidated in the EU policy process and then incorporated in the logic of domestic (national and subnational) discourse, political structures and public policies. (Radaelli 2003, 30).

In this context, the idea of European spatial planning expressed through, amongst others, the European Spatial Development Perspective (CEC 1999) and the Territorial Agenda of the EU is a unique catalyst of change, impacting both the European Union territory as a whole and the individual nation states within it. An empirical description and analysis of this process of change has been at the core of this debate as academics seek to unmask a cause-effect relationship between the EU and national level planning policy arenas and consider whether similarities in effects or processes of change suggest the existence of a possible European-wide process of change. The concept of Europeanisation has been used as a banner for this causal relationship.

The Europeanisation of planning, however, is not limited to European spatial planning discourse as such. As will be developed later, it also results from EU sectoral policies such as regional policy, environmental policy and transport, agricultural and competition policies as well as from all kinds of cooperation programme and, indeed, the concept of European integration as such, which provides a cognitive and normative frame.

Pinning down a specific definition of Europeanisation is problematic. On its own, European Spatial Planning has provided ample material for long lasting academic discussions on its conceptual (in)definition – the examples of polycentric development or territorial cohesion spring to mind (see also contribution of Davoudi in this volume). Europeanisation is, in this sense, similar. 'The conceptual challenge is not primarily that of inventing definitions' (Olsen 2002, 944) but to explore 'the relevance of the concept for inquiring into change' (Gualini 2004, 4). The concept's greater potential is to be understood as a multifaceted phenomenon 'in search of explanation, not the explanation itself' (Radaelli 2004, 2). In this sense our focus concerns the relationship between, on the one hand, the large variety of initiatives, policies and discourses at the European level and, on the other hand, changes occurring in spatial planning practices at national, regional and local level, which eventually may lead to changing planning cultures.

Across Europe, a wave of change can be observed as regards domestic spatial planning practices. An example of this concerns the development of national and regional spatial visions, which in a number of countries and regions (e.g. Portugal, Ireland, Austria, the Walloon region, as well as regions in Spain and Italy; see also contribution of Vettoretto in this volume) happened for the first time. In countries and regions that already had a tradition in spatial visioning, a remarkable change is that visions now explicitly look across the borders and view territory in a wider transnational or even European spatial context. On a more abstract level, it is observed that planning systems evolve over time and that, for example, the French *l'aménagement du territoire*, which was seen as the archetype of the regional economic approach, increasingly adopts elements and approaches from the so-called comprehensive integrated approach of planning, more suggested by the Dutch and Danish planning systems, as well as the other way around (Farinos Dasi/ESPON 2.3.2 2007; Nadin and Stead 2008; see also contributions of Davoudi and Nadin and Stead in this volume). An example of change at the regional and local level is the increasing juridification and technification of planning in the sense that a growing number of planning decisions are made by the courts. This concerns, in particular, planning decisions where environmental issues are at stake (Zonneveld et al. 2008).

We must decide if Europeanisation helps us to understand better the ongoing processes of change simultaneously affecting, in various ways and to various degrees, the domestic spatial planning policy-making of European Union member states. In other words is Europeanisation a feasible research framework for these sorts of changes? Although not an indigenous concept to European spatial planning, Europeanisation is swiftly becoming endogenous to it (e.g. Gualini 2004; Börzel 2002; Faludi 2004; Jensen and Richardson 2004; Giannakourou 2005; Dühr et al. 2007; Böhme and Waterhout 2008; Tewdwr-Jones and Mourato forthcoming). In fact, the last few years have witnessed an increasing number of attempts, focusing directly or indirectly on planning, to explore Europeanisation as an explanatory concept for the changes taking place throughout the multitude of planning systems contained within the EU. But how can this be done?

The Drivers of Europeanisation: How Does It Occur?

In a recent paper, Böhme and Waterhout (2008) consider the Europeanisation of planning from a somewhat broader perspective and identify three sources of Europeanisation: rules, resources and ideas. These three drivers are also considered the key drivers behind processes of institutionalisation and cultural change (Healey 2006; Waterhout 2008). This is not to say that Europeanisation will always produce new or changed institutions, or even culture change, but merely that it evolves along similar lines. Figure 13.1 provides a schematic overview of how the Europeanisation of planning may be taking place.

More specifically in spatial planning EU policies and legislation act as the rules that influence, mostly in an unintended way and most often as an unwanted way, domestic spatial planning practices. Competition policy, dealing with procurement and state aid (Korthals Altes 2006), environmental impact assessments and, in particular, environmental directives, such as the Birds and Habitat Directive, Air Quality Directive and Water Framework Directive, cause important effects and often lead to fundamental changes in decision-making trajectories. However, because each member state is responsible for the way it transposes EU directives in national legislation (as long as the objectives are met), the spatial effects of these directives differ to a great extent from country to country. Unless a comprehensive comparative analysis is performed there can be no definitive answers as to whether this can be explained on the basis of the differences between member states as regards the way: (a) domestic planning systems work; (b) directives are being transposed and interpreted by courts; (c) different national administrative cultures influence the process or (d) a combination of these.

As far as resources are concerned, we can look at transnational cooperation, as stimulated by the INTERREG programme, as a clear example. Since this programme amounts to €1.4 billion for the period 2000–2006 and a more or less similar amount for 2007–2013, this does not imply massive means. But because the programme is explicitly linked to the European Spatial Development Perspective (ESDP) it is an amplifier of the message of Europeanisation it embodies (Pedrazzini 2005). However, INTERREG leads to different solutions in different parts of Europe. For example, polycentric development projects in sparsely populated areas in the north of Europe have a completely different focus from those in urbanised areas (Waterhout and Stead 2007).

Also regarding resources, we should highlight the EU regional policy that represents about a third of the total EU budget, which as Bachtler and Polverari (2007) show has become increasingly spatialised over time. Similarly, other EU spending policies like trans-European network (TEN)-transport and the Common Agricultural Policy can be regarded as having had some impact on domestic spatial development and planning policies. For example, agricultural policy stimulated a more rational way of agriculture which led to large scale

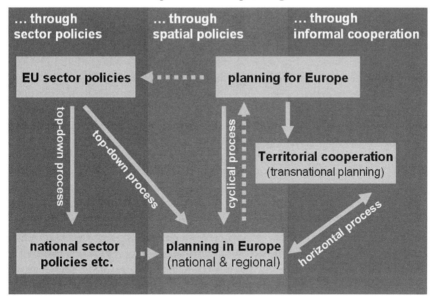

Figure 13.1 Processes and influences underlying the Europeanisation of planning

Source: Böhme and Waterhout 2008: 243.

farming and consequently a change of landscape in parts of Europe (Ravesteyn and Evers 2004; Arkleton Institute/ESPON 2.1.3 2004). Likewise, transport policy and, in particular, the idea of a trans-European network (Buunk 2003) have in many countries led to internal debates and regional pressure to develop large-scale infrastructure projects which link them 'on the network'. European Spatial Planning Observation Network (ESPON) study 2.1.1 on the impact of EU transport policy concludes that the spatial development effects of EU transport policies differ a great deal between member states and that this is primarily because of the inconsistencies between the national, regional and local interpretations of these policies. A general pattern is that in the EU15 the EU transport policies have only marginally influenced domestic schemes, while the member states that joined after 2004 follow EU objectives pretty closely, not least also because they are more likely to qualify for financial support (University of Kiel/ESPON 2.1.1 2004).

Yet, in a number of cases the most important source of Europeanisation is the European spatial planning discourse itself, as a set of ideas about planning. This discussion has been shaped by the ESDP, and has been further elaborated by the recently adopted Territorial Agenda of the EU and the ongoing ESPON project. The development of this discourse has also been referred to as developing 'planning for Europe' (see Figure 13.1). Research on the application of the ESDP reveals the influence of this document as source of inspiration for national and regional planning in European countries.

The ESPON 2.3.1 project observed four types of effect in the application of the ESDP: changes in planning discourse, institutional changes, changes in planning policies and changes in planning practices (as well as a fifth one: no change – e.g. Cyprus, Norway, Poland, the Slovak Republic, Switzerland) (Nordregio/ESPON 2.3.1 2007). Concrete examples of such effects are the already mentioned *hausse* of spatial visions, but also changes in discourse (i.e. Austria, Denmark, Slovenia) which often led to new visual representations showing the country in its wider context. In Flanders, the Czech Republic, France, Ireland, Lithuania, Luxembourg and Spain it was reported that after discursive change policies were adapted.[1] Also various institutional changes were observed ranging from the set-up of new planning institutions (Hungary, Latvia), the strengthening of the regional level (Italy) or the establishment of an International Affairs Unit (Netherlands). Likewise, governance arrangements and administrative structures have been created or reformed in order to deal more effectively with European spatial planning or, for example, the transposition of EU directives (Romania[2]). Furthermore, the ESDP was reported to have played a role in policy changes (Bulgaria and the UK). However, in none of the above situations has the ESDP been identified as the only or major source for change, but as one factor among many others. This reflects the findings of other authors, who nevertheless also concluded that the ESDP has had visible effects on domestic spatial planning (Faludi 2001; Böhme 2002, 2003; Shaw and Sykes 2005; Sykes 2007; Jensen and Richardson 2004; Giannakourou 2005; Janin Rivolin and Faludi 2005).

The label 'idea' may also include the process of European integration as such, and in particular the awareness of domestic actors of a larger framework that inspires them to view their own policies, in this case on planning, in this European context. Institutional reforms such as the EU 1992, the Constitutional Treaty and the 2004 enlargement may have boosted this awareness. As is the case in general with Europeanisation processes, the effects of these policies in terms of changing domestic planning practices differ from country to country and region to region, not only in terms of how they are being translated into national and regional policies, but also as regards the extent of their effects. Some EU directives have had a direct impact on planning in some countries, while others have not. In a similar way the European spatial planning discourse has had an ambiguous impact at the domestic level, in some cases kick-starting an entire sequence of new developments but mostly just creeping into national policies without stakeholders even noticing it. For example, regional planning stakeholders often use 'European' terminology

---

1 For Lithuania, please see also Staniunas's contribution in this volume.
2 For Romania, please see also Puşcaşu's contribution in this volume.

without knowing that it originated at the EU level (Lähteenmäki-Smith et al. 2005; Radaelli 2004). An investigation by the Swedish Association of Local Authorities estimates that about 90 per cent of all local council decisions are in some way informed by EU directives, regulations, recommendations, policy aims or funding (Böhme 2006).

In sum, we distinguish here between four types of process that characterise the Europeanisation of planning: first, the top-down influence of EU policies and directives; second, horizontal processes of Europeanisation, for example, organisational learning through INTERREG cooperation projects and the mutual learning processes that they foster between stakeholders or through the various EU governance committees where representatives meet to discuss EU policy proposals (see also contribution of During et al. in this volume). Third, what Williams (1996) has called spatial positioning, which refers to the ability to view one's position in a larger spatial context, such as the newly developed spatial visions do. A fourth and last type of Europeanisation process is discursive integration (Böhme 2002, 2003) resulting from domestic policy communities interacting through network governance at EU level. Such a round-about process forms the primary explanation for the wide application of the ESDP (Böhme 2002; Böhme and Waterhout 2008; Waterhout and Stead 2007).

Europeanisation: What Impact(s)?

Having established a comprehensive view of the origins and drivers of Europeanisation, the remaining question is to what extent does Europeanisation influence planning? For this question to be answered we should first look at the types of outcome that Europeanisation may produce. As we have seen above, the effects of Europeanisation are not limited to policy, but may very well affect politics and polities as well.

One can then ask if such effects will impart a hegemonic nature to the process of change under analysis, embodying 'the silent development of a discourse of monotopia across the new multi-level field of spatial policy' (Graute 2000, cited in Jensen and Richardson 2004, 179). And, if so, will it be a process characterised, as Jensen and Richardson suggest, by a 'passive adoption' that implies a weak or uncritical adaptational dynamic at the domestic level? The latter is undoubtedly ground for future research, but the suggestion of homogenisation – the suffix '-isation' suggesting a normative bias towards perceiving it as a 'standardisation' of European origin – has not gone unchallenged: 'The Europeanisation of spatial planning in the Mediterranean countries neither follows uniform mechanisms nor produces homogenous domestic structures and spatial planning identities' (Giannakourou 2005, 229).

We agree with Giannakourou, since even if some degree of convergence occurs this does not translate into uniformity across Europe, but into clustered convergence between countries with similar structural characteristics. Nevertheless, even the ESPON 2.3.1 project, which included an explicit hypothesis concerning the application of the ESDP and converging planning cultures, had to conclude that 'planning families' (see also contribution of Stead and Nadin in this volume) did not influence the way in which the ESDP was translated into national and regional planning (Nordregio/ESPON 2.3.1 2007). Yet, as Radaelli (2004) argues, where convergence occurs this can be measured along a continuum.

At a minimum, convergence implies that domestic actors share a common vocabulary. Beyond this one can speak of an ideational convergence in which similar decisions and ultimately similar outcomes form two instances of even stronger convergence. But the latter is unlikely to occur as this would assume a technocratic system of policy implementation, whereas, as Radaelli (2004, 14) argues, in general that 'the whole issue of convergence in the EU should be framed in the context of the principle of subsidiarity'. The previous examples indicate that this argument also applies to the field of planning. Thus the dissemination and influence of the European spatial planning discourse, EU policies and directives and the project of European integration as such clearly feed into the emerging paradigm of Europeanisation in the field of planning studies, but how does this occur?

Seeking further systematisation, Böhme and Waterhout (2008) present a matrix that relates the means and effects of Europeanisation of planning (Table 13.1). An interesting exercise would be to fill in this matrix for each of the 27 EU member states. However, since it is difficult to actually recognise processes of Europeanisation, this is likely to prove less easy than expected. And even if one recognises that change has occurred due to one of the drivers of Europeanisation, one may then ask whether this change is the result of Europeanisation alone, or whether it was a response to a changing domestic environment or simply accelerated by one of the drivers of Europeanisation?

One must also question to whom Europeanisation processes appeal. For example, a study of the Europeanisation of regional planning in the Netherlands suggests that dissimilar processes of Europeanisation take place at national, regional and local levels (Wit 2005). What may appeal to national elites may be less interesting to regional and local planners. In other words, how even are the effects of Europeanisation processes at the domestic level?

Given the unclear extent of Europeanisation effects and the observation that Europeanisation does not lead to convergence per se, one may doubt whether Europeanisation contributes to changing planning cultures and, in the event that it does so, whether these planning cultures all move in similar directions and thus, hypothetically, will this facilitate future transnational cooperation? In other words, does Europeanisation create a common cultural framework for planning in Europe?

Table 13.1   Towards a typology of the Europeanisation of planning

	Rather long-term influence ... → ... rather short-term influence			
Effects (→) Means (↓)	Change of self perception and ones position in Europe	Change of laws, 'daily' practice, procedures, cooperation patterns (organisational learning)	Change in the use of terminology/ temporary application of new terms/concepts	Implementation of single concrete action which would not happen or happen differently without EU influence
Implementation of directive and regulations	Possibly environmental directives in the long run	EU regulations in various sector fields Structural Funds regulations	Formal terminology put down in regulations ...	Application of EU directives in general
Use of EU funding as incentive	ESDP application in INTERREG	- Structural Funds - Organisational learning through INTERREG - LEADER	INTERREG, Structural Funds	Where EU provides co-funding/ infrastructure projects INTERREG
Following of a (hegemonic) discourse set at European level	ESDP application ESPON use	ESDP application at national level in rare cases	ESDP application ESPON	

Source: Böhme and Waterhout 2008, 244.

What Next? The Need for a Systemised Approach to Europeanisation

Europeanisation is an unsettled line of inquiry within planning. There is as yet no general answer regarding the effects of Europeanisation effects on domestic policies. Nevertheless, there is clear and sufficient evidence that where the ESDP, INTERREG or EU policies are concerned it is safe to conclude that observed changes at the domestic level would not have happened without them (see also contributions of Serraos et al. and Vettoretto in this volume).

Although many examples apply to one or just a few EU countries and often do not result in similar outcomes, let alone patterns of convergence, one cannot overlook the significant impact at specific moments and places of processes of Europeanisation. Yet, their diffuse character means that it is unclear how to conceptually deal with these processes and how to treat them from a more theoretical perspective. Literature on Europeanisation in general, and on planning in particular, provides little help in resolving this issue since most authors tend to focus on specific cases of Europeanisation without engaging in systematic attempts to operationalise the concept. So, as Gualini (2004) notes, Europeanisation is not the *explanans* (i.e. the solution or the phenomenon that explains the dependent variables), but the *explanandum* (i.e. the problem that needs to be explained).

However, the typology provided in Table 13.1 may perhaps be a useful first step towards a more systematic analysis of the Europeanisation of planning because it may help us to identify types of outcome as well as to gain a better understanding of the sources of Europeanisation and their potential power to change domestic planning. An important issue in this process concerns the factor of time: what we have seen thus far can be considered just the first examples of Europeanisation, with, perhaps, many more to follow.

In terms of ideas, European spatial planning discourse has been further boosted by the recently adopted Territorial Agenda of the European Union and the Territorial State and Perspectives of the European Union, as well as by the Commission's Green Paper on Territorial Cohesion (CEC 2008). Moreover, the ESPON 2013 programme will play a major role in further developing the discourse and therewith provide a common frame of reference for domestic planners. In fact, the ESPON 2006 programme already acts as such a frame: countries including Austria, Ireland, Germany, Flanders and the Netherlands are in a process of scrutinising ESPON results in order to reflect upon their position in a wider EU spatial context. Regarding resources it is important to mention the continuation of INTERREG as well as the shift of EU funds towards the structural funds programme, which in itself becomes increasingly more spatial. A similar trend is observed in the Common Agricultural Policy where funds are shifted towards Pillar 2, aimed at rural development. In terms of rules, arguably the most indirect yet most fundamental driver of Europeanisation of spatial planning, there will be a steady stream of new and updated directives with an ever increasing level of ambition which may further stimulate processes of 'technification' and 'juridification' of planning. So, assuming that these initiatives and programmes will prove at least as effective as their predecessors, spatial planning practice in Europe can be expected to experience more extensive processes of Europeanisation.

Simultaneously, not only will the Europeanisation of planning continue, also the wider domestic administrative and cultural context in which spatial planning operates will experience, due to similar as well as other drivers, further processes of Europeanisation. As a result, domestic culture in general (and spatial planning culture as a subgroup of it) may change. Hypothesising that in the longer term, with the ongoing European integration and EU and member state policies becoming stronger intertwined, eventually a more apparent EU culture or model of society may emerge, what then will be the effect on planning culture? As has become clear from the above and general literature on Europeanisation, there is no single pattern that explains the direction and degree of change, nor the causal relationship between changing culture and subculture and where change occurs first.

It is probably safe to assume that place-based culture, and planning culture with it, is the result of a combination of EU and national, regional and local (not to speak of global) elements. The harder one looks, the more cultural diversity and refinement between places one finds. Whereas in time planners all over Europe may share an EU-inspired collection of similar planning terms, approaches and even ideologies (in addition to their national, regional and local determined collections), their interpretation and implementation will therefore always remain tuned to local circumstances and cultures. Hypothetically then, convergence between planning cultures due to processes of Europeanisation, will only occur when EU culture acquires relative dominance over domestic cultures. However, given the current trend towards regionalisation and the leading European integration discourse which celebrates and sustains European diversity, such a shift in cultural balance is hard to image. Systemised analysis of Europeanisation of spatial planning, however, can help us to test the hypotheses above and provide us with more definitive answers as regards the effects on planning cultures. The typology presented in Table 13.1 could form a first step in this process.

Concluding Remarks

The concept of Europeanisation entails overlapping meanings and debates as a result of how different disciplines have come to define it. Furthermore, as we have highlighted, Europeanisation is a highly context-dependent concept. We have inquired into the meaning of Europeanisation with a specific focus on its impacts on planning systems and cultures. Although there are clear indicators that Europeanisation may be happening, concrete evidence of it in the domestic planning arena is still too scattered and scarce to make a clear picture.

Whereas we are able to identify the main drivers and processes behind Europeanisation, our knowledge of the causal linkages between these catalysts of change and their effects on planning systems and cultures is still limited. Many examples of Europeanisation can be understood as 'incidents' occurring in time and context specific situations rather than a systematic set of effects.

While we are still struggling to establish a clear picture of Europeanisation, we can already see its effects. To a significant degree Europeanisation can be understood as a bottom-up process reflecting how domestic responses to EU initiatives materialise. Having explained our take on the issue of homogenisation of planning cultures, the Europeanisation of planning can be expected to foster a greater confluence between planning and planning systems in Europe. This confluence cannot disguise the heterogeneity of Europe in terms of governance and government structures, as well as its spatial and cultural diversity, and it may in fact, lead to an increased sense of urgency to further develop planning for Europe (Böhme and Waterhout 2008).

What next? The need for more detailed research is directly connected to the validity of Europeanisation as a concept in the field of planning studies.

Further research may have to leave aside the overall European perspective and first engage in a detailed analysis of individual EU countries (Radaelli 2004). We may then be able to identify, at the level of individual member states, evidence that will support or contradict conceptual explanations for Europeanisation processes. If so it will then be possible to develop a systematic EU-wide comparative framework to analyse the outcomes of Europeanisation and how they may affect planning cultures. Time is of the utmost importance here; research thus far has mainly focused on the process of developing a European planning discourse rather than on the domestic impacts. However, that may be largely because the empirical evidence requires time both for the impacts to manifest and for them to be accounted for.

With the ongoing development of a European territorial cohesion policy, the Europeanisation of planning may soon enter a new phase in which the causal relationship between EU and domestic change becomes more visible and increases the sense of urgency for understanding this process better. Whether the existing and upcoming initiatives will result in long-lasting culture changes or just temporary adaptations is something that only time can tell. Until then, however, the Europeanisation of planning remains visible only to those who are really looking for it and who are actively assessing these newly embedded influences and their outcomes.

Bibliography

Arkleton Institute/Espon 2.1.3 (2004) 'The Territorial Impact of CAP and Rural Development Policy', www.espon.eu.
Bachtler, J. and L. Polverari (2007) 'Delivering Territorial Cohesion: European Cohesion Policy and the European Model of Society', in A. Faludi (ed.) *Territorial Cohesion and the European Model of Society*, Lincoln Institute of Land Policy, Cambridge, MA, 105–28.
Böhme, K. (2002) *Nordic Echoes of European Spatial Planning*, Nordregio, Stockholm.
Böhme, K. (2003) 'Discursive European Integration: The Case of Nordic Spatial Planning', *Town Planning Review* 74(1), 11–29.
Böhme, K. (2006) 'Visst påverkar EU fysisk planering i Sverige', in G. Blücher and G. Graninger (eds) *Planering med nya förutsättningar*, Linköping University Interdisciplinary Studies, 39–56.
Böhme, K. and B. Waterhout (2008) 'The Europeanisation of Planning', in A. Faludi (ed.) *European Spatial Research and Planning*, Lincoln Insitute of Land Policy Cambridge, MA, 225–48.
Börzel, T. A. (2002) 'Pace-Setting, Foot-Dragging, and Fence-Sitting: Member State Responses to Europeanization', *Journal of Common Market Studies* 40(2), 193–214.
Buunk, W. (2003) *The Locus of European Integration*, Eburon, Delft.

Commission of the European Communities (CEC) (1999) *European Spatial Development Perspective: Towards Balanced and Sustainable Development of the Territory of the EU*, Office for Official Publications of the European Communities, Luxembourg.

Commission of the European Communities (CEC) (2008) *Green Paper on Territorial Cohesion, Communication from the Commission*, SEC(2008) 2550, COM(2008) 616 final, 6.10.2008, Brussels.

Dühr, S., D. Stead and W. Zonneveld (eds) (2007) 'Special Issue: The Europeanisation of Spatial Planning through Territorial Cooperation. Introduction to the Special Issue', *Planning, Practice and Research* 22(3), 291–307.

Faludi, A. (2001) 'The Application of the European Spatial Development Perspective: Evidence from the North-West Metropolitan Area', *European Planning Studies* 9(5), 663–75.

Faludi, A. (2004) 'Spatial Planning Traditions in Europe: Their Role in the ESDP Process', *International Planning Studies* 9(2–3), 155–72.

Farinos Dasi, J. and Espon 2.3.2 (2007) *Governance of Territorial and Urban Policies from EU to Local Level*, www.espon.eu.

Featherstone, K. (2003) 'In the Name of Europe', in K. Featherstone and C.M. Radaelli (eds) *The Politics of Europeanization*, Oxford University Press, Oxford, 3–26.

Giannakourou, G. (2005) 'Transforming Spatial Planning Policy in Mediterranean Countries: Europeanisation and Domestic Change', *European Planning Studies* 13(2), 319–31.

Gualini, E. (2004) *Multi-Level Governance and Institutional Change: The Europeanisation of Regional Policy in Italy*, Ashgate, Aldershot.

Healey, P. (2006) 'Transforming Governance: Challenges of Institutional Adaption and a New Politics of Space', *European Planning Studies* 14(3), 299–320.

Janin Rivolin, U. and A. Faludi (2005) 'The Hidden Face of European Spatial Planning: Innovations in Governance', *European Planning Studies* 13(2), 195–215.

Jensen, O.B. and T. Richardson (2004) *Making European Space: Mobility, Power and Territorial Identity*, Routledge, London.

Korthals Altes, W.K. (2006) 'The Single European Market and Land Development', *Planning Theory and Practice* 7(3), 247–66.

Lähteenmäki-Smith, K., S. Fuller and K. Böhme (2005) 'Integrated Multi-level Analysis of the Governance of European Space', *Nordregio Working Paper* 2005:2, Nordregio, Stockholm.

Markusen, A. (2003) 'Fuzzy Concepts, Scanty Evidence, Policy Distance: The case for Rigour and Policy Relevance in Critical Regional Studies', *Regional Studies* 37(6/7), 701–18.

Nadin, V. and D. Stead (2008) 'European Spatial Planning Systems, Social Models and Learning', *DISP* 172, 1/2008, 35–47.

Nordregio/Espon 2.3.1 (2007) *Application and effects of the ESDP in Member States. Final Report of ESPON Project 2.3.1.*, www.espon.eu.

Olsen, J. (2002) 'The Many Faces of Europeanization', *Journal of Common Market Studies* 40(5), 921–52.

Olsen, J.P. (2007) *Europe in Search of Political Order*, Oxford University Press, Oxford.

Pedrazzini, L. (2005) 'Applying the ESDP through INTERREG IIIB: A Southern Perspective', *European Planning Studies* 13(2), 297–317.

Radaelli, C.M. (2003) 'The Europeanisation of Public Policy', in K. Featherstone and C.M. Radaelli (eds) *The Politics of Europeanization*, Oxford University Press, Oxford, 27-56.

Radaelli, C.M. (2004) 'Europeanization: Solution or Problem?', *European Integration online Papers* 8(16), http://eiop.or.at/eiop/texte/2004-016a.htm.

Ravesteyn, N. and D. Evers (2004) *Unseen Europe: A Survey of EU Politics and its Impact on Spatial Development in the Netherlands*, Ruimtelijk Planbureau, The Hague.

Robert, J., T. Stumm, J.M. De Vet, G.J. Reincke, M. Hollanders and M.A. Figueiredo (2001) *Spatial Impacts of Community Policies and the Costs of Non-coordination*, European Commission, Brussels.

Shaw, D. and A. Lord (2007) 'The Cultural Turn? Culture Change and What It Means for Spatial Planning in England', *Planning Practice and Research* 22(1), 63–78.

Shaw, D. and O. Sykes (2005) 'European Spatial Development Policy and Evolving Forms of Territorial Mobilisation in the United Kingdom', *Planning, Practice and Research* 20(2), 183–99.

Sykes, O. (2007) 'Examining the relationship between transnational and national planning: French and British spatial planning and the European Spatial Development Perspective', in P. Booth, M. Breuillard, C. Fraser and D. Paris (eds) *Spatial Planning Systems of Britain and France: A comparative analysis*, Routledge, London, 99–118.

Tewdwr-Jones, M. and J.M. Mourato (forthcoming) 'Europeanisation of Domestic Spatial Planning: Exposing Apparent Differences or Unspoken Convergence?', in W. Zonneveld., L.B. Janssen-Janssen and J. de Vries (eds) *European Territorial Governance*, IOS Press, Amsterdam.

University of Kiel/Espon 2.1.1 (2004) 'Territorial Impact of EU Transport and TEN-Policies', www.espon.eu.

Waterhout, B. (2008) *The Institutionalisation of European Spatial Planning*, IOS Press, Amsterdam.

Waterhout, B. and D. Stead (2007) 'Mixed Messages: How the ESDP's Concepts have been Applied in INTERREG IIIB Programmes, Priorities and Projects', *Planning, Practice and Research* 22(3), 395–416.

Williams, R.H. (1996) *European Union Spatial Policy and Planning*, Paul Chapman Publishing, London.

Wit, A. de (2005) 'Europees denken en handelen – De invloed van de Europese Unie op de provinciale ruimtelijke ordening', Masters thesis, Wageningen Universiteit, Wageningen.

Zonneveld, W., B. Waterhout and J.J. Trip (2008) 'The Impact of EU Regulations on Local Planning Practice: The Case of the Netherlands', paper presented at the ACSP-AESOP 4th Joint Congress, 6–11 July, Chicago.

Chapter 14
A Missing Link in the Cultural Evolution of the European Union: Confronting EU Ideology with INTERREG III Practice Concerning Cultural Diversity

Roel During, Rosalie van Dam, André van der Zande

Introduction

Cultural variety is seen as an important characteristic of Europe. The enlargement of the European Union (EU), globalisation, the decentralisation of the policy process, and the responses within local communities have combined to increase the multicultural character of many countries, adding to the number of languages, religions, ethnic and cultural backgrounds present in regions and cities. Recently, the EU has put more emphasis on a regional approach in its policies, with the aim of bringing Europe closer to its citizens. The European Commission (EC) became aware of the importance of the regional and cultural dimension of European integration for bridging the gap between integration policy, enlargement, and the citizens themselves (Barnett 2001). In this respect, Europe is advocating regional cultural variety as a resource in a pluralist policy approach (Coultrap 1999). 'Unity in diversity' is the appropriated slogan, aiming to bring out the common aspects of Europe's heritage, while respecting cultural, national and regional diversity.

Early ideas of promoting the regional level led to the INTERREG Community Initiative in 1990. This is an EU-funded programme framework that helps Europe's regions to form partnerships to work together on common projects. INTERREG is designed to strengthen economic and social cohesion throughout the EU (see also contributions of Davoudi and Waterhout et al. in this volume), by fostering the balanced development of the continent through cross-border, transnational and interregional cooperation. The INTERREG Community Initiative intends to prepare border areas for a Community without internal frontiers. In practice, however, new cultural dynamics arise when borders are relaxed.

Confronting EU policy and ideology and INTERREG practice raises questions like 'Is the EU really respecting and supporting the cultural diversity of its constituting regions and are the regions recognising the grounding cultural aspects of their planning practice?'

This was the context within which the INTERACT project CULTPLAN was initiated. The CULTPLAN partnership recognised a need for in-depth study of culture and cultural variety in the INTERREG practice of regional planning and development. CULTPLAN focused on exploring the manifestation and mechanisms of culture within INTERREG projects. By collecting narratives how culture affected cooperation and planning practice in projects, the partnership also collected the various field understandings of 'culture' itself. In this chapter we confront the understanding in practice with the concepts of culture in EU policy. In order to do so, our own understanding of culture has to be encompassing and therefore combines value system oriented, semiotic, strategic and participative conceptions of culture. By definition, culture is the community-specific way that thinking and acting influence one another. We will use the empirical results of the CULTPLAN research (CULTPLAN 2007) to confront the EU ideology and policy on culture with the INTERREG practice, and analyse how culture is embedded in policy and practice. It will be shown that, in practice, the desired synergy between cultural diversity and social and economic development is – to some extent – a fairy tale.

Culture and Cultural Diversity in EU Ideology and Policy

From Economic Cooperation to Cultural Integration

The period of EU history that runs from 1990 to 1999 is known as the EU without frontiers. A single market economy, agreed upon in the Single European Act (SEA) in 1987, was supposed to emerge in this period. The goal of this SEA was to remove remaining barriers between countries, and to increase harmonisation, thus increasing the competitiveness of European countries. Because of the collapse of communism across central and Eastern Europe, which began in Poland and Hungary and is symbolised by the fall of the Berlin Wall in 1989, the European nations became closer to one another. In the preceding period, a low response to the elections to the European Parliament in the 1980s has widely been interpreted as a 'democratic deficit' in the EU, caused by a lack of coordination and agreement, the dominance of national over supranational politics and the marginal position of the European Parliament (Coultrap 1999; Decker 2002; Meadowcroft 2002). Reducing this deficit has been the target of many EU policies in this period. In response, the member states wished to supplement the progress achieved by the SEA with other reforms. As a result, the Treaty on European Union was signed in February 1992 and entered into force in November 1993. This Treaty, also known as the Maastricht Treaty, changed the name of the 'European

Economic Community' into 'the European Community', indicating a scope wider than economic growth (European Union 1992).

The Maastricht Treaty introduced the concept of European citizenship, reflecting the shared values on which the European unification is based. Presenting European citizenship as a supplement to national citizenship, the 'European cultural model' accepts both cultural diversity and the defining of a shared cultural entity. In applying the concept of European citizenship, the aim of the EU's cultural policy is to bring out the common aspects of Europe's heritage, while respecting cultural, national and regional diversity (CEC 2002a).

As a result of the Maastricht Treaty, the EU is authorised to undertake actions aiming at preserving, spreading and developing cultural values in Europe. The culture chapter of the Treaty says: 'The community shall take cultural aspects into account in its action under other provisions of this Treaty, in particular in order to respect and to promote the diversity of its cultures' (European Union 1992: Treaty of Maastricht, art. 151:4). Initially its role was limited to enhancing the coordination between cultural actors from the different countries, or supplementing their activities in order to contribute to the growth of the cultures of the participating countries. By focusing on the societal infrastructures involved in the production of cultural events, the conception of culture was limited to 'high-brow culture'. The new cultural programmes Kaleidoscope, Ariane and Raphael were installed directly after 1992, but were eventually evaluated as being based too much on a concept of culture that addressed the higher echelons of society and ignored the cultural aspects of daily life of ordinary citizens. The Commission recognised that, also as a result of the Schengen Convention ensuring the freedom of citizens to travel all over Europe, a more intensive interaction between the daily life cultures present within the EU has emerged. Eventually, the cultural policy of the EU has been seen as an integrated part of the other policy areas and the conception of culture has broadened to the diversity of societal cultures. And this is relevant for discussing the relations between cultural diversity and economic development.

The Commission tried to develop an adequate definition of culture, but did not succeed (Barnett 2001). As a result, different conceptions of culture were introduced during this period. In opposition to the already existing semiotic concept of culture promoting a European flag, anthem and other identifiers (Shore 1996), the Commission advocated a communal view of culture that acknowledged the daily aspects of the society as a whole.[1] In this view, culture should be recognised and addressed in the context of the social economic development of regions, and thus become relevant for all citizens. If prosperity flourishes due to European projects, citizens are assumed to adopt a European identity, and a synergetic social-economic and cultural development

---

1 See also Gullestrup's contribution in this volume.

is proclaimed. Another tendency in the cultural debate was to conceptualise culture in terms of participation. Citizens are assumed to become Europeans because of participation in activities resulting from their own culture and organised in EU-funded projects. The Committee of the Regions – installed in 1994 with the task of advising the Commission in the areas of economic and social cohesion, trans-European infrastructure networks, health, education and culture – is in favour of the participative concept of culture (Barnett 2001). Clearly, all three conceptions are relevant and valid for establishing a European integration that addresses all regions and citizens.

As a result of the accession of eight new member states in May 2004 and the introduction of the Euro, the focus on culture became even stronger in the period of expansion, from 2000 to the present. These trends led to a higher level of cultural interaction between regions and countries. The cultural challenge posed by a larger Europe that is playing an innovative economic role in the world has been proclaimed by the EU and is reflected by the European Commission's policy statement on the role of culture in a globalising world. This statement outlines the current European strategy for the synergy of economic growth and intercultural understanding. It affirms the central role of culture in the process of European integration and proposes a cultural agenda for Europe and for its relations with third countries. The policy statement presents three major objectives that together form a cultural strategy for the European Institutions, the Member States and the cultural and creative sector, viz. promotion of:

1. cultural diversity and intercultural dialogue;
2. culture as a catalyst for creativity in the framework of the Lisbon Strategy;
3. culture as a vital element in the Union's international relations.

This strategy confirms what was already put into practice after the Treaty of Maastricht: a policy of integrating the cultural dimension with social and economic development. INTERREG can be seen as a vehicle of this strategy of the Commission, executed at regional level. INTERREG among others addressed the cultural aspects of the cohesion policy and a better understanding of cross-border, transnational and interregional cultures was considered vital for successful cooperation (see also Davoudi's contribution in this volume). As argued above, three conceptions of culture are espoused by different actors and therefore play a role in INTERREG. These are: a semiotic conception of culture emphasising European signifiers such as an EU flag in an attempt to establish a firm European identity among all citizens; a communal conception leading to synergy and integration of social-economic and cultural development of regional communities; and a participative conception emphasising the inclusion and participation of citizens in EU-funded projects. All three conceptions are valid and may endorse one another, because none of them can establish 'unity in diversity' on their own.

EU Culture Policy and INTERREG

In order to find an appropriate balance between enhancing economic development and respecting cultural diversity in the EU's regional policy, an awareness of cultural dynamics is needed in all EU policies. The Commission intends to ensure that the promotion of culture and cultural diversity is given due consideration whenever culture is at stake in regulatory and financial decisions or proposals, whether directly or indirectly. For example, the structural funds are presented on the European Cultural Internet Portal as an initiative with a specific cultural relevance.[2] This relevance seems to be based on the assumption that the structural funds, and the INTERREG projects they are used for, have a significant impact on regional communities. This would require a participative planning process, a high level of publicity, and public awareness of the projects, or even involvement in running them. The projects are perceived as a vehicle for the diffusion of the EU conceptions of culture delineated above. It is interesting to look at culture from the perspective of the regional policy. Is INTERREG[3] aware that it creates cultural dynamics between regions? And is INTERREG aware of the supposed role of these dynamics in European cohesion? The answer seems to be a decisive 'no'. There is a striking absence of cultural awareness in official publications describing the Regional Policy, such as Working for the Regions (CEC 2001), and in the description of the INTERREG initiative CEC 2002b). Even in the second progress report on economic and social cohesion CEC 2003), a broad view on the cultural aspects of cohesion is lacking and the main focus is on the need for simpler procedures and the inappropriateness of the 'one-size-fits-all' management approach. The regional policy is dedicated to economic growth. At the level of themes for projects, cultural identity is being addressed, but mainly as leverage for achieving more economic growth.

---

2   See http://ec.europa.eu/culture/our-policy-development/doc405_en.htm.

3   The INTERREG Community Initiative, adopted in 1990, intends to prepare border areas for a Community without internal frontiers. It is financed under the European Regional Development Fund (ERDF). INTERREG aims at economic and social cohesion, a balanced and sustainable development of the European territory and territorial integration with candidate and other neighbouring countries. Special emphasis has been placed on integrating remote regions and those which share external borders with the candidate countries. INTERREG III is divided into three strands: A, B and C. Within the strands is a programme structure. The strands aim at improving the cooperation structures, leading to more and higher quality joint projects, and creating synergy between the exchange of best practices and the work in the mainstream structural funds programmes. Strand A aims at local development of social facilities, economy and environment in cross-border cooperation, strand B aims at spatial development strategies, linking cities and management of resources in transnational cooperation and strand C aims at the development of networks and joint structures in interregional cooperation.

So INTERREG is seen as an instrument of EU cultural policy, or at least as relevant to it, only INTERREG doesn't seem to be fully aware of this. INTERREG opts for enhancement of economic development at INTERREG policy level, without embedding culture. For the analysis of interregional cooperation and culture, this is important because it means that cultural dynamics resulting from INTERREG should be seen as unintentional coincidences without a grounding policy framework.

Culture and Cultural Diversity in INTERREG Practice

Culture as a Determinant in INTERREG Evaluations

The relevance of culture in INTERREG can be illustrated by discussions of the evaluation and capitalisation of its programmes. In the formal evaluation of INTERREG II that ran from 1996 to 2003, a major role was assigned to the culture of cross-border collaboration (LRDP LTD 2003). The evaluation states that there is undoubtedly an overarching issue of an insufficiently developed trans-European cooperation culture between public authorities, institutions, citizens and businesses. Both this and other documents (Castelfranchi and Falcone 2001; Inforegio 2005) show that in the practice of transnational, cross-border and interregional cooperation, cultural variety is often perceived as problematic. INTERREG evaluations lack indicators for assessing cooperation processes in general or cultures in particular. Despite an obvious lack of information, culture is mentioned as an important factor. Unfortunately, due to this information gap, we find very few ideas on how culture actually manifests itself. There is no discernible progress in understanding the role of culture, as culture and cultural differences are still mentioned in the mid-term evaluation of INTERREG III (INTERACT 2005) as an important factor in the way programmes are being executed. The evaluation states that administrative cultures may differ considerably, and should be taken into account when judging the performance of programmes. This is a rather cautious description of the role of culture, when we consider the fact that many programmes started late or not at all because of a lack of understanding and shared values (INTERACT 2005).

INTERREG Projects Addressing Culture

A substantial number of projects aim directly at cultural exchange, or use the cultural assets of a region as leverage for economic growth. In the classification of INTERREG projects in an incomplete project database (INTERACT 2007), these projects are categorised under culture (no definition given, but connected to the Lisbon Agenda) and under regional identity and attractiveness. Many of them are executed within the framework of the C strand, aiming at cultural exchange in networks. This is happening despite the fact that culture is not mentioned as a topic of interest in the official description of the C strand (European Union 2004). In the C strand, the category of regional innovative projects, involving regional identity and sustainable development, seems to be the only gateway to establishing projects of cultural relevance. The great majority of projects in the cultural category belong to the B strand. This strand is more focused on planning systems and implementation, with an emphasis on regional identity. Regional identity is the classic theme that deals with the tension between Europeanisation and maintaining regional cultural characteristics. The A strand is focused on softening the internal borders of the EU, between regions. This strand is being executed at a local level and only very limited information is available on central INTERREG websites. Projects in the A-strand are close to the public and focussed on sharing public infrastructures, including cultural ones.

Despite the incompleteness of the database, the reason for this difference may be found at the programme level, as the C strand is pan-European and the B strand is more decentralised. Culture and cultural heritage is explicitly addressed in all thirteen INTERREG III B programmes, each with their own internal structure. It seems that this decentralised decision making leads to more culture oriented projects in the B strand. A similar comparison between the B strand and the A strand would probably show the same tendency: the more decentralised the formulation and execution of a programme are, the more culturally diverse it will be. To substantiate this statement would require an overview of all projects more complete than is provided by the existing database, particularly for the A strand. Nevertheless, the projects in this database clearly show that the regions are interested in projects addressing culture.

Culture within INTERREG Projects

Ideally, in terms of the three conceptions of culture given above, to contribute to the cultural aspects of Europeanisation, projects should strengthen regional identity, combining social-economic and cultural development, or open up new ways of participation in developing its culture for the regional civil society. Simultaneously, signification of project results should contribute to a culture of European citizenship. This would require a thorough understanding of the roles and manifestations of the different cultures at stake in the partnership, and of their context. Practice shows how very difficult it is to understand the cultural differences within a partnership, and this has consequences for the regional exposure and implementation. Besides, practice shows that INTERREG actors also use a limited and rather diffuse conception of culture, focussed on strategy, planning and decision making. This will be illustrated by using a few examples from the CULTPLAN[4] study (CULTPLAN 2007).

When starting a new cooperation, a partner often tries to explain the significance of the project for himself, his institute and his region. Practice shows that it is too easily assumed that the signals of significance are recognised and understood. The start-up meeting in one of the cases was organised in the room where the Treaty of Maastricht had been signed. This signification was not recognised by all partners, because it was not mentioned. When organising meetings or excursions, partners do their utmost to show the importance their region attaches to the project. Only rarely is this recognised by the partners, and often it is seen as boring and time-consuming. Semiotic differences and the time it takes to get acquainted with cultural signals are very much underestimated in cooperation processes.

Differences in mandates frequently cause misunderstandings in a partnership, for example when taking decisions about budgets and measures to achieve goals. In a project dealing with monuments and cultural heritage, one partner has an extremely limited financial mandate and an almost total freedom to determine the measures to be taken to open up a fortification site to the public. In the same project, another partner in exactly the same hierarchical position has a much bigger financial mandate, but only a small role in the negotiation process about the construction of the public site. Because of the small distance and intensive contact between them, they cope with their different points of reference. But uncomfortable situations often arise with other partners in the projects.

Difficulties in understanding the variety of working cultures are illustrated by a project on flooding in which many partners contribute to the process of knowledge exchange in a network. In this project, the degree of cultural understanding directly influences choices about work packages made by the lead partner. The lead partner has a pronounced preference for quick email responses and these are interpreted as dedication and commitment. Another partner in this project does not distinguish between an email and a letter, and will only send emails that are checked at superior and ministerial level. Formulating

---

4 In CULTPLAN, 20 INTERREG projects are culturally analysed. Projects have been selected from strands A, B and C and the project partnerships cover nearly all European countries. In addition to case study analysis, a questionnaire has been sent out to INTERREG officers and practitioners. For further information on methodology and results, see www.cultplan.org. One of the key problems in studying culture in practice is the intangibility of culture as a phenomenon. Some features are attributed to culture because they belong to a specific community or part of the world and not to others. In CULTPLAN this problem has been dealt with by investigating what participants perceive as culture in their project, and in addition asking about the social or daily practice of cooperation and re-analysing the statements using a broad anthropological conception of culture (Gullestrup 2006; see also his contribution in this volume). It has been observed that cross-cultural cooperation leads to a better understanding of one's own cultural peculiarities.

a reaction took some time, which was perceived as a lack of commitment by the lead partner. Moreover, there seems to be no obvious mechanism in the project for achieving a higher level of cross-cultural understanding. On the contrary, cooperation with the partner who responds faster has intensified.

The concept of cooperation is itself subject to different cultural interpretations. In cooperating, southern actors value interaction more highly than writing planning documents. Documents by western partners often are perceived as a signal of unwillingness to debate their contents. Western actors, on the other hand, perceive partners who do not prepare documents in advance as uncommitted. The way the ideas of cooperation in INTERREG have been translated into regulations and formats is not always recognised as appropriate by participants. A poor Italian region which is active in the CADSES programme said that some regions have money and no problems; others have no money and a lot of problems. Western European partners consider it important that there is 'give and take' in a partnership: They object to partners who just 'consume'. There is a tension between the policy aims of INTERREG and the expectations of cooperating partners in practice. The regulative framework of INTERREG supposes consensus about the project aims and the use of project resources within the partnership: A consensus that can only rarely be found at the beginning of a cooperation.

These examples show the complexity involved in understanding cultural peculiarities and the cultural contexts of partners, and in the practice and understanding of working interactively. Understanding the differences takes time and requires flexibility. Specific problems in this respect are the triangular relationships of trust (Castelfranchi and Falcone 2001) between INTERREG, lead partners and other partners, and the perceived inflexibility to deviate from the approved project application. The level of detail in the project application is very high, and it determines many aspects of project organisation and implementation. The cultural issues which have been neglected in the preparation phase crop up during the execution of the project. An adequate handling of the cultural differences would require flexibility in respect to the detailed aims, deliverables, and actions mentioned in the project description. But accountancy controls are a major drawback for flexibility. Project managers are very reluctant to deviate from an approved project application, because they fear getting into trouble with the management and the funding authorities. Trust therefore has to be built in a partnership in a regulative context that is based on mistrust.

Despite the way INTERREG enforces detail and consensus, in the practice of cooperation, projects develop their own project cultures. The first sign of a project culture is the use of predefined concepts which reflect a particular worldview or view on European resources or regulations. Informal contacts outside official meetings may confirm the presence of a specific project culture. Sometimes participants visit each other on their own initiative. The strongest project culture observed has been established by a group of participants who share an ideology about the use of space and aim to systematically convert the world with it. They are aiming at a disciplinary paradigm shift in planning for intensive space use. When a project team migrates from one project to another, often crossing the thresholds between INTERREG programme periods, this is usually based on a strong and positive project culture.

Many projects end up with a strong project culture in which participants tend to see each other as one big family. It can be observed that this takes place in many networking projects, based on weak or moderate interaction with regard to contents. On the other hand, just as many projects are closed having made good progress on their cognitive project aims, but little progress on the recognition and handling of cultural variety. This tends to happen in cognitive oriented projects aiming at the implementation of regional strategies using codified knowledge. In these projects, the interaction concerns the competition between (often unrecognised) culturally embedded practices. The two categories are rarely combined in one project. Immature project cultures may lead to either cognitive or social closure of partnerships, because partners are not fully acquainted with each other's cultures, causing the focus to lie on the partnership itself. And this has consequences for the implementation process, as will be shown below.

Implementing INTERREG Projects in a Regional Culture

Implementing project results means that the outcome has to be confronted with the region's societal and political culture (see also contribution of Knieling and Othengrafen in this volume). The local community's attitude towards the EU plays an important role in this, but so do institutional cultures. In a cross-border project aiming at preventing social exclusion, the local political culture has influenced the project right from the start. The project had been prepared thoroughly in a network of more than two hundred institutions. From this network, five institutions were selected to start and carry out the project. The others were considered to provide a relevant network. However, local politicians considered four of the partners to be too radical and too committed, and replaced them with institutions with a much lower level of commitment. These newcomers had not been involved in the preparation at all. Subsequently, in selecting the day-to-day participants, no terms of reference were used for a shared language. This reflects a low level of commitment among the new institutes. The upshot was that the project was put on ice.

Another interesting example is a project on space use which uses the instrument of 'implementation labs'. The project leader visits the location, and sometimes the local mayor, prior to the event, in search of the right terms with which to address the local politicians. The implementation lab itself goes on for two or three days and a very strong commitment to solving the problem arises during this intensive short period. In some cases, solutions are taken seriously in the local context and culture; in others they are not. Or, as the project leader has been told by a local politician: 'Some ideas are very interesting and will be implemented right away, and some ideas are simply very interesting.' In some cases, these labs have proved to be a strong implementation vehicle.

Another positive example of shared semiotics is that of blood exchange between areas on two sides of a national border in a situation characterised by disrespect and stereotyping. The project resulted in a lot of press attention and eventually to reframing of the border and of the communities. This is one of the very few examples in which a strong local cultural effect can be identified as the spin-off of an INTERREG project.

When surveying implementation practices, one can see that politicians are interested in concrete results that can be implemented straightaway, and do not perceive the interaction between partners of a project as a result in itself. Within the projects studied in CULTPLAN, no exchange of implementation experiences and strategies is organised, because this activity is not scheduled in a project application. Consequently, projects end at the formal deadline for permitted expenditures.

Practice shows that implementation of project results is severely hampered by the time-consuming process of understanding the cultural variety in a partnership. In most cases, the cultural differences have been perceived as problematic for achieving consensus about the project aims and the cooperation processes. The very idea of perceiving cultural differences as a resource – although sometimes mentioned – was hardly ever put into practice.

Conclusions: Are INTERREG Projects Contributing to the Cultural Evolution of the EU?

In the course of the European integration process, culture has increasingly been recognised as a critical factor in public opinion and involvement. It became apparent that Europe should not only become a single market, but should also strive to create a united European citizenship with a diversity of regional cultures. The Treaty of Maastricht has put the European Commission in the position to develop cultural policies and strategies to substantiate this ideology, with certain restrictions. The Commission has chosen not to develop a strong stand-alone cultural policy based on a precise definition of culture, but to improve cultural relevance and awareness in other policy fields. In this respect, the desired synergy between social and economic development and strengthening cultural identity at the regional level has become important. And in view of the cultural policy of the Community, initiatives like INTERREG function as a vehicle to achieve this synergy.

In the regional policy documents concerning social and economic development, there is no sign of recognition of this idea of synergy. This is most remarkable in view of the interest of the Committee of the Regions in a pluralist and participative cultural approach. As a result of this cultural blind spot, culture and cultural diversity are conceived as problematic by-products of interregional cooperation in INTERREG evaluations. Due to a lack of cultural awareness and intelligence, no progress seems to have been made in the subsequent generations of INTERREG programmes.

In regional practice, actors are definitely interested in promoting their local or regional culture and using it to create leverage for economic growth, as can be shown by the focus of many projects. But in the execution of projects, cultural differences create great obstacles to achieving their aims and contributing to the Europeanisation process. The lack of interest at the level of regional and INTERREG policy plays a significant role in INTERREG practice, because the regulative framework does not allow the flexibility that is needed for a time-consuming process of cross-cultural understanding. The presupposition of consensus on project description and the high level of detail required in a project application cause wicked cultural dilemmas, as illustrated in this chapter with a few of the many examples that have been described in the CULTPLAN project.

Underestimating the role of cross-cultural cooperation between regional actors in partnerships prevents the projects from becoming relevant for regional communities in the phase of exposure or implementation. Partnerships tend to focus on the internal processes of cognitive and cross-cultural progress. INTERREG and its projects therefore fail to contribute to the participative culture favoured by Europe and its regions.

This leads to the conclusion that the desired synergy between cultural diversity and social and economic development is a fairy tale, and will remain so as long as regional policy does not acknowledge the vital and pluralistic role of culture. European regional policy has not yet adopted the three conceptions of culture in a new regulative framework, supporting Europeanisation through participation, synergy and signification. Considering the ideology of 'unity in diversity' and its cultural implications, and considering, too, the serious interest of regional actors in cultural development, there is clearly a missing link between EU ideology and EU and INTERREG practice.

Bibliography

Barnett, C. (2001) 'Culture, Policy, and Subsidiary in the European Union: From Symbolic Identity to the Governmentalisation of Culture', *Political Geography* 20(4), 405–26.

Castelfranchi, C. and R. Falcone (2001) 'Social Trust: A Cognitive Approach. Trust and Deception in Virtual Societies', in C. Castelfranchi and Y.-H. Tan (eds) *Trust and Deception in Virtual Societies,* Kluwer Academic Publishers, Dordrecht, 55–90.

Commission of the European Communities (CEC) (2001) *European Union, Regional Policy. Working for the Regions*, Office for Official Publications of the European Communities, Luxembourg.

Commission of the European Communities (CEC) (2002a) *A Community of Cultures: The European Union and the Arts*, Office for Official Publications of the European Communities, Luxembourg.

Commission of the European Communities (CEC) (2002b) *European Union, Regional Policy. Structural Policies and European Territory: Cooperation Without Frontiers*, Office for Official Publications of the European Communities, Luxembourg.

Commission of the European Communities (CEC) (2003) *Second Progress Report on economic and Social Cohesion. Unity, Solidarity, Diversity for Europe, its People and its Territory*, Directorate-General for Regional Policy, Luxembourg.

Coultrap, J. (1999) 'From Parliamentarianism to Pluralism: Models of Democracy and the European Union's "Democratic Deficit"', *Journal of Theoretical Politics* 11(1), 107.

CULTPLAN (2007) *Cultural Differences in European Cooperation. Learning from INTERREG Practice*, final report of the INTERACT project CULTPLAN, ed. R. During and R. van Dam, Alterra, Wageningen UR, Wageningen.

Decker, F. (2002) 'Governance beyond the Nation-state. Reflections on the Democratic Deficit of the European Union', *Journal of European Public Policy* 9(2), 256–72.

European Union (1992) *Treaty of Maastricht on European Union*.

European Union (2004) *European Regional Development Fund 2000–2006*, Community Initiative Programme INTERREG IIIC.

Gullestrup, H. (2006) *Cultural Analysis: Towards Cross-cultural Understanding*, Aalborg University Press, Aalborg.

Inforegio (2005) 'Interreg III A France–Spain Right across the Pyrenees. No Mountain can Divide us', *Inforegio, Panorama 17: Cooperation at the heart of cohesion*, INTERREG in action, Office for Official Publications of the European Communities, Luxembourg.

INTERACT (2005) *A Study of the Mid-term Evaluations of INTERREG Programmes for the Programming Period 2000–2006*, INTERACT, Vienna.

INTERACT (2007) *INTERREG Project Database 2000–2007*, INTERACT.

LRDP LTD (ed.) (2003) *Ex-post evaluation of INTERREG II Community Initiative (1994–1999)*, Brief Report, London.

Meadowcroft, J. (2002) 'The European Democratic Deficit, the Market and the Public Space: A Classical Liberal Critique', *Innovation: The European Journal of Social Sciences* 15(3), 181–92.

Shore, C. (1996) 'Imagining the New Europe: Identity and Heritage in European Community Discourse', in P. Graves-Brown, S. Jones and C. Gamble (eds) *Cultural Identity and Archaeology: The Construction of European Communities*, Routledge, London.

Chapter 15
Territorial Cohesion, European Social Model and Transnational Cooperation

Simin Davoudi

Introduction

This chapter aims to provide a deeper understanding of the concept of territorial cohesion by tracing its roots in two influential but different planning cultures and traditions of France and Germany and by positioning it in the wider debate about the European social model. It suggests that the concept can be interpreted as the spatial manifestation of the European model. Hence, it adds a spatial justice dimension to European spatial policy. The chapter then discusses the pan-European application of territorial cohesion as a spatial concept, suggesting that this is likely to be fragmented and diverse, given the diversity of the national planning systems and their underlying social philosophies and cultural values, However, this is not to deny the significance of the 'softer processes' of transnational collaborative practices in creating a degree of harmonisation in this area.

The Origin of Territorial Cohesion

Two influential French officials are often quoted as key people in promoting a cohesive Europe and in introducing the notion of territorial cohesion, translated from its French original, into the Amsterdam Treaty in 1997. One is Jacques Delors, the former French finance minister and President of the European Commission between 1985 and 1995, and the other is Michel Barnier, the former EU Regional Commissioner. Since then, territorial cohesion has appeared in the Commission's triennial reports *on Economic and Social Cohesion*. First in 2001 in the *Second Report on Economic and Social Cohesion* (CEC 2001), which used the concept to describe the uneven development of the EU territory and particularly the concentration of population and economic activity in the core area of Europe, or as the ESDP called it, the pentagon (CEC 1999);[1] and then in 2004, when the concept was given prominence by its

---

1 This, according to the ESDP, is an area bounded roughly by the metropolises of London, Paris, Hamburg, Munich and Milan, which although covers only 20 per

inclusion in the *Third Report on Economic and Social Cohesion* (CEC 2004). In the wake of the enlargement of the Union from 15 to 25 member states, the *Third Report* highlighted that the challenge of achieving territorial cohesion would be of a different magnitude, as the disparities in the enlarged EU are greater than ever before. Another significant contribution to keep the concept on the agenda came from a six-year research programme under the European Spatial Planning Observation Network (ESPON) (Davoudi 2005b), which was to provide the evidence base for the discussions about territorial cohesion and attempt to measure and identify ways of operationalising it. The concept of territorial cohesion gained further momentum after its appearance in the proposed EU Constitution (later renamed as Lisbon Treaty) which stated that:

> in order to promote its overall harmonious development, the Union shall develop and pursue its action leading to the strengthening of its economic, social and territorial cohesion. In particular, the Union shall aim at reducing disparities between the levels of development of the various regions and the backwardness of the least favoured regions. (Conference of the Representatives of the Governments of the Member States, 2004, Article 220)

The inclusion of territorial cohesion in the proposed Constitution was particularly significant and regarded as the reshuffling of the terminology which was seen to help overcome the issues surrounding the lack of EU competence in spatial planning. Hence, following the decisive 'no vote' in the Dutch and French referenda in 2005, some argued that there would be no mention of territorial cohesion for some time (Hague 2005, quoting Peter Hall). However, the faith of territorial cohesion did not seem to be necessarily dependent on the faith of the proposed Constitution, because it continued to be a key preoccupation for the EU informal ministerial meetings (Nadin and Duhr 2005). For example, during the Dutch Presidency in the second half of 2004, the Dutch Minister, Marjanne Sint, emphasised that 'territorial cohesion means incorporating a spatial planning perspective into decisions that are now made primarily on economic and social grounds' (*Shared Spaces* 2004, 4). The Minister also urged the future presidencies 'to create a clear political agenda for territorial cohesion' (ibid.). The following informal ministerial meeting, held in June 2005 in Luxembourg, concluded that the key challenge 'is to integrate the territorial dimension into EU policies with the aim of achieving a coherent approach to the development of the EU territory, on the basis of the concept of territorial cohesion' (EU 2005, 1).

---

cent of the EU 15 territory, is home to 40 per cent of its population and produces 50 per cent of its GDP (CEC 1999).

While the UK government's priority for the presidency during the second half of 2005 made no mention of territorial cohesion or spatial planning (Foreign Office 2005), the ground had already been laid for the 2007 German Presidency to take the agenda forward. Hence, the *Territorial State and Perspective of the Union: Agenda 2007*, which is considered to be the follow-up to the ESDP, drew on the principles adopted in the Rotterdam informal meeting. These suggest that, 'the incorporation of the territorial dimension, as well as the concept of territorial cohesion can add value to the implementation of the Lisbon and Gothenburg[2] strategy by promoting structured and sustainable economic growth' (EU-IMM 2004). Furthermore, the French Presidency in the second half of 2008 gave central priority to developing the idea of territorial cohesion and indeed saw the publication of a Territorial Cohesion Green Paper, which at the time of writing (November 2008) was going through its consultation process.

The above summary clearly shows that territorial cohesion is here to stay, particularly in the policy vocabulary of the Directorate General on Regional Policy, where it plays a legitimating role for its continuing functions. What is less clear, however, is its exact meaning and ways of implementation. This paper argues that in order to understand the concept of territorial cohesion, we need to situate it within the wider debate about the European social model (see also contribution of Stead and Nadin in this volume).

European Social Model

The general term 'social model' refers to 'ideal types' which, according to Max Weber, are designed to capture the underlying similarities and differences of complex social phenomena (Martin and Ross 2004). Social models conceptualise the ways in which societies construct social interdependence. In market democratic social models, a combination of public policies, market mechanisms and kinship relations are drawn upon to 'distribute obligations amongst interdependent members [who are] differently and unequally located in the division of labour and economically related to each other primarily by market transactions regulated by politically constructed institutions' (Martin and Ross 2004, 11). Social models shape people's access to resources through income from work and welfare state provisions.

However, if we move away from 'ideal types' to reality we will observe as many European social models as there are European countries (Esping-Andersen et al. 2002). In spite of these variations, the European social model

---

2 The Lisbon Strategy (outcome of the European Council meeting in 2000) aims at increasing the EU economic competitiveness and the Gothenburg Strategy (outcome of the European Council meeting in 2001) promotes the integration of the sustainable development objectives in the Lisbon Strategy.

refers to the systems of welfare state and employment relations which share enough commonality, with the exception of Britain, to be distinguished from the American or Anglo-Saxon model. While the former relies on public institutions and collective choice, the latter is dependent on markets and individual choice. In reality, the situation is less polarised and different European countries are positioned at a continuum within these two extremes. Furthermore, their position is dynamic and fluctuates over time (see also contribution of Gullestrup in this volume).

The European model has been referred to by other names, too. Bill Clinton (the former American President) called it the 'Dutch model'; others labelled it: the *poldermodel*, or the 'stakeholder' as opposed to 'shareholder' model. A former director of French planning agency, Michel Albert, called it the 'Rhineland model' as a distinct form of a continental, west European capitalism which is different from the Anglo-Saxon model that is dominant in the United States and Britain (all quoted in Bolkestein 1999). In all these variations, the main argument is that, the European model is a regulated market economy with a comprehensive system of social security which offers greater protection against economic insecurity and inequality than the Anglo-American model. At the heart of both models lie centuries-old contested debates about the relations between the state, market and civic society, between individual liberty and social responsibility, between economic efficiency and social equity, between state as provider and interventionist and state as facilitator and enabler. In short, they raise significant political and normative issues (see also contribution of Knieling and Othengrafen in this volume).

Territorial Cohesion as Spatial Manifestation of the European Social Model

The first proposition in this chapter is that the concept of territorial cohesion adds a new dimension to these debates by extending the application of the principles of 'social models' beyond individuals and social groups to places and territories. Hence, it suggests that different social models not only 'decisively shape the structure of social stratification and the ways individuals are socialised and recruited into different social roles' (Martin and Ross 2004, 12). They also reconfigure the structure of territorial stratification and the ways territories are developed and perform different functions. Within the context of the European social model, territorial cohesion not only brings its embedded political tensions to the fore, it also gives them a spatial dimension. As pointed out by Davoudi (2004), among the myriad of definitions of territorial cohesion offered by various EU publications, none *territorialises* the European model more clearly than the *Third Cohesion Report*. It draws on a simple, yet powerful, rationale to convey the meaning of territorial cohesion, stating that, 'people should not be disadvantaged by wherever they happen to live or work in the Union' (CEC 2004, 27).

This adds a new dimension to the debate about social models. It argues that individual's life chances are not only shaped by the extent to which 'individuals are subjected to and protected from typical biographical risks (unemployment, disability, poverty, illness, old age) throughout their life course' (Martin and Ross 2004, 12). They are also shaped by where they live and work; in other words, by the location and quality of places and territories; by typical spatial risks (such as inaccessibility, isolation, pollution, exposure to natural and technological hazard, place stigma). It suggests that, the quality of places where people live and work can influence their access to economic and social opportunities and the quality of their life. Hence, the concept of territorial cohesion adds a spatial dimension, or in other words *spatialises*, the biographical risks that people face throughout their life course. From this, it can be concluded that social models not only 'conceptualise the ways in which different types of societies construct *social* interdependence' (Martin and Ross 2004, 11 emphasis added), they also construct the ways in which they structure territorial interdependence. Thus, territorial development trajectories are as much dependent on the type of social models as the life chances of individuals.

While the term 'social model' is not itself value-laden, terms such as economic, social or territorial cohesion convey a strong normative dimension. They call for a specific type of social model; one which puts the emphasis on reducing disparities, inequalities and injustices; objectives that are arguably embedded in the European model of society. It is suggested, for example, that:

> the cohesion principle expresses nothing but a concern for rebalancing the uncertain distributive effects of an internal market without borders and, in so doing, avoiding the pernicious risk of Europe disintegrating. (Janin Rivolin 2005, 95)

Therefore, when the cohesion principle was agreed, the implementation of Community policy on territorial and urban issues became indispensable. This is reflected in the Community Strategic Guidelines for Cohesion Policy (CEC 2005) which informs the implementation of Structural Funds in 2007-2013 period. The Strategic Guidelines stress that, 'the territorial dimension of Cohesion Policy' should be taken into account (ibid., 30) and the concept as

> extend[ing] beyond the notion of economic and social cohesion, its objective being to help achieve a more balanced development, to build sustainable communities in urban and rural areas and to seek greater consistency with other sectoral policies which have a spatial impact. (ibid., 27)

It is within this context that the territorial cohesion debate is closely linked to the wider debate about the European social model. It calls for an extension of the underlying principles of the European model from individuals to places and territories. It calls for solidarity not only amongst European citizens but also amongst European territories. It extends the call for work-based social-protection to place-based territorial-protection. Thus, the concept not only has the potential to replace the notion of 'spatial planning' within the EU arenas as some commentators argue (Hague 2005). It also has the potential to re-conceptualise it with emphasising on a new rationality for organising European space. The discourse of territorial cohesion has added a spatial justice dimension to European spatial policy, extending and applying John Rawls' theory of justice (Rawls 1971), with its emphasis on equity, to territorial development (Levy 2003, quoted in Peyrony 2007).

Territorial Cohesion and Two Influential European Planning Traditions

As mentioned earlier, the idea of territorial cohesion has a French origin. It is rooted in the French egalitarian tradition and concerns with equity. This is reflected in the French planning culture of *amenagement du territoire* which is described as the 'regional economic approach' to planning (CEC 1997). Within this approach, great emphasis is put on reducing regional disparities through redistribution of wealth, economic opportunities and development. One of the pioneering contributions to this approach was a book by Jean-Francois Gravier called *Paris et le desert français*, published in 1947. He argued that Paris was sucking the livelihood out of rural France and there had to be a counter-Parisian strategy. His idea was to create *metropoles d'equilibre*, or the growth poles outside Paris, by diverting the resources into French provisional cities and hence countering the negative effects of the free market economy. The aim was to create a territorially cohesive France.

It was this idea that Jacques Delors introduced in the Amsterdam Treaty and was later taken up by the ESDP and its notion of polycentricity (CEC 1999). But, in this transfer of ideas, the redistributive principle which underpinned the French planning tradition as well as the 1960s regional policy, was watered down. In its place, the emphasis was shifted towards maximising endogenous potential of the peripheral regions. The idea, as promoted by the ESDP, is that peripheral regions can be lifted out of decline through comprehensive integrated approach to spatial planning similar to one that has long tradition in Germany (CEC 1997; Davidou 2003).

This leads to the second proposition outlined above, that territorial cohesion combines two influential European planning cultures. The French tradition of regional economic planning underpins its normative ideals of spatial justice and cohesion, while the German tradition of comprehensive integrated planning advocates its mode of implementation and how cohesion can be achieved. This hybrid concept has already been drawn upon in some of the emerging spatial strategies, such as in Ireland. Here, as in Gravier's

France, Dublin is dominant in terms of population and economic activities. Hence, a counter-Dublin spatial strategy has been adopted which is based on maximising the potential of smaller cities without diverting resources away from Dublin (Davoudi and Wishardt 2005).

Hence, the real contestation is not about the normative ideas that the territorial cohesion provokes, but about its mode of implementation. The idea that the state has a right and a duty to correct the social and spatial injustices of the free market economy is embedded in all European social democratic systems. As Hall (2005) suggests, the critical question is not whether the state should interfere, but how much, when and where it should do so. It is at this point that European social models begin to diverge, given their path-dependent trajectory and their diverse cultural and social values. The question emerging in the light of these social and cultural diversities, is whether territorial cohesion can be Europeanised. The short answer is yes, in terms of the ideas that it provokes; but no, in terms of its application (see also contribution of Waterhout et al. in this volume). The problem with pan-European application of the territorial cohesion is that it faces a similar dilemma to the one that has confronted European social model; this is the third proposition presented above.

The Dilemma of Social Europe

The European model and all its variances are the construct of decades of social negotiations and compromises over the balance of relationship between the state, market and the civil society. As a result, the interplay between economic efficiency and social equity has fluctuated over time and in different countries. Despite the general resilience of the model it has not been immune from pressures such as globalisation and challenges such as the shift from manufacturing to services and the slow down in productivity and economic growth. All this has made it difficult for the welfare systems to meet the growing demand which is arising from the changing demographic patterns and family structures (Pierson 2001). These pressures have triggered, and will do so more forcefully in the future, conflicts over distribution of resources along what Martin and Ross (2004, 15) call 'new cleavage lines'.

Among the factors mentioned above, the most relevant and more powerfully exerted is the political decoupling of European economic integration and social-protection issues which, as Scharpf (2002, 646) points out, 'has characterised the real process of European integration from Rome to Maastricht'. Such decoupling would not have happened if the French Socialist Prime Minster, Guy Mollet, had had its way in the Treaty of Rome, and established the harmonisation of social regulations as a precondition for the integration of industrial market. However, if, in 1957, such harmonisation was difficult to achieve among six countries, with more or less similar social models, it is now increasingly difficult when 27 diverse countries, each with different political structures, planning traditions and cultural trajectory, are involved.

This decoupling has created an inherent and persistent tension between the EU economic competitiveness and cohesion policies which tend to creep up every time a new EU initiative or strategy is debated. The conflict reached new heights following the adoption of the Lisbon Strategy in March 2000 by the European Council. This was damned by some political constellations as a move too far towards the Anglo-American 'ultra-liberalism'. Others, however, saw it as a necessary step towards modernising the EU economic policy. For example, just ahead of the Lisbon Submit in a speech to the World Economic Forum in Switzerland, Tony Blair, the then British Prime Minster, criticised the opponents of the European Model, asking

> does Europe continue with the old social model, that has an attitude to social legislation and welfare often rooted in the 1960s and 1970s, or does it recognises that the new economy demands a re-direction of European economic policy for the future?

and urging the European political leaders to 'make a definitive stand in favour of market reform' (quoted in *The Economist* 2000, 17). Similar sentiments enveloped the discussions about the proposed Constitutions with parts of the French and Dutch '"No" Camp' arguing that it was 'too Anglo-Saxon oriented'.

However, this economic emphasis which is seen by some quarters as a new step towards the erosion of the European social model is not new. Indeed, it emerged after the introduction of the Single European Act which among other things liberalised hitherto protected, highly regulated and often state-owned public services including transport, telecommunication infrastructure and energy; sectors that are closely linked to territorial development. All this is the continuation of the hegemony of an economic policy discourse which has framed the European agenda mainly in terms of economic integration and liberalisation (Scharpf 2002). It is this hegemony that has led to continuing investment in developing economic data and indicators at the cost of social ones. This became evident in the course of one of the ESPON research projects which attempted to develop a 'territorial cohesion index' to be used in the future allocation of Structural Funds (Hamez 2005).

As Scharpf (2002, 665) argues, the advancement of EU economic integration since 1950s 'has created a fundamental asymmetry between policies promoting market efficiencies and those promoting social protection and equality', with the former being harmonised and regulated at the EU level while the latter remaining differentiated and regulated at the national level. This asymmetry has largely reduced the capacity of member states to influence the direction of their economies and to realise self-defined socio-political, and by extension spatial, goals. For example, European deregulation policies have taken away the use of public sector industries as an employment buffer at the time of economic decline. Similar dilemma can be observed in the context of territorial cohesion agenda. Here again, such decoupling has had major consequences. For example, the European competition policy has largely disabled the use of state aids in reducing regional disparities and increasing territorial cohesion; an issue which has been at the heart of the political negotiation on the post-2006 distribution of Structure Funds.

The Pan-European Application of Territorial Cohesion?

The asymmetric development of the Europeanisation process has led to an increasing demand for recreating a level playing field and recoupling of social-protection and economic-integration functions at the European level. However, given the diversity of national systems and the political salience of these differences, upon which people have based their life plans, it seems almost impossible to reach a common European solution (Scharpf 2002, 652). The same can be said about territorial cohesion agenda. While the economic drivers of spatial development operate within the market which is increasingly integrated at the EU level, spatial policies continue to be fragmented and subject to national discretion. Hence, achieving a level playing field in this area faces a similar dilemma to that of the EU social policy. Neither the subscription to a European spatial planning Directive nor the harmonisation of the national planning systems seem to be a feasible way forward, given the diversity of such systems and their underlying social philosophies and cultural values. Hence, the application of territorial cohesion will remain a matter for national spatial planning systems. This means that, in the foreseeable future, the EU integration may remain an economic project rather than progressing into a socio-spatial agenda.

Having said that, the significance of ongoing transnational collaborative practices across Europe in creating arenas for learning and exchange of experiences should not be underestimated. These 'soft processes' have played a major part in the wider project of European integration. Different ways of applying the principle of territorial cohesion are debated and exchanged in such arenas; lessons are learnt and good practices are adjusted for different social and cultural contexts. These softer processes of European integration can become particularly effective if 'planning culture' is understood as fluid, multilayered and dynamic; capable of being adjusted and remoulded over time (see also contribution of During et al. in this volume). Hence, while transnational collaborative practices may not provide a road map to universalism in the application of territorial cohesion, they will certainly provide great opportunities for expanding the space of social learning.

Acknowledgement

This chapter draws on an earlier and more detailed discussion presented in Davoudi, S. (2005) 'Understanding Territorial Cohesion', *Planning Practice and Research* 20(4), 433–41.

Bibliography

Bolkestein, F. (1999) 'The High Road that Leads Out of the Low Countries', *The Economist*, 22 May, 115–16.

Commission of the European Communities (CEC) (1997) *The EU Compendium of Spatial Planning Systems and Policies*, Office for Official Publications of the European Communities, Luxembourg.

Commission of the European Communities (CEC) (1999) *European Spatial Development Perspective: Towards Balanced and Sustainable Development of the Territory of the EU*, Office for Official Publications of the European Communities, Luxembourg.

Commission of the European Communities (CEC) (2001) *Unity, Solidarity, Diversity for Europe, its People and its Territory: Second Report on Economic and Social Cohesion*, Office for Official Publications of the European Communities, Luxembourg.

Commission of the European Communities (CEC) (2004) *A New Partnership for Cohesion: Convergence, Competitiveness, Cooperation – Third Report on Economic and Social Cohesion*, Office for Official Publications of the European Communities, Luxembourg.

Commission of the European Communities (CEC) (2005) *Cohesion Policy in Support of Growth and Jobs: Community Strategic Guidelines, 2007–2013*, Luxembourg: Office for Official Publications of the European Communities.

Conference of the Representatives of the Governments of the Member States (2004) *Treaty Establishing a Constitution of Europe* (CIG 87/2/04), Brussels.

Davoudi, S. (2003), 'Polycentricity in European Spatial Planning: From an Analytical Tool to a Normative Agenda', *European Planning Studies* 11(8), 979–99.

Davoudi, S. (2004) 'Territorial Cohesion: An Agenda that is Gaining Momentum', *Town and Country Planning* 73(7/8), 224–7.

Davoudi, S., (2005a) 'Understanding Territorial Cohesion', *Planning Practice and Research* 20(4), 433–41.

Davoudi, S. (2005b) 'ESPON: Past, Present and the Future', *Town and Country Planning*, 74(3), 100–102.

Davoudi, S. and M. Wishardt (2005) 'Polycentric Turn in the Irish Spatial Strategy', *Built Environment* 31(2), 122–32.

EU Informal Ministerial Meeting (2004) Presidency Conclusion, Rotterdam 29/11/2005.
EU Informal Ministerial Meeting on Territorial Cohesion (2005) Presidency conclusions, Luxembourg 20-21/05/2005.
Esping-Andersen, D., A. Gallie and J. Myles (eds) (2002) *Why We Need a New Welfare State*, Oxford University Press, Oxford.
Foreign Office (2005) *White Paper: Prospects for the EU*, Foreign Office, London.
Hague, C. (2005) 'Fighting for European Unity', *Planning*, 8 July, 15.
Hall, P. (2005) 'Fundamental Question for the ESDP', *Town and Country Planning*, November, 330–31.
Hamez, G., (2005) 'Territorial Cohesion: How to Operationalise and Measure the Concept', *Planning Theory and Practice*, 6(3), 400–402.
Hooghe, L. and G. Marks (2001) *Multi-level Governance and European Integration*, Rowman and Littlefield, Lanham, MD.
Janin Rivolin, U. (2005) 'Cohesion and Subsidiarity: Towards Good Territorial Governance in Europe', *Town Planning Review* 76(1), 93–107.
Martin, A., and G. Ross (2004) 'Introduction: EMU and the European Social Model', in A. Martin and G. Ross (eds) *Euros and Europeans: Monetary Integration and the European Model of Society*, Cambridge University Press, Cambridge, 1–19.
Nadin, V. and S. Duhr (2005) 'The Future of Cohesion Policy', *Town and Country Planning* 74(3), 85.
ODPM (Office of the Deputy Prime Minister) (2005) *Conclusions of Bristol Ministerial Informal Meeting on Sustainable Communities in Europe: Bristol Accord*, 6–7 December, ODPM, London.
Peyrony, J. (2007) 'Territorial Cohesion and the European Model of Society: French Perspectives', in A. Faludi (ed.) *Territorial Cohesion and European Model of Society*, Lincoln Institute for Land Policy, Cambridge MA.
Pierson, P. (2001) *The new Politics of the Welfare State*, Oxford University Press, Oxford.
Planning Theory and Practice (2005) Interface On: Territorial Cohesion, 6(3), 387–409.
Rawls, J. (1971) *A Theory of Justice*, Oxford University Press, Oxford.
Scharpf, F. (2002) 'The European Social Model: Coping with the Challenges of Diversity', *Journal of Common Market Studies* 40(4), 645–70.
Schön, P. (2005) 'Territorial Cohesion in Europe', *Planning Theory and Practice* 6(3), 389–400.
Shared Spaces (2004) Newsletter of VROM, The Netherlands ministry of Spatial Planning, Housing and Environment, No. 8, October, 4.
The Economist (2000) 'Europe's New Left, Free to Bloom', 12 February, 17–19.
Town Planning Review (2005) special issue on Territorial Cohesion, 76(1).

PART 6
Conclusions

Chapter 16
Planning Cultures between Models of Society and Planning Systems

Dominic Stead and Vincent Nadin

Introduction

In this chapter we argue that the characteristics of spatial planning systems are embedded in wider models of society, and that the notion of planning cultures sits between the two. We review the parallel dynamics of models of society and models (or typologies) of planning systems and identify the level of correspondence between them. Drawing on evidence from various European countries presented in the various chapters of this book and from elsewhere we show that many planning systems are undergoing similar types of changes despite the fact that the underlying model of society and the nature of the planning system are quite different. We also consider the extent to which these changes in planning systems are leading to convergence.

Our starting point is a comparison of 'models of society' and 'models of planning' (different types of planning systems) and an examination of their parallel trajectories. Models of society are ideal types used to generalise about the diverse values and practices that shape relationships between the state, the market and citizens in particular places. Models of society differ between nation-states (and even within them) but it is generally accepted that it is possible to identify a small number of ideal types. Though abstract concepts, models of society underpin the reality of government approaches to reconciling the competing objectives of economic competitiveness, social cohesion (or social justice) and environmental sustainability. Thus, the form or 'model' of spatial planning and the prevailing planning culture is likely to be interconnected with the model of society. This fits with the assertions that planning culture is 'embedded in the interdependencies of social, economic and political values, norms, rules and laws' (Hohn and Neuer 2006, 293) and has 'evolved with social, political, and economic influences' (Sanyal 2005, 15). Similarly, Vettoretto (this volume) argues that 'planning practices are embedded in another social and cultural character of the welfare state' and observes 'an intertwining among planning, administration and welfare state, ideas of local democracy, and influence of European practices'.

Established models of society are under pressure to change and are in a period of modernisation. Similarly, planning systems and policies in many regions and countries are going through an unprecedented period of adjustment. Planning cultures, positioned between the model of society and the actualities of planning practice, will be influenced by changes in both and may also moderate changes to planning practice. In this context we examine models of spatial planning (ideal types of planning systems) and explore their relationship with models of society and implications for planning cultures.

The chapter begins by examining the concept of the model of society and reviewing different typologies of welfare systems, which we use as a proxy for models of society. Here we compare the groupings of countries that emerge from the different typologies. We then turn to a comparison of typologies of planning systems (or models of planning) and the groupings of countries that result. We summarise some of the broad patterns in the recent evolution of planning and welfare systems in various European countries (both from the contributions in this book and other sources) and relate this to discussions about the convergence of planning systems.

The European Social Model and the European Model of Society

The concept of the European model of society emerged in the 1980s and appeared in various European policy documents from the mid-1990s onwards (Ross 1995; Delanty and Rumford 2005; Faludi 2007a, 2007b; Nadin and Stead 2008). Despite many years of discussion in both academic and political circles, the term has not been defined with any precision (House of Lords 2004; Jepsen and Serrano Pascual 2005; Alber 2006). The European model of society (according to authors such as Albert 1992; Judt 2005; Jepsen and Serrano Pascual 2005) is often used as a term to distinguish European society from other types of society, especially American society. The idea behind the concept is that economic and social progress should go hand-in-hand: economic growth should be combined with social cohesion. For some, the European Model of Society has more than just a social dimension, but also concerns regulations, incentives and innovation (Aiginger and Guger 2006). According to Judt (2005, 748), 'what binds Europeans together, even when they are deeply critical of some aspect or other of its practical workings, is what it has become conventional to call – in disjunctive but revealing contrast with "the American way of life" – the European model of society'.

Typologies and Classifications

Various authors contend that there is not a single European social model but varying social models that reflect substantial differences in conceptualising and constructing social policies, as witnessed by the variety of welfare systems across Europe (Giddens 2005). Publication of Esping-Andersen's 'Worlds of Welfare' thesis (Esping-Andersen 1990) drew attention to some of the differences in national welfare systems and provoked an extensive and ongoing debate about the classification of these systems, including the criteria that are used to differentiate them, the number of distinctive types and the grouping of countries that result (Bambra 2007). Esping-Andersen's 'three worlds of welfare' (summarised in Figure 16.1) has also given rise to a number of competing typologies.

Social-democratic	Extensive high-quality services, open to all irrespective of income; generous (and income-related) transfer payments to those out of or unable or too old to work; strong public support; exemplified by Scandinavian countries.
Liberal, Anglo-Saxon	Basic services, many available only via means testing; limited transfer payments; safety net for the poor so middle-class use and support is limited; both the UK and Ireland are examples, but (compared to, say, the US) only imperfect ones.
Conservative, corporatist	Insurance-based welfare schemes, many of which are administered by unions and employers; strong bias towards support for traditional family structures; Austria, Germany, the Netherlands and other Benelux countries fit neatly into this category, though France and Italy (and rather less easily Spain, Portugal and Greece) can also be included.

Figure 16.1 Summary of Esping-Andersen's three worlds of welfare

Source: Bale 2005.

A variety of criteria have been used to construct different welfare state typologies. These include decommodification[1] (Esping-Andersen 1990), basic income (Leibfried 1992), poverty rates (Ferrera 1996; Korpi and Palme 1998) and social expenditure (Bonoli 1997; Korpi and Palme 1998). The development of these typologies is summarised in Table 16.1. In general, the number of different regime types has increased over time as a consequence of more sophisticated analyses of welfare systems. Since 1990, the number of regime types in Europe has increased from Esping-Andersen's original three (Figure 16.1) to five or six (e.g., Aiginger and Guger 2006; Alber 2006). Across all classifications, some countries are consistently found in clusters with one or more similar countries whereas certain other countries are found in different clusters for each classification. Finland and Sweden, for example, consistently

---

1 The term decommodification refers to the extent to which individuals and families can maintain a normal and socially acceptable standard of living regardless of their market performance.

Table 16.1 Welfare state typologies

Esping-Andersen 1990	Social-democratic DK, FI, SE, NL	Liberal IE, UK	Conservative AT, BE, FR, DE		
Leibfried 1992	Scandinavian DK, FI, SE	Anglo-Saxon UK	Bismarck AT, DE	Latin Rim FR, GR, IT, PT, ES	
Ferrera 1996	Scandinavian DK, FI, SE	Anglo-Saxon IE, UK	Bismarck AT, BE, FR, DE, LU, NL	Southern GR, IT, PT, ES	
Bonoli 1997	Nordic DK, FI, SE	British IE, UK	Continental BE, FR, DE, LU, NL	Southern GR, IT, PT, ES	
Korpi and Palme 1998	Encompassing FI, SE	Basic security DK, IE, NL, UK	Corporatist AT, BE, FR, DE, IT		
Sapir 2006	Nordic DK, FI, SE, NL	Anglo-Saxon IE, UK	Continental AT, BE, FR, DE, LU	Mediterranean GR, IT, PT, ES	
Aiginger and Guger 2006	Scandinavian/ Nordic DK, FI, SE, NL	Anglo-Saxon/liberal IE, UK	Continental/ corporatist AT, BE, FR, DE, LU, IT	Mediterranean GR, PT, ES	Catching-up CZ, HU
Alber, 2006	Nordic DK, FI, SE	Anglo-Saxon IE, UK	Continental AT, BE, FR, DE	Southern GR, IT, PT, ES	New member states CY, CZ, EE, HU, LV, LT, MT, PL, SK, SI	Other LU, NL

Source: authors' own.

appear together in the encompassing/Nordic/Scandinavian/social democratic category, Ireland and the United Kingdom in the Anglo-Saxon/basic security/liberal category, France and Germany in the Bismarck/conservative/ continental/corporatist category and Portugal and Spain in the Latin Rim/ Mediterranean/southern category. Countries such as Luxembourg and the Netherlands on the other hand find themselves together with a different group of countries in almost every classification.

It is important to note here that the various regime types are ideal types which should be contrasted with the idiosyncrasies of particular countries and regions. The allocation of countries to types is not always clear-cut and the reality will inevitably lie somewhere between types. There may also be considerable variation between welfare systems of countries that appear in the same regime type. Even countries with similar sets of welfare institutions are frequently found to display widely divergent patterns of development (Alber 2006). It is also important to note that the classification of countries into regime types is time-dependent: governments, policies and economic activity can all change over time and directly influence the position of a country in the classification system.

European Models of Planning (Planning Systems)

There have been fewer attempts to classify European planning systems compared with welfare systems or social models. Two main approaches are evident. The first starts from other classifications (or families) of the legal and administrative systems within which planning operates. The second seeks to apply a wider set of criteria and produces a set of ideal types. Four specific studies of planning systems are discussed below: two based on families of legal and administrative systems and another two based on ideal types. Table 16.2 presents a summary of the typologies of planning systems in these four studies.

Legal and Administrative Families

Davies et al. (1989) considered planning control in five northern European countries and made a broad distinction between the planning system in England and elsewhere in Europe (following Thomas et al. 1983). This was primarily based on the fundamental differences created by the legal systems within which the planning system operates. The 'legal certainty' provided by systems in continental Europe (at least in the 'ideal sense') based in Napoleonic or Scandinavian legal systems was contrasted with the high degree of administrative discretion in the English system created by the legal framework of English common law. The differences in practice that result include the

Table 16.2 Planning system typologies

Davies et al. 1989[a]	Common law England			Napoleonic codes DK, DE, FR, NL	
Newman and Thornley 1996	British IE, UK		Germanic AT, DE	Napoleonic BE, FR, IT, LU, NL, PT, ES	East European
CEC 1997[b]	Comprehensive integrated AT, DK, FI, DE, NL, SE	Land use regulation IE, UK (+ BE)		Regional economic FR, PT (+ DE)	Urbanism GR, IT, ES (+PT)
Farinós Dasí 2007[c]	Comprehensive integrated AT, DK, FI, NL, SE, DE (+ BE, FR, IE LU, UK) BG, EE, HU, LV, LT PL, RO, SL, SV	Land use regulation BE, IE, LU, UK (+ PT, ES) CY, CZ, MT		Regional economic FR, DE, PT, (+ IE, SE, UK) HU, LV, LT, SK	Urbanism GR, IT, ES CY, MT

Notes:
a Davies et al. do not give a specific name to the two groups but contrast England and other systems based on their legal frameworks.
b The EU *Compendium* identifies 'ideal types' of planning traditions. Each country may exhibit combinations of ideal types in different degrees. The ideal types are dominant in the countries indicated here.
c The ESPON project took the EU *Compendium* traditions as a starting point and examined how countries, including the transition states of central and eastern Europe, were moving between them.

Source: authors' own.

absence of legally binding zoning plans at the local level in England whereas they are commonplace in continental systems.

Zweigert et al.'s (1987) study of legal and administrative families takes a similar approach and has been used widely as a typology for comparing planning systems. Newman and Thornley (1996) for example used this typology to classify planning systems into five legal and administrative families. The Romanistic, Germanic and Nordic legal families, based to greater or lesser degree on the Napoleonic code mixed with other influences, share similar attributes and are sometimes grouped as the western European continental family as identified by Davies et al. (1989). Zweigert et al. (1998) explain how all the continental legal systems share a similar 'legal style': they seek to create a complete set of abstract rules and principles in advance of decision-making. This, they argue, corresponds to particular continental 'mentalities': 'the European is given to making plans, to regulating things in advance, and to drawing up rules and systematising them' (ibid., 71). In contrast, the English common law system does not seek to provide a complete set of legal rules in advance, rather the law is built up on case by case as the decisions of the courts are recorded. Thus, there is much more emphasis on case law than on enacted law, which provides for more administrative discretion.

Using legal families and administrative structures to explain differences among planning systems has obvious validity in that the legal style and the administrative structure of government provide strong frameworks for the operation of planning systems. It helps, in particular, to distinguish between the forms of planning systems where regulation is conducted either through legally binding plans or through the more discretionary approach. The continental civil code legal family tends to produce an approach to planning that seeks to ensure that decisions conform to binding plans made in advance of proposals coming forward. In contrast, the English common law family tends to produce an approach to planning that assesses the performance of development proposals as and when they arise measured against non-binding strategies and performance criteria (Janin Rivolin 2008).

Traditions, Ideal Types and Styles

The EU *Compendium of Spatial Planning Systems and Policies* (CEC 1997) used a larger number of criteria to create four ideal types or 'traditions of spatial planning'. The word 'tradition' was used to emphasise the way that forms of planning are deeply embedded in the complex historical conditions of particular places. The legal family context was used to help distinguish planning systems together with six other variables: (i) the scope of the system in terms of policy topics covered; (ii) the extent of national and regional planning; (iii) the locus of power or relative competences between central and local government; (iv) the relative roles of public and private sectors; (v) the maturity of the system or how well it is established in government and public life; and (vi) the apparent distance between expressed goals for spatial development and outcomes. On the basis of these criteria four major traditions of spatial planning were proposed, recognising that some places might exhibit a strong tendency to one tradition whereas others may exhibit some more complex combination of types of planning. As noted above in relation to the welfare systems, the 'traditions' here are 'ideal types', a synthesis of the real complex mixture of observable phenomena. They serve as measures against which reality can be compared. Inevitably the reality of a planning system and particular actions will exhibit features of more than one ideal type or tradition. A further reflection on how each tradition reflects the seven criteria is given in Table 16.3. Since the ideal type traditions of planning reflect particular assumptions and theories of planning we refer to them as 'models of spatial planning'.

Table 16.3 Traditions and criteria from the EU *Compendium of Spatial Planning Systems and Policies*

	Legal basis	Scope of planning	Scale of planning	Locus of power	Public or private	Maturity of system	Distance between goals and outcomes
Regional economic planning	Mixed	Wide	National planning	Centre and local	Public	Mature	Mixed
Comprehensive integrated	Mixed	Wide	Multi-level planning	Mixed	Public	Mature	Narrow
Land-use management	Discretion	Narrow	Local	Centre	Mixed	Mature	Narrow
Urbanism	Code	Narrow	Local	Local	Mixed	Immature	Wide

The comprehensive integrated planning tradition or model corresponds quite well to the Social-democratic/Scandinavian social model in the geographical area it covers. The name suggests that the planning system explicitly seeks to provide a measure of horizontal and vertical integration of policies across sectors and jurisdictions. This is in contrast to the land-use planning tradition which corresponds well to the Liberal/Anglo-Saxon social model and has the much narrower scope or purpose of regulating land-use change. The other two planning traditions do not correspond so closely to social models. The regional economic planning and urbanism approaches primarily coincide with the Conservative/Corporatist welfare model: the regional economic planning approach is generally more prevalent in the countries to the north of this grouping and the urbanism approaches to the south.

Very much related to the different ideal types or traditions of planning (but not always coincident) is the diversity in professional planning cultures across Europe. Germany, the Netherlands and the UK for example all have a mature planning profession with their roots primarily in the social sciences (Healey and Williams 1993). The planning profession in southern Europe (e.g. Spain and Italy) is on the other hand more closely linked to, and controlled by, the profession of architecture (see also Serraos et al. in this volume in their account about spatial planning in Greece). Meanwhile, planning in certain post-Communist countries in Europe, according to Healey and Williams (1993), is often heavily influenced and rooted in economics, although this does not seem to be the case for Romania and Lithuania, where, according to the accounts of Puşcaşu and Staniunas (earlier in this volume), the planning system in both these countries appears to be closely linked the architecture profession.

ESPON Project 2.3.2 concerning the governance of territorial and urban policies (Farinós Dasí 2006) takes the EU *Compendium* traditions or ideal types of planning (and the limitations this imposes) and 'gives a modest update on the movements that took place since' (ibid., 112). The report seeks to classify each country according to the four traditions, which it renames as styles, because, the report argues, tradition is less relevant for the countries of central and eastern Europe. It gives more emphasis to the distribution of powers relevant to planning among levels of government with a finer analysis of 'state structures' and the decentralisation and devolution of competences, especially the varying forms of regional governance and local powers. It concludes, like the *Compendium*, that variation is the hallmark of planning systems in Europe and that the classification of planning systems is difficult and very much dependent on which criterion is given prominence.

The Evolution of Planning in the Context of Welfare Reforms

Across Europe, welfare systems and planning systems have both experienced various forces of change over recent decades: many of these forces have been felt by both types of systems. In this section, we draw on a review of recent literature, including various contributions to this volume, to examine the recent trajectories of welfare and planning systems within Europe and the key changes that have occurred.

The Evolution of Welfare Systems

Recent pressures on modern welfare systems, according to a review by Korpi (2003), include factors such as population ageing, changing family patterns, new gender roles, decreasing economic growth rates, technological change, internationalisation of the economy, and changing relations between nation states (e.g., as a result of the end of the Cold War and political-economic integration in Europe). As a consequence of these factors, welfare systems across Europe have all experienced change over recent decades. Some authors claim that that the changes in European welfare systems have been small or modest (e.g. Ferrera et al. 2001) whereas others claim that changes have been very substantial, including transformations in welfare paradigms (e.g. Moreno and Palier 2005). Loughlin (2007) points out that, whilst Ferrera et al. (2001) claim that the welfare state in Europe has changed very little in recent years, they then go on to list an impressive array of changes which amount to what is in effect a quite radical transformation of the European welfare states, such as trends in managerialism, privatisation, decentralisation and controls in budgetary expansion. By concentrating on quantitative aspects (e.g. the continuing rise in public welfare expenditure), Loughlin (2007) also argues that authors such as Ferrera et al. (2001) underestimate the importance of very significant changes and miss one of the most important, namely the 'redefinition of the role and functions of the state and of the way in which the different elements of governance that constitute the state are configured' (ibid., 391). These changes are very much mirrored in the evolution of spatial planning (see below).

Looking across four different 'families of welfare' (Scandinavian, Anglo-Saxon, Continental and South European), Ferrera et al. (2001) identify the key social policy reforms in Europe during the 1990s.[2] One striking aspect in their summary of social policy reforms is that certain changes (e.g. pension reform) are common to almost all countries and to all four different families of welfare. Whereas other changes seem to be more specific to certain families of welfare. For example, unemployment benefit reforms took place in all countries in the Scandinavian family of welfare, minimum wage rules were introduced in the Anglo-Saxon countries (Ireland and the United Kingdom), various 'activation' measures to encourage certain groups to participate in employment were introduced in most of the members of the Continental family of welfare (Austria, Belgium, France, Germany, Luxembourg and the Netherlands) and health care reforms were on the political agenda in all countries in the South European family of welfare (Greece, Italy, Portugal and Spain).

Despite these changes, many authors argue that European welfare systems have been resistant to change to a remarkable extent. Ferrera et al. (2001) refer to the 'dynamics of persistence' of the welfare state, which they argue 'clearly overshadow those of convergence' (ibid., 20). Van Kersbergen (2000) asserts that 'while the context of welfare state policies has changed, this has not led to a dismantling of existing welfare state regimes' (ibid., 25). There are also claims that some welfare states have actually expanded in some European countries (e.g. Moreno 2000). The widespread popular support for the welfare state and

---

2   The countries in the four families of welfare identified by Ferrera et al (2001) closely coincide with those falling under four traditions of planning systems identified in the *Compendium of Spatial Planning* (CEC 1997).

the path dependency created by welfare states have both been suggested as possible factors to explain the resilience of welfare systems (Korpi 2003).

The Evolution of Planning Systems

Like welfare systems, Europe's planning systems are also being subject to a range of pressures. Some of these pressures are similar to the pressures on modern welfare systems (outlined above) but others are more specific. According to Healey and Williams (1993), globalisation, sustainable development, economic competitiveness, European integration, economic reforms and demographic change are key issues that are shaping national (and subnational) systems of planning. These are all contributing to various shifts in the objectives, processes, scales and scope of spatial planning. In terms of the recent evolution of territorial governance, Lidström (2007) identifies four general trends:

1. Redefining of the role of the nation-state. The establishment and gradual expansion of what now is the EU has limited the role of national borders and transferred decision-making powers to supranational bodies. In addition, states are challenged from inside, by groups with strong ethnic or regional identities demanding separatism or at least self-government.
2. Strengthening lower levels of self-government. In many countries, functions have been decentralised from central government to local and regional levels of government. In some countries, this has gone hand-in-hand with reorganisations of sub-national levels of government, either by amalgamation of municipalities or regions or by introducing new regional levels of self-government.
3. Accepting increasing diversity, variation and even asymmetry between how territories within the nation state are governed. This tendency towards diversity can be seen as the empowerment of the lower levels of self-government but may also lead to greater differentiation. Not only is the scope for variation between sub-national units greater, some units are also permitted to follow their own paths that may differ quite considerably from the general national pattern.
4. Increasing marketisation of the public domain. Many functions that were seen as fairly stable public responsibilities during the peak of the welfare state era have either been privatised or are run jointly by public and private providers. Public organisations are increasingly limited to 'enabling' other actors to offer services.

As for changes to national planning systems, common features across Europe in the 1980s included trends towards greater flexibility, the loosening of rigid zoning rules and the wider use of conservation designations (Healey and Williams 1993). In the 1990s, there were trends towards a pro-active, strategic approach, based on strategically-oriented plans, often in response to environmental concerns (Healey 1997; Albrechts et al. 2003). More recently, there are claims that there have been trends towards more collaborative and communicative forms of planning, especially in western Europe (Adams 2008). In the case of the United Kingdom, Evans (1995) argues that planning has moved from a 'welfare profession' serving the public interest to a skills-based profession providing a service. According to Hull (2000), whilst the 'hard infrastructure' of the system has for the most part remained intact, there have been significant changes in the 'soft infrastructure': the values, norms and standards which have guided practice. In the Netherlands, it is argued that there has been a shift from 'welfare state spatial planning' to 'development planning' (Zonneveld 2006) while, in France, Loughlin (2007) reports a significant change from top-down to bottom-up governance of spatial planning. Tynkkynen (this volume) suggests a move towards more strategic planning in parts of Russia due in part to influences from western Europe.

Since the 1980s, transnational influences on spatial planning have been accentuated by processes of European integration (Sykes 2008). Planners across Europe are now routinely involved in trans-boundary cooperation networks and inter-regional collaboration initiatives and thus exposed to a variety of planning approaches from other member states (Dühr et al. 2007). The EU's INTERREG Programme is a prime example of the 'Europeanisation' of planning through cooperation between regions and actors (Lähteenmäki-Smith et al. 2005; Böhme and Waterhout 2008; Waterhout et al. in this volume). Various authors suggest that the INTERREG programme has contributed to the emergence of transnational spatial planning practices, the diffusion of certain spatial ideas across European countries and changes in the domestic patterns of spatial planning and regional policies, both in terms of approaches and of institutional capacity (Böhme et al. 2004; Dabinett 2006; Dabinett and Richardson 2005; Giannakourou 2005; Janin Rivolin 2003; Janin Rivolin and Faludi 2005; Pedrazzini 2005; Tewdwr-Jones and Williams 2001).

Given these trends in greater international cooperation on spatial planning and other common pressures for change, we now consider whether this is leading to the convergence of planning systems or models. The ESPON Project 2.3.2 mentioned above suggests that there are some common tendencies, particularly the widespread advocacy of the comprehensive integrated approach (Farinós Dasí 2006). However, there are other forces at work that may outweigh any convergence tendencies. In the same way that welfare systems face 'dynamics of persistence' (Ferrera et al. 2001), so models of planning are resistant to change. They incorporate new ideas and innovate but are tempered by the underlying social model. Ideas are framed according to the underlying 'tradition'. In one sense tradition may hold back innovation but it may also provide for greater continuity and stability. In the longer term, the underlying social model itself will evolve and, if the forces are strong enough, this can occur relatively quickly. In western Europe, the period immediately following the Second World War is a case in point: this was a critical turning point when modern planning was established and welfare systems were extended. For countries in central and eastern Europe, the late 1980s and early 1990s represent a critical turning point. In all cases, the reform and renewal of spatial planning, as with welfare systems, have been confronted with the enduring values and norms that underpin society. In the case of spatial planning reforms in European countries, changes have been shaped by the underlying social model and the values and norms of the prevalent planning culture.

Numerous authors have referred to the confrontation between planning reforms and planning culture in different ways. Healey and Williams (1993) for example have argued that, despite pressures for convergence, the diversity in local planning systems will remain because 'local institutional traditions will always contribute an element of distinctiveness to the way wider economic, cultural and political pressures are interpreted' (ibid., 718). Giannakourou (2005) has argued that the institutional mechanisms and structures of spatial planning in southern European countries are not converging but that Europeanisation is leading to 'alternative paths' of socialisation and learning, causing different degrees of domestic change. This variety is also recognised as a strength: de Jong and Edelenbos (2007) have argued that 'continued variety has a greater potential to offer innovative solutions' (ibid., 704). Moreover, planning models will tend to be influenced, and seek inspiration from, other places that are perceived to have common features that fit with ways of seeing the world. For example, Romania has traditionally been more closely aligned to concepts and ideologies from France and Germany (Puşcaşu in this volume). Similarly, legal, administrative and planning systems in Greece have been historically influenced by French and German models, and more recently by the Anglo-Saxon tradition (see Serraos et al. in this volume). At the European level, Davoudi (in this volume) argues that France and Germany ideologies have been the most dominant influences or 'models' in the development of European territorial cohesion policy. Elsewhere, Janin Rivolin (2008) argues that the European model or principles are counteracted by the prevailing nature of planning systems.

Conclusions

First a note of caution: the discussion about the relation between models of society, spatial planning systems and planning culture should of course be viewed bearing in mind the limitations of general models of welfare or planning systems. Any model will be a considerable abstraction of the true variety that the nation states and regions exhibit. Zweigert et al. (1998) note the dangers in reducing the complexity of variation between countries to a few 'families'. Much depends on the particular criteria employed. The review helps to identify some future research questions on the typologies of models of planning and planning cultures, and the relationship between the planning system and the underlying social model.

Comparison of European social models (and welfare systems) and models of planning systems and their evolution help point to some general conclusions about the connections between them. First, there is reasonable correspondence between the ideal types (or categories) of welfare and planning systems. This is to be expected since the planning system is in part an expression of some fundamental values in a society in relation, for example, to the legitimate scope and aspirations of government, the use of land, and the rights of citizens. The clustering of countries according to ideal types remains similar when different criteria are used, which demonstrates how varying aspects of society are interlinked.

The correspondence of model of society and type of planning system is particularly strong for the British/Anglo-Saxon and the Nordic models. They are consistently distinguished because of their specific characteristics which demonstrate a close association between the dominant model of society and the form of the planning system. There is less consistency between welfare and planning models for continental countries and a few countries like the Netherlands are especially difficult to classify. More attention is certainly needed to incorporate the countries of central and eastern Europe into these classifications for two key reasons. Firstly, these countries have often not been included in previous studies of welfare and/or planning systems. Secondly, many of these countries have experienced rapid changes in their welfare and/or planning systems over recent decades and an up to date assessment of the current situation is needed.

There have been some suggestions of convergence of models and there are clearly common concerns and responses that are strongly influenced by the Europeanisation of spatial planning. However, these common pressures for adaptation are also being shaped (and sometimes counteracted) by planning culture (see also the contributions by Puşcaşu, Vettoretto and Waterhout et al in this volume). Here the comparison with studies into changing welfare systems is instructive. There is evidence of significant welfare reforms in practice but the underlying models remain quite distinctive and influential. We suggest that this may also be the situation in the case of spatial planning: significant reforms are taking place to systems across Europe but outcomes are variable and strongly influenced by the prevalent planning culture and social model. Further research into this suggested relationship would be a very useful contribution to the academic debate.

Bibliography

Adams, N. (2008) 'Convergence and Policy Transfer: An Examination of the Extent to which Approaches to Spatial Planning have Converged within the Context of an Enlarged EU', *International Planning Studies* 13(1), 31–49.

Aiginger, K. and A. Guger (2006) 'The Ability to Adapt: Why it Differs between the Scandinavian and Continental European Models', *Intereconomics* 14(1), 14–23.

Alber, J. (2006) 'The European Social Model and the United States', *European Union Politics* 7(3), 393–419.

Albert, M. (1992) *Kapitalismus contra Kapitalismus*, Campus Verlag, Frankfurt/New York.

Albrechts, L., P. Healey and K.R. Kunzmann (2003) 'Strategic Spatial Planning and Regional Governance in Europe', *Journal of the American Planning Association* 69(2), 113–29.

Arts, W. and J. Gelissen (2002) 'Three Worlds of Welfare or More?', *Journal of European Social Policy* 12(2), 137–58.

Bale, T. (2005) *European Politics. A Comparative Introduction*, Palgrave Macmillan, London.

Bambra, C. (2007) '"Sifting the Wheat from the Chaff": A Two-dimensional Discriminant Analysis of Welfare State Regime Theory.', *Social Policy and Administration* 41(1), 1–28.

Böhme, K. and B. Waterhout (2008) 'The Europeanisation of Planning', in A. Faludi (ed.) *European Spatial Research and Planning*, Lincoln Institute of Land Policy, Cambridge, MA, 225–48.

Böhme, K., T. Richardson, G. Dabinett and O.B. Jensen (2004) 'Values in a Vacuum? Towards an Integrated Multilevel Analysis of the Governance of European Space', *European Planning Studies* 12(8), 1175–88.

Bonoli, G. (1997) 'Classifying Welfare States: A Two-dimension Approach', *Journal of Social Policy* 26(3), 351–72.

Commission of the European Communities – CEC (1997) *The EU Compendium of Spatial Planning Systems and Policies, Regional Development Studies*, Office for Official Publications of the European Communities, Luxembourg.

Dabinett, G. (2006) 'Transnational Spatial Planning – Insights from Practices in the European Union' *Urban Policy and Research* 24(2), 283–90.

Dabinett, G. and T. Richardson (2005) 'The Europeanisation of Spatial Strategy: Shaping Regions and Spatial Justice through Governmental Ideas', *International Planning Studies* 10(3/4), 201–18.

Davies, H.W.E., D. Edwards, A.J. Hooper and J.V. Punter (1989) 'Comparative Study', in H.W.E. Davies (ed.) *Planning Control in Western Europe*, HMSO, London, 409–42.

de Jong, M. and J. Edelenbos (2007) 'An Insider's Look into Policy Transfer in Transnational Expert Networks', *European Planning Studies* 15(5), 687–706.

Delanty, G. and C. Rumford (2005) *Rethinking Europe: Social Theory and the Implications of Europeanization*, Routledge, London.

Dühr, S., D. Stead and W. Zonneveld (2007) 'The Europeanisation of Spatial Planning through Territorial Cooperation', *Planning Practice and Research* 22(3), 291–307.

Esping-Andersen, G. (1990) *The Three Worlds of Welfare Capitalism*, Polity Press, Cambridge.

Evans, B. (1995) *Experts and Environmental Planning*, Avebury, Aldershot.

Faludi, A. (2007a) 'The European Model of Society', in Faludi, A. (ed.) *Territorial Cohesion and the European Model of Society*, Lincoln Institute of Land Policy, Cambridge, MA, 1–22.

Faludi, A. (2007b) 'Territorial Cohesion Policy and the European Model of Society', *European Planning Studies* 15(4), 567–83.

Farinós Dasí, J. (ed.) (2006) *ESPON Project 2.3.2: Governance of Territorial and Urban Policies from EU to Local Level*, ESPON Coordination Unit, Luxembourg.

Ferrera, M. (1996) 'The Southern Model of Welfare in Social Europe', *Journal of European Social Policy* 6(1), 17–37.

Ferrera, M., A. Hemerijk and M. Rhodes (2001) *The Future of Social Europe: Recasting Work and Welfare in the New Economy. Report for the Portuguese Presidency of the European Union*, European University Institute, Florence.

Giannakourou, G. (2005) 'Transforming Spatial Planning Policy in Mediterranean Countries: Europeanisation and Domestic Change', *European Planning Studies* 13(2), 319–31.

Giddens, A. (2005) 'The World Does Not Owe Us a Living!', *Progressive Politics* 4(3), 6–12.

Healey, P. and R. Williams (1993) 'European Urban Planning Systems: Diversity and Convergence', *Urban Studies* 30(4/5), 701–20.

Healey, P. (1997) 'The Revival of Strategic Spatial Planning in Europe', in P. Healey, A. Khakee, A. Motte, and B. Needham (eds) *Making Strategic Spatial Plans: Innovation in Europe*, UCL Press, London, 3–19.

Hohn, U. and B. Neuer (2006) 'New Urban Governance: Institutional Change and Consequences for Urban Development', *European Planning Studies* 14(3), 291–8.

House of Lords (2004) *European Union. Twenty-Ninth Report*, HMSO, London.

Hull, A. (2000) 'Modernizing Democracy: Constructing a Radical Reform of the Planning System?', *European Planning Studies* 8(6), 767–82.

Janin Rivolin, U. (2003) 'Shaping European spatial planning: How Italy's experience can contribute', *Town Planning Review* 74(1), 51–76.

Janin Rivolin, U. (2008) 'Conforming and Performing Planning Systems in Europe: An Unbearable Cohabitation', *Planning Practice and Research* 23(2), 167–86.

Janin Rivolin, U. and A. Faludi (2005) 'The Hidden Face of European Spatial Planning: Innovations in Governance', *European Planning Studies* 13(2), 195–215.

Jepsen, M. and A. Serrano Pascual (2005) 'The European Social Model: An Exercise in Deconstruction', *Journal of European Social Policy* 15(3), 231–45.

Judt, T. (2005) *Postwar: A History of Europe Since 1945*, Random House, London.

Korpi, W. (2003) 'Welfare-State Regress in Western Europe: Politics, Institutions, Globalization, and Europeanization.', *Annual Review of Sociology* 29, 589–609.

Korpi, W. and J. Palme (1998) 'The Paradox of Redistribution and the Strategy of Equality: Welfare State Institutions, Inequality and Poverty in the Western Countries' *American Sociological Review* 63(5), 661–87.

Lähteenmäki-Smith, K., S. Fuller and K. Böhme (2005) *Integrated Multi-level Analysis of the Governance of European Space*, Nordregio, Stockholm.

Leibfried, S. (1992) 'Towards a European Welfare State', in Z. Ferge and J.E. Kolberg (eds) *Social Policy in a Changing Europe*, Campus-Verlag, Frankfurt, 245–79.

Lidström, A. (2007) 'Territorial Governance in Transition', *Regional and Federal Studies* 17(4), 499–508.

Loughlin, J. (2007) 'Reconfiguring the State: Trends in Territorial Governance in European States', *Regional and Federal Studies* 17(4), 385–403.

Moreno, L. and B. Palier (2005) 'The Europeanisation of Welfare: Paradigm Shifts and Social Policy Reforms', in P. Taylor-Gooby (ed.) *Ideas and Welfare State Reform in Western Europe*, Palgrave Macmillan, Basingstoke, 145–75.

Moreno, L. (2000) 'The Spanish Development of Southern Welfare', in S. Kuhnle (ed.) *The Survival of the European Welfare State*, Routledge, London, 146–65.

Nadin, V. and D. Stead (2008) 'European Spatial Planning Systems, Social Models and Learning', *DISP* 44(1), 35–47.

Newman, P. and A. Thornley (1996) *Urban Planning in Europe: International Competition, National Systems, and Planning Projects*, Routledge, London.

Pedrazzini, L. (2005) 'Applying the ESDP through INTERREG IIIB: A Southern Perspective', *European Planning Studies* 13(2), 297–317.

Ross, G. (1995) *Jacques Delors and European Integration*, Polity Press, Cambridge.

Sanyal, B. (2005) 'Hybrid Planning Cultures: The Search for the Global Cultural Commons', in B. Sanyal (ed.) *Comparative Planning Cultures*, Routledge, London, 3–38.

Sapir, A. (2006) 'Globalization and the Reform of European Social Models', *Journal of Common Market Studies* 44(2), 369–90.

Sykes, O. (2008) 'The Importance of Context and Comparison in the Study of European Spatial Planning', *European Planning Studies* 16(4), 537–55.

Tewdwr-Jones, M. and R.H. Williams (2001) *The European Dimension of British Planning*, Spon, London.

Thomas, H.D., J.M. Minett, S. Hopkins, S.L. Hamnett, A. Faludi and D. Barrell (1983) *Flexibility and Commitment in Planning*, Martinus Nijhoff Publishers, The Hague/Boston/London.

van Kersbergen, K. (2000) 'The Declining Resistance of Welfare States to Change?', in S. Kuhnle (ed.) *Survival of the European Welfare State*, Routledge, London, 19–36.

Zonneveld, W. (2006) 'Planning in Retreat: The Changing Importance of Dutch National Spatial Planning', paper presented at the Conference of the European Group of Public Administration, 6–9 September, Università Bocconi, Milan.

Zweigert, K. (author), H. Kötz (author) and T. Weir (translator) (1987) *An Introduction to Comparative Law*, 2nd edn, Clarendon Press, Oxford.

Zweigert, K. (author), H. Kötz (author) and T. Weir (translator) (1998) *An Introduction to Comparative Law*, 3rd edn, Oxford University Press, Oxford.

Chapter 17
Planning Cultures in Europe between Convergence and Divergence: Findings, Explanations and Perspectives

Joerg Knieling and Frank Othengrafen

Introduction

All contributions in this volume describe planning cultures, each using different kinds of evidence and specific forms of argumentation to explore the concept of planning culture. However, in general they all refer to the central questions set out by the editors in their introduction. Thus, the main purpose of the conclusion is to reconsider the framework presented by the 'culturised planning model' and its (analytical) cultural dimensions (see earlier contribution of Knieling and Othengrafen in this volume), to find answers to the questions posed earlier and to identify further topics that might be worthy of future research.

Planning in a Culturised Future

As the contributions to this volume demonstrate, the planning cultures of different European countries show that each national or regional planning context is characterised by particularities of history, beliefs and values, political and legal traditions, different socio-economic patterns and concepts of justice, interpretations of planning tasks and responsibilities, as well as different structures of governance. In other words, social processes are characterised by the way they are embedded in specific cultural contexts, referring to territorial traditions and historic developments, norms, institutions, values and attitudes.

Planning can be described as one of these social activities and is thus framed by the same conditions. Planning is also embedded in economic, political and socio-cultural contexts, which define a framework that has to be considered when analysing and comparing planning systems and practices. The experiences from various European countries show that, despite the unifying and culturally homogenising power of global economic interconnections, processes of internationalisation and the increasing global orientation of policies, a wide range of culturally affected ways and strategies remain for nations or regions to react towards the global challenges. This is true in particular for urban and regional development where it becomes obvious that cultural diversity has a spatial component (e.g., Cook et al. 2000), as it is visualised by different meanings and understandings of territory and spatial planning, planning objectives as well as specific spatial planning systems, strategies and instruments.

Against this background, awareness of local, regional and national (cultural) contexts comes to the fore and can be interpreted as a sign of a 'culturised future' (e.g., Young 2008). Concerning globalisation, awareness that space is no longer a neutral category that can be interpreted as a 'container' for economic and social processes, as it was regarded from the 1960s until the 1980s, is growing. Space is, rather, the result of social relations among people living in a certain area or region (territory as socially-constructed space) so that culture and cultural influences play a crucial role.

The second sign of a 'culturised future' can be found in cultural and organisational sciences, especially in the field of cross-cultural studies, as authors such as Hofstede, Gullestrup and Schein have shown (see also earlier contribution of Knieling and Othengrafen in this volume). From this point of view, the concept of culture is used in a systematic way to identify differences in preferences, values, norms, rules and attitudes to be able to manage (cultural) differences successfully, for example, in internationally operating enterprises as well as in internationally oriented cities and regions. Against the background of an increasingly diverse workforce and population and the (internal) internationality of enterprises, it has become a major challenge to adapt to this diversity and to use its potential in terms of innovation and global connectivity. Thus, 'diversity management' of cultural differences is seen as a key issue for the competitiveness of enterprises as well as of cities and regions.

Third, the importance of culture has been recognised in international politics. The European Commission, for example, has emphasised the role of culture within its policy documents such as the European Agenda for Culture and the Programme of Territorial Cooperation with its strong focus on cross-cultural exchange (During et al. in this volume). In particular the 'culture chapter' of the EU Treaty accentuates the significance of culture by claiming that the 'Union shall take cultural aspects into account in its action under the provisions of the Treaties, in particular in order to respect and to promote the diversity of its cultures' (EU 2008). An increasing recognition of culture and cultural contexts is also found at the level of the United Nations and the World Bank which have both put more emphasis on spatial planning or development opportunities that are based on specific cultural conditions (see introduction to this volume by Knieling and Othengrafen).

These different but complementary developments are part of a 'cultural turn' in politics as well as in planning theory and practice. They recognise the role of culture for spatial development and aim at enhancing the role of culture in national or regional (planning) policies, recognising the knowledge of cultural, ethnic, linguistic and religious diversity.

European Planning Cultures and the Need to Recognise Culturally Embedded Practices

Various EU policy documents, programmes and initiatives highlight the role of culture for the European integration process. In this context, the recognition of culture is seen as a contribution to the economic and social cohesion throughout the EU by fostering a balanced development of the continent (e.g., through cross-border, transnational and interregional cooperation) which is based on 'a united European citizenship with a diversity of regional cultures' (During et al. in this volume). This shows the necessity of analysing the 'cultural contexts' of such concepts and programmes in which spatial planning and development are embedded and operate to implement European programmes as well as the European integration process successfully.

However, as During et al. have shown on the basis of INTERREG practices, there seems to be a gap between cultural diversity and potential on the one side and the social and economic development on the other side. In other words, the cultural embedding of development practices is not really recognised by the actors involved, with the consequence of 'cognitive or social closures of partnerships because partners are not fully acquainted with each other's cultures'. Besides friction in the process of international cooperation, this might result in difficulties in the implementation of project results (During et al. in this volume).

One conclusion is to focus more on comparing contemporary urban and regional planning to identify cultural influences on spatial development and to provide a scientific basis to use cultural diversity for the development of the European territory (e.g., Faludi 2002a). Against this background, it seems necessary to redefine spatial planning and development in the context of global interconnections and EU integration policies.

The 'Culturised Planning Model' and its Three Dimensions

Many authors in this volume (e.g., Fürst's, Staniunas' and Vettoretto's contributions) have emphasised the importance of cultural contexts and 'mental environments' (Staniunas in this volume) that frame spatial planning. But despite the mentioned 'cultural turn' and the increasing recognition of culture as a concept in various other fields, planning and planning theory hardly ever seem to consider culture as a significant contribution for analysing or comparing planning principles, objectives, systems, and processes. Fürst (in this volume) accentuates that 'planning culture [is] a neglected dimension in international comparative studies on planning systems'.

However, Fürst and other authors (e.g., During et al. in this volume) recognise that 'culture' and 'planning culture' are difficult to define and to operationalise as scientific concepts. Therefore, it is important to develop a theoretical model that is based on a consistent set of criteria and explains the enduring phenomenon of culture and its impact on contemporary spatial planning practices (see earlier contribution of Knieling and Othengrafen in this volume). A first theoretical approach to operationalise culture has been developed by Gullestrup. He distinguishes between a 'horizontal' (immediately visible cultural traits) and a 'vertical' dimension (hidden, taken-for-granted assumptions and fundamental legitimating cultural traits) of culture. 'The horizontal and vertical dimensions of culture thus make up a kind of "skeleton"' (Gullestrup in this volume), which enables observers to understand or analyse cultural influences in societies. From his point of view, the analytical model might also assist planners to describe different (European) planning practices and to understand the reasons or culturally embedded practices why there are different approaches regarding spatial planning and development.

Based on Gullestrup's distinction between 'horizontal' and 'vertical', the 'culturised planning model', which was developed in this volume and served for analysing planning practises in different European countries, contains (analytical) categories of possible interrelations between cultural theories and (postmodern) planning theories to explain the influences of culture on planning procedures and practices. Therefore, the model consists of the following three analytical dimensions (see Knieling and Othengrafen earlier in this volume):

1. 'planning artefacts', describing visible planning products, structures and processes which can easily be recognised and understood; for example, urban structures and master plans, etc.;
2. 'planning environment', referring to assumptions and values that are specific for actors being involved in spatial planning (e.g., urban and regional planners, urbanists, geographers etc.); for example, objectives and principles planning is aiming at, planning traditions, the scope of planning (comprehensive planning vs planning by projects), and political, administrative, economic and organisational structures.), etc.;
3. 'societal environment', representing underlying, unconscious assumptions which affect urban and regional planning as specific societal backgrounds; for example, the (self-) perception of planning or people's acceptance of planning, but also the consideration of nature, different concepts of justice and impacts of socio-economic or socio-political models about planning, etc.

Planning Cultures in Europe between Convergence and Divergence 305

In this sense, the 'culturised planning model' with its (analytical) dimensions describes elements for a culture-based planning paradigm, which can provide the framework for the analysis and description of planning practices and cultures. Based on a consistent system of dimensions and criteria, the model contributes to the development of a wider theoretical basis and a conceptual framework for a systematic comparison of different planning cultures (planning models and practices related to an institutional and social context).

Planning Culture as a Scientific Concept: Findings and Explanations

The theoretical conception of a 'culturised planning model' outlined above offers the opportunity for a systematic analysis and comparison of the influences culture has on planning processes, practices and outcomes. Nevertheless, the questions emerge which practical or empirical findings the theoretical model explains, which results will be achieved by using the theoretical model, how these findings can be used, and what its potentials and strengths as well as weaknesses and restrictions are?

To answer these questions, this chapter summarises and valuates the cultural paradigm, which is the basis of the culturised planning model by analysing the case studies of this volume. Therefore, some of the findings and results will be summarised with regard to the three dimensions, then a general appraisal of the model will follow. The objective of this volume is to decode the role of culture for spatial planning. According to Breulliard and Fraser (2007, xiv) this means that the emphasis of the work is not to describe what is happening in each country's professional practice but to highlight and compare the role culture has on the organisation, structures, processes and outcomes of spatial planning.

Planning Artefacts: Findings and Explanations

The first dimension of the 'culturised planning model' delineates the 'planning artefacts', meaning the visible planning products, structures and processes when encountering a foreign (planning) culture. In this context, all contributions marked how spatial planning and development functions in specific cities, regions or countries and how these are physically structured or shaped.

One impression concerning the structure of cities and regions is the division between countries where spatial development follows either a more coordinated way or those where rules are more or less coincidental. The northwestern European countries, for example, comply with the first category, i.e. spatial development follows a system of controlled rules and regulations. In contrast, spatial development in southern European countries and, to a lesser extent, in Eastern Europe, does not seem to follow such patterns. There, uncoordinated developments and 'creative' planning or construction activities appear to be a daily occurrence, as the examples of Athens, Istanbul and St Petersburg indicate. Against this background, Vettoretto (in this volume) argues that the 'Italian planning culture is depicted as quite different from other European cultures and traditions which are informed by responsiveness, social support and acceptance'.

Besides urban structures and spatial patterns, the dimension of 'planning artefacts' consists of urban and regional plans and development concepts. These also belong to the 'visible' planning products because they can easily be discovered when encountering a foreign (planning) culture. The Urban Development Plan of Vienna, for example (see Dangschat and Hamedinger in this volume), is not legally binding but serves as an important instrument for guiding the future development. It aims at improving the quality of life, social justice and urban design; but it also focuses on issues such as competitiveness, deregulation and liberalisation to strengthen Vienna's position. Serraos et al. (in this volume), in comparison, highlight the legally binding character of the General Urban Plans in Greece for public authorities and private actors, at least after they have been approved by the Minister for the Environment, Spatial Planning and Public Works. When looking at the planning culture and planning traditions, there is a huge difference compared to the Urban Development Plan in Vienna. This also refers to the contents and objectives of the plans. In contrast to the Urban Development Plan of Vienna with its broad approach, which also includes procedural elements and aspects of deregulation and liberalisation of development, the General Urban Plan in Athens seems to be more strictly oriented to its 'original' task of 'providing general guidelines for its spatial development' (Serraos et al. in this volume). These differences might be due to the organisation of spatial planning at the national level: Greece belongs to the highly centralised countries in Europe where decision-making mainly takes place at the national level, so that principles and objectives are determined in a national plan. In contrast, Austria is a federal state where the competence for spatial planning is provided to the states or regions so that their plans can follow a broader approach, than the General Urban Plans in Greece can. This is the case, for example, especially in Vienna, which is both a city and a federal state.

In her contribution, Dühr also outlines the different objectives of spatial plans and the different cartographic representations. Concerning a particular field of spatial planning diversity, she articulates the role of culture for understanding the design and the use of cartographic representations in spatial planning. Following her argumentation, maps and cartographic representations serve as illustrations of spatial policies. The visualisations differ from country to country (or sometimes from region to region) in the way in which they symbolically represent their territories. This, of course, is due to the 'unspoken rules of map production that reflect the values of the culture within which the map has been produced' (Dühr in this volume). In other words, the visualisation is deeply rooted in historical, geographical and cultural contexts, which have evolved over time and have developed specific planning practices.

For a better and systematic understanding of planning cultures in Europe, these aspects offer a good starting point, so that the analytical dimension of 'planning artefacts' may be useful for decoding the role of culture for spatial planning and for comparing planning cultures. However, the descriptions concerning the 'planning artefacts' cannot explain the occurrence of different spatial patterns and they are not able to explain the multiplicity of planning structures or processes and their contemporary transformations. Therefore, the 'culturised planning model' provides the analytical dimensions of 'planning environment' and 'societal environment'.

Planning Environment: Findings and Explanations

The 'planning environment' is one of the analytical dimensions of the 'culturised planning model' which aims at exploring reasons for the varying spatial structures and spatial planning structures or products. By referring to the shared assumptions and cognitive frames, practices and values that are taken for granted by members of the planning profession, the objective is to figure out cultural values, traditions, attitudes and habits which have a significant influence on planning structures, processes and outcomes but that are not that easily recognised.

When looking at the division of countries in which spatial development follows either a more coordinated path or in which rules of spatial development are more coincidental, there are various rationales – given by the case studies in this volume – which belong to the dimension of the 'planning environment'. Germany, for example, follows a scientific-rational way of planning which is part of the German intellectual style (see Fischer in this volume). Spatial planning in Germany, generally speaking, seems to be more regulatory than in other countries and is based on scientific and rational methods, as, for example, shown by Christaller's spatial concept or by the preparation and visualisation of cartographic maps (see Fischer and Dühr in this volume).

Although the Russian planning culture pursued a similar scientific-rational approach, which was based on the use of data and the role of planners as experts (Tynkkynen in this volume), nowadays the Russian 'planning environment' has to deal with the stronger role of the private sector compared to the German characteristics. Due to the collapse of the former Soviet Union and a focus towards the market economy, the public sector, including spatial planning, has to share competencies with the private sector. As Staniunas, Tynkkynen and Puşcaşu (in this volume) argue, the clientelistic relations between private actors and politics are a driving force for new planning and construction activities that are influencing the structure and shape of cities and regions. In consequence, planners are reduced to acting as 'mechanical formulators of blueprints and construction permits' (Tynkkynen in this volume). This might be a reason why urban and regional development, at least in the St Petersburg region, sometimes appear to be uncoordinated.

In Athens and Istanbul it became obvious that the planning of the Olympic facilities (see Serraos et al. in this volume) and of the French Street area (see Prehl and Tuçaltan in this volume) was not related either to existing regulatory plans or to a wider strategic policy. In both countries, the process of the 'ratification' of urban plans is a highly complicated and political process. That might be one reason why projects are not embedded in wider spatial policies or regulatory plans, which might lead to a kind of uncontrolled development. In Turkey this is even more complicated as 'most of the legislation has an open part that can be revised due to the low level of standardisation' and urban plans are only legally binding for a short time (Prehl and Tuçaltan in this volume). Prehl and Tuçaltan conclude that the uncoordinated development in Turkey, demonstrated by the example of French Street, could occur because municipalities have never had functions of coordinating and controlling, which are mainly tasks of the government – a similar situation to that in Greece.

The latter aspect also points to administrative and decision-making structures which affect planning practices. The examples of Austria, Greece, and Italy show the high concentration of decision-making processes in the administration and, for example, in Vienna, within the extended structure of the ruling party (Dangschat and Hamedinger in this volume). Thus, hierarchical decisions (state-centred) and clientelistic (selective and fragmented) relations seem to be characteristic in these countries and have a huge impact on the way planning is performed.

An example of the hierarchical way of planning is found in Greece. There, the Ministry for Environment, Spatial Planning and Public Works has been responsible for the development of urban plans in all Greek municipalities during the 1990s and still is responsible for the approval of urban plans, which nowadays are developed by the municipalities. Another approach has emerged in Eastern Europe, where unofficial networks play an important role in decision-making processes. Many decisions are the result of 'clientelistic relations' between private actors and politicians (see contributions of Tynkkynen, Staniunas and Puşcaşu). Consequently, spatial planning focuses more on construction permits for private actors and to a lesser extent on strategic and comprehensive approaches, which are not appreciated by the political sphere. However, if more comprehensive plans are developed and approved, this happens 'without considering whether it is possible to realise the actions provided in plans' (Staniunas in this volume). To some degree these practices show decisive differences compared with western European countries.

In many countries of Southern and Eastern Europe, strategic planning has only recently gained more emphasis. This might be due to the fact that spatial planning has not been an independent profession in these countries. As the examples of Greece, Italy, Lithuania, Russia and Romania show, spatial planning is often a field for architects and civil engineers, who focus on other aspects but not on strategic or 'comprehensive' planning. Their emphasis on projects and constructions is stronger, so comprehensive planning has only limited influence.

Another aspect which is also related to the shared assumptions and cognitive frames, practices and values that are taken for granted by members of the planning profession is the 'legitimation' or 'role' of planning. As Vettoretto has elaborated for Italy (in this volume), spatial planning is more important for the political consensus-building process than for the regulation of land-use issues. In contrast, Serraos et al. (in this volume) point out that spatial planning controls land use but only has a weak strategic orientation. A third approach is provided by Staniunas, Tynkkynen, as well as Prehl and Tuçaltan (all in this volume), who describe the role of planning as a 'supportive actor' – sometimes even reduced to the technical means – in the decision-making of politicians and private actors.

The introduction of the analytical dimension of the 'planning environment' aims at exploring cultural values, traditions, attitudes and habits which have a significant influence on planning structures, processes and outcomes but are not immediately obvious. As the findings and explanations indicate, the analytical dimension of the planning environment – representing the shared assumptions that are taken for granted by members of the planning profession – can help to analyse the role of culture in spatial planning and to compare planning cultures. However, there are further aspects which have an impact on planning practices. The next section explains findings that belong to the more general norms, rules, traditions, values and attitudes of a society.

Societal Environment: Findings and Explanations

The 'societal environment', as the third dimension of the 'culturised planning model', describes underlying assumptions that are more difficult to perceive but which affect urban and regional planning by forming the specific societal background. By referring to the mental predispositions, i.e. the unconscious, taken-for-granted societal norms, beliefs, perceptions, thoughts and feelings (e.g., people's acceptance of planning, different concepts of justice, impacts of socio-economic or socio-political models on planning or the consideration of nature), this dimension aims at exploring the multiplicity of political and social practices and cultural frames that shape spatial planning.

When looking at the role of spatial planning in the Eastern European countries, it became obvious in the previous section that planning is more or less reactive or responsive to 'external proposals' but does not initiate or control spatial development by itself. This might stem from scepticism about or even rejection of planning after the collapse of the former Soviet Union. All kinds of planning have been related to negative associations concerning the centrally planned economy of the Soviet period, so that planning is no longer very popular (see Staniunas' and Tynnkynen's contributions). Staniunas, when describing the Lithuanian planning culture, discovers that the question 'Why do we have to deal with planning?' is crucial for those post-Soviet societies oriented towards the West and market economy. This might explain why only scant attention has been devoted to planning and why the public significance of planning declined.

Vettoretto and Serraos et al. (both in this volume) describe another reason why planning lacks acceptance. Greece is a highly centralised state where most competencies refer to the national level. But Serraos et al. indicate that people tend to resist hierarchical state decisions 'when they are forced to do things they are not inspired by'. This seems to be linked to the inefficiency of national government: on the one hand, national government is not able to consider local needs adequately, so that uncontrolled, informal and sometimes illegal activities take place to meet local needs. On the other hand, if unwanted, uncontrolled or illegal planning or construction activities occur, national government does not stop them. On the contrary, spatial planning often legitimises these activities afterwards. This resistance to hierarchical decision-making is not only related to the 'planning environment', it seems to be a general Greek societal attitude. As Serraos et al. summarise, 'the stronger the role of the state the more ineffective spatial planning becomes' (Serraos et al. in this volume).

In comparison, Vettoretto highlights the role of 'familism' and clientelism in Italy. Due to the inefficiency of the state and the centralised institutions, the family or similar local networks fulfil an important task with regard to the provision of social services. People do not expect the state – in terms of public administrations and other public bodies – to take care of them; they have more confidence in their family and neighbourhood to provide them with social services and facilities. Following Vettoretto's argumentation, these customs are deeply rooted in the Mediterranean countries' culture. Here, clientelism and familism 'hampered the constitution of a modern public sphere', including the spatial planning domain. This attitude might be a further reason that spatial plans, as a public domain, do not achieve an adequate steering capacity (Vettoretto in this volume).

In contrast to the cultural customs in the Mediterranean countries, Fischer identifies other cultural attitudes in Germany which are important for the shape of German planning culture. He shows that former Prussian values such as accuracy, order and discipline affected, and still affect, the 'societal environment' (see Fischer's contribution). These attitudes are culturally deeply rooted within the society so that public rules and norms – including guidelines for spatial plans – reach a high degree of legal commitment. Thus, illegal developments with regard to spatial development are rare. However, this might also reflect the society's higher confidence in the (federal) state.

Finally, the question of 'social justice' and its influence on planning practices is worth consideration. Germany, Austria and most of the Scandinavian countries emphasise the reduction of regional disparities, the provision of equal living conditions and nationwide comprehensive public approaches and services. This is rooted in the specific social model of these countries which, again, is embedded in cultural traditions, attitudes and values (see Stead and Nadin in this contribution). In contrast, the question of 'social justice' does not yet appear to be particularly clear in the Eastern European states. Nor is the 'role of the public' clearly defined (Staniunas in this volume), including the social model and its implications. The impacts on future spatial strategies and developments also remain unclear.

Summarising, we can say that, besides the shared assumptions that are taken for granted by members of the planning profession ('planning environment'), the 'societal environment' includes further unconscious, taken-for-granted beliefs, perceptions and thoughts that are deeply rooted in each society and affect planning structures, processes and outcomes. As this section's findings and explanations indicate, this analytical dimension is necessary to explain cultural influences on spatial planning and for understanding and comparing planning cultures.

Planning Cultures in a Dynamic Perspective

However, planning cultures are not static, they are subject to change because both – 'planning' and 'culture' – are subtle and complex in nature and are based on fluid and abstract concepts. As a consequence, planning cultures are 'exposed to a perpetual pressure to undergo changes' (Gullestrup in this volume) caused by external and internal factors.

External and Internal Change-initiating Factors

Following Gullestrup, the internal change-initiating factors occur 'within' the observed culture. This refers to, among other things, changes in the political-administrative system and in political attitudes, but also to changes in the shape of norms, rules, attitudes and values and in the scientific priorities of a society. With regard to planning culture, it can be summarised that the recognition of the role and involvement of politics in planning processes (this refers particularly to the scientific-rationalistic view of planning where politics did not play an important role) marked such an internal change, as Vettoretto and Tynkkynen describe in their contributions. Another internal change-initiating factor is the shift from government to governance. Dangschat and Hamedinger, as well as Vettoretto (all in this volume), emphasise current public strategies to involve the public in planning processes, due to the increasing awareness and willingness of citizens to engage in urban development projects.

Referring to Gullestrup, external change-initiating factors are even more important than internal factors. External change-initiating factors, consciously or unconsciously, are assessed and adapted by an existing culture, but they remain foreign elements to that culture. As various authors have shown in their contributions, globalisation as an external factor has had a significant impact on spatial policies. This is primarily proved by the urban development strategies of Athens, Istanbul, St Petersburg and Vienna which have all focused on competitiveness and the extension of the territorial advantages or strengths of their city-regions (Dangschat and Hamedinger, Tynkkynen, Prehl and Tuçaltan, Serraos et al. in this volume) which were not necessarily part of the planning culture in former times. Together with the ongoing trends of deregulation, deconcentration and privatisation (Fürst in this volume), it can furthermore be summarised that private developers and enterprises are gaining more influence and power in planning processes (e.g., Prehl and Tuçaltan, Tynkkynen, Staniunas, Dangschat and Hamedinger in this volume). Especially in the Eastern European countries, there is a distinctive orientation towards neoliberal approaches, not least because of the collapse of the former Soviet Union, with its embedded principles of a centrally planned economy. As a backlash, public planning has a difficult status in these societies because of its negative, historically influenced image. Clientelistic relations between private actors and politics have become more common – as, for example, Tynkkynen and Staniunas and also Prehl and Tuçaltan show (all in this volume) – which sets the agenda for the further development of the territory. From the point of view of cultural change it will be worth analysing what influence the current economic crises and the increasing criticisms of neoliberal politics, especially with regard to its social ignorance, will have on attitudes towards public planning and – overall – towards the steering capacity of the state with respect to the relationship between politics and the economy overall.

European Planning Cultures between Convergence and Divergence

An important external change-initiating factor is the concept of 'Europeanisation' (Waterhout et al. in this volume). As Gullestrup argues, the creation of the EU and the ongoing cooperation processes across the inner European borders in particular (During et al. in this volume) have been responsible for various change-initiating factors within the EU member states.

Nevertheless, to discuss the effects or impacts of Europeanisation on planning culture and the related issue of convergence or divergence it becomes necessary to define the concept of Europeanisation first. In this context,

> Europeanisation consists of processes of a) construction, b) diffusion, and c) institutionalisation of formal and informal rules, procedures, policy paradigms, styles, 'ways of doing things' and shared beliefs and norms which are first defined and consolidated in the EU policy process and then incorporated in the logic of domestic (national and subnational)

discourse, political structures and public policies. (Radaelli 2003, 30; see also contribution of Waterhout et al. in this volume)

The influence of the EU is recognisable in at least three ways. First, the EU affects the administrative and organisational structure of some of the EU member states, as Puşcaşu, Vettoretto as well as Serraos et al. have shown in their contributions (in this volume; see also Beck and Thedieck 2008). Second, the introduction of visions, scenarios and strategic planning changes the regional (or national) spatial planning practices. This is the case in Lithuania, Greece and Italy (see Staniunas, Serraos et al. and Vettoretto in this volume) as well as in Portugal, Spain, Ireland and Austria (see Waterhout et al. in this volume). Third, Europeanisation leads to a shift of spatial policy contents. The ESDP, for example, introduced and fostered European spatial planning principles such as polycentric development and sustainability, which the EU member states, in particular the new member states, are trying to follow (see Puşcaşu and Waterhout et al. in this volume; see also Faludi 2002b). Besides, planning these processes affect far more aspects of national as well as regional and local cultures; the interpretations of these processes vary between regret about loss and hope for a better future (e.g., Pollack 2005; Raabe and Sznajderman 2006).

The EU mattered in Southern Europe especially (Featherstone and Kazamis 2001) and still matters, particularly in policy-making processes in Central and Eastern European member states. One reason for this is the fact that the applicants had to fulfil the obligations of EU membership, including the transfer of EU rules, procedures and policy paradigms into their domestic system (Grabbe 2006, 42–6). Additionally, Staniunas, Tynkkynen and Puşcaşu (see contributions in this volume) point out that the Central and Eastern European countries have incorporated into their planning systems planning elements which did not grow within their planning cultures traditionally, but which were popular in the Western European states.

The impact of globalisation and Europeanisation is closely associated with the concept of convergence. As Turner and Green (2008, 13–14) summarise:

> Europeanisation is arguably the most directly important [factor] ... it provides both agency and structure to the process of policy convergence: not only is the EU by itself a source of convergence, but its institutions ... act as a highly significant forum for the promotion of policy transfer and convergence.

However, what exactly does 'convergence' mean and how can we work out if Europeanisation really leads to a convergence of planning cultures in Europe? Following Turner and Green (2008, 5) again, policy convergence can be defined as any increase in the similarity between one or more characteristics of a certain policy (e.g. policy objectives, policy instruments, policy settings), across a given set of political jurisdictions (supranational institutions, states, regions, local authorities) over a given period of time. Policy convergence thus describes the end result of a process of policy change over time towards some common point, regardless of the causal process.

Against this background, the contributions in this volume show some common features that can be interpreted as related to Europeanisation and which might be considered as 'precursors' to policy convergence. In detail, this implies:

- the internationalisation of planners' education (see Fürst in this volume) that leads to planners' acquiring similar knowledge, skills and competences worldwide;
- the harmonisation of spatial planning policies such as territorial cohesion, where the French and German approaches, for example, seem to be moving towards each other (see Davoudi in this volume);
- the influence of European programmes as URBAN and INTERREG, which conveyed the involvement of the public into planning processes (for Austria and Italy see Dangschat and Hamedinger as well as Vettoretto in this volume);
- EU rules, regulations, norms and directives, which aim at providing similar subjects (e.g., polycentric development, sustainability and accessibility as described in the ESDP) and structures (see Fürst and Waterhout et al. in this volume); and
- comparable characteristics of European cultural values, for example, the 'money-based economic reality perspective' or 'nature as an objectified object' (Gullestrup in this volume).

The influence of Europeanisation on policy convergence is thus recognisable but there are also other impacts to be considered. The 'path dependence', i.e. the significance of local, regional or national cultural contexts, remains an important resisting factor. Planning cultures, planning systems and 'spatial policies continue to be fragmented and subject to national decision' (Davoudi in this volume). As the contributions in this volume show, the maintenance of differences ('forces of divergence') can mainly be ascribed to

- the different effects of globalisation on national structures and economies (status quo) and the related strategies;
- the different effects of Europeanisation on national (and regional) spatial planning systems and strategies (status quo); Fürst, for example, concludes that Europeanisation leads to a common vocabulary among

planners but that the European concepts and strategies nevertheless are implemented and interpreted in various ways (Fürst in this volume);
- the sustained power of the state (e.g., Page 2008, 185) and national institutional resilience, which slow down the Europeanisation process (see also Doria et al. 2006);
- the sustained power of culture, i.e. the specific cultural context of any area with its traditions, norms, habits, attitudes and values, which lead to different interpretations of the ESDP and the Territorial Agenda and thus to different priorities when implementing these concepts; and
- different (intellectual) ways and styles (see Fischer's contribution in this volume) which influence the way of dealing with uncertainty, EU specifications, emerging theories and paradigms etc. that again leads to different approaches to spatial planning and development.

Recent comparisons of various policy fields of the UK and Germany lead to similar results. As Page (2008, 184–5) concludes, there is only one major policy arena, that of immigration, where policy convergence takes place; in all other fields of policy rather divergent forces are active. In the field of political studies, where research on the impact of Europeanisation has a longer tradition, the general tenor is not to overestimate the EU's influence (e.g., Grabbe 2006, 42). Europeanisation never follows uniform mechanisms nor does it produce homogeneous domestic structures and spatial planning identities or cultures (Davoudi, Stead and Nadin, as well as Waterhout et al., in this volume). With Page (2008, 184), we can conclude that 'the resultant force seems to be predominantly continued divergence' (Page 2008, 184). With regard to the impact of globalisation on local cultures we find a similar line of argument at Friedman (2006, 506–7): 'Indeed, it is becoming clear that the flat-world, while it has the potential to homogenize cultures, also has ... an even greater potential to nourish diversity to a degree that the world has never seen before'. In his opinion 'local cultures have a much better chance of being preserved' because in the range of globalisation new forms of communication and innovation allow 'to take your own local culture and upload it to the world'. But Friedman concedes that his view is quite an optimistic one and that there are many arguments pointing into the opposite direction.

Perspectives: Culture as an Organising Principle in Planning Theories

The 'culturised planning model' and its (analytical) dimensions describe elements for a culture-based planning paradigm that provides a critically viable and practically usable approach for the analysis and description of planning cultures and practices. In detail, the model is supposed to:

- contribute to the scientific exploration and establishment of the term 'planning culture' to become aware of diversity in planning, for example, different planning contexts and cultures, and to question its hidden values as well as practices; and
- improve planning practices and – through policy evaluation – to contribute to policy development by enriching and stimulating a professional discourse on planning cultures which are considered important for the territorial, economic and social cohesion of the European Union (see also contributions of Waterhout et al., During et al. and Davoudi in this volume).

Furthermore, the model contributes to advancing the understanding and use of (postmodern) theories in planning and promoting new approaches to planning theories by combining elements of cultural and organisational studies with planning theories to explain differences and peculiarities among EU member states. Following Chettiparamb (2006, 72), the derivation of planning theories either results from the empirical analysis of planning practices or from 'theoretical advances in planning-related disciplines'. The latter is regarded, for example, by Hillier and Healey (2008, 405), as essential to get new impetus into the field of spatial planning and planning theory. The 'culturised planning model' belongs to this approach by introducing culture as an organising principle for the analysis of spatial planning. The aim of this approach is to achieve a more systematic discussion about functional structures and mechanisms, planning systems and planning styles with regard to the cultural context of different countries and societies. This stands in line with other theoretical approaches, which stress the importance of a situated and contextualised understanding of planning (e.g., Schönwandt 2002, 2008; Archibugi 2008; Byrne 2003; Cettiparamb 2006). Hillier and Healey (2008, 407) recognise such theoretical approaches as focusing on 'complexity analysis of spatial planning practices' towards a 'big picture' of planning theory 'where phenomena can be explained causally and in which there is a 'whole' that exists as a system'.

This 'system' approach is not new in the field of planning theory (e.g., McLoughlin 1969). Rational planning theories of the 1960s and 1970s emphasised the scientific concepts of system and structure to analyse cities or regions as complex entities using a 'linear approach' (e.g., Byrne 2003, 172). However, the linear approach and its focus on 'benign' or 'innocent' planning problems was seen as one of the failures 'of planning to validate its "scientific understanding" through achievements in practice' (ibid.). Despite the failure of the 'linear approach' in complex systems

> the ... concepts of system and structure are essential for social analysis, but only if we concede that a system is not itself an object which globally defines local (e.g. small scale) interactions, but the product of local interactions, and

that structures are important because of their content and not their form. (Fischer 1994, 76)

This self-conception of planning sciences is integral for the 'culturised planning model', which considers planning as a social activity being embedded in a wider cultural, socio-political and socio-economic context of a specific region or territory. Similar to the theoretical considerations of the 'culturised planning model' (Schönwandt 2002, 2008) has introduced a 'system-environment paradigm', emphasising that planning as a core activity of the system is structurally connected with its direct environment. Consequently, Schönwandt distinguishes between the 'planning world' and the 'everyday world' (Schönwandt 2008, 29). With their knowledge, skills and competences in theories and methods, actors involved in planning processes compose the planning environment, i.e. the organisational and theoretical background of planning (ibid., 57–8). The planning environment is embedded in the 'broader' context of the societal environment and is affected by a specific agenda of topics and actors. In the 'culturised planning model' Schönwandt's systematic finds its counterpart in the distinction between the dimensions of 'planning artefacts' and 'planning environment' on the one side, and 'societal environment', on the other.

By combining these two analytical dimensions, Schönwandt (2002, 30) outlines a 'third generation' of planning theory which, in his opinion, might:

- embrace the complexity of planning processes and practices (i.e. spatial, social, political, economic or ecological aspects);
- consider the restrictions of the cognitive skills or demands of planners; and
- cover theoretical approaches towards planning, especially in the field of semiotic, epistemological and ethnic studies (see also Archibugi 2008; Chettiparamb 2006; Byrne 2003).

Against this background, the outlined 'culturised planning model' aims at contributing to the planning theory discussion. By considering and encoding cultural phenomena of planning not only on the visible surface but also on a 'hidden' level and by introducing the (analytical) dimensions of: (1) 'planning artefacts'; (2) 'planning environment'; and (3) 'societal environment' the model follows an integrated and comprehensive approach of planning. This is in line with the theoretical concept of a 'rethought planning' (Allmendinger 2001, 189), where the concept of complexity is one of the key principles to provide planners with a more systematic understanding of spatial planning (Archibugi 2008, 9; Byrne 2003, 174; Allmendinger 2001, 197–8). By introducing the 'culturised planning model' with its underlying assumption of culture as one of the organising principles for spatial planning, it combines various aspects which 'have remained until now very separate' (Archibugi 2008, 9) but which are important for understanding spatial planning processes and practices. The 'culturised planning model', with its three dimensions, might contribute to a better understanding of the structure, processes and results of planning practices and the relations between these phenomena by introducing a more comprehensive analysis.

Evaluation of the 'Culturised Planning Model': Potential and Shortcomings

The field of spatial planning and planning culture appears multifaceted and highly complex. It is characterised by a multiplicity of political and social practices and cultural frames that shape spatial practices and which, at the same time, complicate a systematic analysis of these multiple culturally embedded influences on spatial planning. With regard to the 'culturised planning model', the assumption is that there are elements which are immediately obvious, as well as elements which belong to the underlying norms of morality and social structures being more difficult to observe (see earlier contribution of Knieling and Othengrafen in this volume; see also Dühr, Vettoretto, and Staniunas).

Thus, the 'culturised planning model' aims at covering not only the 'facade' (see Staniunas in this volume) of spatial planning and development but also at explaining deeper cultural layers and assumptions. Again, it is not the objective of the model to describe what is happening in each country's professional practice but to systematically decode and compare the impact culture has on the organisation, structures, processes and outcomes of spatial planning. As shown by the case studies in this volume, the 'culturised planning model' therefore offers adequate tools.

- It contributes to the scientific exploration and establishment of the term 'planning culture' to become aware of the diversity in planning.
- It reduces the multiplicity of aspects on spatial planning practices and cultures by introducing the three analytical dimensions 'planning artifacts', 'planning environment' and 'societal environment'. This offers the opportunity for systematic analysis and comparison of (European) planning cultures.
- It makes planning processes and outcomes more transparent. As a consequence, it improves planning practices and, through policy evaluation, contributes to policy development by enriching and stimulating a professional discourse about planning cultures which are considered increasingly important for the territorial, economic and social cohesion of the European Union.
- It introduces the concept of culture into the field of spatial planning. By combining cultural theories and planning theory it might give new impetus to the field of spatial planning and planning theory. This particularly refers to some postmodern theories which search for a 'big

picture' planning theory 'where phenomena can be explained causally and in which there is a 'whole' that exists as a system.

However, some open questions and critical points concerning the 'culturised planning model' remain.

- The empirical analysis has to be deepened in further applications of the model. Only when further case studies have been analysed will a more profound evaluation of the 'culturised planning model' become possible. This also refers to possible applications of the model in practice.
- The case studies in this volume represent different spatial levels (city, city-region, nation) and specific topics with regard to planning culture. This variety complicates a systematic analysis and comparison of planning culture on basis of the developed criteria. However, systematic and comprehensive examination and reflection is necessary to enhance the model as a whole (e.g., by enhancing the set of criteria for each of the analytical dimensions).
- The analysis and integration of cultural theories needs to be reflected in wider contexts to guarantee that there are no conflicting theoretical approaches in the field of (anthropological) cultural studies or organisational sciences and to stabilise a broad theoretical basis of the 'culturised planning model'.

Nevertheless, the model appears to contribute to a better understanding of the relationship between the cultural context (including the specific socio-economic patterns and related cultural norms, values, traditions, and attitudes) and spatial planning as an operative instrument of territorial policy. By introducing culture as the organising principle, the model enables us to decode the cultural phenomena of an area in a systematic way. Against this background and by emphasising the 'cultural turn' with regard to spatial planning, the model might stimulate ongoing discussion in the field of (postmodern) planning theories.

Furthermore, all the contributions to this volume deal with European planning cultures. Certainly, the subject of planning cultures is not limited to the European borders but it opens the field for research on a much more far-reaching international scale. However, the European integration and enlargement process offers a politically important and scientifically interesting challenge. Reaching a better understanding of the diversity of Europe, evaluating this as a potential for future European development and integrating the knowledge about planning cultures into the practice of European interregional cooperation appears to be a significant factor for the success of the integrated and sustainable development of the European Union. We hope that the model and discussions around it can contribute to this overall goal.

Bibliography

Allmendinger, P. (2001) *Planning in Postmodern Times*, Routledge, London and New York.

Archibugi, F. (2008) *Planning Theory. From the Political Debate to the Methodological Reconstruction*, Springer, Milan and Berlin.

Beck, J. and F. Thedieck (eds) (2008) *The European Dimension of Administrative Culture*, Nomos, Baden-Baden.

Breulliard, M. and C. Fraser (2007) 'Preface', in P. Booth, M. Breuillard, C. Fraser and D. Paris (eds) *Spatial Planning Systems of Britain and France, A Comparative Analysis*, Routledge, London, xiii–xv.

Byrne, D. (2003) 'Complexity Theory and Planning Theory: A Necessary Encounter', *Planning Theory* 2(3), 171–8.

Chettiparamb, A. (2006) 'Metaphors in Complexity Theory and Planning', *Planning Theory* (5)1, 71–91.

Cook, I., D. Crouch, S. Naylor and J.R. Ryan (eds) (2000) *Cultural Turns/ Geographical Turns: Perspectives on Cultural Geography*, Pearson Education, Harlow.

Doria, L., V. Fedeli and C. Tedesco (eds) (2006) *Rethinking European Spatial Policy as a Hologram. Actions, Institutions, Discourses*, Ashgate, Aldershot.

EU (2008) *Consolidated Version of the Treaty on the Functioning of the European Union*, Office Journal of the European Union, 9 May, Brussels.

Faludi, A. (2002a) 'The European Spatial Development Perspective (ESDP): An Overview', in A. Faludi (ed.) *European Spatial Planning*, Lincoln Institute of Land Policy, Cambridge, MA, 3–18.

Faludi, A. (ed.) (2002b) *European Spatial Planning*, Lincoln Institute of Land Policy, Cambridge, MA.

Featherstone, K. and G. Kazamias (2001) *Europeanization and the Southern Periphery*, Routledge, London.

Fischer, M.D. (1994) 'Modelling Complexity and Change: Social Knowledge and Social Process', in C.M. Hann (ed.) *When History Accelerates. Essays on Rapid Social Change, Complexity and Creativity*, The Athlone Press, London, 75-94.

Friedman, T.L. (2006) *The World is Flat. The Globalized World in the Twenty-First Century*, Penguin Books, London.

Grabbe, H. (2006) *The EU's Transformative Power. Europeanization Through Conditionality in Central and Eastern Europe*, Palgrave Macmillan, Houndsmills.

Hillier, J. and P. Healey (2008) *Contemporary Movements in Planning Theory*, Critical Essays in Planning Theory, ,ol. 3, Ashgate, Aldershot.

McLoughlin, J.B. (1969) *Urban and Regional Planning: A Systems Approach*, Faber and Faber, London.

Page, E.C. (2008) 'Conclusions', in E. Turner and S. Green (eds) *Policy Convergence in the UK and Germany, Beyond the Third Way?*, Routledge, London, 184–90.
Pollack, M. (ed.) (2005) *Sarmatische Landschaften. Nachrichten aus Litauen, Belarus, der Ukraine, Polen und Deutschland*, Fischer, Frankfurt/Main.
Raabe, K. and M. Sznajderman (ed.) (2006) *Last & Lost. Ein Atlas des verschwindenden Europas*, Suhrkamp, Frankfurt/Main.
Radaelli, C.M. (2003) 'The Europeanisation of public policy', in K. Featherstone and C.M. Radaelli (eds) *The Politics of Europeanization*, Oxford University Press, Oxford, 27–56.
Schönwandt, W.L. (2002) *Planung in der Krise? Theoretische Orientierungen für Architektur, Stadt- und Raumplanung*, Kohlhammer, Stuttgart.
Schönwandt, W.L. (2008) *Planning in Crisis? Theoretical Orientations for Architecture and Planning*, Ashgate, Aldershot.
Turner, E. and S. Green (2008) 'Understanding Policy Convergence in Britain and Germany: Towards a Framework for Analysis', in E. Turner and S. Green (eds) *Policy Convergence in the UK and Germany, Beyond the Third Way?*, Routledge, London, 1–21.
Young, G. (2008) *Reshaping Planning with Culture*, Ashgate, Aldershot.

Index

architects 65, 83, 115, 142–4, 182–3, 190, 193, 231, 309
architecture 69, 71–2, 74, 77, 79, 86–7, 142–4, 175, 182, 191, 193, 232, 291
attitudes xxiv–xxv, xxviii, xxx, 7, 17, 24–6, 29, 32, 39, 43, 49, 52–4, 56, 66, 197, 227, 301–2, 307, 309–12, 315, 319
Austria xxx, 45, 95–110, 209–10, 241, 244, 248, 285, 292, 306, 308, 310, 313–14
   Vienna xxx, 95–110, 306, 308, 312
   Red Vienna 96, 109

Belgium 45, 116, 209, 210, 292
beliefs xxiv, xxx, xxxiii, 26, 31, 39, 42–3, 48–9, 56, 75, 198, 240, 301, 309, 311–12
   shared xxxiii, 198, 240, 312
Britain *see under* United Kingdom
Bulgaria 244

cartographic representations 113, 114–15, 119, 123, 125, 131–3, 306
Central European Core Region (CENTROPE) 107–10
clientelism xxxii, 97, 109, 223, 307, 308, *see also* patronage
co-action 5, 6, 9
cohesion
   social xxvi, 95, 110, 132, 255, 258–9, 273, 283–4, 303, 316, 318
   territorial xxiii, xxxiii, 44, 240, 248, 250, 269–77, 295, 314
collectivism 50, 51
communism 87, 152, 160, 174, 178–9, 181, 256, 291
communities 26, 39, 40, 152–3, 170–71, 180, 190, 201, 223–4, 226, 245, 255, 258–9, 265–6, 273
competitiveness 33, 50, 56, 95, 103, 110, 129, 164, 256, 271, 276, 283, 293, 302, 306, 312

economic 56, 95, 129, 271, 276, 283, 293
conflicts 23, 32, 70, 83, 158, 159, 160, 164, 195, 275
convergence xxix, xxxiii–xxxiv, 24, 30, 108, 133, 163, 179, 239, 246–7, 249, 283–4, 292, 294–6, 301–19
cooperation xxiii, xxvi–xxvii, xxxi, 4, 5, 9, 20, 23, 31, 44, 65–6, 75, 96, 101, 103–5, 107–8, 110, 113, 126, 134, 180, 183, 222, 240, 242, 245–7, 255–6, 258–60, 262–3, 265–6, 269–77, 294, 303, 312, 319
   cross-border xxvi, 44
   cross-cultural 262, 266
   intercultural 20, 75
   international 4, 31, 65–6, 294, 303
   interregional xxvi, 44, 255, 258–60, 266, 303
   regional 105, 110, 319
   territorial 113
   transnational xxvi, xxxiii, 44, 242, 246, 259, 269–77
cooperatism xxxi, 96, 109
'co-opetition' 102, 107
CULTPLAN 26, 29–0, 256, 262, 265–6
cultural contexts xxiii–xxv, xxvii–xxxiv, 5, 29, 39, 42–3, 53–5, 239, 248, 263, 277, 301–3, 307, 314–16, 319
cultural dimensions xxiii, xxx, 5, 51, 59, 301
cultural diversity xxv–xxvii, xxix–xxx, xxxiii, 33, 52, 54, 249, 255–66, 302–3
cultural influences xxiii, xxvii, xxix, 23, 302, 303, 304, 311
cultural turn xxiv–xxv, 24, 51, 302–3, 319
culture
   concept of xxix, 3–5, 40–41, 43, 49, 51, 53, 55, 257–8, 302, 318
   corporate 24

dimension 5, 6, 7
layers 7, 8, 9
political 24, 25, 97, 109, 264
regional 264
culturised planning model xxx, xxxiv, 57–9, 301, 304–5, 307, 309, 315–19
Czech Republic 107, 244

decentralisation 27, 31–2, 209, 224, 234, 255, 291–2
democracy xxxi, 8, 83–4, 103, 160–61, 192, 201–2, 227, 283
democratisation 84, 224, 227, 234
Denmark 3, 4, 12–13, 41, 209–10, 241, 244
deregulation 27, 31, 95, 103, 198, 222–4, 227–8, 233, 277, 306, 312
development
  economic 45, 97, 104, 118, 132, 196, 198–200, 221, 224, 256–60, 265–6, 303
  regional xxiv–xxv, xxvii, xxix, 28, 42, 100, 110, 159, 164, 175, 180, 206, 302, 308
  spatial xxiv, xxvii, xxix, 100, 113, 117, 126, 131, 134, 205, 207, 209, 218, 239, 242–3, 259, 277, 290, 303, 305–7, 309, 310
  sustainable 28, 30, 33, 141, 145, 206, 259, 261, 271, 293, 319
  territorial xxiii, 132, 273–4, 276
  urban xxiv–xxv, xxvii, xxix, xxxi, xxxiii, 42, 74, 77, 83, 86, 87, 97, 100, 102, 103, 104, 110, 178, 207, 210, 223, 227, 233, 302, 306, 308, 311, 312
devolution 118, 192, 200, 224–5, 234, 291
divergence xxix, xxxiv, 301–19

emics 5, 8, 55
England *see under* United Kingdom
environmental protection 30, 56, 100, 103, 132
etics 5, 55
European Commission (EC) xxvi, 44–5, 180, 255, 257–8, 265, 269, 302

Compendium of Spatial Planning Systems and Policies 44–6, 48, 189, 288–92
Lisbon Strategy 258, 271, 276
European Council 271, 276
Europeanisation xxxiii, 182, 192, 197–9, 201, 239–50, 261, 266, 275, 277, 294–6, 312–15
European Parliament 256
European Spatial Planning Observation Network (ESPON) 241, 243–4, 246–8, 270, 276, 288, 291, 294
European Union (EU) xxiii–xxiv, xxvii, xxix, xxxii–xxxiii, 4, 16, 19, 27, 30, 31, 44, 45, 46, 47, 65, 97, 99, 102, 106, 108, 113, 139, 179, 180, 18, 1989, 210, 224, 225, 228, 232, 239–50, 255–66, 269–72, 274, 276, 288–91, 293–4, 302–3, 312–16, 318–19
  Cohesion Policy 179, 273
  Committee of the Regions 258, 265
  INTERREG xxvi, xxxiii, 23, 199, 242, 245, 247–8, 255–66, 294, 303, 314
  directives 31, 242, 244, 245, 247
  European Spatial Development Perspective (ESDP) xxiii, xxvii, 27, 180, 240, 242–7, 269, 271, 274, 313–15
  Objective 2 102, 106
  Structural Funds 199–200, 247, 273, 276
  Territorial Agenda xxiii, xxvii, 240, 243, 248, 315
  Treaties
    Lisbon 270
    Maastricht 256–8, 262, 265, 275
    Rome 275
  URBACT xxvi
  URBAN xxvi, 102, 199–200, 314
expertise 152, 154, 157, 159, 161–2, 164, 183, 193, 202

family 16, 196, 310
familism xxxii, 196–7, 310
feudalism 84, 170, 171, 172
Finland 41, 209, 210, 285

France xxxiii, 23, 29, 45, 48, 115, 177, 180, 209, 210, 244, 269, 274, 275, 285, 287, 292, 294, 295
French Street Urban Transformation Project *see under* Turkey

gender 104–5, 291
gentrification 226, 228–9
geographic information systems (GIS) 131, 132, 133, 183
Germany xxx–xxxi, xxxiii, xxvii, 13, 23, 25–7, 29, 41, 45, 48, 65–90, 97, 113, 115–19, 123–6, 129, 131–2, 177, 180, 182–3, 208–10, 239, 248, 269, 271, 274, 285, 287, 291–2, 295, 307, 310, 314–15
   National Socialism 70–72, 78, 83
   Prussia 77–8
globalisation xxiii, xxiv, xxv, xxxii–xxxiii, 30, 95–6, 181–2, 197, 201, 221–35, 255, 275, 293, 302, 312–15
governance xxiv, xxv, xxviii, xxx, 24, 26, 28, 30, 32–3, 39, 95–6, 101, 106, 109–10, 116, 153–5, 159, 160, 163, 198–200, 223–4, 227, 234, 239, 244–5, 249, 291–4, 301, 311
Great Britain *see* United Kingdom
Greece 205–19, 285, 291–2, 295, 306, 308, 310, 313
   Athens xxxii, 205–19, 306, 308, 312
gross domestic product (GDP) 97, 212, 270

harmonisation 224–5, 256, 269, 275, 277, 314
Heimat 74, 84, 86, 87, 89
heritage xxvi, 108, 128–9, 190, 193–4, 201, 206, 255, 257, 261–2
Hungary 107, 244, 256

ideal types 86, 271, 283–4, 287–91, 296
ideology(ies) xxxi–xxxiii, 6, 15, 41, 87, 95, 98, 160, 163, 180–81, 189–90, 193–4, 197, 202, 249, 255–66, 295
individualism 50, 51
industrialisation 83–4, 96, 222
information and communications technology (ICT) 127, 129, 132

infrastructure, xxv, 103–4, 108–9, 118, 127–9, 132, 147, 153, 156, 175–7, 205, 209, 212–13, 215, 218, 227, 243, 258, 276, 294
integration xxiii–xxiv, xxvii–xxix, 6, 10, 25, 30, 39, 52, 54–5, 98, 109, 116, 129, 199, 240, 244–6, 248–9, 255, 258–9, 265, 271, 275–7, 290–91, 293–4, 303, 319
   European xxiii–xxiv, xxvii–xxix, 240, 244, 246, 248–9, 255, 258, 265, 275, 277, 293–4, 303, 319
   EU xxvii, 30, 277, 303
internationalisation 31, 223, 291, 301, 314
INTERREG *see under* European Union
Ireland 45, 210, 241, 244, 248, 274, 285, 287, 292, 313
Italy xxxii, 23, 29, 48, 189–202, 209, 210, 241, 244, 285, 291–2, 308–10, 313–14

knowledge xxiii, xxiv, xxv, 3, 10, 12, 17, 19–20, 24, 33, 40–42, 45, 47, 55–6, 58, 75, 95, 127, 139–43, 148, 151, 160, 182, 189, 194, 249, 262, 264, 303, 314, 317, 319

language 6, 7, 23, 25, 27, 41, 119, 139, 145, 176, 183, 264
laws 45–6, 58, 66, 100, 118, 145, 148, 154, 169, 177–8, 190–91, 195–6, 198–201, 206, 224–7, 234–5, 239, 247, 283
   see also regulations, rules
LEADER 199–200, 247
liberalisation 84, 103, 222–4, 227–8, 233, 276, 306
liberalism 179, 221
Lisbon Strategy *see under* European Commission
Lithuania xxxi, 139–48, 244, 291, 308, 310, 313
Luxembourg 244, 270, 287, 292

media 17, 133, 170
models of society xxxiv, 283–96
modernisation xxx, 83, 95–6, 101, 103, 106, 176, 178, 190, 193, 222, 225, 283

narratives 30, 54–5, 59, 191, 256
  master-narratives 52–3
nature xxviii–xxxiv, 4–5, 8–9, 12, 17–19, 30, 45, 49, 56, 83–4, 86, 119, 124, 128–9, 131, 146–7, 163, 170, 173, 183, 200, 218, 240, 245, 283, 295, 304, 309, 311, 314
neoliberalism xxiv, xxxii, 30, 116, 152, 221, 223, 225, 226, 312
Netherlands xxvii–xxxi, 26, 45, 65, 113, 115,–19, 123–6, 129, 131–2, 182, 189–91, 209–10, 239, 241, 244, 246, 248, 270, 272, 276, 285, 287, 291, 292, 294, 296
norms xxvii–xxviii, xxxiii, 4, 7, 24–6, 32, 39, 41–2, 49, 56, 58, 82–3, 86, 139, 160, 169, 198, 240, 283, 294–5, 301–2, 309–12, 314–15, 318–19
  behavioural 25, 49
  moral 4, 7, 41
Norway 244

Ottoman Empire 171, 222, 230, 233

participation 23, 25, 43, 56, 97, 102, 104–6, 109–10, 141, 160–61, 199–201, 227, 233–4, 257–8, 261, 266
patronage xxxii, 97, 195–7, 200
  see also clientelism
planners xxiii, xxxi, xxxiii, 6–7, 20, 25, 28, 30–33, 42, 48, 56, 65, 71–2, 101, 114, 118–19, 129, 131, 133, 142–3, 146, 151–2, 154–64, 183–4, 189–90, 193–4, 198–9, 208–9, 221, 234–5, 246, 248–9, 304, 307, 314–15, 317
planning
  economic 45, 169, 174, 193, 274, 290
  land-use 42, 151, 153, 156–9, 164, 196–7, 290
  national xxxii, 134, 244, 246, 289
  reformist 192–3, 195–8
  regional xxiii–xxiv, xxvii–xxix, xxxii, 3, 25, 33, 39–40, 42–3, 53–4, 56, 58, 107, 119, 132, 134, 151–5, 159, 162, 175, 177, 193, 197, 200–201, 206, 244, 246, 256, 289, 301, 303–4, 309
  spatial xxiv, xxvi–xxix, xxxi–xxxiv, 3, 6, 25–7, 28–9, 31, 33, 44–8, 54–7, 59, 78, 100–10, 113–19, 125–6, 129, 132–4, 169–78, 180–83, 189–90, 196, 199, 201, 205–11, 224, 239–46, 248–9, 270–71, 274, 277, 283–4, 289–96, 302–11, 313–19
  strategic 30, 33, 42, 102–3, 116, 151, 161, 179, 198, 227, 294, 308, 313
  territorial 139–40, 142, 144–5, 147, 169, 180
  transnational xxxi, 113, 294
  urban xxiii–xxiv, xxvii–xxix, xxxi–xxxii, 3, 25, 29, 39–40, 42–3, 53–4, 56, 58, 66, 71, 78, 97, 101–5, 110, 115, 151, 152–6, 158, 160, 163–4, 170–71, 177, 181, 193, 197, 206–7, 221, 226, 234, 303–4, 309
planning artefacts xxx, xxxiv, 55, 58, 304–7, 317
planning education 31, 118, 131, 134
planning environment xxx, xxxiv, 56, 58, 304, 307, 309–10, 311, 317–18
planning theory xxviii, 43, 51, 53–4, 151, 164, 302–3, 316–19
Poland 81, 244, 256
politics xxxii, 83–4, 116, 152, 156, 174, 192, 198, 221, 223–4, 227, 234, 245, 256, 302, 307, 311–12
pollution 15, 212, 273
Portugal 45, 209, 210, 241, 285, 287, 292, 313
postmodernism xxv, xxx, 52–4, 59, 67, 69–70, 160, 162, 164, 304, 316, 318–19
privatisation 31, 222–4, 227–8, 233, 292, 312
public sector 18, 45, 224–5, 228, 277, 307

rationality xxxi, 15, 19, 53, 159, 164, 190, 194–5, 274
'reality' 3–4, 10, 11, 20
Realpolitik xxxi, 152, 157–8, 163
reformism xxxii, 189–202
Regional Spatial Strategies (RSSs) 118–19, 124–5, 131–2

regulations 27–8, 31, 100, 116, 139, 146, 172, 174, 191, 195–8, 208–9, 225, 227, 232, 234–5, 239, 245, 247, 263, 275, 284, 305, 314
  see also laws, rules
rhetoric 105, 114, 158, 199
Romania xxxii, 169–84, 244, 291, 295, 308
rules xxvii–xxxiii, 7, 27, 32, 39–40, 42–3, 49–50, 54, 75, 114, 171–2, 177, 183, 189, 196, 198, 234, 240, 242, 248, 283, 289, 292–3, 302, 305–7, 309–14
  socially-constructed 114
  see also laws, regulations
Russia xxxi, 41, 151–65, 294, 182, 307–8
  St Petersburg xxxi, 151–65, 306, 308, 312
  see also Soviet Union, USSR

science 3, 18, 24, 66, 78, 83, 84
Second World War *see* World War II
secularisation 174, 222
Single European Act (SEA) 30, 256, 276
Slovakia 107, 244
societal environment xxx, xxxiv, 56, 58, 304, 307, 309–11, 317–18
Soviet Union xxxi, 151–4, 160, 163, 221, 307, 309, 312
  see also Russia, USSR
space xxiii, xxiv, xxv, xxvii, xxxiii, 5, 19, 52, 126, 129, 133, 142, 158, 171–2, 174, 180, 182, 189, 208, 218, 226, 234, 264, 274, 277, 302
  residential 222
  socially-constructed xxiii, 302
  urban 218, 226
Spain 241, 244, 285, 287, 291–2, 313
sustainability xxxi, 56, 105, 152, 197, 199, 201, 224, 283, 313–14
Sweden 13, 209, 210, 245, 285
symbols 30, 41–2, 71, 72, 114, 125, 129, 230

technology xxxii, 6, 9, 18–19, 83–4, 127, 129, 148, 183

territory xxiii–xxv, xxvii, xxix, xxxi, 44, 56, 113–14, 124, 129, 131–3, 146, 158, 169–71, 172, 174, 178–9, 182, 201–2, 207, 210, 240–41, 259, 269–70, 302–3, 312, 317
  European xxvii, xxix, 259, 303
tourism 126, 175, 180, 206, 212
traditions xxiii–xxv, xxvii–xxviii, xxxi–xxxiii, 24, 31–2, 39, 42–7, 52–4, 56, 58, 65–6, 71, 77, 84, 113–14, 116, 119, 132–4, 139, 143, 151–64, 181, 189–90, 225, 269, 27, 276, 288–92, 295, 301, 304, 306–7, 309, 311, 315, 319
  administrative xxviii, 39
  cultural xxxii, 46, 311
  economic 39
  historic xxxii
  legal xxiv, xxviii, 39, 301
  planning xxvii, xxx, 31, 58, 113–14, 116, 119, 133–4, 189, 225, 276, 288, 290, 304, 306
  political xxiv, xxviii, 39, 301
transport 20, 42, 95, 104, 108–9, 118, 127, 129, 212, 240, 242–3, 276
transportation 9, 20, 175–6, 178, 194, 196, 213, 215
  public 196, 213
Turkey xxxii, xxxiii, 221–35, 308
  Istanbul xxxii, xxxiii, 221–35, 306, 308, 312
    French Street Urban Transformation Project xxxii, 221–35

United Kingdom (UK)/Great Britain 11, 45, 47, 115, 118, 191, 200, 208, 210, 244, 271–2, 285, 286–8, 291, 292, 294, 315
  England 113, 116–119, 123, 125–6, 131, 132, 177, 180, 287–9
  Northern Ireland 118
  Scotland 118
  Wales 118
United Nations (UN) 4, 224, 302
  Convention for the Safeguarding of the Intangible Cultural Heritage xxv

Convention on the Protection and
   Promotion of the Diversity of
   Cultural Expressions xxv
Universal Declaration on Cultural
   Diversity xxv
United States of America (USA) 14, 28,
   41, 69–70, 80, 155, 156, 183, 208,
   272, 276, 284
URBACT *see under* European Union
URBAN *see under* European Union
urbanism 45, 56, 115, 169, 175, 177–8,
   182–3, 189, 290
urban renewal 97, 102–3, 105–6, 110,
   207
USSR xxxii
   see also Russia, Soviet Union

values xxiv–xxv, xxvii–xxx, xxxiii, 4, 7,
   10–12, 15–46, 48–9, 52–6, 58, 95,
   114, 139, 183, 189, 192–5, 199, 222,
   228, 257, 260, 269, 275, 277, 283,
   294–6, 301–2, 304, 306–7, 309–11,
   314–16, 319
  cultural xxxiii, 14, 54, 56, 222, 257,
   269, 275, 277, 307, 309, 314

welfare state 31, 196, 201–2, 221, 271–2,
   283, 285, 292–4
welfare systems 275, 284–5, 287, 290–6
World Bank xxv, 224, 302
World War I 96, 174
World War II 70, 89, 96, 97, 174, 178,
   191, 192, 196, 210, 295